T0181432

Organizational Behaviour in Healthcare

Series Editors
Jean-Louis Denis
School of Public Health
University of Montreal
Montréal, QC, Canada

Justin Waring
Nottingham University Business School
University of Nottingham
Nottingham, UK

Paula Hyde
Birmingham Business School
University of Birmingham
Birmingham, UK

Published in co-operation with the Society for Studies in Organizing Healthcare (SHOC), this series has two strands, the first of which consists of specially selected papers taken from the biennial conferences held by SHOC that present a cohesive and focused insight into issues within the field of organizational behavior in healthcare.

The series also encourages proposals for monographs and edited collections to address the additional and emergent topics in the field of health policy, organization and management. Books within the series aim to advance scholarship on the application of social science theories, methods and concepts to the study of organizing and managing healthcare services and systems.

Providing a new platform for advanced and engaged scholarship, books in the series will advance the academic community by fostering a deep analysis on the challenges for healthcare organizations and management with an explicitly international and comparative focus.

More information about this series at
http://www.palgrave.com/gp/series/14724

Peter Nugus · Charo Rodriguez ·
Jean-Louis Denis · Denis Chênevert
Editors

Transitions and Boundaries in the Coordination and Reform of Health Services

Building Knowledge, Strategy and Leadership

Editors
Peter Nugus
Institute of Health Sciences Education
McGill University
Montréal, QC, Canada

Charo Rodriguez
Department of Family Medicine
McGill University
Montréal, QC, Canada

Jean-Louis Denis
School of Public Health
University of Montreal
Montréal, QC, Canada

Denis Chênevert
Department of Human Resource
Management
HEC Montréal
Montréal, QC, Canada

ISSN 2662-1045 ISSN 2662-1053 (electronic)
Organizational Behaviour in Healthcare
ISBN 978-3-030-26686-8 ISBN 978-3-030-26684-4 (eBook)
https://doi.org/10.1007/978-3-030-26684-4

This Palgrave Macmillan imprint is published by the registered company Springer Nature Switzerland AG
The registered company address is: Gewerbestrasse 11, 6330 Cham, Switzerland

Preface: Studying Coordination, Specialisation and Complexity in Health Systems

Researchers of the organisation of health services have increased attention to how health system reforms can and should serve the health needs of communities, in relation to the specialised services individuals need, including when, where, how and by whom they need it. Such reform efforts can be seen as attempts to coordinate increasingly complex and specialised services, and optimise and learn from the mutual influence of deliberate and system-wide policy interventions with local adaptations and innovations. This book, featuring contributions and data from Australia, Canada, France, Norway, the UK and the US, brings together seminal contributions from the 14th Organisational Behaviour in Healthcare (OBHC) Conference, held in Montreal, Canada, in May 2018. In all, 13 different countries were represented at the conference, among more than 190 participants. The OBHC Conference is the official conference of the UK-based Society for Studies in Organising Healthcare (SHOC). The Montreal conference theme was: *Coordinating Care across Boundaries and Borders*, culminating in this collection, which joins the OBHC book series of Palgrave Macmillan, edited by Jean-Louis Denis, Justin Waring and Paula Hyde.

The book is divided into four parts. Part I features chapters that document efforts by policy-makers, health services and healthcare teams to coordinate care across professional and organisational boundaries, and sectoral boundaries including primary, community and acute care. The chapters in Part II exemplify conceptual innovations in health organisational research, showing how the field spans ideological, learning and practice boundaries. In seeking to integrate policy reforms with locally responsive innovations, the chapters in Part III show that health system leadership is a question of reconciling strategy, identity, knowledge and change. Part IV moves the discussion of boundary-work into potential health system interventions, focusing on strengthening the self-organising capabilities of boundaries themselves. We conclude by arguing that the reconciliation of coordinative efforts with the needs of the individuals and societies who pay for health services, depends on understanding work that happens within as well as across boundaries of healthcare workers, and health and social services and systems.

The translation of initial ideas of OBHC Conference contributors to this book is a substantial team effort. For their wisdom and support, we thank our colleagues on the Scientific and Organizing Committee of the OBHC Conference, Jamie DeMore, Samer Faraj, Ann Langley, Maud Mazaniello-Chézol and Diana Ramos. Maud Mazaniello-Chézol, in particular, was the linchpin of the conference coordination, continuing her contribution through post-conference publication. We wish also to thank Mark Exworthy, the President of SHOC for his ongoing support and sage advice, and the SHOC Committee. We thank Valérie Thomas, Emille Boulot, Allison Ford and Laura Rojas-Rozo, whose support and assistance were indispensable. Editing by Donetta Hines and Richard Cooper was most valuable, detailed and educational. Thanks are due to our hard-working colleagues in the international health organisational research community for providing anonymous reviews of the chapters. Last, but not least, we thank our patient editors at Palgrave Macmillan, Liz Barlow and Lucy Kidwell for meticulous guidance in the production of this book. These combined efforts have been central to this book's contribution to understanding healthcare coordination and change.

Healthcare delivery is becoming increasingly complex, and demands for greater accountability to patients and citizens are increasing.

The efforts of our health organisational studies community are directed toward advancing our understanding of healthcare coordination, as it is and how it can and should be. We invite you to share the leg of the journey that this book represents. Our colleagues in Manchester in the UK are sharpening the focus on the relationship between broader health systems and their constituent parts, with the theme: *Managing Healthcare Organisations in Challenging Policy Contexts: Integration or Fragmentation?* We look forward to tackling this challenge at the OBHC Conference in Manchester in 2020.

Montreal, Canada   Peter Nugus
2019   Charo Rodriguez
                                                       Jean-Louis Denis
                                                       Denis Chênevert

Introduction

Health systems worldwide are grappling with, but at least recognising, the centrality of coordinating difference in an increasingly complex care environment. Experiments in organising specialised care span disciplines, occupations, organisations and sectors. A central theme of this book is the relationship between strategic and organic change and what this means for the way we organise health work. How can we wittingly and optimally design healthcare delivery at policy and organisational levels that foster connections to localised practices, communities and consumers? How do we monitor the interests that various organisational choices serve? This book addresses these questions by focusing on how we codify healthcare work both in empirical analyses of practical interventions and through conceptual debate. What is evident in this snapshot in the evolution of organisational studies of healthcare is increasing recognition of the intersection of leadership, strategy and change. Furthermore, new ways of organising knowledge are shedding new light on how particular knowledge and types of knowledge are afforded credibility, and challenges posed to understanding the various identities of those who work, are treated and have a stake in, healthcare. We conclude by fusing questions of heedful boundary negotiation, in real times and places, with the conditions and activities that promote the sustainability of renewed and collaborative boundary practices themselves.

Part I presents empirical studies of care coordination that bring us up close to their opportunities and challenges. To open the contributions, Maniatopoulos and colleagues discuss new models of care (NCMs) through which the National Health Service (NHS) England has endeavoured to improve care quality, cost and outcomes. They focus on a "vanguard program" to implement new care models (NCMs) to integrate care more effectively and efficiently across healthcare sectors. In this work, the tensions between centralisation and local empowerment show that, without appropriate incentives guiding institutional and individual action, local practitioners disproportionately bear the burden of policy-practice contradictions. Bridges and colleagues then share an inside view of an organisational journey from planned policy to practice. We see starkly the extent to which and how external factors influence the effectiveness and sustainability of planned interventions, and must be taken account of. This journey of a planned intervention brings us face to face with the apparent tensions between target-driven organisational culture and lofty rhetoric about compassionate care. Dickinson and colleagues then offer us a laboratory of cross-provider negotiation in the form of NGOs partnering with governments—in this case to seek to eradicate a disease rarely seen in a developing country—in Australia's Northern Territory. Scabies, an infestation associated with skin infections, may yet withstand the cultural and institutional boundaries that such diverse organisations represent. Vulnerability is couched in organisational terms in Goldberg and Mohan's subsequent chapter. The very boundaries that impede care delivery to vulnerable people are shown to be surmountable by appropriately specialised organisational input, whose collaboration and partnership is mediated by leadership, culture and resources. Not only is inter-organisational collaboration central to the success of their model; formal education through the Guided Interprofessional Focused Teaching (GIFT) Model infuses formal education and reflexive collaboration.

Part II conveys ideas that have shaped and potentially could shape care coordination across boundaries. Malone commences this section by aligning abstract theory with boundaries of health policy and practice. He posits critical realism as an appropriately abstract and action-oriented theory that is adept at explaining complex phenomena such as healthcare, which involves a bewildering cast of players from different perspectives. Marchand and colleagues then model for us how theory has been used to contextualise research and innovation in healthcare. The notion of "governmentality" has been used variously, in studies of health systems and networks, as an epistemology, framework and specific form of governance. The variety of such uses points to the importance of clarifying the conceptual status of a particular theory, and also serves to highlight the significant impact, and necessity, of theory in organisational health research. Uniquely spanning from political ideology to policy, Kvåle and colleagues map ideologies of collectivism and individualism in Norwegian government attempts to redress social inequality, showing their manifestation and organisational consequences in healthcare policy. The authors argue that the cyclical pattern of ideological flux shows how policy influences could be better balanced to maximise structured solutions and the promotion of healthy lifestyle choices. Moralee and Bailey then draw on longitudinal qualitative educational data to argue that the concept of "hybridity" of the identities of the professional and the manager might be too simplistic to explain the degree to which and manner in which identities are subsumed into managerialist agendas.

Part III focuses on strategic change, and its relationship to knowledge and worker identity. What contribution can and do middle managers make in relation to strategic change? The extensive review presented by Gutberg and colleagues shows that middle managers have a greater contribution than thought to advance strategic change, and indeed to thwart it. Such capability by middle management is subject to conditions that engage managers consciously and early in strategic change processes. In the absence of an overt and strategic focus, middle managers might struggle to transcend pre-existing organisational power relations. In the following chapter, Wiggins redefines leadership as a boundary-specific mechanism of "tempered tenacity": that is, reflexively-inspired, emergent and shared meanings by which relatively stable and different cultures and practices are transgressed. Kislov and colleagues then unearth hidden modes by which particular forms of knowledge become embedded in institutions and are held as more credible than others, i.e. "chains of codified knowledge". Such forms of knowledge hence have a greater impact on practice, which open up contextualised, "bottom up" forms of knowledge, and opportunities for practice to be perceived as credible evidence.

Part IV addresses sustainability and the enactment of self-organising capacities of boundaries. Lennox and colleagues build a creative and extensive empirical study to examine the impact of a Long Term Success Tool (LTST) to indicate and prompt sustainability improvement interventions. The tool signaled threats to and opportunities for sustainability of the improvement interventions, drawing explicit attention to diverse opinions, direction needed and actions to be taken. Thus, they foreshadow the greater attention needed by conceptual researchers of organisational studies in healthcare to the space between tacit collaborative working and conscious awareness. This volume, then, represents increasing engagement with stakeholder responses to concrete "toolkits" and other devices of knowledge translation. For Sharp and colleagues, toolkits can be seen as tangible boundary objects, to satisfy the apparent need to reconcile differing audiences. Framing toolkits as boundary objects provides a realistic frame around which to identify what a "toolkit" can and cannot realistically accomplish. In aligning contexts, interventions, mechanisms and outcomes, the in-depth case study presented by Côté-Boileau and colleagues shows that, under conditions of change, the mobilisation of relational capacities becomes all the more important. Allowing the academic mission of a health service to expand across units or services which function differently, but which rely on each other for continuous care, will help build bridges across organisational boundaries. In the final chapter, French and colleagues enrich our understanding of the socio-cultural context of quality improvement, examining its local and cross-boundary manifestations. In their extensive case study, pragmatic boundary work was supported by boundary interactions by knowledge brokers across the different communities. Although quality improvement (QI) tools were still treated critically by colleagues, such localised interaction was, in many ways, more productive than "top-down" initiatives because they were more likely to be adaptable and adapted to local situations. Taken together, the four parts of the book help us to develop a broad understanding and promising perspectives on the integration and coordination of healthcare. We conclude by positioning coordination in terms of its systemic boundaries, and advocate for broader and more diverse perspectives in health organisational research. In essence, this edited collection challenges us to support and enact reform across disciplinary, institutional and conceptual boundaries to render our health delivery systems ever more efficient, effective, accessible, just and equitable.

Peter Nugus
Charo Rodriguez
Jean-Louis Denis
Denis Chênevert

Contents

Editors and Contributors

About the Editors

Peter Nugus is a sociologist and ethnographer, and Associate Professor in the Institute of Health Sciences Education and the Department of Family Medicine at McGill University, Montreal, Canada. Peter is also Acting Director of the McGill University Practice-based Research Network (PBRN). Peter's published ethnographic and participatory research in emergency departments and various hospital and community settings across six countries, and teaching, has focused on workplace and organisational learning, care coordination, culture and identity in complex organisations, and translation and mobilisation of knowledge across knowledge producers and users. Peter held a Fulbright Post-doctoral scholarship at the University of California Los Angeles and an Australian government Endeavour Post-doctoral scholarship at Columbia University, and was a Postdoctoral Fellow at the Netherlands Institute for Health Services Research (NIVEL). Peter has publications in leading journals, such as the *British Medical Journal, Social Science & Medicine* and *Sociology of Health & Illness.*

Charo Rodriguez is Full Professor in the Department of Family Medicine and Director of the Family Medicine Educational Research (FMER) Group, at McGill University, Montreal, Canada. Charo completed her studies in Medicine at the University of Alicante, Spain. She obtained an M.Sc. in Public Health (Management) at the University of Valencia, Spain, and completed a Ph.D. in Public Health (Health Care Organization) at the University of Montreal. With funding from competitive grants offered by the Canadian Insitute's of Health Research, and the Fonds de Recherche du Quebéc, among other agencies, Charo's research interests and publications are in professional and organisational identity, medical education, power, organisational discourse, inter-organisational and interprofessional collaboration, information technology implementation processes in health care organisations.

Jean-Louis Denis is Full Professor of Health Policy and Management at the School of Public Health, Université de Montréal, researcher at the Research Center of the CHUM (CRCHUM) and holds the Canada research chair (tier I) on health system design and adaptation. He is a visiting professor at the Department of Management, King's College London. His current research looks at healthcare reforms and health system transformation, innovations in academic health centres and the role of medical doctors in health policy. In recognition for his academic contribution to the field of health policy and management, he was nominated member of the Academy of Social Sciences of the Royal Society of Canada in 2002, fellow of the Canadian Academy of Health Sciences in 2009 and Fellow of Academy of Social Sciences (FAcSS) in 2019. Recent papers have been published in *Academy of Management Annals, Implementation Science, Journal of Public Administration Research and Theory, Public Administration and Perspectives on Public Management and Governance*. He is co-editor of the Palgrave series on *Organizational Behaviour in Healthcare*.

Denis Chênevert is a Full Professor at HEC-Montréal. He researches and teaches primarily in strategic human resources management, workforce and compensation, in particular as it relates to health care. He widely published, including in international scientific journals such as *International Journal of Human Resources Management, Group & Organization Management* and *Industrial Relations*. He regularly serves as an invited speaker on human resource management issues. Denis received his Ph.D. from the University of Toulouse, France.

Contributors

Simon Bailey is Sociologist based in the Centre for Health Services Studies, University of Kent, UK. His research interests are in the critical study of medical work, knowledge and organisation, notably the adoption of new knowledge, practices, technologies and roles and the manner in which these become embedded and institutionalised within healthcare organisations. His research expertise is in qualitative, ethnographic and arts-based methods; it is strongly interdisciplinary, spanning medical and organisational sociology, work and employment studies, education, and knowledge mobilisation and implementation.

G. Ross Baker is Professor in the Institute of Health Policy, Management and Evaluation, Dalla Lana School of Public Health, at the University of Toronto and led the development of an innovative Masters in Quality Improvement and Patient Safety at the Institute. Ross is widely published on the epidemiology, organisation analysis and policy issues related to patient safety and quality improvement. His recent research includes case studies of patient engagement strategies in healthcare organisations, an evaluation of an innovative approach to monitoring and measuring patient safety, research on integrated care strategies and an analysis of interprofessional team dynamics in quality improvement. In October 2017, Ross Baker received the Barer Flood Prize from the Institute of Health Services and Policy Research of the Canadian Institutes of Health Services Research in recognition of his "outstanding contributions to health services and policy research in Canada".

Whitney Berta is Professor with the University of Toronto's Institute of Health Policy, Management & Evaluation. She holds a Ph.D. from the Rotman School of Management, M.B.A. from McGill University and a B.Sc. in Biology-Human Genetics from the University of British Columbia. Dr. Berta has a sustained interest in the role of knowledge in organisational performance: How its acquisition, generation, use, non-use and disuse relate to organisational performance. In particular, she is interested in contributing to understanding of why, how and when workers in organisations generate or acquire new knowledge, how they collectively learn about and use new knowledge and why some organisations are highly effective in applying new knowledge to enhance their performance while others are less adept at doing so. Her work chiefly draws from, and aims to contribute to, the literature on organisational learning and knowledge transfer originating in the organisation and management sciences and relates to the concept of learning health systems.

Ruth J. Boaden is the Director of the NIHR CLAHRC for Greater Manchester (2014–2019)—a collaboration of NHS providers, commissioners, industry and third sector partners in Greater Manchester with the University of Manchester. Ruth is also Professor at the Alliance Manchester Business School, University of Manchester where her research covers a wide range of areas within health services management, including implementation science and knowledge mobilisation, along with quality and improvement. Ruth chairs research funding panels for the Alzheimer's Society and has been a member of the NIHR Knowledge Mobilisation Research Fellowships and NIHR Health Services and Delivery Research Board. Ruth is the independent academic advisor to the GM Health and Social Care Partnership Evaluation Programme. She wants research to make a difference.

Jackie Bridges is Professor of Older People's Care at the University of Southampton, England. She is a registered nurse and applied social scientist leading a major programme of research focused on professional work and organisational change related to older people's care. Her research has a particular focus on identifying the modifiable factors that promote or inhibit the delivery of responsive health care for older people with complex needs and on developing, implementing and evaluating interventions aimed at manipulating these factors.

Élizabeth Côté-Boileau is a doctoral candidate in the health sciences research programme at the Université de Sherbrooke (Quebec, Canada). She is also a doctoral fellow of the Fonds de recherche Santé—Québec (FRQS, 2017–2020). Her main research interests regard the governance and capacity building dynamics of large-scale health system transformations, with a particular focus on performance and innovation management. Her thesis project focuses on integrated performance management systems and behaviours towards value-based public healthcare systems. Élizabeth cumulates several pan-Canadian research collaborations, mainly through her work as a consultant for the Canadian Foundation of Healthcare Improvement (CFHI) and Health Standards Organization (HSO). She is also a board member of the *Canadian Association for Health Services and Policy Research (CAHSPR)* as the Student Working Group Co-Chair, co-founder of the *Early Career Hub—The Society for Organizational Studies in Healthcare (SHOC)*, and an active member of the *Hub-Health: Politics, Organizations and Law (H-POD)* from University of Montreal.

Greta Cummings is Dean of the Faculty of Nursing, University of Alberta, Canada. She leads the CLEAR (Connecting Leadership Education and Research) Outcomes Research Program, focusing on leadership practices of healthcare decision-makers to achieve better health outcomes in the healthcare system and for providers and patients. She has published more than 200 papers and was a 2014 Highly Cited Researcher in Social Sciences (Thomson Reuters) for papers arising from her leadership research.

Helen Dickinson is Professor of Public Service Research and Director of the Public Service Research Group at the School of Business, University of New South Wales, Canberra. Her expertise is in public services, particularly in relation to topics such as governance, leadership, commissioning and priority setting and decision-making. Helen has published eighteen books and over sixty peer-reviewed journal articles on these topics and is also a frequent commentator within the mainstream media. She is co-editor of the *Journal of Health, Organization and Management* and *Australian Journal of Public Administration*. Helen is also a board member of the Consumer Policy Research Centre. In 2015, Helen was made a Victorian Fellow of the Institute of Public Administration Australia, and she has worked with a range of different levels of government, community organisations and private organisations in Australia, UK, New Zealand and Europe on research and consultancy programmes.

William G. Dixon is Professor of Digital Epidemiology, Director of the Centre for Epidemiology Versus Arthritis at the University of Manchester and an honorary consultant rheumatologist at Salford Royal NHS Foundation Trust. He qualified from Guy's and St. Thomas' Hospitals, London, trained as a rheumatologist in Manchester, UK, and has higher degrees from the University of Manchester and McGill University, Montreal. His interests are medication safety (pharmacoepidemiology) and using technology to support clinical care and research to improve patients' lives, including the collection and analysis of electronic health record data, collecting patient-generated health data using consumer devices and analysis of social media data.

Michelle Dowden is Registered Nurse Midwife with 25 years' experience conducting health programmes that focus on good clinical outcomes and the social determinants of health. The main focus of her work has been with remote Indigenous communities and other large Indigenous health services throughout Australia, both in research and in service delivery. She has a strong background in continuous quality improvement and currently is the CEO for One Disease which is not-for-profit organisation working to eliminate Crusted Scabies from Australia. In 2006, she completed the Masters in Public Health at Charles Darwin University Treatise topic, Factors Affecting Uptake of CQI.

Anna Ehrenberg is professor of nursing and head of research in health and welfare in the School of Education, Health and Social Studies, Dalarna University, Sweden. Her research is in the area of implementation of evidence-based practice, patient safety and nursing informatics to support nursing knowledge in assessments of patient care needs and clinical decision-making.

Jonathan Erskine is Honorary Fellow at Durham University, where he worked from 2014 to 1016 in health policy research, specialising in large-scale change in health systems and organisation development in the UK's NHS. He has published journal articles and book chapters on new care models in the English NHS, transformational change in health systems, the built infrastructure of health care, Lean management in health organisations and culture change in the health and social care sectors. He is Executive Director of the European Health Property Network, a pan-European knowledge hub for organisations involved in the strategic planning and design of healthcare facilities, and he is currently a non-executive director on the board of an NHS Hospital Foundation Trust in the north-east of England.

Jane Frankland is Senior Research Fellow in the School of Health Sciences at the University of Southampton, England. She is an experienced mixed methods researcher, with particular expertise in qualitative methods and evaluation of complex interventions. Her research career spans health service and public health research. Her interests lie in the everyday experiences and work of health and illness; self-care and self-management; help-seeking; and the acquisition of health knowledge and skills.

Catherine E. French is a health service manager and researcher specialising in developing organisational approaches and capacity building to translate research into practice. Catherine's research background is in social science, and her interests include knowledge mobilisation, academic healthcare organisations and qualitative methodology. Catherine was awarded an NIHR Doctoral Research Fellowship to undertake her Ph.D. at UCL (researching boundary spanning processes in Academic Health Science Centres) which she completed in November 2016. Catherine has over 15 years' experience in operational management, programme management, capacity building and service improvement roles in the NHS across acute care, commissioning and mental health, including from 2104 to 2018 as Collaborative Learning and Partnerships lead at CLAHRC Northwest London where she was responsible for developing a quality improvement capacity building programme informed by an action research approach. Since 2018,

Catherine has been leading a programme of transformation to integrate clinical care and research across a large university and NHS partnership.

Karen Gardner is Senior Research Fellow at the University of New South Wales Canberra where she leads the complex systems research theme in the Public Services Research Group at the School of Business. Before moving into academia, she worked in practice and policy roles in the non-government sector and in government, in the areas of youth health and homelessness, and primary healthcare reform. This galvanised her interest in the study of change in complex real-world settings and her commitment to working in partnership with service providers and those whose health and well-being are at stake. Recent projects have focused on the implementation of continuous quality improvement programmes, primary care performance measurement and commissioning processes, and the evaluation of complex health interventions in Aboriginal and Torres Strait Islander communities.

Wendy Gifford is Associate Professor in the School of Nursing, Faculty of Health Sciences, University of Ottawa, Canada, and Codirector of the Center for Research on Health and Nursing. Her programme of research focuses on implementation leadership and knowledge translation with healthcare providers and includes working with Indigenous communities in Canada.

Dr. Debora Goetz Goldberg is Associate Professor in the Department of Health Administration and Policy at George Mason University. She is a mixed methods researcher with an emphasis on survey and qualitative research methodologies. Her research focuses on primary care practice transformation, patient experience and care for the underserved. Her teaching experience includes courses on the US healthcare system, change management and leadership, evaluation and outcomes research methodology, and qualitative research methods. Before entering academia, she worked in healthcare management consulting serving commercial and government clients.

Peter Griffiths is Chair of Health Services Research at the University of Southampton, England, and Senior Investigator of the UK's National Institute for Health Research (NIHR). He is lead of the fundamental care in hospitals research theme of the NIHR Collaboration for Leadership in Applied Health Research and Care (Wessex). His research focuses on the nursing workforce and factors influencing safe and effective nursing care delivery. He has published widely on safe nurse staffing and has worked closely with the National Institute for Health and Care Excellence and NHS Improvement on their work to develop guidance for safe nurse staffing levels and systems.

Jennifer Gutberg, M.Sc. is a Ph.D. candidate at the Institute of Health Policy, Management and Evaluation at the University of Toronto. She holds a Master of Science in Administration from the John Molson School of Business at Concordia University and a Bachelor of Arts in Psychology from McGill University. Her research interests are in the organisation and management of health care, with particular focus on organisational culture, leadership and patient safety. She is additionally interested in and has conducted research exploring models of integrated care from an organisational lens, particularly through the use of qualitative methods. Jennifer's dissertation explores the role of middle managers and front-line providers in strategic patient safety culture change efforts. Her research is supported by the Fonds de recherche du Québec—Santé, as well as the Health System Performance Research Network.

Gill Harvey is Professorial Research Fellow in the Adelaide Nursing School, University of Adelaide, Australia. Previously, she was professor of health management in the Alliance Manchester Business School, University of Manchester, UK. She has a professional background in nursing, and her research interests are in the field of knowledge translation and implementation. She was recognised for work in this field in 2014 with a listing as a Thomson Reuters highly cited researcher in the social sciences category.

Bob Hudson is Honorary Professor in Public Policy in the Centre for Health Services Studies at the University of Kent. Prior to this, he worked at the Open University, the Nuffield Institute for Health, University of Leeds, the University of Durham, University of Glasgow and New College Durham. Bob has been involved in several major research and consultancy projects on health and social care over the past thirty years and has written about these widely in the academic and professional press and wider media.

David J. Hunter graduated in political science from Edinburgh University. His academic career spans over 40 years researching complex health systems with a focus on how health policy is formed and implemented. Between 1999 and July 2017, David was Director of the Centre for Public Policy and Health at Durham University. The Centre was designated a WHO Collaborating Centre in Complex Health Systems Research, Knowledge and Action in 2014. In August 2017, he transferred to the Institute of Health & Society, Newcastle University and became an Emeritus Professor in August 2018. He is Visiting Professor, University of Chester. Former positions include: non-executive director, National Institute of Health and Care Excellence (NICE) (2008–2016); Appointed Governor, South Tees Hospitals NHS Foundation Trust (2009–2017); and special advisor to the UK Parliamentary Health Committee. He is Honorary Member of the UK Faculty of Public Health and Fellow of the Royal College of Physicians (Edinburgh).

Janet Kelly is a nurse researcher in South Australia who works collaboratively with Aboriginal community members, health carers and researchers in urban, rural and remote areas to improve healthcare experiences and outcomes. She develops patient journey mapping tools and case studies that identify barriers and enablers to care from multiple perspectives. These tools assist healthcare professionals in developing ground-up evidence and comparing their practice to patient priorities, health service guidelines and standards.

Charlotte Kiland is Associate Professor in Political Science at the Department of Political Science and Management at University of Agder, Norway. She has coordinated a bachelor and master programme in public health for several years. Her research and publications have focused on organisational change in local government, inter-municipal cooperation, public sector reforms and the relationship between political and administrative leadership. Her current research interests also include health system governance and implementation of public health policies.

Roman Kislov is Senior Research Fellow in the Alliance Manchester Business School, University of Manchester, UK. He conducts qualitative research on the processes and practices of knowledge mobilisation, with a particular interest in communities of practice, intermediary roles, organisational learning and implementation of change. Before joining academia, he worked as a doctor for a gold mining company in Central Asia, combining clinical work with a managerial post.

Alison Kitson is the inaugural Vice President and Executive Dean of the College of Nursing and Health Sciences, Flinders University, Adelaide, South Australia. Prior to this appointment, she was dean and head of school at Adelaide Nursing School at the University of Adelaide. Alison has published more than 300 peer-reviewed articles and in 2014 was acknowledged in the Thomson Reuters list of highly cited researchers for her work on knowledge translation.

Gro Kvåle is Associate Professor in Organization and Management at the Department of Political Science and Management, University of Agder, Norway. She has taught organisation theory, public administration and research design among other things for more than 20 years at all levels of higher education. Kvåle's research and publications are mainly in organising, change and reforms in the public sector. Governance, legitimacy and identity concerning public organisations in particularly public welfare and health organisations are of special interest along with the important and fascinating field of public health policy.

Laura Lennox is the Associate Lead for Improvement Science and Quality Improvement at CLAHRC NWL within the Department of Primary Care and Public Health at Imperial College London in the UK. Prior to joining Imperial College in 2011, she worked as a registered nurse in Ontario, Canada, and obtained a Master's in Public Health from the London School of Hygiene and Tropical Medicine. Laura is passionate about understanding how healthcare systems can maximise investments and reduce waste to produce long-term change for patient care. Laura currently works with healthcare teams to study how improvement takes place in practice, evaluating how effectively

QI methods are applied and exploring how their use can be improved. Laura was awarded her Ph.D. in 2019. Her doctoral work explores the process of achieving sustainability in healthcare improvement initiatives and investigates how sustainability can be influenced with the use of specific strategies and interventions.

Paula Libberton is Principal Teaching Fellow in the School of Health Sciences at the University of Southampton. She is a registered mental health nurse, and her research involves the study of relational capacity of ward nursing teams to deliver compassionate care which supports both physical and mental health.

Antoine Malone is a Ph.D. student at Ecole Nationale d'Administration Publique (ENAP) in Montreal and young researcher at Université de Montréal's H-POD. He is Director of Research for the French Hospital's Federation (Paris).

His research interests include comparative healthcare policies, knowledge management in healthcare organisations, policy and transformative capacity in health care and clinical integration. He regularly teaches at Sciences Po Paris, on healthcare reforms.

As Director of Research for the French Hospitals Federation, he is currently charged with developing and implementing a large-scale clinical integration and population health project.

Gregory Maniatopoulos is Senior Research Associate at the Institute of Health & Society, Newcastle University, UK. His research interests lie primarily in the broad area of health systems, policy implementation and change, in particular exploring how organisational, technological and policy factors shape processes of appropriation of innovations in healthcare practice. Previous research on this area has embraced a variety of innovations and settings, and his most recent work has focused upon the implementation of new care models, innovative health technologies and the transitions of care. He has been involved as researcher, Co-Investigator and Principal Investigator in several research projects for the National Institute for Health Research (NIHR), the Engineering and Physical Sciences Research Council (EPSRC), the European Commission and a number of UK government departments and local authorities.

Jean-Sebastien Marchand is a post-doctoral researcher at *Faculty of medicine and health sciences* of *Universite de Sherbrooke* (Canada) and *Centre de recherche Charles-Le Moyne—Saguenay–Lac-Saint-Jean sur les innovations en santé* (CR-CSIS, Canada). He is also lecturer in *Ecole nationale d'administration publique* (ENAP, Canada) and research associate at *Health Management Innovation Research Centre* (HMI Lab) of *ESCP Europe* (France). His primary research interests are the performance and management of public healthcare organisations. He also focuses on the governance and structuration of hybrid networks in public administration and the comparative performance of emergency departments. His works have been published in peer-reviewed journals, most recently the *International Review of Administrative Sciences* and the *Journal of Clinical Oncology*. As a *Health System Impact Fellow* of the *Canadian Institutes of Health Research* (CIHR), he works closely with healthcare executives and policy-makers to improve the performance of the Canadian healthcare system.

Carl May is Professor of Medical Sociology at the London School of Hygiene and Tropical Medicine, England. He is a medical sociologist and implementation scientist with a wide range of research interests across the sociology of health technologies and of human relations in the healthcare systems of the advanced economies. This work has ranged from very applied evaluation studies in health services research (especially in qualitative studies nested within randomised controlled trials) through studies of the social construction of professional-patient relations and different disease entities, to fundamental social science research on the dynamics of human agency under conditions of constraint. Carl is one of the key architects of Normalization Process Theory.

Akhilesh Mohan is completing a DDS degree at the Herman Ostrow School of Dentistry at the University of Southern California (USC). He completed a Master of Health Administration in Health Systems Management (MHA) at George Mason University in 2017. While at Mason he was the President of the MHA Healthcare Leaders of Tomorrow (MHALT) student organisation and a research assistant in the Department of Health Administration and Policy. He also holds a master's level degree in Dental Surgery specialising in Orthodontics from M R Ambedkar Dental College & Hospital in Bengaluru, Karnataka, India.

Simon Moralee is an organisational sociologist based in the Health Management Group, part of the Alliance Manchester Business School, the University of Manchester, UK. His career background is in health economics and health service management, before turning to academia in 2007. His research interests are in the study of management and leadership education in the medical profession, as well as in health policy within the wider health and social care sector. His research expertise is in qualitative approaches and is strongly focused on impact for practitioner groups in health and care roles.

Marie-Andrée Paquette is a research professional at the Center for Action in Work Disability Prevention and Rehabilitation (CAPRIT), Université de Sherbrooke. As such, she contributes to develop and evaluate practical knowledge and tools aiming to support healthcare practitioners and other stakeholders involved in the work rehabilitation process. She is also responsible of managing and coordinating the activities of the Research Chair in Rehabilitation at Work (J-Armand Bombardier and Pratt & Whitney Canada). Initially trained in political science, public health and public administration, she has developed great research interests and expertise in healthcare systems governance, as testified by recent publications in the *International Journal of Integrated Care*, the *International Journal of Public Administration* and *Health : An Interdisciplinary Journal for the Social Study of Health, Illness and Medicine*.

Tyrone A. Perreira, Ph.D., M.Ed. is Assistant Professor at the Institute of Health Policy Management and Evaluation, Dalla Lana School of Public Health at the University of Toronto. Dr. Perreira's research is in the field of micro-organisational behaviour. His areas of interest include work psychology, psychometrics and research methods. Collaborating with the Ontario Medical Association, the Ontario Hospital Association and Health Quality Ontario, current projects include physician engagement, well-being and quality improvement. For the past 20 years, Dr. Perreira has worked across the continuum of care. He has collaborated on international projects with world-renowned scholars. His early research involved performance measurement and randomised controlled trials in cardiac and trauma resuscitation. Dr. Perreira obtained his doctorate in Health Services Research from the University of Toronto and holds a Master of Education.

Lena Pettersson is Research Coordinator at Dalarna University, Sweden. Previously, she was research management and governance manager at Clinical Research Network Eastern, Cambridge, UK. Her professional background is nursing with a bachelor's degree in nursing from the Red Cross School of Nursing in Stockholm, Sweden, and a master's degree in health promotion from the University of East London.

Julie E. Reed is the Deputy Director and Academic Lead for the National Institute of Health Research (NIHR) Collaboration for Leadership in Applied Health Research and Care (CLAHRC) Northwest London. Julie is also Senior Research Fellow at Imperial College and was in the first cohort of Improvement Science Fellows funded by the Health Foundation. Julie's research interest covers a wide range of topics associated with the emerging field of Improvement Science. Julie is at the forefront of defining this new field working with international colleagues to define the Frontiers of Improvement Science, to establish principles of Improvement in Organisations and to advance thinking about how to evaluate complex interventions in complex systems.

Caroline M. Sanders is Professor of Medical Sociology at the University of Manchester and has a professional background in nursing. She has expertise in health services research and qualitative research methods. Her interests include the collection and use of patient experience data, the negotiation of trust and privacy online, and the impact of digital innovations on healthcare interactions and inequalities. She leads the "Marginalised Groups (Patients & Carers)" research theme within the NIHR funded Greater Manchester Patient Safety Translational Research Centre. She is also Director for Public and Patient Involvement and Engagement (PPIE) at Health Innovation Manchester and has expertise in participatory methods for co-design of healthcare interventions.

Charlotte A. Sharp is a specialist rheumatology trainee in the North West of England, with undergraduate degrees in Medicine and Healthcare Ethics and Law. Her current doctoral research is based at the Alliance Manchester Business School and focuses upon knowledge mobilisation products derived from healthcare research (e.g. toolkits), asking why and how they are developed and how this might influence their potential application. Charlotte's research is funded by the National Institute for Health Research Collaboration for Leadership in Applied Health Research and Care (NIHR CLAHRC) Greater Manchester and the Connected Health Cities programme. Research and practice interests include knowledge mobilisation, implementation science and quality improvement. In 2018, she led the development of the British Society for Rheumatology Choosing Wisely UK recommendations.

Dag Olaf Torjesen is Associate Professor in Organization at Department of Political Science and Management, University of Agder, Norway. Torjesen has more than 20 years teaching and supervision experience and is heading an executive master programme in health management at University of Agder. Torjesen is supervising the Ph.D. project, "Local adaption to a national health care reform". He is also involved in comparative research within the Nordic region, such as engaging in research and publications on political and administrative leaders in Nordic Local Government, and governance and institutional change in Nordic healthcare systems, including on the role of patients in health care delivery.

Dominique Tremblay holds an academic position at the Faculty of Medicine, Université de Sherbrooke. With her research team, she produces new knowledge to improve clinical and organisational practices. For example, she analyse the implementation of cancer networks and the impact on timely access to quality and cost-effective care. Modernising health services delivery for cancer patients and their loved ones is an imperative worldwide. Dr. Dominique Tremblay, Research Chair in Quality and Security of Care for Cancer Patients, is seeking to develop, implement and evaluate promising interventions to enhance each patient and family experience at all stages of the cancer journey.

Dr. Tremblay works closely with patients, managers, clinicians and policy-makers to identify opportunities for improvement in cancer care and to design tailored interventions. Her goal is to join individual and collective efforts to reduce the cancer burden.

Naomi van der Linden is Health Economist, working at AstraZeneca the Netherlands as Market Access and Health Economics Manager. She has a multidisciplinary background in Medicine (Drs.), Clinical Epidemiology (M.Sc.), Organisational Anthropology (B.Sc.) and Health Economics (M.Sc.), with a Ph.D. in the use of real-world evidence to inform reimbursement decisions. Her post-doctoral research includes work in infectious diseases, oncology, cardiovascular and renal conditions, diagnostics and emergency medicine. Naomi is passionate about realistically capturing the value of interventions in health economic models, to inform decision-making.

Lars Wallin is professor of nursing in the School of Education, Health and Social Studies, Dalarna University, Sweden. His research programme focuses on the study of implementation and knowledge use. It includes systematic literature reviews, instrument development and intervention studies. He has also contributed to national and international cluster randomised trials investigating the effectiveness of facilitation and reminder systems as implementation strategies.

Liz Wiggins is Associate Professor of Change and Leadership at Ashridge Executive Education, Hult International Business School in the UK where she co-leads the GenerationQ Masters in Leadership (Quality Improvement). She has over twenty-five years' experience working with leaders in the UK, Europe and Asia as an executive coach, change consultant and facilitator. Much of her current work is with healthcare organisations in the UK and the Middle East. She was Vice President Communications at Unilever and on the board of the change consultancy, Smythe Dorward Lambert. Liz has two master's degrees and a Ph.D. in Organizational Psychology from Birkbeck College, University of London. Her current research interests are exploring what it takes to shift cultures and examining the nature of power and politics.

Paul Wilson is Senior Research Fellow in the Alliance Manchester Business School, University of Manchester, UK. His research interests are focused on evidence-informed decision-making in health policy and practice and the development and evaluation of methods to increase the uptake of research-based knowledge in health systems. He is the co-editor-in-chief of Implementation Science.

List of Figures

List of Tables

Part I

Coordinating Care Across Organisational and Sectoral Boundaries

This first Part orients the book with a series of conceptually-informed innovations in policy and practice that aim to contribute to care coordination across organisational and sectoral boundaries. The first chapter, contributed by Maniatopoulos and colleagues, focuses on initiatives in the National Health Service of England, to support system-wide lessons of care organisation among a select group of "Vanguard" sites. In the second chapter, also from the UK, Bridges and colleagues trace the contextual factors that are central to embedding compassionate care interventions and micro and meso organisational levels. The following chapter, contributed by Dickinson and colleagues, stands outside conventional health services, showing how a single Australian organisation, One Disease, is able to optimise various and diverse networks that might be less easy for embedded health services to reach. Finally, Goldberg and Mohan's study, from the US, shows the dexterity of local health services to be able to respond uniquely and appropriately, through multi-sector collaboration, relationship-building and embedding professional training opportunities, to the health and social needs of vulnerable communities.

1

Implementing the New Care Models in the NHS: Reconfiguring the Multilevel Nature of Context to Make It Happen

Gregory Maniatopoulos, David J. Hunter, Jonathan Erskine and Bob Hudson

List of Abbreviations
ACC: Acute Care Collaboration Vanguard
ACO: Accountable Care Organisations
CCG: Clinical Commissioning Group
EHCH: Enhanced Health in Care Homes

G. Maniatopoulos (✉) · D. J. Hunter
Institute of Health and Society, Newcastle University,
Newcastle upon Tyne, UK
e-mail: gregory.maniatopoulos@newcastle.ac.uk

D. J. Hunter
e-mail: david.hunter2@newcastle.ac.uk

J. Erskine
Durham University, Durham, UK
e-mail: jonathan.erskine@durham.ac.uk

B. Hudson
Center for Health Services, University of Kent, Canterbury, UK
e-mail: b.hudson-278@kent.ac.uk

© The Author(s) 2020
P. Nugus et al. (eds.), *Transitions and Boundaries in the Coordination
and Reform of Health Services*, Organizational Behaviour in Healthcare,
https://doi.org/10.1007/978-3-030-26684-4_1

GP: General Practice
ICP: Integrated Care Partnerships
MCPs: Multispeciality Community Providers
MDT: Multidisciplinary Team
NCMs: New Care Models
NHS: National Health System
PACS: Primary and Acute Care Systems
PbR: Payments by Results
STPs: Sustainability and Transformation Partnerships
UEC: Urgent and Emergency Care
UK: United Kingdom
5YFV: NHS Five Year Forward View

Introduction

With health systems globally facing new and complex challenges, policy-makers are increasingly preoccupied with and thus prioritize transforming the way services are organised and provided to meet rapidly changing conditions (Hunter 2016; Hunter et al. 2015; WHO 2016, 2018). In the UK, the health and social care system faces mounting pressures to improve outcomes and reduce inequalities despite increasing financial stringency and uncertainty.

Following publication of the *NHS Five Year Forward View* (5YFV) in 2014, a Vanguard programme was introduced by NHS England (the executive non-departmental public body of the Department of Health and Social Care oversees the NHS) to test different approaches to health and social care service delivery (NHS England 2017). The reform programme has constituted the most significant and ambitious set of changes experienced by the health and social care sectors in England in recent years. In particular, the changes are not concerned primarily with structures or top-down reform edicts; rather, they seek new ways of working and joining up care across a whole system, driven by those on the front line. These reform initiatives have typically taken place under the banner of "Triple Aim" thinking, focusing on population health, effective patient-centred care, and per capita cost (Berwick et al. 2008). The NHS invited individual organisations and partnerships, including those with voluntary and community sector involvement, to apply to become pilot sites for the Vanguard new care models (NCMs) programme. In this context, the term "Vanguard" signifies a new care model that is exemplary in its innovative capacity to optimise the health of individuals and the population, through and while providing efficient health care. Overall, 50 Vanguards were established across England, tasked with designing and delivering a range of NCMs to tackle deep-seated problems typical of all health systems to a greater or lesser degree.

The NCMs include managing rising demand on accident and emergency services, keeping people out of hospital, effecting rapid discharge for those no longer in need of acute care, integrating health and social care, reducing silo working, and giving higher priority to prevention. The reform is intended to foster greater engagement of frontline staff by providing innovative ways of working that connect care and lessons across other services and indeed the whole health system, rather than rely solely on top-down reform edicts.

Against this background, we explore factors shaping the implementation of five Vanguard pilot sites for the NCM programme in the North East region of England. We draw upon an evaluation study, conducted over 12 months, which explored the implementation arrangements of the following Vanguards: Multispecialty Community Providers (MCP); Integrated Primary and Acute Care Systems (PACS) Vanguard; Acute Care Collaboration (ACC) Vanguard; Enhanced Health in Care Homes (EHCH) Vanguard; and Urgent and Emergency Care (UEC) Vanguard (see Appendix A for a brief description of each Vanguard). The evaluation was conducted during a time of ongoing policy changes, notably developments surrounding Sustainability and Transformation Partnerships (STPs), Accountable Care Organisations (ACOs), and Integrated Care Partnerships (ICPs).

In seeking to understand the changes and the likelihood of success, we draw upon Pettigrew et al.'s (1992a) "receptive contexts for change" framework, which we combine with more recent theoretical developments aiming to address the multilevel nature of context (Maniatopoulos et al. 2015; Greenhalgh et al. 2017). Despite its emphasis on the complex, multifaceted nature of implementing changes, we consider that the framework of "receptive contexts" acquires even greater nuance when framed in terms of multiple levels of context (macro-, meso-, and micro-) which has gained increasing currency among organisational and healthcare researchers (ibid.). Our purpose here is to broaden the scope and scale of analysis across the multiple levels of context shaping both process and outcomes of health systems transformation.

Implementation, Context, and Change: Towards a Multilevel Contextual Analysis

Theory and research addressing the diffusion of changes in healthcare organisations have accelerated and developed across a large, diverse, and complex literature, related frameworks, and disciplines, seeking to explore the contextual factors shaping the implementation process (Greenhalgh et al. 2004, 2005; Dopson and Fitzgerald 2005; Kaplan et al. 2010; Aarons et al. 2011; Bate 2014; Greener et al. 2014; Fulop and Robert 2015; Squires et al. 2015; May et al. 2016; Kyratsis et al. 2012; Nilsen 2015). Various conceptualisations of context reflect the different perspectives exploring the recursive relationship between human action and the wider organisational and system context (Greenhalgh et al. 2016; Damschroder et al. 2009).

Pettigrew et al.'s (1992a) "receptive contexts for change" framework was one of the first attempts to explicitly recognise the complex, multifaceted nature of implementing changes in practice. Such a perspective challenges the conventional split between policy formulation and implementation by viewing these processes not as discrete but as interactive (Pettigrew 1990; Pettigrew et al. 1992b). Its basic proposition is that any analysis of change should focus not solely on the content of the change initiative, but also on the process (including actions and interactions of key players) and on the context (both local or "inner" context and the "outer" context of national and regional policies and events) (Pettigrew et al. 1992a). This requires viewing change as a multifaceted process, involving social, political, cultural, environmental, and structural dimensions. As such, "receptive contexts" are defined as situations where there are features of both context and individual action that seem to be favourably disposed to change. Conversely, non-receptive contexts are those situations where a combination of conditions effectively creates blockages or resistance to change. The key factors comprising the "receptive contexts for change" framework are summarised in Table 1.1.

Recent theoretical developments have attempted to explore further the interdependent relationships between different structural elements of the context across a multilevel set of practices (Maniatopoulos et al. 2015; Greenhalgh et al. 2016, 2017; Robert et al. 2010). Such perspectives recognise the mediating role of context, not just at the immediate level of implementation but at the policy, systems, and organisational levels, where the complexities associated with the political economy of health care (e.g. funding and commissioning) are important determinants of the success, or failure, of implementation (Maniatopoulos et al. 2015). The focus on the local and more distant social, political, and economic influences plays a key role in the so-called theories of social practice which aim to produce rich theorisations of the process of implementation as an outcome of social practice (Greenhalgh et al. 2017).

Drawing upon wider intellectual resources, such approaches aim to move away from viewing context as a layered and unidirectional set of influences with pre-existing "top" and "bottom" structures by highlighting the dynamic nature of context; that is to say, context is seen as evolving and changing over time (Maniatopoulos et al. 2015; Dopson and Fitzgerald 2005). Accordingly, the boundary between inner and outer context, far from being given or fixed, becomes both socially configured and reconfigurable, thus allowing alternative ways of reshaping organisational change. From this perspective, implementation is seen as an emergent and contingent process of contextual and relational organising through "sense-making" (Weick 1995; Peck and 6 2006). Such an approach reinforces previous attempts to reassess models of policy implementation in the "congested state", notable for multilevel governance and a need to align both vertical (centre-local) and horizontal (central-central and local-local) axes (Exworthy and Powell 2004). While previous research (e.g. Pettigrew et al. 1992a) has highlighted the complex, multifaceted nature of implementing change, we argue

Table 1.1 "Receptive contexts for change" framework

Factors	Description	Focus of analysis	Empirical focus
Quality and coherence of policy	Evidence-based policy and alignment between goals, feasibility, and implementation requirements at both national and local levels	Macro-level	The role of policy priorities for improving health care
Environmental pressure	Environmental conditions for transformational change, including political context	Macro-level	The role of financial and public concerns to service improvement
Supportive organisational culture	Organisational support and commitment for change	Meso-level	The role of shared values, beliefs, and patterns of behaviour
Change agenda and its locale	Local political culture and support for organisational changes	Meso-level	The role of local pressures to improve health services
Simplicity and clarity of goals and priorities	Identified goals, priorities, and a pathway for change that is sustainable over time	Meso-level	The role of multiple priorities at both national and local level
Cooperative inter-organisation network	Joined-up thinking/partnership arrangements across organisational and professional boundaries—formal and informal	Meso-level	The role of partnerships, alliances, or other collaborations between professionals and organisations working together
Managerial–clinical relations	High-trust managerial–clinical relationships	Micro-level	The role of relationship-building through multidisciplinary teams
Key people leading change	Leadership and adoption of a shared vision, values, and beliefs	Micro-level	The role of credible change agents/champions to lead change/system leadership

that implementation science can advance in the practical lessons it can offer decision-makers by understanding better how change is implemented in regard to the multiple levels of context (macro-, meso-, and micro-) and, crucially, to how reconfigurations across a multilevel set of practices shape implementation and change. Drawing upon the multilevel nature of context, we distil lessons from an exploration of factors shaping the implementation of five Vanguard pilot sites for the NCM programme in the North East region of England.

Understanding the Implications of New Care Models

Data collection involved semi-structured interviews (66 in total; see Table 1.1) conducted between December 2016 and May 2017 with key informants at each site, and a detailed review of Trusts' internal documents and policies related to the implementation of each Vanguard. Participants were purposively selected according to their role and involvement in the implementation of each Vanguard and included clinicians, chief executives, commissioner managers, project managers, and other specialists. Participants were provided with information sheets in advance, and they signed consent forms prior to the commencement of the interviews. Interviews lasted around one hour and were digitally recorded and transcribed (Table 1.2).

Transcribed interview data were analysed using thematic analysis to generate category systems and repeated themes (Boyatzis 1998). This involved an iterative process of refining codes to more abstract themes to characterise the data and make their lessons transferable. To ensure analytical rigour, two members of the research team independently coded and analysed the qualitative data. These were then reviewed and discussed at wider research team meetings, with any discrepancies resolved through discussion. Following the analysis within each Vanguard site, a comparative case study approach (Ragin and Becker 1992) was used to compare and contrast factors shaping the implementation arrangements across all five Vanguards. For confidentiality, all participants have been anonymised.

Table 1.2 List of interviewees

Vanguard	No. of interviews	Interviewees
MCP Vanguard	7	Senior Manager, CCG
MCP Vanguard	1	Senior Manager, LA
MCP Vanguard	3	Senior IT Manager, CCG
PACS Vanguard	11	Senior Manager, CCG
PACS Vanguard	2	Senior IT Manager, CCG
ACC Vanguard	7	Senior Manager, CCG
ACC Vanguard	3	Senior IT Manager, CCG
Enhanced Health in Care Homes Vanguard	14	Senior Manager, CCG
Enhanced Health in Care Homes Vanguard	3	Senior IT Manager, CCG
Urgent and Emergency Care Vanguard	11	Senior Manager, CCG
Urgent and Emergency Care Vanguard	4	Senior IT Manager, CCG
Total	**66**	

New Care Models in Practice

This section discerns factors shaping the implementation of five Vanguard pilot sites as they engaged with the multiple levels of context ranging from the macro policy level and the organisational responses at a meso-level to the micro-level setting of workforce redesign. Although inevitably there are multiple nuances between sites, our primary focus is on common issues and concerns across all five Vanguards. Unless otherwise stated, the quotations used reflect the general thoughts and views expressed by our interviewees.

Negotiating Uncertainty Around Policy and Government Targets

All five sites recognised that the Vanguard programme provided a significant opportunity for the region to improve the way services are organised and delivered, to meet the rapidly changing needs of their populations. Moreover, they felt that the programme provided an invaluable opportunity to develop a shared vision for the regional healthcare system, ranging from clinical workforce redesign to digital technology and patient empowerment. Despite these opportunities, each Vanguard had different aims, purposes, local arrangements, and practices. These factors had to be set against a wider context of significant financial tensions, uncertainty around the direction of policy, and fundamental questions about the future, including the impact of more recent policy developments that, as noted earlier, dominated the agenda. Therefore, the success of the programme would ultimately depend on the reconciliation of these macro-, meso-, and micro-levels of action. From a policy perspective, the rapid pace of policy development in the NHS led some interviewees to assert that actions or changes imposed by government can negatively affect progress.

> *I think we've had so many central directive changes over the last 18 months that it really hasn't helped with trying to get buy-in. From new care models becoming very much NHS- driven programmes, to Sustainability and Transformation Partnerships superseding local plans, to various things that just create layer upon layer of uncertainty; really – a lot of goal- post changes.* (EHCH-Senior Manager 6, CCG)

For some participants, the pace of such change is particularly concerning. The following comment is typical:

> *I think one of the challenges has been the speed that we've had to go; the pressure that we've had from NHS England, because of being part of a national programme. I think that the speed and the pressure have suited other work streams, rather than it has mine.* (EHCH-Senior Manager 10, CCG)

Despite the *5YFV*'s emphasis on "local flexibility" (NHS England 2014, p. 4) to support implementation, there was a perception that government targets and undue emphasis on performance could hinder progress:

> *We've been influenced heavily though by the national direction of travel around standards and improvements and national must-dos, which at times has conflicted with what we've been attempting to do.* (UEC-Senior Manager 5, CCG)

Essentially, all five Vanguards held similar views on the influence of the wider context within which they operated. They were critical in various ways of NHS England, particularly of the unrealistic pressure placed upon them to deliver efficiency savings and improved outcomes. Participants sensed neglect at the meso-level, limiting the ability of local actors to fulfil the Vanguard programme's ambition. There was a sense in which the pressure they felt was forcing the Vanguards to deliver without the appropriate substantive change being in place or sufficiently embedded and without being able to show sufficient or adequate evidence to support change.

> There's been a lot of pressure from NHS England for certain things to be done on frameworks and time series and delivery plan sort of thing. So, there is often a push from the office-based vanguard staff that we need to get certain things done... (EHCH, Senior Manager 14, CCG)

The uncertainty around the direction of policy developments surrounding STPs, ACOs, and more recently ICPs accompanied by growing financial pressures on the NHS raised issues and concerns about the sustainability of the positive developments underway across the NCM national programme.

Legitimating Return on Investment and Measuring Performance

All sites acknowledged that the Vanguards provided a platform for regional collaboration, innovation, and the sharing of best practice with the potential to strengthen the scale and pace of change and to do so more cost-effectively. There appeared to be a considerable degree of technology/digital innovation and sharing of optimal or promising practice, most notably in relation to information sharing. In this regard, a number of interviewees pointed to the benefits of being able to draw upon the support from the national programme, but there was evidence of a tension between national pressures and the need to maintain locally driven change. As a participant in the MCP Vanguard commented:

So, the demand to see efficiencies to deliver...feels very top-down – from a very high level...particularly in the last year, as opposed to the few years before that, when we've had time to do a bottom-up drive for designing change. (MCP-Senior Manager 2, CCG)

Although interviewees believed that hitherto national policy, and the NCM programme, had been of benefit, others spontaneously spoke of their fear that the *"rug would be pulled"* from under them with, for example, one model being recommended over all of the others, or alternatively, there would be a major change in policy.

From a national driver point of view, what's around the corner? What's going to be the flavour of the month? So, we put all this effort into the Five Year View, New Care Models and I think that for me is the main [concern]. (MCP-Senior Manager 4, CCG)

In this context, discussions regarding the national (i.e. English) NHS agenda tended to fall broadly into a number of categories. There was a minority group of respondents who acknowledged the invaluable support they believed they had received by being part of the Vanguard. For most, however, this was thought to come at a price. As one respondent in the PACS Vanguard commented:

There's an incredible level of scrutiny on you to be successful. I think the politics of it play out in the sense of trying to give you enough time to see results, but, at the same time, wanting results really fast so that they can roll models out nationally... (PACS-Senior Manager 3, CCG)

A number of interviewees criticised the Vanguard programme's ambitious plans for sustainable transformation during a period of significant financial pressures and uncertainty over the future of the NHS. Within all Vanguards, there were concerns that too much was being expected too soon, in terms of demonstrating a "return on investment" in digital capacity.

Nothing really gets time to bed in before the next initiative comes along – they give you £1 m and want to know the return on investment is £1.0325! (UEC-Senior IT Manager 2, CCG)

Availability of resources was considered a central factor for the successful implementation of each Vanguard. However, uncertainty around the availability of funding was evident across all sites. For example, cuts in the anticipated funding to digital developments have already made an impact:

> *Vanguard funding for urgent and emergency care is absolutely off the table. It has allowed us to get to this point but there is a lot more that could be done* (UEC-Senior IT Manager 1, CCG)

The need to legitimate return on investment and an undue emphasis on performance, then, represented a stark tension between macro- and other levels of social action, with frontline staff, at the micro-level, most strongly suffering the contradictions of unrealistic expectations from policy-makers.

Managing Different Structures and Governance Arrangements Across Care Settings

At an organisational level, participants felt that the Vanguard initiatives have the potential to address the problem of silo working across organisations. However, they also conveyed that current organisational arrangements could sometimes be a barrier to successful joint working. As one interviewee in the Care Home Vanguard commented:

> *At the moment, there's a boundary line that comes in between each thing that you do: 'that's health; that's social work.' It shouldn't be like that. It should be everybody working together for one outcome for the patient or the service user.* (EHCH-Senior Manager 7, CCG)

In this context, it was felt that variations in organisational, structural, and governance arrangements across different providers could serve as a barrier to the delivery of the programme's aims and objectives. As an interviewee in the UEC Vanguard stated:

We have two acute trusts and the focus in each acute trust is very different, and the pressures in each acute trust are very different, and they conflict. (UEC-Senior Manager 3, CCG)

Although interviewees reported how successfully relationships had been developed with different sectors, a focal point of discussions concerned the difficulties that the work and nature of the Vanguards could cause with external partners. For example, in the case of the ACC Vanguard, the apparent competitiveness of hospital trusts ran somewhat counter to acute care collaboration and at times was thought to promote suspicion and mistrust.

Then, there needs to be a bit of a behavioural shift, because by nature hospital trusts are competitive with each other and counter to the collaborative approach, which is what acute care collaboration is about. Generally, it can be quite parochial. (ACC-Senior Manager 1, CCG)

It had been more difficult to convince potential partners that the relationship would be built upon collaboration, rather than competition or, indeed, acquisition. Although such difficulties were highlighted, most felt that lessons had been adequately learned. The following view is typical.

I think it is going back to prior to the Vanguard we were going through a process to acquire [Rural Hospital]. I think that learning has helped us to understand some unintended consequences that we wouldn't want to repeat around culture, and how, during major change, cultures collide, and what we would do differently. (ACC-Senior Manager 1, CCG)

The challenge of managing different governance structures across the Vanguards is a stark example of the potential tension between macro- and meso-level policy interventions and reforms. More complex was balancing collaboration efforts with different partners from different sectors, since the concept was clearly not aligned with the profit-making motives of commercially based organisations.

As soon as you start developing models with organisations such as Rovera, PWC, Metronics, they have a slightly different incentive. So, [we have to ensure that] we have the right balance, and we keep patients at the heart of it, which is what we hope to achieve … but you can absolutely understand that [it] will always be a challenge to get to the right place. (ACC-Senior Manager 7, CCG)

The challenge of managing different governance structures across organisations inhibited collaboration and often served as a barrier to the delivery of each Vanguard's aims and objectives.

Reconfiguring Inter-organisational Relations and Practices

The development of multidisciplinary teams (MDT) to facilitate successful implementation of each Vanguard was viewed as one of the most important benefits across all sites. It was felt that sharing aims and learning about the viewpoints of others helped to combat the silo working, for which health and social services have long been accused and often found guilty. Participants also conveyed an increasing recognition that joint working was the only way to operate during times of severe budget constraints and cuts. Although multiagency and multidisciplinary input, and the ability to bring in other experts were valued, it was felt that there could be problems when new organisations or new representatives became involved in service delivery. It was perceived to be difficult to acquaint new service providers and partners with the intentions and progress of the Vanguard. For some participants, the inclusion of many different organisations could also add unnecessary complexity.

You're pulling together lots of different employers and areas of work … Although all the people in the room might be very up for all working together, once you bring the bigger beasts in, it's not as simple as that … You're wrestling, then, with lots of different sets of values, ability to change, flexibility… (EHCH-Senior Manager 5, CCG)

Although trust between agencies was considered essential, participants recognised that strong relationships often took time to develop. In this regard, MDT working was seen to require clarification of purpose, stratification of patients, and appropriate management. All Vanguards widely shared the view that they needed adequate support across, and within, the relative organisations, employing both personal connections and available structures to varying degrees.

Despite these challenges, relationship-building between care settings clearly characterised all the Vanguards. Continual organisational re-structuring, and hence changing personnel, enhanced the need for inter-professional communication.

> *I think, if you can create some relationships and friendships way before you start any project, you [are] always going to do better than just launching straight in. I think creating the right system and the right relationships make it work... It is essentially then understanding and emphasising with your colleagues [the importance of relationships] and actually looking at where the ability for joint working is.* (ACC-Senior Manager 6, CCG)

Even though relationships between health and social care services had been built up over many years, participants thought those relationships were inadequately developed. One respondent found particular challenge in managing the contrast between working within the "flat structure" of the Clinical Commissioning Group compared to the bureaucratic and hierarchical structure of the Foundation Trust and local authority. Many interviewees believed, despite co-location of those in different health and social care settings, that they lacked understanding of others' professional roles.

> *So, the people who would be my equivalent colleagues – we don't spend any time together – we don't really understand what each other is doing and whether there is any crossover or conflict.* (PACS-Senior Manager 4, CCG)

Difficulties in operational relationships were also evident between the acute and community sectors and in the seeming lack of enthusiasm among acute clinicians for working in the community.

We still haven't cracked the relationship and models of care about how we pull our secondary care colleagues out [to work in] the community more. [We've] done some decent pilots of it at a local level...but what we haven't done is [started] looking at that integration of relationships across the whole county that [makes that happen]. (PACS-Senior Manager 3, CCG)

Although there were concerns that inter-professional communication and understanding remained a challenge, generally it was felt by many that this was improving.

We have pockets of it in primary care; it's brilliant. ... I think we are conquering quite a lot of the organisational stuff, but what we haven't landed yet is the culture and mindsets of how clinicians can work together in different ways. (PACS-Senior Manager 2, CCG)

The need for, and importance of, relationship-building was common to all five sites, but in each, there appeared to be different obstacles to progress. It was suggested that the Vanguards helped individual sites to build inter- and intra-organisational relationships. Nonetheless, common to all five was the significant amount of effort and time that had been put into creating better relationships among partners.

Building Capacity and Resources

Participants valued the Vanguard initiatives for the "pump priming" that had allowed plans to commence and be supported earlier than would have happened otherwise. In particular, participants acknowledged that the resources provided through each Vanguard supported the local testing and implementation of innovation, but also helped to maximise the opportunities to build upon previous achievements.

[The Vanguard programme] brings some extra capacity into the system to actually do some of the work...I don't think that would have happened without the financial resource that the Vanguard was able to bring to bear. (UEC-Senior Manager 2, CCG)

However, as described by many of those we interviewed, the Vanguard work was not part of their "day job". For some, this created a potentially irreconcilable tension. As one participant in the ACC Vanguard remarked:

> *My role is not the Vanguard ... and that's sometimes the tension, because the day job is the day job... but everybody is incredibly pressurized, and if you don't keep an eye on the day job, the day job gets worse.* (ACC-Senior Manager 2, CCG)

Many of the interviewees were highly critical of a reduction in financial support for serving as a Vanguard and that there had been no guarantee of funding over the three years.

> *Sometimes, to do a transformational change, you do need a bit of pump priming – when you are getting half the funding that you need. That is a bit difficult... I think the challenges are [that] the initial excitement has been a bit tamped down because ... the funding allocations were cut in subsequent years.* (ACC-Senior Manager 1, CCG)

There was, additionally, a common perception that the short-term investment of the Vanguard programme was insufficient to sustain its ongoing work and development. Participants feared that once the Vanguard support disappeared, the programme would continue but that the pace would slow considerably.

> *I am not confident with it coming to a sudden end ... because, if they are not providing any money or any funds, how are they going to keep up the impetus on delivery? I don't think we'd stop because we've got that relationship with organisations now. I just don't know if it would continue as extensively as it is doing now.* (ACC-Senior Manager 4, CCG)

Apart from material resources, time and "back-fill" of staff were considered to be major barriers to successful performance and innovation as a Vanguard. Further, staff had to see the value and benefit of the team.

I think the biggest issue about MDT working is creating the time … (P)eople, I think, are working exceptionally hard. There isn't an additional workforce that you can put in because there is nobody to back-fill… It is less about the money and more about the workforce. (PACS-Senior Manager 1, CCG)

Those professionals whose time was funded, to enable them to be involved in local Vanguard initiatives, felt protected time allowed them to attend MDT meetings and participate to a greater extent in the broader collaborative aims of the Vanguard project. As a participant at the Care Homes Vanguard remarked:

One of the benefits is having the time to think about what is useful. Normally as a [General Practitioner – GP], you don't get much time to reflect on the value of what you are doing or why you are doing it, or how you might be doing it. (EHCH-Senior Manager 12, CCG)

However, there appeared to be some resentment that not everyone's time was covered and that, for many, the tasks undertaken and meetings attended were assumed to be part of their everyday responsibilities. As a participant at the Care Homes Vanguard stated:

Why was it allowable to pay for GP and consultant time, but not to give something to care homes for their involvement? (EHCH-Senior Manager 6, CCG)

Availability of capacity and resources was considered to be a key factor for the successful implementation of each Vanguard. However, there were tensions between the need for real investment in terms of capacity, capability and finance, the accompanying risk, and the ability to deliver outcomes. In particular, concerns were raised over the lack of additional resources to support transformation efforts within each Vanguard.

Securing Commitment and Engagement

Among all Vanguards, there was considerable praise for the high levels of commitment shown by staff involved in local change initiatives. Such recognition was believed to promote better outcomes, with people eager to meet objectives and to share experiences and lessons. As one interviewee in the Care Homes Vanguard remarked:

> *Everyone in there wants to be there, I think, and wants to make a difference, and wants to work on behalf of their organisations to start building bridges and improving systems.* (EHCH-Senior Manager 1, CCG)

Buy-in from organisations or particular professional groups was also considered vital for success of the Vanguard programme, but was often difficult to achieve. As one participant in the Urgent and Emergency Care Vanguard stated:

> *I think what helps the Vanguard project is the buy-in ... getting some of the understanding, and [getting] the buy-in from some of our local authority partners has been very challenging.* (UEC- Senior Manager 7, CCG)

Despite apparent commitment among many staff members across the region, interviewees lamented that such commitment among staff of the Vanguards was irregular. In particular, concerns were raised in the PACS Vanguard that some Trusts had not yet agreed to participate in the ACO:

> *The elephant in the room is the fact that we have a great big hospital trust which still sits in the area... It is a bit of a concern because, from a needs perspective, the people that go to that hospital tend to be more affluent... We are just going, 'oh that's a bit hard, let's concentrate on the easy stuff', rather than looking at the whole thing.* (PACS-Senior Manager 4, CCG)

Some participants argued that the programme had been left to focal individuals. Furthermore, engagement was seen to be inconsistent, as were the interplay of organisational and personal relationships.

> *I mean the challenge, which we think we crack but we don't really crack is engagement...I would say it is a fragile thing, engagement from leaders to healthcare workers, particularly GPs, it has to be developed.* (PACS-Senior Manager 9, CCG)

> *I think the key relationships were very strained at the beginning...there was a clash of personalities, a clash of priorities and just a clash of focus.* (PACS-Senior Manager 8, CCG)

Thus, structured organisational relationships and fleeting interpersonal relationships both advanced and inhibited collaboration.

Implications of the Enactment of New Care Models

Drawing upon recent theoretical developments on the multilevel nature of context (Maniatopoulos et al. 2015; Greenhalgh et al. 2017), we explored factors shaping the implementation of five Vanguard sites for the NCM programme in the North East of England. Our analysis advances the study of large-scale health system implementation in three ways. First, it broadens the scope and scale of analysis across the multiple levels of context that contributed towards the successful implementation of large-scale health system change initiatives (Maniatopoulos et al. 2015; Greenhalgh et al. 2016, 2017; Robert et al. 2010). In this study, we have not examined those factors shaping the implementation of NCMs in a particular context, but rather have explored the interdependent relationships among different structural elements of the context across a multilevel set of practices, ranging from the macro-policy level and the organisational responses at a meso-level to the micro-level setting of individual action/workforce redesign.

Second, our theoretical positioning stresses the importance of being sensitive to the broader political context of policy implementation in which large-scale health system transformation takes place (Hunter et al. 2015; Navarro 2011; Jones 2017). Much of the extant literature around health systems implementation has decontextualized it from the wider setting and focused on the structural elements of the systems, or on the processes and relationships between elements of the systems, rather than exploring the surrounding political environment within which the changes being implemented are taking place (Hunter et al. 2015). However, we show that health system change initiatives in themselves are not neutral; they reflect particular political values, beliefs, and ideologies, although these underlying political assumptions are rarely specified by their proponents. Achieving whole system change is particularly vulnerable to the vicissitudes of day-to-day politics, especially where that system, like the UK NHS, is itself subject to those very same pressures. Within all the Vanguards, there were concerns that government targets dominated local initiatives and displaced objectives, such as the opportunity for shared learning. Our findings demonstrate how the implementation of the NCMs in England is framed within a climate shaped by a strong and persistent audit culture, new public management practices, and a neoliberal set of ideas with an emphasis on the delivery of quick efficiency savings, measuring performance, and the containment of public spending on services.

Finally, this study moves the debate about health system reform beyond the single-site and timeframe implementation of health policy by exploring the implementation of the NCM programme within a wide range of organisations and related stakeholders involved in the delivery of an NHS strategy. Undoubtedly, single-site implementation studies provide a valuable tool for studying in a vertical way the impact of health policy on practice. They have enabled the assembly of rich and detailed local ethnographies of the adaptive response by single organisations to the translation of policy into practice. However, to view large-scale health system transformation principally at the point where a single organisation encounters, if inadequately theorised and sampled, it risks missing the wider context of policy implementation which, in turn, could lead to somewhat partial understandings of these complex processes. Furthermore, single-site studies risk downplaying important influences and interdependencies between organisations and settings. We argue that if we are to understand the full implications of large-scale health system change initiatives, then there is benefit in studying how health policy implementation is played out over multiple time frames, organisations, and settings. To understand the shaping of reform and policy implementation, therefore, requires researchers to go beyond the study of policy implementation at a single locale or moment and, rather, attempt to follow it through space and time. Given that complex change represents a continuous journey rather than a phenomenon that occurs at a single defined point in time, there is great merit in seeking to evaluate such developments over time, taking into account myriad factors and pressures that can be evident in wider contexts. Future research ought to consider such large-scale reforms, not only across sites but across time, and focus also on the lessons that variations among sites can offer the research agenda on reform and implementation.

Acknowledgements This chapter presents independent research that was funded by the National Health Service England (NHS) through the support of the North East Commissioning Support Unit (NECS). This funding is gratefully acknowledged as is the support received from NECS for the duration of the study. Ethical approval was gained from Newcastle University Research Ethics Committee (ref: 01216/2016). NHS Research Ethics approval was not required for this study.

Appendix A—Vanguard Sites

Vanguard	Aim of programme
Multispecialty Community Providers (MCPs)	The Vanguard aims to move care out of the hospital into the community. It involved the implementation of an out of hospital model of care focusing on people staying independent and well for as long as possible; people living longer with a better quality of life with long-term conditions; people supported to recover from episodes of ill health and following injury; resilient communities; and high levels of public satisfaction. The MCP Vanguard began in April 2015 although pre-Vanguard elements began implementation from 2013
Primary and Acute Care Systems (PACS)	The Vanguard aims to develop a new variant of "vertically integrated" care allowing single organisations to provide joined-up GP, hospital, community, and mental health services. It involved the development of a new Urgent and Emergency Care Hospital and the development of an "enhanced care teams" pilot and new workforce models (Transforming Primary Care). The PACS Vanguard began in June 2015, and the Trust became the first Accountable Care Organisation in the region—effective from April 2017

(continued)

Vanguard	Aim of programme
Acute Care Collaboration Vanguard (ACC)	The Vanguard aims to link local hospitals together to improve their clinical and financial viability, reducing variation in care and efficiency. It aims to widen the support and services (i.e. commercial/contractual services, consultancy/advisory as well as a range of clinical and corporate services) the Trust can provide to other parts of the NHS through acquiring and/or merging with other hospital Trusts. The ACC Vanguard was finalised in January 2016
Enhanced Health in Care Homes Vanguard (EHCH)	The Vanguard aims to offer older people better, joined-up health, care, and rehabilitation services. It aims to develop a sustainable, high-quality new care model for people in community beds and receiving home-based care services across a metropolitan area with a new outcome-based contract and payment system that supports the development of the Provider Alliance Network (PAN) delivery vehicle. The Vanguard started in March 2015 although some features had been implemented pre-Vanguard status
Urgent and Emergency Care Vanguard (UEC)	The Vanguard aims to improve the coordination of urgent and emergency care as a whole system, ensuring people can access the most appropriate service, the first time. The Vanguard status was awarded in July 2015, and the programme has been fully operational since November 2016. Most initiatives went live in December 2016

References

Aarons, G. A., Hurlburt, M., & Horwitz, S. M. (2011). Advancing a conceptual model of evidence-based practice implementation in public service sectors. *Administration and Policy in Mental Health and Mental Health Services Research, 38*(1), 4–23.

Bate, P. (2014). *Context is everything*. London: The Health Foundation.

Berwick, D. M., Nolan, T. W., & Whittington, J. (2008). The triple aim: Care, health, and cost. *Health Affairs, 27*(3), 759–769.

Boyatzis, R. E. (1998). *Transforming qualitative information: Thematic analysis and code development*. Thousand Oaks, CA: Sage.

Damschroder, L. J., Aron, D. C., Keith, R. E., Kirsh, S. R., Alexander, J. A., & Lowery, J. C. (2009). Fostering, implementation of health services research findings into practice: A consolidated framework for advancing implementation science. *Implementation Science, 4*, 50.

Dopson, S., & Fitzgerald, L. (2005). *Knowledge into action: Evidence-based healthcare in context*. Oxford: Oxford University Press.

Exworthy, M., & Powell, M. (2004). Big windows and little windows: Implementation in the 'congested state'. *Public Administration, 82*(2), 263–281.

Fulop, N., & Robert, G. (2015). *Context for successful quality improvement*. London: The Health Foundation.

Greener, I., Harrington, B. E., Hunter, D. J., Mannion, R., & Powell, M. (2014). *Reforming health care: What's the evidence?* Bristol: Policy Press.

Greenhalgh, T., Robert, G., Bate, P., Macfarlane, F., & Kyriakidou, O. (2005). *Diffusion of innovations in health service organizations*. Oxford: Blackwell.

Greenhalgh, T., Robert, G., Macfarlane, F., Bate, P., & Kyriakidou, O. (2004). Diffusion of innovations in service organizations: Systematic review and recommendations. *Milbank Quarterly, 82*(4), 581–629.

Greenhalgh, T., Shaw, S., & Wherton, J. (2016). SCALS: A fourth-generation study of assisted living technologies in their organisational, social, political and policy context. *British Medical Journal Open, 6,* e010208.

Greenhalgh, T., Wherton, J., Papoutsi, C., Lynch, J., Hughes, G., A'Court, C., et al. (2017). Beyond adoption: A new framework for theorizing and evaluating nonadoption, abandonment, and challenges to the scale-up, spread, and sustainability of health and care technologies. *Journal of Medical Internet Research, 19*(11), e367.

Hunter, D. J. (2016). *The health debate* (2nd ed.). Bristol: Policy Press.

Hunter, D. J., Erskine, J., Small, A., McGovern, T., Hicks, C., Whitty, P., et al. (2015). Doing transformational change in the English NHS in the context of 'big bang' redisorganisation. *Journal of Health Organisation and Management, 29*(1), 10–24.

Jones, L. (2017). Sedimented governance in the English NHS. In M. Bevir and J. Waring (Eds.), *De-centring health policy: Learning from British experiences in healthcare governance*. London: Routledge.

Kaplan, H. C., Brady, P. W., Dritz, M. C., Hooper, D. K., Linam, W. M., Froehle, C. M., et al. (2010). The influence of context on quality improvement success in health care: A systematic review of the literature. *Milbank Quarterly, 88*(4), 500–559.

Kyratsis, Y., Ahmad, R., & Holmes, A. (2012). Making sense of evidence in management decisions: The role of research-based knowledge on innovation adoption and implementation in healthcare. *Implementation Science, 7,* 22.

Maniatopoulos, G., Procter, R., Llewellyn, S., Harvey, G., & Boyd, A. (2015). Moving beyond local practice: Reconfiguring the adoption of a breast cancer diagnostic technology. *Social Science and Medicine, 131,* 98–106.

May, C. R., Johnson, M., & Finch, T. (2016). Implementation, context and complexity. *Implementation Science, 11,* 141.

Navarro, V. (2011). The importance of politics in policy. *Australian and New Zealand Journal of Public Health, 35*(4), 313.

NHS England. (2014). *Five year forward view.* NHSE.

NHS England. (2017). *Next steps on the NHS five year forward view.* NHSE.

Nilsen, P. (2015). Making sense of implementation theories, models and frameworks. *Implementation Science, 10,* 53.

Peck, E., & 6, P. (2006). *Beyond delivery: Policy implementation as sense-making and settlement.* Basingstoke: Palgrave Macmillan.

Pettigrew, A. M. (1990). Longitudinal field research on change: Theory and practice. *Organization Science, 1*(3), 267–292.

Pettigrew, A. M., Ferlie, E., & McKee, L. (1992a). *Shaping strategic change.* London: Sage.

Pettigrew, A. M., Ferlie, E., & McKee, L. (1992b). Shaping strategic change: The case of the NHS in the 1980s. *Public Money and Management, 12*(3), 27–31.

Ragin, C. C., & Becker, H. S. (1992). *What is a case? Exploring the foundations of social inquiry.* Cambridge: University Press.

Robert, G., Greenhalgh, T., MacFarlane, F., & Peacock, R. (2010). Adopting and assimilating new Non-pharmaceutical technologies into health care: A systematic review. *Journal of Health Services Research & Policy, 15*(4), 243–250.

Squires, J. E., Graham, I. D., Hutchinson, A. M., Michie, S., Francis, J. J., Sales, A., et al. (2015). Identifying the domains of context important to implementation science: A study protocol. *Implementation Science, 10,* 135.

Weick, K. E. (1995). *Sensemaking in organizations.* Thousand Oaks: Sage.

World Health Organization. (2016). Health system transformation: Making it happen. In *Expert meeting.* Madrid, Spain, December 17–18, 2015. http://www.euro.who.int/data/assets/pdf_file/0014/318020/Madrid-Report-HST-making-it-happen.pdf?ua=1. Accessed 12 Dec 2017.

World Health Organization. (2018). Leading health system transformation to the next level. In *Expert meeting.* Durham, UK, July 12–13, 2017. http://www.euro.who.int/en/health-topics/health-systems/health-services-delivery/publications/2017/leading-health-sytem-transformation-to-the-next-level-2017. Accessed 4 July 2018.

2

Coordinating Compassionate Care Across Nursing Teams: The Implementation Journey of a Planned Intervention

Jackie Bridges, Jane Frankland, Peter Griffiths, Paula Libberton and Carl May

Introduction

Delivering care that combines compassion with clinical and cost-effectiveness is a priority for health systems globally and in the UK. We define compassionate care as care that focuses on the patient or client as an individual person, with needs and desires, and worthy of dignity, rather than exclusively as a task-focus of health work. In the UK, the findings of the Francis inquiries into care failures at Mid Staffordshire NHS Foundation Trust have been the stimulus for renewed attention

J. Bridges (✉) · J. Frankland · P. Griffiths · P. Libberton
School of Health Sciences, University of Southampton,
Southampton, UK

J. Frankland
e-mail: j.l.frankland@soton.ac.uk

P. Griffiths
e-mail: peter.griffiths@soton.ac.uk

© The Author(s) 2020
P. Nugus et al. (eds.), *Transitions and Boundaries in the Coordination
and Reform of Health Services*, Organizational Behaviour in Healthcare,
https://doi.org/10.1007/978-3-030-26684-4_2

on compassionate care (Francis 2010, 2013). As Francis' findings reflected, older people in hospital are a group at particular risk of a lack of compassion in their care. A recent study into NHS wards with high numbers of older patients in two hospitals reported that 10% of all staff–patient social interactions are negative (Barker et al. 2016). Addressing the problem of promoting health professionals' delivery of compassionate care has largely focused on interventions that encourage individual professional behaviour change (Blomberg et al. 2016). However, the results of these interventions are uneven, and the evidence base to support them is underdeveloped. Against this background, our understanding of how to embed such interventions at a whole system level (across a team, clinical directorate, or whole hospital) is limited. While there is evidence about the role of contextual factors in shaping health professional–patient interactions, such research has tended to focus on the ways that contexts place constraints on practice, particularly the way that work is defined, and workload distributed and organized. Nevertheless, context can also be considered as elements in one's environment that influence individual action, such as policies, norms, technology, and resources. Therefore, without a more complete understanding of the role of contexts, further development of interventions that aim to engender individual behaviour change on their own is unlikely to support the promotion of compassionate care in hospital.

Research that focuses on implementation of planned interventions indicates that contexts (e.g. role definitions, organizing logics, material, and informational resources for practice) can be understood as both sources of complexity (May 2013; May et al. 2016) and dynamic resources for improvement (Cammer et al. 2013; Hawe et al. 2009; Pfadenhauer et al. 2017; Rycroft-Malone 2008). Discerning how

P. Libberton
e-mail: p.libberton@soton.ac.uk

C. May
London School of Hygiene and Tropical Medicine, London, UK
e-mail: c.r.may@soton.ac.uk

individual behaviour change processes among hospital-based professionals are shaped by dynamic structural and relational elements of context can lead to improved knowledge of how interpersonal, person-system, and person-technology interactions can lead to normative and relational restructuring in the wider health system (Bridges et al. 2007; Hawe 2015; Hawe et al. 2009; Hewison and Sawbridge 2015; Hewison et al. 2018; Martin et al. 2012; May 2013; May et al. 2016). Most importantly, the development and evaluation of interventions that mobilize elements of contexts in which professionals encounter patients are likely to increase the capacity of whole systems to support improvements in care.

Compassionate nursing care interventions tend to be focused on staff training, staff support, or introducing new models of care (Blomberg et al. 2016). Yet, our systematic review of studies to evaluate the effectiveness of compassionate nursing care interventions found that the quality of evaluation in this field tended to be poor, with mainly small-scale before-and-after studies (Blomberg et al. 2016). Although a small number of additional studies have used qualitative methods to evaluate the mechanisms for the change and impact of the intervention and often include an analysis of the enablers and barriers to change, these studies do not examine in depth the process of implementation itself. As such, these studies are unable to systematically identify the contexts in which successful implementation is more likely to occur, or, in cases where contexts are unreceptive, how resources, relationships, and norms in the wider system may need purposeful restructuring to support implementation and sustain longer-term change (Bridges et al. 2018). This chapter seeks to more thoroughly investigate the processes and outcomes of implementing an intervention, Creating Learning Environments for Compassionate Care (CLECC), aimed at supporting the delivery of compassionate care by hospital teams. This detailed study is guided by Normalization Process Theory (NPT), an implementation theory that identifies, characterizes, and explains empirically demonstrated factors that shape implementation processes and their outcomes (May et al. 2018).

CLECC is underpinned by workplace learning principles to inform leadership and team practices (such as dialogue, reflective learning, mutual support, and role modelling) that support the ongoing relational capacity of individual team members (Bridges and Fuller 2015; Fuller 2007; Fuller and Unwin 2004; Wenger 1998). We define relational capacity here as the capacity to embed and sustain compassionate caring practices within a complex and dynamic organizational context. We build on the assumption, from our previously published work, that relational capacity is a property of the necessary ward-level conditions that support caring work and thus improve patient experiences (Bridges et al. 2013; Bridges and Tziggili 2011). CLECC's focus on the work team draws on research indicating associations between work group mechanisms that promote shared norms, social and practical support for individual members, and care quality (Bolton 2005; Maben et al. 2012; Parker 2002; Patterson et al. 2011).

CLECC (Bridges et al. 2009; Bridges and Fuller 2015) was implemented in each of the four ward settings over a four-month period, with a view to embedding and sustaining new practices (Table 2.1). Implementation was facilitated by a senior practice educator, a clinically trained member of the hospital staff seconded to the ward team. The intervention consisted of a set of:

a. Regular CLECC meetings between the ward manager and matron to enrol individuals in CLECC.
b. Action learning sets to facilitate ward managers to explore their role in leading and supporting CLECC in their teams.
c. Team learning activities, including study days and twice weekly reflective discussions on results from team exercises, including climate analysis, values clarification, and peer observations of work with patients.
d. Mid-shift five-minute cluster discussions to support each other's well-being through social support and rebalancing individual workloads when needed.
e. Team-developed learning plans to share with senior hospital managers; learning plans included sustainability measures for practices that underpin the delivery of compassionate care, such as identifying and requesting resources needed for ward managers to continue to attend action learning sets.

Table 2.1 CLECC set activities

Activity	Month 1	Month 2	Month 3	Month 4
Ward manager action learning sets	Session 1: Set up action learning set, establish ground rules	Session 2: Focus on workplace climate, team values, valuing staff	Session 3: Focus on enhancing team capacity for compassionate care	Session 4: Focus on influencing senior managers
Team learning plan	Introduce and discuss learning plan	Discuss ward leader drafts	Finalize, identify resources needed to support, present	Senior manager gives feedback on team plan
Ward manager/matron meetings	Introduce and discuss	Ongoing—every two weeks	Ongoing—every two weeks	Ongoing—every two weeks
Peer observations of practice	Identify two volunteer observers from staff team	Train observers	Observe practice	Give feedback on observations of practice
Team study day (all staff)	Team analyses workplace climate, clarifies values	–	–	–
Mid-shift cluster discussions (all staff)	Ongoing	Ongoing	Ongoing	Ongoing
Reflective discussions (twice weekly) (all staff)	'I feel valued at work when…' exercise	Team values clarification exercise; BPOP activities (Bridges et al. 2009)	BPOP activities (Bridges et al., 2009); Team learning + service user feedback plan discussions	Reflections on feedback from observations of practice

Each practice educator worked simultaneously with two wards in their allocated hospital, organizing specified CLECC activities.

Gauging Perspectives on a Planned Intervention

A qualitative process evaluation of CLECC was undertaken, guided by NPT (May 2013; May and Finch 2009; May et al. 2016). We sought to understand the dynamics of implementing a complex relational intervention and to explain the extent to which CLECC was incorporated into existing work practices. Recognizing that little is understood about identifying and mobilizing elements of context in health care interventions, we applied NPT to our analysis of CLECC, a theory developed from multiple studies of many different health care systems. NPT provides a robust framework for analysis of system implementations in that it 'identifies, characterises, and explains mechanisms that have been empirically demonstrated to motivate and shape implementation processes and affect their outcomes' (May et al. 2018, p. 2). Because NPT focuses on outcomes of individuals and groups, rather than intentions or beliefs in outcomes, we apply its four dynamic processes (coherence, cognitive participation, collective action, and reflexive monitoring) that motivate and shape implementation processes (May and Finch 2009).

Part of a wider feasibility study of CLECC implementation and evaluation (Bridges et al. 2018), our evaluation of the implementation of the complex relational intervention focused on:

1. Exploring how and in what ways the new practice was initially received, how people conceptualized and made sense of it individually, collectively, and in practice (coherence).
2. Assessing the degree of ownership of and participation in the new practice by key individuals and teams (cognitive participation).
3. Identifying the work that individuals and teams did to enact the new practice (collective action).
4. Exploring the perceived impact of the new practice on staff work and on patient outcomes (reflexive monitoring).

The CLECC intervention was introduced to four inpatient wards in two general National Health Service (NHS) hospitals in England. Wards with relatively high proportions of older patients (medicine for older people and orthopaedics) were recruited through ward manager agreement.

Individual face-to-face semi-structured interviews were undertaken with staff over a 12-month period beginning in May 2015, at the outset of the implementation period, followed by two further interview rounds (at 3–6 months and 7–12 months) (Fig. 2.1). Purposive sampling was used to capture variations in staff grade and ward. Participants were invited to take part in repeat interviews so that variations in implementation over time could be tracked. Where there was attrition, new participants were recruited to maintain ward and grade variation. Senior nursing managers were invited to an interview in the final phase. Interview schedules reflected NPT dynamic processes and changed over time to reflect implementation stages. Interviews were conducted by university researchers and lasted on average 46 minutes. Interviews were audio-recorded and transcribed verbatim. Practice educators leading CLECC implementation kept detailed field notes. A sample of CLECC learning activities was also observed by researchers ($n = 7$ over 26 hours). Staffing data were gathered through a ward manager questionnaire.

Data analysis involved reading, familiarizing, and open coding, undertaken independently by research team members and then collaboratively in data analysis workshops. A preliminary coding frame focused on implementation and mechanisms of impact. All interview data were

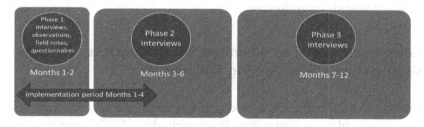

Fig. 2.1 CLECC process evaluation timeline

coded against this frame. The use of constant comparison enabled the generation of new categories and the comparison of data in relation to these categories. Narrative data summaries and matrix/charting techniques were then used to facilitate comparison with the NPT framework to test and refine emerging theories of implementation processes (Pope et al. 2013). All data from observer and practice educator field notes, and from quantitative analyses of staffing data, were then systematically interrogated and compared against these emerging theories, the purpose being to use multiple perspectives to elicit more complex and situated understandings (Richardson 2000). Ethical approval for the study was granted by the Social Care Research Ethics Committee 14/IEC08/1018.

Enacting the Planned Intervention

In total, 47 interviews were conducted with ward managers ($n=4$), deputy ward managers ($n=2$), registered nurses (RNs) ($n=8$), health care assistants (HCAs) ($n=7$), senior hospital nurses ($n=2$), and practice educators ($n=2$). Ward-based interviewees had worked on their current ward between two weeks and 14 years, on average for four years. Two study days and five action learning sets were observed in full.

Findings illustrate the work that staff needed to do, individually and collectively, to implement CLECC in practice. While many of the individual elements of CLECC were possible to implement during the implementation period, sustaining such work beyond this time was difficult for some ward teams to achieve. The findings that follow explain how and why this was the case.

Coherence: CLECC as a Limited Set of Concrete Practices Versus as an Underpinning Philosophy

Interview and observation data clearly indicated that all care staff were able to articulate activities associated with the CLECC intervention. Staff valued the principles behind many concrete CLECC activities, appreciating the focus on staff well-being and consequent impact on patient care quality. For RNs, the CLECC principles resonated with their aspirations for successful teamwork and patient care. For HCAs, the intervention was a new and welcomed way of thinking about their workplace. Nevertheless, beyond the activities staff were directly involved in, they struggled to explain the purpose and potential of CLECC. Even so, staff tended to associate CLECC with cluster discussions that took place part-way through each shift, thus providing an opportunity to gather as a team and check on each other's well-being.

> *So, whereas before they might know that orange bay is heavier* [in workload] *than green bay, they might not necessarily have volunteered to go and help. Now they are much more aware that if [staff in orange bay]are going 'well actually we're struggling'; [we realize] 'well, we're not, we'll come and help you'. And I think that's because of the [clusters] and the fact that we're all sitting down and going 'is there anything we can do to help you?' And if they are going 'well actually I've got a really poorly patient, so I've been struggling with the others'; [we say] 'right, well then, we'll come and help you'. And it's made them more aware of each other.* **N003**[1] (HCA, Hospital A)

All staff attended the study days and, on prompting, were able to associate these sessions with CLECC. Furthermore, participating in a study day where only other team members were present was considered unusual and was welcomed. Staff saw the study day as a way of ensuring that they were working together and as an opportunity to engage with the ward vision, which was not previously explicit. The most important aspect of the study day was the chance to get to know each other, which staff reported they had not had the opportunity to do previously. As a result, the study days served to promote coherence or sense-making work around CLECC, but also team cohesion.

> *We had the study days and they were all very good, and I found that I got to know the different people within those study days, or how they felt and I thought: 'oh, I didn't know that'. So that was useful.* **N001** (Staff Nurse, Hospital B)

The ward managers and practice educators charged with facilitating CLECC were involved in a wider range of CLECC activities; these individuals and the senior nurse managers were generally able to provide a more articulate philosophy of CLECC and to identify associated behaviours.

> To me, CLECC is about giving staff tools to ensure that they support themselves to do a hard job. So it's about providing a nurse with the knowledge of what they need to deliver ... compassionate care or high-quality person-centred care, whatever you want to describe it as – every day, at a high quality standard, [That] is what we have to aim for, but also with you having some insight into how your behaviour affects both your patient and your staff. **SN002** (Senior Nursing Manager, Hospital B)

On average, over one-third of staff left over the course of the study, and this turnover rate was consistent with other (control) wards we were monitoring. There was, however, no provision for this turnover in the design of CLECC delivery through a one-off implementation period, which limited the opportunity for staff arriving after this period to make sense of CLECC. In summary, although ward staff appreciated the potential value of CLECC, their understanding of CLECC was limited to and shaped by the concrete activities that they participated in.

Cognitive Participation: Staff Keen to Participate but Not Sure Who Should Drive It Forward

Staff were keen to participate in CLECC, but there were varied levels of clarity between the teams and hospitals about whose responsibility it was to ensure CLECC was implemented. Each practice educator took a different approach to their role, and these differences were enabled by the relative flexibility of the intervention. Such differences in practice educator approach, and their interactions with existing ward cultures, influenced the ward staff's degree of ownership of the intervention. For example, one practice educator (in Hospital B) was perceived to have a relatively autocratic style of leadership, seeing her role as informing teams how to do things, rather than working alongside them to support them in changing practice. In this way, the practice educator passed the responsibility for CLECC to teams before they had learned how to take ownership.

[The practice educator] was very adamant that it wasn't her responsibility to [make sure the cluster discussions were convened]; it could have been anybody's [responsibility].... N008 (HCA, Hospital B)

After the implementation period, staff on these wards reported that cluster discussions were no longer taking place, attributing the cessation to the fact that no one was actively implementing them. In contrast, another practice educator (Hospital A), who was perceived to have a more democratic style of working, actively worked with staff to make CLECC more flexible and fit better with resource pressures.

It [cluster meeting] doesn't always stick to that time. It kind of depends how it's going. So we've had, like, busy days when stuff's been happening on the ward. At one point they [nursing staff] kind of ask permission to make it [cluster meeting] later. It's kind of sad. But I'm like...'yeah, do it whatever time it works in the ward. If we can do it, that's a bonus.' So, quite often it's the [HCAs] asking for it [cluster meeting]. N035 (Practice Educator, Hospital A)

Although this practice educator and more senior team members initially originated the cluster discussions, as the intervention became embedded over time, other team members, including HCAs, initiated cluster discussions without waiting for more senior direction. The cluster discussions on these wards continued to run after the implementation period.

They [HCAs] will remind whoever is in charge of the ward, and say "Are we having a [cluster] today?" I've seen that quite a few times. N035 (Practice Educator, Hospital A)

CLECC also gave staff in all participating teams, including HCAs, the opportunity to see themselves as innovators, providing a mechanism through which individuals could articulate their ideas for improving practice on the ward. As a result, staff felt more empowered than before to respond to ideas and to implement change. They approached the ward manager and the matron simultaneously, when previously communication was directed through the ward manager.

> *Quite a few of the staff have [become] involved in various different things that have come out of the study days – what they wanted to change, and thought they could do better. And they've gone off [in] sort of little groups, or twos and threes, and are bringing that stuff back, passing it through the matron. N030 (Ward Manager, Hospital B)*

However, not all ideas were implemented in practice, and this appeared to be linked with uncertainty in certain teams about whose role it was to realize or authorize the implementation of particular ideas that emerged. In one team in Hospital B, since staff clearly expected that the ward manager or matron had the requisite authority to realize proposed ideas, their lack of 'follow through' evidenced in later interviews was demoralizing for the staff involved.

> *Some of them felt a little bit disappointed that they'd made these suggestions and [the staff] took their time to [develop the ideas], and then no one really followed it through or said 'yes, we can use that or no we can't'. It just got left. N001 (Staff Nurse, Hospital B)*

Nevertheless, all interview participants conveyed that they saw CLECC as a way to build the team and improve care, and this ethos underpinned their participation in prescribed activities. Consequently, study days and action learning sets were all well attended across the teams. Even so, fortnightly CLECC meetings between ward managers and their matrons did not proceed in one hospital site (Hospital B), indicating a lack of clarity about the role of the matron in implementing CLECC activities.

> *Both ward [managers] felt that there has been a negative impact [on CLECC implementation] from the lack of support from the matron. Items identified by the nursing teams that were considered areas requiring improvement were*

unsupported, and even, in some instances, rejected. **N036** (Practice Educator field note, Hospital B)

The early establishment and continuation of meetings between ward managers and their matrons at the other hospital site (Hospital A) appeared to be linked with a more proactive matron role in supporting CLECC.

So my matron's been very supportive the whole way through; we've kept in regular contact. She's been asking for updates, she's known about the interventions that we've done on the ward and has been really supportive. **N034** (Ward Manager, Hospital A)

Furthermore, levels of cognitive participation varied between the ward managers, and this shaped CLECC implementation by their teams. In Hospital A, the Ward A manager was initially sceptical about CLECC, but found it a helpful way to manage continuity through the disruption caused by two major ward relocations and changes in team membership during the project. Ward B manager (Hospital A) was new to the ward and her post and embraced CLECC enthusiastically as a way to establish the team and guide her leadership. Ward D manager (Hospital B) expressed a high level of support for CLECC and attended all the study days and action learning sets but struggled with team cohesion owing to a large influx of new staff that outnumbered the original team members. The manager of Ward E (Hospital B) kept a distance from CLECC, sending her deputy in her place to the study days and the ward manager action learning sets. Consequently, while the majority of staff were eager to participate, the extent to which individuals saw it as their role to undertake specific CLECC activities varied between teams and hospitals.

Collective Action: Participation Shaped by Organizational Context

Whether or not the activities went ahead as planned was mediated by the extent to which the proposed activity harmonized with the priorities of the wider hospital organization and resources available to the ward team. A particular influence was the organizational priority afforded to material patient care activities over CLECC activities in the context of high patient care workloads. Although staff in all teams reported struggling to find the time to engage with the five-minute cluster discussions, the planned 20-minute reflective learning sessions were perceived to be impossible to integrate into ward practice. CLECC's flexibility enabled staff to develop strategies that partly overcame time barriers.

Because [the clusters are] five minutes you can work it and actually if you're having a day where you're too busy to run them, then that's the day that you realise that you need to go round and make sure everyone's okay... And I think that's definitely been my biggest struggle throughout it all – it's just being able to release staff to do things. **N005** (Ward manager, Hospital A)

Despite these struggles, staff reported that senior hospital managers in both hospitals had endorsed the work that had resulted from the CLECC intervention, suggesting that the benefits were visible and valued outside of the immediate ward team.

They seemed to be really positive about it and [the visiting senior manager] said – 'if this is working for you, continue.' **N009** (HCA, Hospital B)

Nonetheless, staff's participation in CLECC activities was viewed as of secondary importance to providing direct patient care. In Hospital B, in spite of a supportive senior manager, ward staff and the practice educator reported a lack of support from the matron for the participating wards. This lack of support was also suspected by the senior manager.

I assumed that my matron was working with the ward [managers] on a weekly basis, but I doubt it was what I expected it to be. So, we should have put more nursing leadership resources into it, just to provide that support and recognize it. **SN002** (Senior Nursing Manager, Hospital B)

Interestingly, many cluster discussions proved possible to integrate into the working day and went ahead during the implementation period. However, across all teams, cluster discussions were less readily convened when patient care demands were particularly high and staffing resource was low. CLECC properties of plasticity enabled staff to develop and adapt practices that suited local circumstances, but were constrained by the available resources and priorities of the wider organization.

Reflexive Monitoring: Valued by Staff but Challenging to Sustain

Staff from all four participating teams reported benefits to personal well-being and capacity to care from CLECC participation. They spoke of engaging more consciously and deliberately with patients as individual people, prioritizing such personalized attention over the completion of tasks. Although staff reported that their practice was already compassionate, CLECC had given them opportunities to prioritize compassionate practices and to further commit to compassion.

> *CLECC, for me, is about giving the staff the empowerment to feel like they can sit and do things with patients that are compassionate rather than task orientated, so rather than just doing the [observations] and just doing the washes, just having a chat with the patient about their life, their family or sitting and doing an activity with them; rather than just: 'we've got to get the washes done, we've got to get the observations done' – which do still need to be done, but it's about giving the staff that empowerment of being able to say: 'let's do something a bit different'.* **N034** (Ward Manager, Hospital A)

CLECC was associated with an improvement in staff morale and staff well-being and viewed as impacting positively on patient care. The legitimacy for CLECC practices seemed to come partly from the fact that staff were part of a named programme and perhaps because they were also part of a research study. One interviewee cited an instance in which a senior manager (Hospital A) visiting the ward came across a cluster discussion, which was also used by some teams to make sure that staff had a drink of water. This shared concern for colleagues belied appearances, initially being seen as simply taking an unscheduled break.

> *I don't know who it was, but someone very high in the hospital [came to the ward] and was like, 'why are people standing and drinking in the corridor?'* **N025** (HCA, Hospital A)

Once the manager was told the cluster discussion was part of CLECC, she was reported to have then understood the purpose behind an activity considered unusual enough to remark upon. Furthermore, the improved teamwork reduced the burden for some staff and provided opportunities to undertake activities that previously would have been rare occurrences.

> *... Because of the task orientated work, we've managed to go, 'right, we've finished, [they] haven't' and then so we can go 'right, we'll give you guys a hand and then we can all be finished together.' And then that means we've got more time to do things that we might not be able to normally do, like, wash someone's hair, do their nails."* **N009** (HCA, Hospital B)

The principles of compassion and concern that underpin CLECC continued to be understood and valued across the teams, even several months after the implementation period. Hospital A ward teams continued with the cluster discussions, a concrete marker of CLECC's sustained impact. Although Hospital B wards had not continued, their overall attention to supporting each other appeared to have increased the relational capacity of individual team members and the team as a whole, at least setting a memorable norm for working more closely together.

Implications for Compassionate Care of Planned Intervention

The CLECC intervention was feasible in practice, welcomed across the teams, and served as a broader stimulus to collective action. CLECC developed cultures, at least temporarily, in which reflection, learning, mutual support, and innovation were more legitimate within the work team and in which expertise was seen to be distributed more widely among team members. However, the findings also indicated that the degree of impact and sustainability were highly context-specific and were mediated by factors at ward-team level and at other levels of the organization.

Staff at all levels of the hierarchy were able to identify the benefits to patient care of ward staff engaging in CLECC activities, echoing other findings that the creation of unmanaged spaces for work-team members to 'take shelter' provides the potential for valued learning and social support for difficult work with clients (Bolton 2005, p. 134; Parker 2002). Furthermore, our findings confirm that intervening at work-team level can be successful, corroborating an association indicated in other research (Bridges and Fuller 2015; Maben et al. 2012; Mimura and Griffiths 2003; Patterson et al. 2011). Despite high workloads, CLECC empowered managers and frontline care staff to reflect on local norms governing team practice, on the relationships and resources that aligned with them, and to make some changes. Thus, interventions at work-team level can play a part in shaping relational capacity (Billett 2004). However, we also found that implementation was uneven between hospitals and teams, particularly over the longer term, reinforcing the value of both tailoring intervention to particular contexts and paying attention to the sustainability of complex interventions beyond initial set-up (Bridges et al. 2007, 2017; Martin et al. 2012; May 2013).

Team-specific factors, and factors outside of the direct influence of the ward teams, mediated the impact and sustainability of the intervention. Such factors included norms regarding the legitimacy and nature of nursing work; staff learning and staff support; interpretation of key stakeholder roles, particularly the ward manager and matron role in supporting implementation; workforce characteristics such as staffing levels in relation to patient workload; and stability of workforce over time. We saw how these factors influenced the extent to which planned CLECC intervention activities consistently took place and were sustained over time. Some factors were related to the busyness and priorities of acute care contexts, including changes in team membership between shifts and over time, while others varied across the individual settings, such as the participation of individual ward leaders.

While CLECC draws on principles of democratic working, its longer-term success relies on consistent cognitive participation from more senior members of the hierarchy. Since such cognitive participation is, in turn, shaped by structural and relational elements of context, further study would be helpful here to better understand these specific features and their impact. Overall, our findings indicate the need for more study to better understand the scope, sources, and impact of variation, including a wider range of settings than studied here, to enable more systematic study of contextual layers beyond the individual teams.

Framing interventions such as CLECC as events within complex, adaptive systems focuses attention, not only on the properties of the intervention, or the actors' contributions, or lack of contribution, to implementation, but also on the dynamic properties of the system itself (Hawe 2015; Hawe et al. 2009). A successful intervention is one that leaves a 'lasting footprint', one that is able to trigger new and sustained structures for interaction and new shared meanings (Hawe et al. 2009, p. 270). The extent to which interventions such as CLECC can sustainably transform the system depends on their engagement with their contexts and the capability this creates. Successful intervention, therefore, depends on a thorough understanding of context, as prescribed by NPT, but may well also include a deliberate harnessing of system properties to support implementation, in advance of and alongside the introduction and support of the intervention package.

Conclusion

This case study of a compassionate care intervention illustrates a number of implications for intervention design and implementation. Our analysis of CLECC, guided by NPT, sought to identify the dynamics of human agency in complex health care systems. In particular, the study reinforced the value of both tailoring interventions to particular contexts and paying attention to the sustainability of complex interventions beyond initial set-up. Despite staff from all participating teams reporting benefits to personal well-being, team building, and the capacity to care from the CLECC participation, many participants noted challenges in sustaining intervention adoption. Sustainability and success of the intervention required consistent cognitive participation from all levels of the health care service hierarchy, but particularly the engagement and participation from more senior members. Intervention implementation also required clearly defined roles and responsibilities for programme implementation, given that the extent to which individuals took responsibility for CLECC implementation and operation varied between teams and hospitals. Clearly defined roles and responsibilities would also have the additional benefit of contributing to succession planning, as participants noted that CLECC did not provide for ensuring continuity following attrition in the design of CLECC delivery. This limited the opportunity for staff commencing after the initial implementation period to make full sense of CLECC.

Despite the discourse on compassionate care often primarily focused on individual caregiver disposition and agency, our findings from CLECC highlight that complex health care programs also require the support of resources, norms, and relationships located in the wider system. Successful intervention design and delivery in complex adaptive systems, such as health care, should include the careful identification and mobilization of relevant elements of context. As our case study of CLECC demonstrates, it may be necessary to undergo extensive organizational restructuring, both culturally and structurally, to re-shape the conditions in which people are able to act and adopt change.

Acknowledgements The authors would like to thank all NHS staff who participated in the study.

Funding The CLECC study was funded by the National Institute for Health Research (NIHR) Health Services and Delivery Research programme (project number 13/07/48) and supported by NIHR Collaboration for Leadership in Applied Health Research and Care Wessex.

Disclaimer The views and opinions expressed are those of the authors and do not necessarily reflect those of the Health Services and Delivery Research programme, NIHR, NHS, or the Department of Health and Social Care.

Copyright Information Sections of this chapter are reproduced from Bridges et al. (2017). This is an Open Access article distributed in accordance with the terms of the Creative Commons Attribution (CC BY 4.0) licence, which permits others to distribute, remix, adapt and build upon this work, for commercial use, provided the original work is properly cited. See: http://creativecommons.org/licenses/by/4.0/.

Note

1. *N* denotes nursing team membership, *SN* denotes senior nursing manager, and number represents order of entry into study.

References

Barker, H., Griffiths, P., Gould, L., Mesa-Eguiagaray, I., Pickering, R., & Bridges, J. (2016). Quantity and quality of interaction between staff and older patients in UK hospital wards: A descriptive study. *International Journal of Nursing Studies, 62,* 100–107.

Billett, S. (2004). Learning through work: Workplace participatory practices. In H. Rainbird, A. Fuller, & A. Munro (Eds.), *Workplace learning in context* (pp. 109–125). London: Routledge.

Blomberg, K., Griffiths, P., Wengstrom, Y., May, C. R., & Bridges, J. (2016). Interventions for compassionate nursing care: A systematic review. *International Journal of Nursing Studies, 62,* 137–155.

Bolton, S. C. (2005). *Emotion management in the workplace.* Basingstoke: Palgrave Macmillan.

Bridges, J., Fitzgerald, L., & Meyer, J. (2007). New workforce roles in health care: Exploring the longer-term journey of organisational innovations. *Journal of Healthcare Organization and Management, 21*(4/5), 381–392.

Bridges, J., Flatley, M., Meyer, J., & Brown Wilson, C. (2009). Best practice for older people in acute care settings (BPOP): Guidance for nurses. *Nursing Standard, 24*(10).

Bridges, J., & Fuller, A. (2015). Creating Learning Environments for Compassionate Care (CLECC): A programme to promote compassionate care by health and social care teams. *International Journal of Older People Nursing, 10*(1), 48–58.

Bridges, J., May, C. R., Fuller, A., Griffiths, P., Wigley, W., Gould, L., et al. (2017). Optimising impact and sustainability: A qualitative process evaluation of a complex intervention targeted at compassionate care. *BMJ Quality & Safety, 26*(12), 970–977.

Bridges, J., Nicholson, C., Maben, J., Pope, C., Flatley, M., Wilkinson, C., et al. (2013). Capacity for care: Meta-ethnography of acute care nurses' experiences of the nurse–patient relationship. *Journal of Advanced Nursing, 69*(4), 760–772.

Bridges, J., Pickering, R. M., Barker, H., Chable, R., Fuller, A., Gould, L., et al. (2018). Implementing the Creating Learning Environments for Compassionate Care programme (CLECC) in acute hospital settings: A pilot RCT and feasibility study. *Health Services and Delivery Research, 6*(33), 1–196.

Bridges, J., & Tziggili, M. (2011). Piloting discovery interview technique to explore its utility in improving dignity in acute care for older people. *International Practice Development Journal, 1*(2), Article 4.

Cammer, A., Morgan, D., Stewart, N., McGilton, K., Rycroft-Malone, J., Dopson, S., et al. (2013). The hidden complexity of long-term care: How context mediates knowledge translation and use of best practices. *The Gerontologist, 54*(6), 1013–1023.

Francis, R. (2010). *Independent inquiry into care provided by Mid Staffordshire NHS Foundation Trust January 2005–March 2009.* London: The Stationary Office. https://www.gov.uk/government/uploads/system/uploads/attachment_data/file/279109/0375_i.pdf. Accessed 18 Feb 2017.

Francis, R. (2013). *Report of the Mid Staffordshire NHS Foundation Trust public inquiry.* London. http://webarchive.nationalarchives.gov.uk/20150407084003/http://www.midstaffspublicinquiry.com/report. Accessed 18 Feb 2017.

Fuller, A. (2007). Theories of learning and communities of practice. In J. Hughes, N. Jewson, & L. Unwin (Eds.), *Learning in communities of practice* (pp. 17–29). London: Routledge.

Fuller, A., & Unwin, L. (2004). Expansive learning environments: Integrating organizational and personal development. In H. Rainbird, A. Fuller, & A. Munro (Eds.), *Workplace learning in context* (pp. 126–144). London: Routledge.

Hawe, P. (2015). Lessons from complex interventions to improve health. *Annual Review of Public Health, 36,* 307–323.

Hawe, P., Shiell, A., & Riley, T. (2009). Theorising interventions as events in systems. *American Journal of Community Psychology, 43*(3–4), 267–276.

Hewison, A., & Sawbridge, Y. (2015). Organisational support for nurses in acute care settings: A rapid evidence review. *International Journal of Healthcare, 1*(1), 48–60.

Hewison, A., Sawbridge, Y., Cragg, R., Rogers, L., Lehmann, S., & Rook, J. (2018). Leading with compassion in health care organisations: The development of a compassion recognition scheme-evaluation and analysis. *Journal of Health Organization and Management, 32*(2), 338–354.

Maben, J., Peccei, R., Adams, M., Robert, G., Richardson, A., Murrells, T., et al. (2012). *Exploring the relationship between patients' experiences of care and the influence of staff motivation, affect and wellbeing. NIHR Service Delivery and Organisation programme.* http://www.netscc.ac.uk/hsdr/files/project/SDO_FR_08-1819-213_V01.pdf. Accessed 18 Feb 2017.

Martin, G. P., Weaver, S., Currie, G., Finn, R., & McDonald, R. (2012). Innovation sustainability in challenging health-care contexts: Embedding clinically led change in routine practice. *Health Services Management Research, 25*(4), 190–199.

May, C. (2013). Towards a general theory of implementation. *Implementation Science, 8*(1), 18.

May, C., & Finch, T. (2009). Implementing, embedding, and integrating practices: An outline of normalization process theory. *Sociology, 43*(3), 535–554.

May, C. R., Johnson, M., & Finch, T. (2016). Implementation, context and complexity. *Implementation Science, 11*(1), 141.

May, C. R., Cummings, A., Girling, M., Bracher, M., Mair, F. S., May, C. M., et al. (2018). Using normalization process theory in feasibility studies and process evaluations of complex healthcare interventions: A systematic review. *Implementation Science, 13*, 80.

Mimura, C., & Griffiths, P. (2003). The effectiveness of current approaches to workplace stress management in the nursing profession: An evidence based literature review. *Occupational and Environmental Medicine, 60*(1), 10–15.

Parker, V. A. (2002). Connecting relational work and workgroup context in caregiving organizations. *The Journal of Applied Behavioral Science, 38*(3), 276.

Patterson, M., Nolan, M., Rick, J., Brown, J., Adams, R., & Musson, G. (2011). From metrics to meaning: Culture change and quality of acute hospital care for older people. *NIHR SDO Programme Project, 3*(1501), 93.

Pfadenhauer, L. M., Gerhardus, A., Mozygemba, K., Lysdahl, K. B., Booth, A., Hofmann, B., et al. (2017). Making sense of complexity in context and implementation: The Context and Implementation of Complex Interventions (CICI) framework. *Implementation Science, 12*(1), 21.

Pope, C., Halford, S., Turnbull, J., Prichard, J., Calestani, M., & May, C. (2013). Using computer decision support systems in NHS emergency and urgent care: Ethnographic study using normalisation process theory. *BMC Health Services Research, 13*(1), 111.

Richardson, L. (2000). Writing: A method of inquiry. In N. K. Denzin & Y. S. Lincoln (Eds.), *Handbook of qualitative research* (pp. 923–948). Thousand Oaks: Sage.

Rycroft-Malone, J. (2008). Evidence-informed practice: From individual to context. *Journal of Nursing Management, 16*(4), 404–408.

Wenger, E. (1998). *Communities of practice: Learning, meaning and identity.* Cambridge: Cambridge University Press.

3

Driving Change Across Boundaries: Eliminating Crusted Scabies in Northern Territory, Australia

Helen Dickinson, Karen Gardner, Michelle Dowden
and Naomi van der Linden

Introduction

Collaboration is recognised as a central feature of high-quality health systems (Williams 2012; Dickinson and O'Flynn 2016). This chapter contributes to what we know about the intersection of collaboration

H. Dickinson (✉) · K. Gardner
Public Service Research Group, School of Business,
University of South Wales Canberra, Canberra, Australia
e-mail: h.dickinson@adfa.edu.au

K. Gardner
e-mail: karen.gardner@unsw.edu.au

M. Dowden
Registered Nurse Midwife, Darwin, NT, Australia
e-mail: michelle.dowden@onedisease.org

N. van der Linden
Health Economist at AstraZeneca, The Hague, The Netherlands
e-mail: naomi.vanderlinden@chere.uts.edu.au

© The Author(s) 2020
P. Nugus et al. (eds.), *Transitions and Boundaries in the Coordination and Reform of Health Services*, Organizational Behaviour in Healthcare,
https://doi.org/10.1007/978-3-030-26684-4_3

with the notion of boundary work. 'Boundary work' refers to the efforts made to build, enhance or respond to formal aspects of discursively constructed organisational or professional demarcations (Allen 2000). Collaboration within organisations and across the boundaries of other organisations and sectors is even more important in the face of 'wicked issues'. Wicked problems are those so complex and embedded that their very nature requires joint working from a number of partners (Head and Alford 2015). This chapter draws on, as a case study, the wicked problem of crusted scabies (CS) in Indigenous populations living in remote communities in Australia's Northern Territory (NT). The 'wickedness' of CS is evident in its significant biological, economic and socio-economic dimensions. These dimensions include the fragmentation and lack of coordination of health care, the remote living conditions of the population, climate, sustained political will and health and economic inequities of Indigenous people across the region (Barber et al. 2014). This chapter reports on a programme seeking to improve identification and on-going management of CS in pursuit of elimination of the condition in the longer term, the collaborative effort mobilised to address this problem and the collaborative lessons it yields.

Scabies is a skin condition endemic within remote Aboriginal communities in the NT, where communities have among the highest reported rates in the world (Romani et al. 2015). Caused by the mite *Sarcoptes scabiei*, scabies often results in severe itching, and in patients with compromised immunity, it may progress to CS, which is a severe variant of scabies caused by a hyper infestation of the same mite (Strong and Johnstone 2007). The fissures associated with CS provide a portal of entry for bacteria and, if left untreated, can result in secondary infections, glomerulonephritis, rheumatic heart disease, sepsis and death (Thornley et al. 2018).

Community-based scabies control programmes have operated with some success in NT communities since the late 1990s, but sustaining treatment interventions is difficult because treated patients often become re-infected (Carapetis et al. 1997). High prevalence in the community, as well as heat, humidity, overcrowding and movement between households and communities, presents significant challenges for sustaining the reductions achieved (Hay et al. 2012). Despite being relatively straightforward and inexpensive to treat, both scabies and CS in remote Aboriginal communities are a major cost burden for communities already struggling to deal with a significant burden of ill health.

CS was recently identified as a priority for elimination by a not-for-profit organisation working as an external agent to influence health sector improvements in diagnosis, management and follow-up support for self-management. The NT government has also recently listed CS as a notifiable disease, providing an additional public health response and increasing opportunities for elimination (Quilty et al. 2017). Elimination is a major challenge for a wicked problem like CS that has biological, economic and socio-economic dimensions, which require coordinated action and multi-dimensional system changes across institutional and organisational boundaries if efforts are to be successful. As well as meeting biological and economic criteria for elimination, political will and a sustained health system response are required (Dowdle 1999). Such a response will involve significant collaboration across different levels of the health system, with families and communities, between Indigenous and mainstream health organisations, and between health agencies, local government and other public health interests.

In the next section, we provide an overview of the One Disease (OD) programme, followed by a discussion of the Australian health system and the different forms of collaboration implemented in pursuit of eliminating CS. We consider the boundaries that need to be crossed to establish the new approach. As we suggest, overcoming this wicked issue is a significant challenge given the range of different boundaries that must be traversed. However, the challenge is even greater in this case since the reform effort is being driven by a not-for-profit organisation that sits outside of the 'formal' health system. This raises a question as to the degree to which a philanthropic organisation can strategically intervene in the design and organisation of health services. Having set out this background, we move on to provide a short overview of the methods adopted in this research. In the findings section, we provide an overview of some of the contested boundaries identified during the research and the techniques developed to support working across them. We conclude that the OD programme was successful largely because of the relationships its organisers managed to create with a range of different stakeholders and their ability to put time and energy into an issue that is complex in nature and does not come under the jurisdiction of any one organisation.

The One Disease Crusted Scabies Elimination Programme

OD is a non-government, not-for-profit, philanthropically funded organisation. As its name suggests, it was established to focus on one disease and is now focused on CS, with the short-term aim to improve detection, diagnosis and management of CS and to prevent re-occurrence in clients who have been successfully treated. This is a first step towards the longer-term aim of eliminating CS from Australia by 2022.

OD works with existing health services and uses medical and public health approaches and community development principles to facilitate more coherent coordination among services for the detection and management of CS. This includes the following strategies:

- Conduct audits of primary healthcare (PHC) clinics against CS case definition to improve detection,
- Promote a care coordination approach to improve access to services and continuity of care for patients with CS between primary and secondary care services,
- Embed integration of CS management into PHC clinics and hospitals,
- Support timely and comprehensive treatments, including providing individual case management,
- Follow-up treated CS clients in PHC centres to ensure on-going prevention and management,
- Maintain a focus on household-level strategies that address the health of the household by treating all members and supporting the achievement and maintenance of a 'scabies-free zone'.

The mission of this organisation is ultimately to make itself redundant by embedding new processes into the existing health service delivery systems, both community-controlled and State government-run.

The programme promotes better understanding of CS through education so that individuals work with local clinics to self-manage their condition and prevent recurrences over time.

Cross-Boundary Working in the Elimination of Crusted Scabies

The Australian healthcare system has been described as one of the most fragmented in the world (Dickinson and Ledger 2017), with responsibilities for planning, delivery and funding split between different levels of government (local, state/territory, federal/commonwealth), in addition to non-government sectors. Australia has universal health care through the Medicare scheme, but private insurance and provision also play an important part in the delivery of care. Across the country, Aboriginal Community-Controlled Health Services (ACCHS) are funded by the federal government to provide PHC services that are initiated and operated by local Aboriginal communities to deliver comprehensive and culturally appropriate care to the communities that control it through a locally elected management board. The ACCHS model is Australia's only model of comprehensive primary health care formally based on Alma Ata principles of the centrality of primary health care for individual and societal well-being, and it is significantly different from general practice or community health. By world standards, Australia has a 'good health system for reasonable per capita health expenditure' (McKeon et al. 2013, p. 9), but lags behind other colonial nations in achieving Indigenous health equity (Freeman et al. 2016). Aboriginal and Torres Strait Islander peoples experience significant health inequities and present a major burden of chronic conditions (Australian Institute of Health and Welfare 2015).

The fragmentation and complexity of the health system pose challenges for those with complex and chronic diseases (Commonwealth of Australia 2015). Indigenous people in remote communities who contract CS typically have a range of chronic conditions that require treatment from various parts of the health system. Disease elimination programmes do not rely solely on drug treatments, but also need to involve hospital, public health, education partners, housing providers and a range of other stakeholders. In this case, the collaboration required to address this wicked issue is both horizontal and vertical. Collaboration in the face of such entrenched problems requires working vertically between specialists, hospitals and PHC clinics to improve access to services and continuity of care for clients across the treatment spectrum and horizontally between clinics, community and environmental health and households, to support scabies-free households and improve management and lifelong follow-up in PHC. The OD programme must, therefore, operate across a number of different boundaries and borders within the health system and beyond, including institutions, health and community sector organisations, professions, Western and Indigenous knowledge systems, cultures and others.

An extensive literature has developed around the concept of cross-boundary working (Williams 2012; O'Flynn 2014). It stresses that boundary-crossing is central to designing and delivering high-quality healthcare services and addressing the difficulties involved in working collaboratively. Although significant effort and investment have gone into developing collaborative arrangements across health care in general, there is still something of a lack of evidence to demonstrate that this type of working has had a substantial impact on the outcomes of those accessing these services (Dickinson and O'Flynn 2016).

The existing literature suggests that collaboration is a difficult enough task, but it is potentially even more challenging for the OD programme, as this organisation sits outside of the formal health system. OD does not deliver services under contract to the Australian government but is trying to influence change within services with which they work. The evidence suggests that such organisations can sometimes struggle in these types of initiatives, as their role can go unrecognised or under-recognised by public authorities (Giarelli et al. 2014). It can be difficult for external agencies to drive changes of practice through the health system (Roy et al. 2017). Even where organisations are successful in changing practices, the sustainability of these changes after these external agents leave is a pertinent question (Dyer 2006). Most research about how collaboration occurs across boundaries overlooks the different strengths of boundaries within and across organisations. Therefore, this project sought to explore the degree to which or how a philanthropic organisation, or one outside the boundaries of the main health system, can strategically intervene in the design and organisation of health services and with what effect.

Understanding Change Across Boundaries

The data presented in this chapter are derived from an evaluation of the OD programme in the NT (Gardner et al. 2018). The evaluation was mixed methods in approach, drawing on qualitative and quantitative data from key reports and documents, interviews and focus groups with key stakeholders and programme staff and an audit of patient records. It explored the impact of the programme on improving detection and management of CS, including the prevention of recurrence in patients and the creation of scabies-free household environments, as well as the overall cost of illness of CS in the NT. The project further sought to identify model components that need to be in place should the programme be rolled out to other Australian jurisdictions.

In this chapter, we present only one component of the larger project, drawing on published literature, programme documentation and the perspectives of health professionals to explore the programme approach to collaborations established for crossing boundaries and working to promote coordination. For the present research, 19 health professional staff of health services participated in individual interviews, an additional five staff in a remote health clinic participated in a focus group, and three OD staff also participated in a separate focus group. With the permission of the participants, interviews were digitally recorded and transcribed verbatim, then uploaded into NVivo 11, which was used to assist with data management, including coding and analysis. Data were analysed thematically against the evaluation questions and then compiled by stakeholder type and region for comparison. Key barriers to implementation of the programme strategies were analysed inductively to identify boundary issues that signified contestation and the techniques adopted to work across boundaries.

Collaborative Efforts for Cross-Boundary Change

Overall, the research project showed that the OD programme had largely been successful and was well regarded by those stakeholders who were interviewed (Gardner et al. 2018). The project showed improvements in diagnosis and treatments, reflected in patients' staying longer in hospital to complete treatment and more continuous follow-up in the community. However, maintaining a scabies-free zone was challenging for those returning home after completing hospital treatment. In the context of overcrowded housing and endemic scabies in the community, elimination efforts require on-going coordination of care across the health delivery spectrum (primary, secondary and specialist). Coordination is particularly important at discharge when household contacts who have simple scabies must be treated so they cannot re-infect individuals returning home from hospital. Education and support for self-care over the long term are also needed for people who have previously had CS in order to prevent its recurrence.

Efforts to achieve coordination therefore require collaboration among staff and patients that cuts across traditional vertical approaches to providing medical care. Interview data highlighted four areas in which existing boundaries had to be negotiated to support a collaborative approach. First, working from the 'outside in' as a not-for-profit organisation within a publically funded health sector highlighted different values and expectations and raised questions about the role of not-for-profit organisations (or 'not-for-profits') in the community-controlled health sector and the potential for further fragmentation of funding. Second, while organisational boundaries between hospitals, primary care and community health must be spanned if care is to follow the client, negative previous experiences of patients can prevent people from seeking care and completing treatments. Negative experiences of Indigenous people raise questions about the types of coordination and support required, and the skills and attributes health professionals need to work across personal and cultural boundaries. A third, related boundary is the professional role of Aboriginal health practitioners in elimination of CS, their specific cultural knowledge and their potential role in building relationships between health services and households. Lastly, CS is a condition associated with overcrowding and poor living conditions. The extent to which health policy and practitioners can impact housing conditions is a long-standing and well-recognised barrier to addressing the social determinants of health. We briefly provide an overview of these different contested boundaries and then move on to explore the ways in which OD sought to work across them.

Contested Boundaries

Various aspects of the diagnosis and treatment of individual patients with CS exacerbate the challenges of collaboration. Many people experience stigma and shame associated with having CS, and this can make them reluctant to seek care. Extended treatment periods of 3–4 weeks in a hospital isolation ward away from their community are also difficult for many people, and it is common for patients not to complete hospital treatment. Once home, there can be limited opportunities for privacy in overcrowded households, and poor housing hardware presents significant barriers to administering treatments and maintaining on-going prevention. As a result, coordination of care for people with CS involves providing education and practical support as well as medical care.

OD staff not only worked across organisational boundaries to facilitate links between hospital, PHC and households, they needed to adopt supportive strategies that could assist patients to overcome the structural barriers they face in accessing care, as well as helping to address emotional and personal issues involved. Clinical care pathways, discharge planning processes and electronic care plans and recall systems were embedded in clinical information systems to improve care processes. Training was also provided to support staff to adopt new practices. However, outreach into the community is also required to build trust and encourage people to seek and complete treatment. This is a significant gap in existing care arrangements.

Many staff interviewed commented on the need to work in the community outside of the health clinic. One remote area nurse summed up the significance of working in the community for a patient who was repeatedly re-infected with CS. She noted that had there been more outreach services, staff could have identified problems earlier and provided assistance to prevent the patient's recurrences.

> *I remember one patient in particular. The whole reason why she kept getting re-infected was that her washing machine broke down, and that wasn't identified until [the OD nurse] went out there, and she sourced, like, a new part for the washing machine, which meant she could wash her clothes, which meant she wasn't re-infecting herself. So, I mean, just something so simple like that… was a bit of a game changer, you know. And, you know, it's not stuff that's hard, but it's just stuff that you can look for, and it's stuff that you get from just visiting the house itself.* (Remote area nurse)

Competing priorities and the high demands of acute and chronic care were repeatedly identified by primary care staff as major barriers to continuing outreach support once OD is no longer providing it. Many commented that the demands of acute and chronic care in PHC clinics make it difficult to find time.

> *While it relies on one person doing surveillance and the staff on the ground doing the work, with all the competing priorities, it's always fraught. And whilst we all know its core business and it's part of what we need to do, the reality of service delivery is that 10 other things will come up on the same day. And it's hard to make people on the ground aware of that priority when they might see another priority. So, they might agree with you—'yeah, it's a priority'—but I'm just so busy. And we run an emergency service too.* (PHC Director)

Time is a constant theme in discussions regarding health programme delivery in remote communities. One child health nurse commented on the value of unrestricted time working with communities.

> *The One Disease programme has a wonderful ability in that when they're in the community, the constraints on their time are not so strict. So, for example, if we're referring families with recurrent scabies in six months or three times, let's say, the ability that she had was she could go back multiple times and just*

spend time building a relationship with that family, and then taking as long as it needed to have discussions and find out if there's other family members... whereas the clinic staff are so over-run that time is really hard to get that extra support.

Beyond the perceived limitation of time, effective support for people with CS depended on an ability to develop trusting relationships based on respectful engagement and supportive interactions. An experienced Medical Director expressed the view that there is sometimes limited understanding of the effects of dispossession on Aboriginal people and little knowledge of how to work with Aboriginal people and their communities. He said,

... when people come to hospital, they feel very disempowered, racially profiled and very uncomfortable. And this is affecting our ability to provide services .... There is a misunderstanding of ... what really are the effects of dispossession and being a non- dominant culture in a very dominant culture world.

This statement captures the significance of respectful engagement and also points to the importance of cultural knowledge and the role of Aboriginal and Torres Strait Islander health workers (AHWs) *vis-à-vis* general practitioners and nurses in providing an outreach function and working with communities. As one community worker noted:

They [PHC Clinics] can't work without the Aboriginal workers with them. [They] need equal numbers to the clinical staff. Otherwise it is just going to be band-aid stuff; [the problems] will repeat and repeat.

The ability to develop strong inter-organisational and inter-sectoral relationships relies not only on having a larger Aboriginal health workforce, but also on the community having the capacity to engage in a community development approach. One Aboriginal health practitioner commented:

You need strong people in the community to be involved. To get the message out there and to keep it going. There are not many strong elders ...

Material resources are just as important in building a community development approach in communities:

> You need washing machines and mattresses that are affordable. [A] community development approach ... is needed.... Put a washing machine in the ladies' centre—come in, have a cup of tea, do the washing. Even just have a laundromat. There isn't one here. Not even clothes lines and washing machines in some places. ("Strong Women" programme worker)

While resources are critical, poor housing and overcrowding are major factors in the transmission of scabies and CS in remote communities in the NT. Addressing these problems may increase the impact of programmes on reducing transmissions. Yet there is limited capacity in the current system for health departments and services to influence housing and other policies.

The boundary between health and housing providers was discussed by numerous stakeholders, especially the Strong Women workers in ACCHS. They argued that without crossing the boundary into housing, it will be very difficult for the health sector alone to eliminate CS.

> What is the root of the problem? This is important to think about. If you don't have running water or a fridge or a washing machine ... How many people in houses? Thirty plus people living in a three-bedroom house. All these things need to be addressed in conjunction with the skin stuff.... Housing is always going to be an issue. The overcrowding. If you don't sort this, then you can't get rid of scabies. ("Strong Women" programme worker)

Following from this, one medical practitioner pointed to the complexity of negotiating actions to address complex health problems in a siloed policy environment. He said:

> And as health services, and as One Disease ... we don't actually have control over education or housing, or food security, or things like that. So, it's always looked at [as] the health sphere [that is] responsible for elimination [of scabies or CS]. And I know that these organisations do advocacy and stuff, but ... there's not the same buy-in if it's not a health organisation, because, more broadly in government, the social determinants aren't considered as important—doesn't have the same level of importance as health staff [does].

Ways of Working Across Boundaries

The techniques and methods used by OD staff for working across boundaries were often relational in nature. In addition to the formal partnerships that established the programme's values and principles, and clinical pathways and care plans that were embedded into health system architecture as part of programme implementation, OD staff sought to build networks and relationships with multiple stakeholders as a way of mobilising effort to work across the many boundaries they faced.

A Director of Nursing in a large community-controlled organisation described the type of engagement as involving a lot of contact and discussion.

> So we met up really early on, and just had a good few meetings about how we'd work together, and establishing avenues for her to be able to audit our data, and then look into our individual client records, and provide support to the clinic. So she's done a couple of visits out there. And then we talked a lot in the preliminary stages of development of the position.

This same Director commented that it was the extensive experience of working within the PHC sector that enabled OD staff to negotiate aspects of implementation. As well-respected individuals with extensive knowledge of 'the rules of the game', OD staff were able to negotiate across different sets of values and imperatives to find ways of overcoming obstacles that might otherwise have interfered with working together. He said:

> I mean [X] has been great in that space, really pragmatic and goes: 'Yeah, I see where you're coming from.' She's been working in this area for so long and she's not got rose-colored glasses.… So it's great to have her in that role to be able to have those frank conversations.… I think [this is better than] if you had a … different person come into that role, not understanding the context, not necessarily being pragmatic and realistic, and [tell] us how it's got to be and how we can eliminate this. Whereas you can have your say and say: 'These are our challenges,' and she goes, 'I know them all, I'm totally cool with that, and this is how we can work together, and let's try and do that. (PHC Director)

The approach to working with patients was similar to that of working with staff, in terms of the centrality of collaboration, problem-solving and respectful relationships. One Senior Medical Officer described such engagement as a collaborative personalised approach and reflected on the degree of time and investment required to implement it:

> *So the approach is an organised approach. It's driven by knowledge of which patients are affected. It's a collaborative approach with health centre managers and doctors. And its protocol driven, I believe. And it features, in my experience, availability in excess of what we normally have in our clinical services. And, in my experience, it features good collaboration with other service providers within the community health centres and health teams.... And it also offers a service that is responsive with respect to time. So I've observed that. One Disease personnel can attend to review a patient in a much shorter time frame than we would get people from other services to attend.* (Senior medical officer/manager NT Health)

The strong relationships that OD staff were able to develop with patients are perceived as a major strength of the programme.

> *One of the key things is the relationship that is developed with the patients. I've seen that the OD staff demonstrate good support of relationships with affected people. And I've been struck by how that differs from the broader relationships [patients have] with clinicians. So, the personal relationship element is certainly a strength.* (Senior Medical practitioner/manager)

This was reinforced by one Strong Woman worker:

> *She [the OD nurse] was good. And she could talk and we know each other. And she always came to visit and she always kept asking me for my family, ask how your family's going.... And also she's [the OD nurse] good for two-way learning. She listens and asks us questions and learns from us.*

Others highlighted the problem-solving, navigation and coordination aspects of the role as critical to its success.

It's that coordinator who says, 'I'm going to facilitate this patient being seen'; or maybe they're going to have access to the CIS to put a recall in. Maybe they're going to monitor the recall. Maybe they're going to ring the doctor and the health centre manager from the community and say, 'Your patient is coming home, this is what's happened and this is what we need to do, would you be able to get to have that recall done?' That sort of stuff. In bigger communities where there's possibly a number of people with this condition, you would almost [always] have a community-based worker, who might be a health worker, or they might be a mentor. (Senior Medical officer)

Perhaps because their remit is not as prescribed and limited as that of formal health organisations, OD could be agile and deal with issues as they arise. As one senior medical practitioner/manager observed, this could be incredibly mobilising, because these workers would be expected to come into organisations and take efficient action:

They've provided motivation. Let's get up; let's do something about this. Let's get down to the house and have a look and pick them up, and see how they're going. OD had said, 'Look she needs to have a bath, and she needs to be covered with this lotion.' And the worker was going, 'I don't want to do that.' But within a few days I saw her and she said [that] I brought her up and I'm giving her a bath here in the clinic and I'm putting the stuff on her. And I think that the support, keeping the motivation going, was really good.

Sustaining Change Across Boundaries

Considerable progress in implementation has resulted from working across multiple forms of boundaries. The broad lesson of this research is that the further away from the existing service system a potentially influential operator is, the firmer the boundary will be, and the greater the on-going, inter-personal work will be to bridge those boundaries. This project demonstrates that in addressing wicked issues, effective collaborative work is extraordinarily time-consuming and involves continuous effort so that functioning partnerships can be developed (Gardner et al. 2018). Formal partnership arrangements articulate the roles, responsibilities and values underpinning the collaboration, including a recognition of self-determination and community control, and formalised care pathways and electronic records provide the architecture for implementation. However, the programme was unlikely to have succeeded to the extent that it did without the significant focus on building trust and supportive, respectful relationships to assist services and people with CS in overcoming the many barriers that inhibit patient-centred care.

As Dickinson (2014) argues, effective cross-boundary working is less a science than an art. It involves significant investment in relationships if it is to work well, and this effort and activity are often missed in formal processes of care. OD, as an outside organisation, was able to influence treatment completion and reduce recurrences of CS by bringing additional resources to bear and by working to establish respectful relationships. These actions led some providers to question whether there is a role for outsiders to 'shine a light' periodically on issues that do not achieve the prominence they deserve in the context of highly stretched services and a population that carries a major burden of disease. OD was able to focus on this one area and worked with individuals within the health system to navigate it in a way that no existing health organisations were able to do. However, it is important to recognise that while CS is an area of interest to the various different organisations involved in care in these areas, it is not the sole responsibility of any single organisation. Furthermore, the numbers presenting with this condition are not so large that CS has, as yet, caused a significant crisis in the health system. OD was therefore afforded some degree of latitude in operating around this area, because other partners did not feel that they 'owned' the space. The size and scale of the OD operation allowed them to support a focus on CS patients and be agile in supporting them to navigate the health system. Their depth of knowledge and understanding of both the health system and the different partners within it, however, meant that the approach may not be as simple or straightforward to replicate easily in other areas. There are also questions as to the sustainability of the approach once OD ceases operating in the locality, even though they are working hard to embed practices within the health system.

Conclusions

Eliminating CS from remote Aboriginal and Torres Strait Islander communities in the NT is a major effort involving communities, individuals and the health sector in working together across organisational, institutional, professional and cultural boundaries. OD has embarked on a long-term venture to build relationships, engage stakeholders and work with a range of providers to develop, trial and embed a new approach to detection, treatment, on-going prevention and self-management of CS.

This case study illustrates that focus on respectful collaboration, education, place-based responsive care and the establishment of health service systems and tools are the foundations of permeating and creating increasingly permeable boundaries across organisations. Such on-going inter-personal actions can improve capacity for action and embed new processes that can lead to sustainable improvements in care and the creation of scabies-free household environments. This early investigation of the OD programme and preliminary snapshot of findings indicate attitudinal changes and health centre system improvements within a broader policy context that lacks sufficient focus on the socio-economic determinants of health. This case study highlights the importance of cross-sector collaboration across boundaries and the importance of considering and addressing place-based and systemic social and economic health determinants.

References

Allen, D. (2000). Doing occupational demarcation: The 'boundary-work' of nurse managers in a district general hospital. *Journal of Contemporary Ethnography, 29*(3), 326–356.

Australian Institute of Health and Welfare. (2015). *The health and welfare of Australia's Aboriginal and Torres Strait Islander peoples: 2015.* Canberra: AIHW.

Barber, J. T., Brolan, C. E., & Hill, P. S. (2014). Aboriginal medical services cure more than illness: A qualitative study of how indigenous services address the health impacts of discrimination in Brisbane communities. *International Journal for Equity in Health, 13,* 56.

Carapetis, J., Connors, C., Yarmirr, D., Krause, V., & Currie, B. (1997). Success of a scabies control program in an Australian aboriginal community. *The Pediatric Infectious Disease Journal, 16,* 494–499.

Commonwealth of Australia. (2015). *Reform of the federation: Discussion paper.* Canberra: Commonwealth of Australia.

Dickinson, H. (2014). Making a reality of integration: Less science, more craft and graft. *Journal of Integrated Care, 22,* 189–196.

Dickinson, H., & Ledger, J. (2017). Accelerating research translation in healthcare: The Australian approach. In A. McDermott, M. Kitchener, & M. Exworthy (Eds.), *Managing improvement in healthcare: Attaining, sustaining and spreading quality.* Basingstoke: Palgrave Macmillan.

Dickinson, H., & O'Flynn, J. (2016). *Evaluating outcomes in health and social care.* Bristol: Policy Press.

Dowdle, W. R. (1999). The principles of disease elimination and eradication. *CDC MMWR, 48,* 23–27.

Dyer, O. (2006). In search of a sustainable philanthropy. *Bulletin of the World Health Organization, 84,* 432–433.

Freeman, T., Baum, F., Lawless, A., Labonte, R., Sanders, D., Boffa, J., et al. (2016). Case study of an aboriginal community-controlled health service in Australia: Universal, rights-based, publicly funded comprehensive primary health care in action. *Health and Human Rights Journal, 18,* 93–108.

Gardner, K., Van Gool, K., van der Linden, N., Agostino, J., Campbell, M., Dickinson, H., et al. (2018). *Evaluation of the one disease crusted scabies elimination project.* Canberra: Public Service Research Group, Business School, University of New South Wales.

Giarelli, G., Annandale, E., & Ruzza, C. (2014). The role of civil society in healthcare systems reforms. *Social Science and Medicine, 123,* 160–167.

Hay, R., Steer, A., Engelman, D., & Walton, S. (2012). Scabies in the developing world—Its prevalence, complications, and management. *Clinical Microbiology and Infection, 18,* 313–323.

Head, B. W., & Alford, J. (2015). Wicked problems: Implications for public policy and management. *Administration & Society, 47,* 711–739.

McKeon, S., Alexander, E., Brodaty, H., Ferris, B., Fraxer, I., & Little, M. (2013). *Strategic review of health and medical research.* Canberra: Department of Health.

O'Flynn, J. (2014). Crossing boundaries: The fundamental questions in public management and policy. In J. O'Flynn, D. Blackman, & J. Halligan (Eds.), *Crossing boundaries in public management and policy: The international experience.* London: Routledge.

Quilty, S., Kaye, T., & Currie, B. (2017). Crusted scabies in northern and central Australia—Now is the time for eradication. *Medical Journal of Australia, 206,* 296.

Romani, L., Steer, A. C., Whitfield, M. J., & Kaldor, J. M. (2015). Prevalence of scabies and impetigo worldwide: A systematic review. *Lancet Infectious Diseases, 15,* 960–967.

Roy, M., Baker, R., & Kerr, S. (2017). Conceptualising the public health role of actors operating outside of formal health systems: The case of social enterprise. *Social Science and Medicine, 172,* 144–152.

Strong, M., & Johnstone, P. (2007). Interventions for treating scabies. *Cochrane Database Systematic Reviews, 18*(3), Cd000320.

Thornley, S., Marshall, R., Jarrett, P., Sundborn, G., Reynolds, E., & Schofield, G. (2018). Scabies is strongly associated with rheumatic fever in a cohort study of Auckland children. *Journal of Paediatrics and Child Health, 54,* 625–632.

Williams, P. (2012). *Collaboration in public policy and practice: Perspectives on boundary spanners.* Bristol: Policy Press.

4

Bridging the Safety Net: A Case Study of How the MAP Clinics Use Collaboration to Meet the Needs of Vulnerable Patients

Debora Goetz Goldberg and Akhilesh Mohan

Introduction

Despite recent advances in health insurance coverage in the United States, 29.3 million individuals, out of a population of approximately 300 million, were uninsured for health care in 2017. The largest subgroups of uninsured populations include individuals who are poor, aged 25–34, and of Hispanic and Latino American ethnicity (Cohen et al. 2018). Poverty, racial/ethnic minority, lack of health insurance, chronic illness and disability, and migration status are some of the most significant factors associated with a vulnerability to healthcare disparities

D. G. Goldberg (✉)
Department of Health Administration and Policy,
George Mason University, Fairfax, VA, USA
e-mail: dgoldbe4@gmu.edu

A. Mohan
Herman Ostrow School of Dentistry, University of Southern California,
Los Angeles, CA, USA
e-mail: ashikari@gmu.edu

© The Author(s) 2020
P. Nugus et al. (eds.), *Transitions and Boundaries in the Coordination and Reform of Health Services*, Organizational Behaviour in Healthcare,
https://doi.org/10.1007/978-3-030-26684-4_4

(Grabovschi et al. 2013; Shi and Stevens 2005). Vulnerable populations experience greater risk factors, less access to care, and increased morbidity and mortality rates in comparison with the general population (Joszt 2018). Thus, caring for vulnerable populations and addressing disparities in care are essential in achieving population health. However, individual organizations face certain challenges in improving the health status of vulnerable populations because of issues with chronic illness management, related social and economic needs, and the high cost of providing care.

A report from the National Academy of Medicine (NAM) stresses the importance of collaborative, intersectoral efforts for improving population health (Institute of Medicine 2012). We define collaboration as a group of organizations voluntarily joining forces to accomplish a purpose over time. Collaboration can be described as a process and an outcome that cannot be addressed by any single individual and instead is accomplished best by interested parties (Gray 1989). To this extent, our definition of collaboration extends beyond the everyday, common-sense meaning of the word, which can imply simply working on the same task, often by compulsion or necessity. Voluntary engagement of interested and affected parties is central here. The rationale for collaboration is that separate entities can enhance the likelihood of achieving their goals by working together rather than independently (Roberts 2004). Collaboration can build relationships and structures that are sustainable over time and prove useful in future endeavors, such as coalescing behind a common mission and goal, developing joint strategies, sharing control, joint accountability, and sharing in the results (Mattessich et al. 2001). Collaborations can add new capabilities and opportunities, streamline processes, gain administrative efficiencies, achieve greater economies of scale, enter new geographies, provide new services, or reach new beneficiaries (Glanz et al. 2008).

Challenges in service provision can be viewed through the lens of resources, which is why our study is guided by Resource Dependency Theory (RDT). RDT has been used in the health industry to examine organizational structures and behaviors that reflect adaptation intended to secure a stable flow of resources (Oliver 1990). RDT examines the ways in which organizations deal with resource constraints and pressures from the environment. It holds that organizations experience pressure on the basis of the availability of critical resources and adopt strategies to acquire resources to survive and function. This may include developing a dependency on other organizations for resources (Pfeffer and Salancik 1978). The theory thus examines resource availability, exchange of resources between organizations, constraining effects such as dependence on other organizations, and efforts by organizational leaders to manage dependence, and it has been used to explain why organizations establish strategic relationships between government, public, and professional organizations (Garpenby 1999).

There is a need to more fully understand how resources influence multisector collaborations for primary and preventive health care (Schepman et al. 2015), specifically the provision of health-related services to vulnerable populations. The goal of this research is to articulate a care model for vulnerable populations and illustrate how intentional collaboration, beyond accidental or compulsory working on the same project, can be useful in addressing the health and social needs of underserved groups. The case study provides detailed information on a particular experiment of collaboration, based on the Mason and Partners (MAP) clinics, its partner organizations, and the support provided by partners that contributes to the success and sustainability of this clinic's model. The detailed case study description is intended to help other educational institutions and healthcare organizations establish a similar model for vulnerable populations.

The Map Clinic Case Study

While Northern Virginia possesses some of the United States' wealthiest counties, within these counties are pockets of poverty that have an immense effect on minority residents. The median per capita personal income in 2015 was around $67,000 (USD) in counties and cities in Northern Virginia (Virginia State Government 2017). Despite this high per capita income for Northern Virginians, the Commonwealth of Virginia falls behind in providing a safety net infrastructure to protect and ensure affordable health care to residents, particularly those without health insurance, and for individuals living with multiple chronic conditions and mental illness. The average life expectancy ranges from 71 to 89 years across Northern Virginia. Neighborhoods with lower life expectancy tend to have other poor health outcomes, such as illnesses and injuries among children and adolescents, as well as higher rates of physical disease, mental illness, and premature death among adults (Woolf et al. 2017).

Northern Virginia's high cost of housing and other goods contributes to the high rates of poverty in the area. Researchers at the University of Virginia created a "Virginia Poverty Measure" that improves the standard poverty measurement by incorporating contemporary spending patterns, accounting for regional differences in the cost of living, and including the effects of taxes, government programs, and medical costs (Gunter 2013). Considering these factors, Northern Virginia exhibits a 12% poverty rate of residents who are in economic distress. Northern Virginia has over 500 census track regions with 15 areas known as "islands of disadvantage" on the basis of social and economic indicators. For example, in one census track region, 57% of adults lack health insurance coverage, 52% are single-parent households, and only 40% of adults have a high school education. In another census track region, there is a 49% child poverty rate, and 29% of individuals live in households with limited English (Woolf et al. 2017).

One potential reason for these pockets of poverty is the high number of immigrants who live in this region. In 2012, one in every nine Virginians was foreign-born and of all foreign-born residents, more than two-thirds (68%) live in Northern Virginia, accounting for nearly one quarter (23%) of the area's population. Northern Virginia and other parts of the Washington, DC metropolitan area experience a high number of unauthorized immigrants. "Unauthorized immigrants" are defined by the US Department of Homeland Security as foreign-born non-citizens residing in the country who are not "legal immigrants." It is estimated that Virginia has 275,000 unauthorized immigrants (Passel and Cohn 2014), many of whom live in the Northern Virginia area.

Description of the MAP Clinics

The MAP clinics are an academic-practice partnership based on strategic collaboration between academic institutions, local governments, and non-profit organizations. The mission of the MAP clinics is to improve the health status of vulnerable populations while giving nursing and allied health students a hands-on healthcare experience through interprofessional community-based learning. The clinics provide free school physicals, screenings, and mental health services to uninsured and low-income residents. The clinics were developed on the principle of partnership, and as a result, they have extensively collaborated with local health departments, health systems, and public schools to provide free care.

The MAP clinics opened as makeshift clinics in October of 2013 in Manassas Park's Costello Community Center. Since then, the MAP clinics have transformed into stand-alone clinics adjacent to various community centers across the Northern Virginia area. The clinics have grown considerably over the last several years and now operate seven health centers. They have treated over 11,000 patients and have provided over $3.5 million worth of free services to vulnerable populations.

The main source of external funding for the MAP clinics has come from the Health Resources and Service Administration (HRSA), an agency of the US Department of Health and Human Services, with the aim of supporting the education and training of students in an interprofessional environment. HRSA's funding, however, is not enough to support the entire program. The clinic's leaders collaborate with numerous government and community organizations to share resources. For example, MAP's clinical spaces are largely provided by the county government and located in community centers or schools, and most of the MAP service providers and staff are employees of academic partners. A small amount of operational costs are covered by educational course offerings and student tuition. Other costs, such as medical equipment, supplies, and patient educational materials, are funded by partner organizations or charitable donations (Sutter-Barrett et al. 2015a).

A Partnership Model

Patients who do not have access to regular healthcare may experience a quick decline in their conditions and end up using costly health services such as being treated at emergency departments. The MAP clinics seek to bridge this gap by providing temporary acute and chronic illness care as well as linking patients to community resources. The MAP clinics are based on the Bridge Care model, which is an innovative approach to improving access to health care for low-income, underserved, and uninsured patients (Sutter-Barrett et al. 2015b). The Bridge Care model comprises short-term, low-cost health management services for patients who later transition to a more permanent source of medical care. The Bridge Care model, illustrated in Fig. 4.1, consists of nurse-managed health clinics (NMHCs) connected to academic nursing schools and other allied health educational programs (Sutter-Barrett et al. 2015b).

In line with the Bridge Care model, the MAP clinics connect primary health care with social and behavioral health services. The integration of these services is critical to the well-being of underserved populations in Northern Virginia because many of these individuals are new immigrants who face challenges in obtaining health care, accessing safe and affordable housing, and socializing because of communication barriers, stigma, and marginalization. Patients who are treated at the MAP clinics

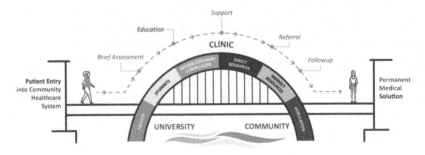

Fig. 4.1 The Bridge Care Model

are screened for social and economic needs, including housing and employment, access to food, mental health, and substance abuse, as well as other medical and dental needs. Patients can be treated by the clinics for up to 18 months; however, most patients are stabilized and referred to other sources of care in a much shorter timeframe. The MAP clinics maintain a strong referral network with well-organized care pathways that identify potential referral sites according to patients' income, immigration status, transportation, and disease/illness. Referrals are based on diagnosis and classified as either medical, women's health, behavioral, immunization, dental, vision, or nutritional. This model of care for vulnerable people provides both individualized patient services and group visits, with a focus on health education and management of chronic care conditions.

Understanding Clinics' Efforts to Support Vulnerable Patients

This research is a qualitative case study of an exemplary model for providing care to extremely vulnerable populations. The case is a clinical model that brings together academic institutions, community organizations, government agencies, and others to meet the health and social needs of vulnerable populations in Northern Virginia. The study received Institutional Review Board (IRB) approval by George Mason University in 2016.

Case Study Research

Case study research is an empirical investigation of a phenomenon using multiple sources of evidence (Hancock and Algozzine 2011). The descriptive case study method was chosen to present a detailed description of the clinical model including contextual information (Yin 1994).

The case study approach enables us to better understand how innovation can come about in complex, real-world contexts and can shed light on how these innovations fail or succeed (Stake 2006). Information that can be gained from a detailed case study provides an initial understanding of factors that influence success, of challenges incurred, and of what strategies organizations use to overcome those challenges. Specific questions explored in this research include: What role do dedicated resources have in the success of such a model? What is the culture for cooperation in the local environment across sectors and how does this influence intended outcomes? What is the relationship between leading stakeholders concerning intensity, formality, cooperativeness? How do relationships between stakeholders influence intended outcomes? This qualitative case study begins to address these questions.

Sampling Methods

Purposeful sampling was used to select an information-rich case for in-depth analysis of a clinical model for providing care to vulnerable populations. The case was carried out by interviewing leaders in the Northern Virginia area who included faculty at educational institutions, Department of Health officials, and local healthcare executives. The MAP clinics were chosen as a case study for in-depth exploration because of their ability to address a major population health issue in Northern Virginia—improving access to health care and social services for individuals who are both low income and have no source of insurance coverage. Success of the MAP clinics was measured by the growth of the clinics in the last several years, which is based on both the number of unique patients seen, the number of new clinic sites, and sustainability of the clinics.

Data Collection

The research team conducted on-site visits and in-depth, semi-structured interviews with key informants to explore stakeholders' views on resource needs and constraints, partner relationships, partner goals and objectives, facilitators and barriers of collaboration, and the role of collaboration to advance the goals of the MAP clinics. The study also used document review of project reports, news articles, and collaboration manuscripts to identify the history of the collaboration, discussions between stakeholders, challenges experienced, and methods of resolution.

Data collection was directed by a semi-structured interview guide and a document review guide that were developed from literature discussing collaborations and innovations in primary care delivery. On-site visits were conducted multiple times at two MAP clinic sites to observe clinic operations and conduct interviews. All interviews were conducted in person, lasted approximately one hour and were either audio or video recorded, then transcribed for data analysis. A total of fourteen interviews were conducted with MAP clinic faculty and students, as well as leading stakeholders in the collaboration who included executives and frontline managers at local health systems, non-profit social service organizations, public health departments, insurance companies, and healthcare foundations.

A sample of specific questions asked during interviews is presented in Table 4.1. Utilization data and patient demographic data were also collected to identify growth in clinic visits, types of visits, and characteristics of the patient population.

Table 4.1 Sample interview questions

Who (person and organization) is generally accepted as the leader of the clinical model and what is their influence on how stakeholders work together?
What organizations and/or groups are involved in this clinical model? Briefly explain the role of each collaboration partner
What is the relationship between key partners as far as intensity, formality, and cooperativeness?
What role do dedicated resources have in the success of the clinical model?
What is the local/regional environment and culture for working together across sectors? How does this influence the outcomes of the clinical model?
Does competition for healthcare patients impede collaboration efforts?
What are the agreed-upon indicators of success for this clinical model?

Data Analysis

During data analysis, the project team first studied the case in terms of its situational issues and developed a detailed description of the case and themes within the case. Analysis of data involved a combination of inductive and deductive coding to conduct a thematic analysis. Interview notes were uploaded into the qualitative analysis software, *QSR International NVivo version 11*. An initial coding scheme was created to reflect important components of the literature and the interview guide, and new codes were added as important information emerged from the interviews.

The project team took specific measures to increase the validity and credibility of the study. First, the sample included a mix of individuals from various disciplines and professions as well as from various organizations involved with the MAP clinics. This method of triangulation helped to ensure that multiple perspectives were captured. Second, findings from the data analysis were reviewed by external researchers to reduce the potential for investigator bias. Finally, member checking was used by providing a mini case study that was presented to several research participants to review and provide feedback.

Factors Shaping the Collaborative Potential of Academic-Practice Partnerships

We identified major factors in establishing successful academic-practice partnerships drawing on the MAP clinics case study. The findings illustrate the particular importance of collaboration in cross-sector partnerships and in securing critical resources to provide health-related services to vulnerable populations, aimed at helping patients enter a more permanent medical environment.

Engagement

As a general comment on the remainder of our findings, the MAP clinics could be said to have successfully reached out to vulnerable people in the provision of health care. According to descriptive statistics conducted by our research team, the MAP clinics have progressively treated more patients in each clinic over time, as listed in Table 4.2. Since 2013, MAP clinics have treated over 11,000 patients, 44.53%, below

18 years of age, and 27.7% between 35 and 54 years of age. As for patients' country of origin, 65.8% of patients who visited MAP clinics were of Hispanic/Latino background, as shown in Table 4.3. Overall, 53% of patient visits were for acute illnesses, and 33% were for school physicals, which is a common trend among uninsured populations.

Collaboration

Collaboration is central to long-term success in the *Bridge Care* model. The model requires that leading community stakeholders share a common vision for the program and understand their responsibilities, which include providing resources, program development and implementation, as well as program evaluation (Sutter-Barrett et al. 2015b). Many

Table 4.2 MAP clinic utilization data: 2014–2017

Utilization data	% (n)
Total visits by clinic location	
Franconia	23.6 (2757)
Manassas	35.6 (4136)
Culmore	24.9 (2915)
CSB	9.5 (1104)
PWHD	1.2 (144)
FCPS	2.4 (283)
Unknown	2.9 (344)
Visits per year	
2014	13.8 (1616)
2015	24.6 (2871)
2016	31.9 (3726)
2017[a]	28.6 (3343)
Visit type	
Acute	52.4 (6121)
Behavior health	1.8 (216)
Follow-up	9.1 (1006)
Pharmacy	1.9 (222)
School physical	32.4 (3794)
Sport physical	2.18 (255)
Social work	0.5 (9)

[a]Data includes January 2017 to October 21, 2017

Table 4.3   MAP clinic patient demographics: 2014–2017

Demographic variable	Survey sample % (n)
Participant age	
<18	44.5 (5203)
19–25	4.2 (496)
26–34	10.6 (1241)
35–54	27.7 (3243)
55–64	8.0 (936)
65+	4.3 (505)
Gender	
Male	43.5 (3437)
Female	56.4 (4455)
Country of origin	
Hispanic or Latino	65.8 (4007)
Not Hispanic or Latino	31.8 (1938)
Patient declined to specify	2.3 (142)

individuals interviewed for this project conveyed that they depended on strong relationships between participating partners and stressed the importance of collaborations. As one nurse faculty member commented: "It's all about making connections." Other interviewees specifically discussed the importance of communication between collaboration partners, such as this statement from a health system community outreach representative; "communication is the number one thing."

Interviewees described collaboration according to three distinct functions. The first is collaboration between supporting partners with the same mission to care for vulnerable populations in Northern Virginia. These partners include local public health departments, healthcare systems, and insurance companies, each of which plays a unique role in supporting the clinics. Regional insurance companies represent an example of this type of partnership by having representatives on-site during clinic sessions to assist patients with Medicaid insurance enrollment. Insurance companies also provide funding and human resources for local health fairs focused on health and wellness education.

The second type of collaboration concerns the educational mission of the clinics, which is central to the optimal use of the intellectual resources on which collaboration depends. The clinics are based on the Guided Interprofessional Focused Teaching (GIFT) Model of Group Care, which depends on collaboration with other university departments and external educational institutions to provide care. The clinics simultaneously expand interprofessional education and practice opportunities for Advanced Practice Nursing (APN) and other students from nursing, nutrition, social work, psychology, health informatics, and health systems management. These interprofessional community-based learning experiences can help students understand their own professional identity while gaining an understanding of other professionals' roles on the healthcare team (Bridges et al. 2011). Multiple departments at George Mason University participate in the MAP clinics to offer community-based learning experiences for students. Another example is the University of Virginia Medical School, in which Ophthalmology faculty and residents provide telehealth services for diagnosing diabetic retinopathy. In our study, a number of individuals discussed the need for interprofessional education and collaboration across disciplines. An executive from one health system partner stated: "Education needs to change so that we learn to work with different professionals and levels." A lead nurse practitioner at the MAP clinics stated:

> It's about connecting our most vulnerable of patients with existing health resources and connecting graduate students in nursing, psychology, nutrition, and social work with the goal to provide them with community-based learning experiences to better prepare them for the workforce.

The third type of collaboration is with referral partners. Such partners include local social service organizations, free clinics, health departments, and other healthcare providers who are willing to care for patients after they are seen at the MAP clinics. "The power in partnering is about connections to help people get what they need—that is community partnering," stated a lead nurse practitioner at the MAP clinics who described the importance of collaboration in referring patients to outside health care and social services.

Ongoing Challenges

The MAP clinics face many challenges related to funding, lack of space, electronic health records (EHRs), Internet access, and patient data reporting. Even though they receive grants from the federal government, the amount is very low relative to the volume of patients who need care. The lack of space and permanent structure for some of the clinics has made it difficult to treat a high volume of patients. The EHR used by the MAP clinics is available for free; however, the system is not compatible with the EHRs of referral partners. Patient data reporting has also been a considerable challenge, because the EHR system does not allow for efficient reporting. Moreover, many patients served by the clinics are unable or unwilling to provide personal information or a medical history on which collaboration depends, making it difficult to follow up with patients and to coordinate care.

Collaborative Structures and Processes to Support Vulnerable Patients

In assessing the structural and organizational factors that characterize the MAP model of cross-sector care, we refer back to resource dependence theory (RDT) (Oliver 1990). This research showed that strategic or intentional collaboration, beyond mere co-presence on projects or in workplaces, requires proactively engaging with human, material, technological, and intellectual resources of others to optimize both the specialized services that particular individuals or organizations provide and the integration of those services. The application of organizational theory to studies of care delivery models for vulnerable populations can provide insight into the structure, functioning, and success of such initiatives. RDT is thus useful in understanding how and why organizations may be willing to participate in collaborations for vulnerable populations. Future case studies drawing on RDT can also shed light on organizational behaviors and functioning that leaders use to secure resources.

Healthcare organizations in Northern Virginia, like the MAP clinics, that provide care to vulnerable populations exist in an environment with scarce resources characterized by a lack of services, providers, and funding to meet the needs of this population. The MAP clinics are therefore highly dependent on partnerships with other government and non-governmental organizations for resources. This case study revealed that organizations with similar missions and goals to care for vulnerable populations or to educate professionals in a community setting were more likely to participate actively and dedicate resources to the MAP clinics. Other organizations with competing interests for limited resources, such as specific local health systems and public health agencies, were less actively involved in supporting the MAP clinics.

The success of the MAP clinics, in terms of growth in the number of individuals treated and the number of clinic sites, supports the premise that such clinics satisfy demands from partner organizations and are in turn dependent on those organizations for continued support. While many NMHC efforts fail on account of a dependence on a limited source of funding, the MAP clinics, and future clinics like them, may succeed because of their widespread and intentional efforts to draw resources from a variety of stakeholders in the community.

There are many reasons for the success or failure of a health initiative. Organizational factors such as regulatory and financial structures and organizational culture may influence whether health initiatives are sustainable and reach their mission and goals (Davies et al. 2000; Donaldson and Gray 1998). Structural features also include the organizational configuration, technological support, communication methods, and processes for problem-solving and quality improvement. Organizational culture is about the shared learning experiences and assumptions held by members of a group or organization (Schein 2004). The organizational culture of each partner may influence the success and sustainability of cross-sector organizations such as the MAP clinics as well as attitudes to strategic collaboration itself.

Leaders of the MAP clinics were able to develop a coherent vision of the clinical model as well as strategically plan clinic locations and partnerships with other organizations. Some of this success may be due to the personal individual traits of MAP clinic leaders and other stakeholders. Leadership traits, such as high engagement, resiliency, communication, and team-building skills, as well as an innovative spirit, which can influence partner participation and support (Huxham and Vangen 2000; Sullivan et al. 2012). Nevertheless, our research indicates that a carefully developed collaborative model of care can assist in meeting the health and social needs of vulnerable communities.

Conclusion

This study showcases the benefits and conditions underpinning multisector collaboration and interprofessional education in meeting the health care and social needs of vulnerable populations. The MAP clinics, in line with the Bridge Care model, leveraged collaboration with partner organizations, referral organizations, and educational departments and institutions to secure resources to survive and function. Such a multisector model of care has the potential for replication by other educational institutions and health service delivery organizations to meet the needs of vulnerable populations, taking into account the specific needs of sponsor organizations and patient populations. As this case study has shown, strategic collaboration is central to success, because improving the health status of vulnerable populations requires optimization and integration of unique and varying contributions from government, educational institutions, hospitals and health systems, community organizations, community health centers, and local clinics.

References

Bridges, D. R., Davidson, R. A., Odegard, P. S., Maki, I. V., & Tomkowiak, J. (2011). Interprofessional collaboration: Three best practice models of interprofessional education. *Medical Education Online, 16.* https://doi.org/10.3402/meo.v16i0.6035.
Cohen, R. A., Zammitti, E. P., & Martinez, M. E. (2018). *Health insurance coverage: Early release of estimates from the National Health Interview Survey, 2017.* National Center for Health Statistics. https://www.cdc.gov/nchs/data/nhis/earlyrelease/insur201605.pdf.

Committee on Integrating Primary Care and Public Health; Board on Population Health and Public Health Practice; Institute of Medicine. (2012). *Primary care and public health: Exploring integration to improve population health*. Washington, DC: National Academies Press (US).

Davies, H. T. O., Nutley, S. M., & Mannion, R. (2000). Organisational culture and quality of health care. *BMJ Quality and Safety, 9*, 111–119.

Donaldson, L. J., & Gray, J. A. (1998). Clinical governance: A quality duty for health organisations. *Quality in Health Care, 7*, S37–S44.

Garpenby, P. (1999). Resource dependency, doctors and the state: Quality control in Sweden. *Social Science and Medicine, 49*(3), 405–424.

Glanz, K., Rimer, B. K., & Viswanath, K. (2008). *Health behavior and health education, Part 4* (pp. 293–300). San Francisco, CA: Jossey-Bass.

Grabovschi, C., Loignon, C., & Fortin, M. (2013). Mapping the concept of vulnerability related to health care disparities: A scoping review. *BMC Health Services Research, 13*, 94.

Gray, B. (1989). *Collaborating*. San Francisco: Jossey-Bass.

Gunter, M. (2013). U.Va. Demographers' new measure finds poverty rate in northern virginia high. *UVA Today*.

Hancock, D. R., & Algozzine, B. (2011). *Doing case study research: A practical guide for beginning researchers* (2nd ed.). New York, NY: Teachers College Press.

Huxham, C., & Vangen, S. (2000). Leadership in the shaping and implementation of collaboration agendas: How things happen in a (not quite) joined-up world. *Academy of Management Journal, 43*(6), 1159–1175.

Joszt, L. (2018). Vulnerable populations in healthcare. *American Journal of Managed Care*. Available at: https://www.ajmc.com/newsroom/5-vulnerable-populations-in-healthcare.

Mattessich, P. W., Murray-Close, M., & Monsey, B. R. (2001). *Collaboration: What makes it work*. Saint Paul, MN: Amherst H. Wilder Foundation.

Oliver, C. (1990). Determinants of interorganizational relationships: Integration and future direction. *Academy of Management Review, 15*(2), 241–265.

Passel, J. S., & Cohn, D. (2014). *Unauthorized immigrant totals rise in 7 states, fall in 14: Decline in those from Mexico fuels most state decreases*. Washington, DC: Pew Research Center's Hispanic Trends Project.

Pfeffer, J., & Salancik, G. R. (1978). *The external control of organizations: A resource dependence view* (p. 60). New York: Harper & Row.

Roberts, J. M. (2004). *Alliances, coalitions and partnerships: Building collaborative organizations*. Gabriola Island, BC, Canada: New Society Publishers.

Schein, E. (2004). *Organizational culture and leadership*. San Francisco, CA: Wiley.

Schepman, S., Hansen, J., de Putter, I. D., Batenburg, R. S., & de Bakker, D. H. (2015). The common characteristics and outcomes of multidisciplinary collaboration in primary health care: A systematic literature review. *International Journal of Integrated Care, 15*, e027.

Shi, L., & Stevens, G. D. (2005). *Vulnerable populations in the United States* (p. 312). San Francisco: Jossey-Bass/A Wiley Imprint.

Stake, R. (2006). *Multiple case study analysis*. New York, NY: Gilford Press.

Sullivan, H., Williams, P., & Jeffares, S. (2012). Leadership for collaboration. *Public Management Review, 14*(1), 41–66.

Sutter-Barrett, R. E., Sutter-Dalrymple, C. J., & Dickman, K. (2015a). Bridge care nurse-managed clinics fill the gap in health care. *The Journal for Nurse Practitioners, 11*(2), 262–265.

Sutter-Barrett, R. E., Sutter-Dalrymple, C. J., & Peppard, L. (2015b). Introducing bridge care: A powerful partnership between academia and community. *Clinical Scholars Review, 8*(1), 49–58.

Virginia State Government. (2017). *Virginia performs*. Available at: http://vaperforms.virginia.gov/indicators/economy/personalIncome.php.

Woolf, S. H., Chapman, D. A., Hill, L., & Snellings, L. K. (2017). *Getting ahead: The uneven opportunity landscape in Northern Virginia*. Northern Virginia Health Foundation.

Yin, R. (1994). *Case study research: Design and methods* (2nd ed.). Beverly Hills, CA: Sage.

Part II
Reaching Across Ideological, Learning and Practice Boundaries

Part II of this book expands the notion of boundaries from health services to the intersection of boundaries at levels of theory, learning and practice. Antoine Malone's chapter commences Part II, drawing on the case of healthcare policy design in France. Malone applies critical realism as a way to understand relations of influence that shape and produce effects in the complex, cross-boundary work of healthcare. Marchand and colleagues, from Canada, then empirically consider various uses of the theory of governmentality in health organisational research. The authors argue that healthcare coordination can be better informed with reference to a variety of perspectives that underpin healthcare reform efforts. In the following chapter, Kvåle and colleagues compare broad ideas of public-collectivist versus private-individualist healthcare and responsibility, in a discourse analysis of healthcare policies in Norway. Moralee and Bailey's study from the UK concludes Part II by extending how professional identities manifest as hybrid identities, as a way of reconciling the complex work involved in care coordination.

5

Making Sense of System Boundaries: Critical Realism and Healthcare Policy Design

Antoine Malone

Introduction

Health systems and services have been characterized in terms of complex adaptive systems (CAS)—otherwise known as complexity theory or complexity science. This means that they are said to produce outcomes which are the effects of interactions among networks of agents (Plesk and Greenhalgh 2001; Roy et al. 2010); although CAS are inherently self-organizing (Tan et al. 2005), they are subject to change if any component of the system undergoes alteration. Since organized healthcare delivery systems are composed of multiple stakeholders who coordinate to engage in healthcare provision for a complex array of patient needs, each hospital, clinic, or other health service is a CAS, comprised

A. Malone (✉)
École Nationale d'Administration Publique (ENAP),
Quebec City, QC, Canada
e-mail: a.malone@fhf.fr

© The Author(s) 2020

P. Nugus et al. (eds.), *Transitions and Boundaries in the Coordination and Reform of Health Services*, Organizational Behaviour in Healthcare, https://doi.org/10.1007/978-3-030-26684-4_5

93

of interacting networks of actors. If an individual health service is a complex system, then the macro-level of healthcare systems would certainly exhibit an even greater degree of complexity. Among the human (not to mention non-human), elements of such larger complex networks surrounding healthcare provision are politicians and their staff, government administration, trade unions, professional organizations, interest groups, knowledge producers of different types, patients, and so on. A myriad of forces interacts in a highly complex process that eventually leads to the formation of a policy—desirable, undesirable, or in between, depending on one's perspective. Large, healthcare reforms have been researched through a CAS framework (Best et al. 2012). However, there is considerable debate about the localized dynamics through which policy-makers seek to design better-coordinated health care (Van Gestel et al. 2018). This conceptual chapter, which draws on an illustrative case study, aims to bring clarity to this debate.

To analyze the complex processes of healthcare policy design across multiple organizations and institutions, a useful first step is to integrate complexity into the study of the policy design process through policy advisory systems (PAS). PAS is an analytical tool that takes account of the various sources of input into policy-making. Instead of focusing on a single actor, research on PAS focuses on the interaction among many types of actors, the result of which would lead to a specific outcome. CAS and PAS go hand in hand, for the latter provides an analytical tool to make sense of complex interaction in the policy design process at the macro-level of a complex adaptive healthcare system.

Although both CAS and PAS enable us to *describe* the healthcare systems, we still lack a theoretical framework that explains the dynamics within these systems. In other words, even if CAS and PAS allow us to discern relationships between agents, or the shape of systems, they cannot tell us why these relationships take the form they take and why they endure or disappear over time, nor the specific outcomes they produce. In other words, we still need a way to identify the patterns by which agents in the policy-making produce influence each other.

We propose critical realism (CR) as a theoretical framework well suited for such a task. With its emphasis on generative mechanisms nested inside a layered reality, CR can be used to give a deeper understanding of the dynamics that shape a given system and its outcomes. With an emphasis on the process of seeking insight into the manifestation of system interrelationships, we suggest using CR as an effective theoretical approach when studying healthcare policy design. We begin by sketching the main features of CAS and PAS research and their advantages and shortcomings. We briefly present the main feature of CR and its main operational components. We then use an example drawn from a current research project to illustrate how a CR informed approach can help characterize the shape of a given PAS and the impact its mechanisms could have on the shape of healthcare reforms. Finally, we discuss the merits of CR in providing a theoretical framework for the study of boundaries in health care.

Systems in Health Care

Conceptualizing healthcare systems as CAS is becoming more and more common in healthcare services research. Among the key drivers for such a shift in conceptualization is the realization that linear models commonly used to describe the behavior—both enacted and expected—of healthcare systems are far too simplistic to encompass the inherent complexity of healthcare organizations (Brathwaite et al. 2017). Instead of focusing on a single actor within these systems, complexity science calls for studying systems as such, drawing attention to the fact that a given phenomenon is the result of complex interactions among many different sets of actors and the contexts within which they evolve. That is to say, phenomena *emerge* through these interactions. Among the key features of CAS is the fact that they are path-dependent and sensitive to initial conditions. In other words, although people possess agency, agency is bounded by structures, such that the shape and dynamics of these systems are strongly shaped by the cultural context in which they evolve (Brathwaite et al., op. cit.). Complexity theory has been employed to analyze both small- and large-scale interventions in health care. Less is known about how such efforts relate to health care. This is important, because healthcare reform needs to take account of the professional and organizational boundaries that characterize contemporary health care. Therefore, the aim of this chapter is to understand the way a CAS perspective can account for healthcare policy design.

Systems in Policy-Making: Policy Advisory Systems

If a complexity approach is recognized as a suitable analytical tool for healthcare systems, then a systemic approach should also be used to analyze healthcare policy processes. The term "policy advisory systems" (PAS) was introduced by Halligan in 1995, as a way to characterize and analyze the multiple sources of policy advice utilized by governments in policy-making processes. In PAS, policy-makers sit at the center of interconnected knowledge production systems which generate policy options and recommendations (Hustedt and Veit 2017). Members of such systems are researchers, advocacy groups and NGOs, professionals, political operators, citizen organizations, consultants, and so on (Craft and Howlett 2012), as is also the case of healthcare policy (Contandriopoulos et al. 2017). Specifically, two factors have been identified as crucial for any healthcare policy to have a chance to produce *effective and sustainable reform*: the ability to inform policy choices with credible evidence based on research findings and the ability to generate and sustain a wide coalition of actors in support of the reform proposal (Forest et al. 2015; Gleeson et al. 2009; Best et al., op. cit.). This implies the successful reconciliation of work across boundaries in terms of different roles and services. In short, an open and diverse PAS seems to be a prerequisite in designing successful policy in health care.

Research on PAS tends to take one of two approaches: either analyzing the capacity of a given set of actors in a given location, such as the level of training of policy analysts in a ministry (Bernier and Howlett 2017), or analyzing the level of interaction between given members of a PAS (Evans and Wellstead 2009). Although such approaches illuminate the functioning of a given PAS, research on PAS still suffers from being essentially descriptive. Furthermore, even though politicization and externalization have been identified as key mechanisms conducive to the emergence of PAS, we still have little evidence regarding the forces that shape these systems and little empirical research into the actual workings of PAS (Ouimet et al. 2017). Nonetheless, and in line with research on CAS, there is consensus that the shape and dynamics of PAS heavily depend on cultural, national, and social aspects and on the policy domain under scrutiny (Van den Berge 2017; Hustedt 2013). But *how* precisely do these factors come into play?

Making Sense of Systems: Critical Realism

We propose critical realism (CR) as an ontological framework that allows for a coherent approach to this question. For critical realists, reality consists of three overlapping domains: the empirical, the actual, where social phenomena take place, and the real, where generative mechanisms that produce outcomes in a specific context can be found (Bhaskar 2017). For Ackroyd and Karlsson (2014), a critical realist approach "[s]hould account for key social processes which are at work beneath surface appearances and explain puzzling outcome" (need p. 21). As such, critical realism (CR) is essentially concerned with causality in an open system (Collier 1994) (Fig. 5.1).

Because open systems contain many interacting factors, it can be challenging to determine how various elements interact in an open

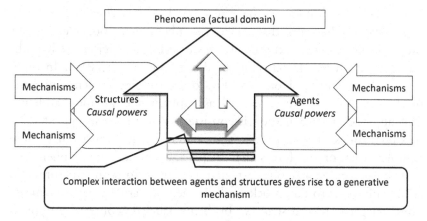

Fig. 5.1 Causality in critical realism

system. Furthermore, such mechanisms exist in the domain of the real, and they occur in and across the boundaries of other systems. Yet the effectiveness of interventions depends on the character of particular interaction among structures (such as policies, financial incentives, and organizational cultures) and agents, who have their own free will. Although such structures and agents are ontologically distinct, they both have causal power, which in turn gives rise to a mechanism, leading to the emergence and shape of a given phenomenon (Elder-Vass 2010). Mechanisms, such as path dependency (Pierson 2000) and layering (Thelen 2004), are often used as explanatory devices in social science. For example, Fraser et al. (2017) found that "holding the line" was a key mechanism in the success of a major emergency service reconfiguration operation, whereas Jones and Hexworthy (2015) state that "framing" was the key to a successful redeployment of hospital services in the face of strong opposition. Homophily—the tendency to build relatively strong relationships with those similar to oneself—is another mechanism that explains why disciplines and clinical specialties organize themselves into silos (Brathwaite et al. 2017).

The key question in a CR approach is "what needs to exist in order for these phenomena to have happened happen the way they did," This CR question leads, secondly, to a "backward" research strategy called retroduction that starts with the observed phenomena and then proceeds to an in-depth study of the context in which it takes place. The third step of CR involves the researcher hypothesizing one or more generative mechanisms that make the phenomena possible. Finally, the researcher looks for empirical clues to solidify or reject the hypothesized mechanisms (Fletcher 2016; Blom and Moren 2011). In other words, the researcher looks for clues or converging evidence that the mechanism indeed exists, as well as explains the situation at hand. This approach to explanation is consistent with the mainstays of complexity theories, in that it rejects linear models in favor a much more complex view of the forces that shape and define a given phenomenon. Furthermore, assigning explanatory powers to both structures and agents allows us to take stock of ill-defined but crucial factors that are often relegated to the shadows by being labeled "context." Although complexity theory recognizes that elements of context have causal power, CR is unique in providing a theoretical framework capable of integrating these elements into the search for explanatory mechanisms.

To illustrate the utility of a CR approach to causality within a complex system, we turn to the dynamics of the healthcare policy advisory system in France. We focus on two important issues for any healthcare system: explaining the discrepancy between a large number of reforms yet limited change in the actual delivery of services (Forest and Denis 2012) and exposing the links between the way healthcare policies are designed and their capacity to drive healthcare transformation. This latter issue is closely linked with research on policy capacity in healthcare systems, intended to guide the improvement of healthcare coordination (Savoie 2003; Forest et al. 2015).

The Core of a French Policy Advisory System: The Welfare Elite

Genieys and Hassenteufel have variously provided a compelling description of the PAS at work in France through their work spanning almost 20 years on the "Welfare Elite." Their explanation for the trajectory of the French healthcare system for the last 30 years is the presence of a closely knit group of high civil servants who share the same programmatic vision and who, through their successive occupation of strategic locations, have been able to implement that vision (Hassenteufel et al. 2010). The shared programmatic vision had been implemented through successive reforms over the last 25 years that established the State as the core "regulator" of the French healthcare system (Palier 2010). Especially noteworthy is that this civil servant group has pursued their vision with remarkable continuity, despite several changes in parties in power (Genieys and Smyrl 2008).

One of the striking features of this Elite is that they do not originate in the health sector: They are neither health professionals nor health managers. Rather, they originate from ENA (National School for Administration) and are mainly members of only two administrative corps—the *Cour des Comptes* (Equivalent to National Audit Office) and the General Inspectorate for Social Affairs (IGAS). It should also be noted that *ENA* is strictly a professional school, not a university—this means that for the most part, members of the "Welfare Elite" do not have a training in research and scientific methodology. In addition, during their careers, these administrators occupy a number of positions considered important in PAS: They serve as ministerial advisers, then go on to serve in government advisory bodies, and then move to lead government administrations (Genieys 2005).

Such clues point to a closed PAS in the France where these Elite essentially function in a closed loop, producing knowledge in government-controlled advisory bodies that use such knowledge to craft and progress policies when there is a political window of opportunity (Hassenteufel et al. 2008). This closed-loop account of healthcare policy design raises several questions, especially in light of complexity science. The first question revolves around the capacity of this Elite to function in apparent isolation from other powerful groups in French health care. These include medical professions and political actors—especially considering that city mayors chair the boards of public hospitals in France; trade unions who technically "own" the National Sickness Fund; the research community; and finally citizens themselves. The second question deals with the impact that such a way of functioning has on policy capacity in health care. Engaging and mobilizing an open PAS are generally considered a key ingredient in successful reform and that would be true in the case of France, where the State, at least in the healthcare sector, is considered to have a limited powers and legitimacy (Tabuteau 2013). If that is true, then an open PAS would at first sight be a prerequisite for change.

Collecting Empirical Clues on a Closed Policy Advisory System

In the research of Genieys and Hassenteufel on the Welfare Elite, we found little trace of interaction between members of this Elite and—what would be—key actors in a healthcare PAS. For instance, Hassenteufel et al. (op. cit.) point out that researchers are kept at bay from the policy design process. What is clear, however, is that the main intellectual material used to design healthcare policy comes from three knowledge-producing institutions (the *Cour des Comptes, IGAS and Haut Conseil pour l'Avenir de l'Assurance Maladie*), all of which are State-controlled and closely linked with the Elite. Indeed, when we conducted a preliminary analysis of more than 75 programmatic reports produced over nine years by these institutions to find traces of engagement with "usual suspects" in PAS (medical professions, research community, professional organizations, etc.), we found almost none. Furthermore, few of these reports had a formal bibliography, footnotes, or formal references to scientific work and almost no international examples. There was, however, almost without fail, a list of the interviewees for the purpose of the report. Whereas civil servants figured prominently on this list, we identified few clinicians and even fewer researchers. In terms of substantive content, the recommendations of these reports were overwhelmingly consistent with the programmatic vision described by Genieys and Hassenteufel, notably the idea that the role of the State has to be reinforced.

We then looked at actual policies designed by this Elite, in particular a recent reform that brings together 930 public hospitals into 135 territorial groupings. This "Groupements hospitaliers de Territoires" (GHT) reform was presented by Hubert and Martineau (2016) as the most far-reaching structural reform conducted to this day in France. However, upon closer analysis, one can also say that the reform was tailored to go *around* the major players in the field. For instance, in GHTs, the hospitals are not merged, meaning that mayors chair the boards of hospitals and clinicians have no binding obligations, that human resources remain under the control of each hospital, and that the director of the "main" hospital has no authority over colleagues form the smaller hospitals. Even though the reform was part of a major piece of legislature, we found almost no trace of public consultation nor serious engagement with important stakeholders such as the medical professions, professional organizations, and major political stakeholders on the topic of hospital organization. Furthermore, although three official reports were commissioned to prepare the reform, and public consultations were organized in several French regions, none of these reports mentions the prospect of GHTs. Most significantly, the official transcript of the public consultations, prepared by the General Inspectorate for Social Affairs, an institution closely linked with the Elite, mentions that "regional consultations *did not* touch on the subject of the organization of public hospitals" (IGAS 2014, emphasis added). We then looked at parliamentary records and found that there were only two questions on GHTs, both of which were explained away on the basis that this was only a technical reform. Therefore, not only does the policy design process seem to be shrouded in secrecy, the policies also seem to be designed *around* the major players.

Hypothesizing a Generative Mechanism: Boundary Control

In essence, our application of the key critical realist (CR) question is "*what must exist for the Welfare Elite to be possible?*" On an empirical level, this case of the French health system shows limited evidence of engagement with what are usually considered the major actors of an open PAS, and policies designed *around* these actors. In our analysis of the actual domain—the domain in which events occur—however, there is evidence of a closed PAS. Finally, in the domain of the *real*, one or several mechanisms make this closed PAS possible (Fig. 5.2).

Our research leads us to believe that the main mechanism that allows the Elite to maintain its position and to enforce a closed PAS is a mechanism of boundary control. Hassenteufel et al. (2010) have previously shown that the Welfare Elite were able to differentiate themselves from their colleagues in the Budget Ministry. In doing so, they were able to build a boundary. Essentially, boundary control is a mechanism by which those who exert local domination seek to protect themselves from external influence. It is part of a larger family of mechanisms of power reproduction by which "[E]lites preserve power by securing successors of the same persuasion, promoting institutional change to enhance power, defending from encroachment by outsiders" (Falleti and Lynch 2009, p. 1150). As such, boundary control has been identified as a generative mechanism in other settings: as a defensive strategy for peripheral culture, as an explanation for the dynamics

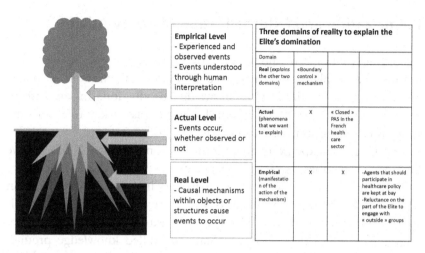

Empirical Level - Experienced and observed events - Events understood through human interpretation	Three domains of reality to explain the Elite's domination			
	Domain			
	Real (*explains* the other two domains)	«Boundary control» mechanism		
Actual Level - Events occur, whether observed or not	Actual (phenomena that we want to explain)	X	« Closed » PAS in the French health care sector	
Real Level - Causal mechanisms within objects or structures cause events to occur	Empirical (manifestation of the action of the mechanism)	X	X	-Agents that should participate in healthcare policy are kept at bay -Reluctance on the part of the Elite to engage with « outside » groups

Fig. 5.2 Domains of reality and policy advisory systems (PAS) (*Source* Adapted from Fletcher [2016])

of research disciplines, as a way for local potentates to preserve their power from the center, and as an explanation for the place of Italian "University barons" (Falleti and Lynch 2009; Raadschelders 2011). In each case, a particular subgroup has been able to differentiate itself from a larger group, thereby preserving and augmenting its autonomy within the system.

The Emergence of a Mechanism: Causal Powers of Structures and Agents

What gives rise to the emergence of a generative mechanism like boundary control in a CR approach is the complex interplay among structures and agents and their respective causal powers. We therefore proceeded to identify key structures that would have causal efficacy in the emergence of a boundary control mechanism. These structures, which may even contain their own underlying mechanisms, are often conflated into "context" in complexity theory, thereby obfuscating the explanatory dynamics in PAS.

Politicization and Externalization of Policy Advice

According to Howlett and Craft (2013), there are two main mechanisms that explain the emergence of PAS, politicization of policy advice, and externalization of knowledge production. In the case of France, ministerial staff and political advisors play a key role not only in agenda setting, but also in knowledge production and even technical work, at the expense of the administration (Rouban 2007). As we have seen, members of the Elite occupy key positions in successive ministerial staffs, despite changes in parties in power. Externalization of knowledge production, which is also a driver conducive for PAS, is well documented in France. However, this externalization is quite specific and mainly directed toward State-controlled knowledge producers. In the case of health policy, such knowledge producers would be the Cour des Comptes, IGAS and *Haut Conseil pour l'Avenir de l'Assurance Maladie*. In short, externalization of knowledge production was done at the expense of the administration, but *not* in favor of "outside" knowledge producers such as researchers, think tanks, civil society, and so on.

France's Knowledge Regime and Politico-administrative System

The third structural factor is France's specific knowledge regime, where the State has a preference for knowledge produced within itself, and by government-controlled advisory bodies and data producers (Brookes and Le Pendeleven 2014): Advocacy groups, think tanks, and the research community either do not have sufficient means or the habit of directly engaging in policy design (Campbell and Pedersen 2014). Such boundedness goes hand in hand with France's politico-administrative system. In this system, a very small number of elite schools, first among them being the ENA (National School for Administration), hold a monopoly over the top echelon of the administration and their elite administrative corps who also staff the key knowledge-producing institutions and key positions on ministerial staff. This closed system allows for a highly homogenous profile among top civil servants, as well as close interpersonal links, since all of them have been to the same school (Suleiman 2008).

Fragmentation as a Key Factor

Compared with other healthcare systems, the French system is highly fragmented (Nay et al. 2016). Representation within the sector reflects such fragmentation. For instance, 95 organizations were officially represented in the committee assembled for the "Devictor" report on territorial health services (2014). The lack of a single dominant player in the field allows the State to play one against the other, but also made the "steering" of the system relatively complicated (Rochaix and Willford 2005) (Fig. 5.3).

Such structural factors enable the emergence of a strong boundary control mechanism. However, for this mechanism to exist and operate, structural causal powers have to be mobilized by agents, particularly the members of the Welfare Elite. Members of the Elite share the same programmatic vision, which they wish to see translated into actual reforms (Hassenteufel et al. 2010). Our close working relationship with prominent members of the Elite spanning almost 15 years suggests that the following ideas would come into play in generating and sustaining a

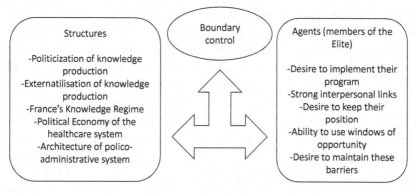

Fig. 5.3 The emergence of a boundary control mechanism

boundary control mechanism: the desire of the members of the Elite to implement their program; their desire—conscious or not—to preserve their monopoly over the top positions; their ability to use political windows of opportunity to push through specific pieces of policy; and their desire to implement and maintain these barriers, whether consciously or not.

Critical Realism in Practice: Consequences of Boundary Control

Engaging a CR [inspired approach] allows us to hypothesize a boundary control mechanism that is instrumental in generating and sustaining a closed PAS in the French healthcare sector. In other words, the "Welfare Elite" is able to maintain its dominant position because of this mechanism, which itself emerges from a complex interaction among a number of structural factors and the agents' ideas. This mechanism has several real-life effects. The first is that boundaries have two sides. Maintaining boundaries between the Elite and other powerful groups in the sector allows the Elite a certain amount of autonomy within these frontiers. This means that if the Elite were to step out of these boundaries into another group's territory, it would generate a reaction. Boundary control allows each group a large amount of autonomy within their own territory. For instance, few countries offer such overt professional autonomy to the medical profession. In fact, the only two times in the last 20 years where a reform project had a direct impact on actual clinical practice and autonomy, the strong reaction by doctors compelled the government to back down (Hassenteufel 2015). The same can be said about patients, who maintain considerable freedom of choice of their providers (Nay et al., op. cit.). Furthermore, even though the overall number of hospital beds has diminished in France, compared with other countries, the number of hospital closures in France has been minimal (DREES 2016). Nevertheless, each hospital board, as mentioned, is chaired by the mayor, who is generally considered to be the second most powerful political figure in France after the President (d'Harcourt 2014): Closing a *hospital,* instead of just closing *beds* inside a hospital, would involve a major political battle, which has so far been avoided by the Elite. Finally, even though the National Sickness Fund remains a private organization, and as such is a competitor to the Ministry of Health (Cour des Comptes 2015), the Elite have so far refrained from a frontal attack. This is probably because such a direct attack would spark a major confrontation with trade unions, who control the board of the Fund as well as its local branches. In short, the most visible aspect of a strong boundary control mechanism is *paradigm freeze* (Lazar and Forest 2013). In order to have lasting change, the Elite would have to engage seriously with the major players in the field: doctors, citizens, research community, worker's unions, and the political class. Yet, in doing so, they would lose some of their autonomy over policy design and implementation and probably their monopoly over the highest positions in healthcare administration: therefore, boundaries which are necessary for the system to exist in the way it does insure that the system as a whole remains frozen.

The existence of a boundary control mechanism explains two things: First, it explains why and how a small programmatic Elite is able to preserve its domination over the top positions of the French healthcare system, even though it has limited legitimacy in the domain. Second, it explains why there is so little real change in the system, even though it has undergone several major reforms. In essence, the boundary control mechanism is, at the same time, a condition of the survival of a given system and an explanation for the inertia in the same system.

Indeed, the French case is a textbook-worthy example: The context and ideas of key groups allow for the emergence of a strong boundary control mechanism. Nevertheless, the potential for boundary closure always exists, especially in healthcare policy. The idea of "boundary spanning" keeps appearing in the healthcare literature, whether it be for small-scale improvement projects (Sims et al. 2015), large-scale transformations (Best et al. 2012), or major reforms (Denis et al. 2015). Yet boundaries can sometimes have puzzling origins and functions. In order to dismantle boundaries, one has to know where they stand and why they exist. If the causal factors that generate and sustain them are not well understood, interventions aiming to bring them down may miss the mark. In the case of France, for instance, it is quite possible that both "reformers" and "reformees" (health professionals, patients, mayors, and so on) are more or less satisfied with the existing situation, even if they feel that the system as a whole is quickly degrading. The current system allows for stability and independence, even if the overall result is far from satisfying.

For the study of PAS, our approach helps to overcome one of the shortcomings of the field: the gap that exists between the level of a given capacity and the actual use of that capacity in a policy design process. For instance, there is no shortage of health professionals, researchers, and Ph.Ds in France. Yet they are seldom used to inform policy design. Nor is there a shortage of interest on the part of political stakeholders, such as mayors. Yet they are not often involved more in policy design, either. In short, a CR informed approach helps to understand the dynamics of PAS and policy design more generally.

Understanding Complex Systems: A Critical Realist Point of View

The advantage of a complexity approach to healthcare systems is that it reveals the interdependencies among actors and their boundaries, their capacity for adaptation to a given situation, the role of non-formalized rules, and the dynamic nature of a system. It helps to take stock of "contextual" factors and their sensitivity to initial conditions. The dynamic interactions across boundaries that characterize specialized contemporary health care call for study of the underlying dynamics and emergent behaviors in a system. Yet an important question remains: "What *causes* things to happen"? What *needs to exist* for this specific shape of system to be possible?

This is where a critical realist (CR) approach is especially helpful. By stratifying reality into three layers, CR helps provide analytical clarity. Explanatory mechanisms emerge through generative mechanisms that are situated in the domain of the *real*. They exist independently of our knowledge, but are activated through the complex interaction between structures and agents, each possessing causal powers. The same mechanism will not produce the same effect in a different context, for its effectiveness is contingent on such complex interaction. By ontologically separating structures and agents, CR allows for a structured analysis of the elements of "context" that have causal powers, whereas in PAS "context" and "structures" are often left in a black box while overemphasizing the role of agency. On the other hand, CR also helps to sidestep another shortfall—namely attributing overriding causal power to institutional structures. Explanation, in that sense, is necessarily contingent. Linear explanation is impossible in an open system, where the conjunction between the agent's ideas and beliefs and the structures possessing causal powers and mechanisms is in constant flux. It is only through an in-depth knowledge of a given situation that the reproduction or reverse work toward revealing causal mechanisms becomes possible.

The main drawback of critical realism, however, is that it is essentially an ontology, a way to conceive reality, and not an epistemology, a way of knowing. This means that critical realist research involves, by necessity, combining the insights of CR with a more applied theoretical tool. In this paper, we combined CR with a PAS analytical lens to make sense of the dynamics that drive the policy design process. Yet since policy design is only part of the policy process, other theoretical models should be mobilized to shed light on this much wider subject. Perhaps a promising way forward would be to combine a CR ontology with the model developed by Van Gestel et al. (2018), bringing three "traditional" models of policy processes into an integrated model based on the role of ideas, institutions, and timing in shaping major policy decisions.

This leads to the second drawback of CR, in that there is no ready-made and simple tool to operationalize a CR informed research study. Reflecting the complexity of causality in an open system, a critical realist approach implies crossing boundaries between academic disciplines, to gain a highly detailed view of a particular case or phenomenon. The present case will, in the future, draw on semi-structured interviews of key stakeholders of policy reform, including health professionals, patients, researchers, and policy-makers. As we have seen in our illustrative example, one needs to dig into history, public administration, sociology, political science, and so on. This makes CR research resource intensive, because the search for complex causal mechanisms inside CAS is detailed and complicated. In that sense, CR's greatest appeal, according to Reed (2009), is that "it can offer organizational researchers the required intellectual framework and tools that they need to rediscover the sense of intellectual challenge and excitement that Mills identified at the core of the 'sociological imagination'" (need 445#). Inasmuch as healthcare systems are recognized as CAS, then the search for causality within these systems is bound to be complex: It will require "sociological imagination." But the reward seems to be well worth the price. Identifying and understanding generative mechanisms, such as boundary control, allow for a deep understanding of the dynamics of healthcare systems. Boundaries, and the need to work across them to make change happen, are the core subject of this book. But in order to bring down boundaries, one first has to know where they are and why they exist in the first place.

References

Ackroyd, S., & Karlsson, J. C. (2014). Critical realism, research techniques and research design. In P. K. Edwards, J. O. O'Mahoney, & S. Vincent (Eds.), *Studying organizations using critical realism: A practical guide* (pp. 21–45). Oxford: Oxford University Press.

Bernier, L., & Howlett, M. (2017). The policy analytical capacity of the Government of Quebec: Results from a survey of officials. In M. Howlett, A. Wellstead, & J. Craft (Eds.), *Policy work in Canada: Professional practices and analytical capacities* (pp. 77–87). Toronto: Toronto University Press.

Best, A., & Greenhalgh, T. (2001). The challenge of complexity in health care. *British Medical Journal, 323,* 625–628.

Best, A., Greenhalgh, T., Lewis, S., Saul, J. E., Carroll, S., & Bitz, J. (2012). Large-system transformation in health care: A realist review. *The Milbank Quarterly, 90*(3), 421–456.

Bhaskar, R. (2017). *The order of natural necessity: A kind of introduction to critical realism* (G. Hawke, Ed.). London: CreateSpace Independent Publishing.

Blom, B., & Moren, S. (2011). Analysis of generative mechanisms. *Journal of Critical Realism, 10*(1), 69–79.

Brathwaite, J., Curruca, K., Ellis, L. A., Long, J., et al. (2017). *Complexity science in health care—Aspirations, approaches, applications and accomplishments: A white paper.* Sydney: Australian Institute of Health Innovation, Macquarie University.

Brookes, K., & Le Pendeleven, B. (2014). *L'État innovant (2): diversifier la haute fonction publique* (44 pp.). Paris: Fondation pour l'Innovation politique.

Campbell, J. L., & Pedersen, O. K. (2014). *The national origins of policy ideas: Knowledge regimes in the United States, France, Germany and Denmark.* Princeton: Princeton University Press.

Collier, A. (1994). *Critical realism: An introduction to Roy Bhaskar's philosophy.* London: Verso.

Contandriopoulos, D., Benoit, F., Bryant-Lukosius, D., Carrier, A., et al. (2017). Structural analysis of health-relevant policy-making information exchange networks in Canada. *Implementation Science, 12,* 116.

Cour des Comptes. (2015). La stratégie et le pilotage central de l'organisation du système de soins: une refonte nécessaire. In Cour des Comptes. *Rapport Annuel sur l'application de la loi de financement de la Sécurité sociale* (pp. 217–244). Paris: Cour des Comptes.

Craft, J., & Howlett, M. (2012). Policy formulation, governance shifts and policy influence: Location and content in policy advisory systems. *Journal of Public Policy, 32*(2), 79–98.

Devictor, B. (2014). *Le Service Public Territorial de Santé (SPTS), Le Service Public Hospitalier (SPH): Développer l'approche territoriale et populationnelle de l'offre en santé.* Paris: Ministère des Affaires sociales et de la Santé.

d'Harcourt, H. (2014). Le lobby des maires. *Pouvoirs, 148,* 71–80.

DREES. (2016). *Les établissements de santé* (186 pp.). Paris.

Elder-Vass, D. (2010). *The causal powers of social structures.* Cambridge: Cambridge University Press.

Evans, B., & Wellstead, A. (2009). Policy dialogue and engagement between non-governmental associations and government. *Central European Journal of Public Policy, 7*(1), 60–87.

Falleti, T. G., & Lynch, J. F. (2009). Context and causal mechanisms in political analysis. *Comparative Political Studies, 42*(9), 1143–1166.

Fletcher, A. J. (2016). Applying critical realism in qualitative research: Methodology meets method. *International Journal of Social Science Research Methodology, 20*(2), 181–194.

Forest, P.-G., & Denis, J.-L. (2012). Real reform in health systems: An introduction. *Journal of Health Politics, Policy and Law, 37*(4), 575–586.

Forest, P.-G., Denis, J.-L., Brown, L. B., & Helms, D. (2015). Health reform requires policy capacity. *International Journal of Health Policy Management,* 4(5), 2–3.

Fraser, A., Baeza, J. I., & Boaz, A. (2017). Holding the line: A qualitative study of the role of evidence in early phase decision making in the reconfiguration of stroke services in London. *BMC Health Research Policy and Systems, 15,* 45.

Genieys, W. (2005). La constitution d'une élite du *Welfare* dans la France des années 1990. *Sociologie Du Travail, 47,* 205–222.

Genieys, W., & Smyrl, M. (2008). Inside the autonomous sphere: Programmatic elites in the reform of French health policy. *Governance, 21*(1), 75–93.

Gleeson, D., Legge, D. G., & O'Neil, D. (2009). Evaluating health policy capacity: Learnings form international and Australian experience. *Australia and New-Zealand Policy, 6*(3), 1–15.

Halligan, J. (1995). Policy advice and the public service. In G. B. Peters & D. J. Savoie (Eds.), *Governance in a changing environment* (pp. 138–172). Montréal: McGill-Queen's University Press.

Hassenteufel, P. (2015). Les médecins contre le Plan Juppé: une mobilisation dans la durée. *Les Tribunes de la Santé, 46,* 49–56.

Hassenteufel, P., Genieys, W., Moreno, J., Smyrl, M., Beaussier, A.-L., & Hervier, L. (2008). *Les nouveaux acteurs de la gouvernance de la protection sociale en Europe (Allemagne, Angleterre, Espagne, France).* Paris: Rapport de recherche de la MIRE.

Hassenteufel, P., Smyrl, M., Genieys, W., & Moreno-Fuentes, F. J. (2010). Programmatic actors and the transformation of European health care states. *Journal of Health Politics, Policy and Law, 35*(4), 517–538.

Howlett, M., & Craft, J. (2013). The dual dynamics of policy advisory systems: The impact of externalization and politicization on policy advice. *Policy and Society, 32,* 187–197.

Hubert, J., & Martineau, F. (2016). *Mission Groupements Hospitaliers de Territoire, Rapport de fin de mission.* Paris: Ministère des Affaires Sociales et de la Santé.

Hustedt, T. (2013). Analyzing policy advice: The case of climate policy in Germany. *Central European Journal of Public Policy, 7*(1), 88–110.

Hustedt, T., & Veit, S. (2017). Policy advisory systems: Change dynamics and sources of variation. *Policy Science, 50*(1), 41–56.

IGAS. (2014). *Synthèse des débats régionaux.* Paris: Ministère des Affaires Sociales et de la Santé.

Jones, L., & Hexworthy, M. (2015). Framing in policy process: A case study from hospital planning in the National Health Service in England. *Social Science and Medicine, 124,* 196–204.

Lazar, H., & Forest, P.-G. (2013). Prospects for health care policy reform. In H. Lazar, J. N. Lavis, P.-G. Forest, & J. Church (Eds.), *Paradigm freeze: Why it is so hard to reform health-care policy in Canada* (pp. 219–252). Kingston: Queen's University Press.

Nay, O., Béjean, S., Bénamouzig, D., Bergeron, H., et al. (2016). Achieving universal health coverage in France: Policy reforms and the challenge of inequalities. *The Lancet, 387*(10034), 2236–2249.

Ouimet, M., Bédard, P.-O., & Léon, G. (2017). Inside the black box of academic researchers-policy analyst's interaction. In M. Howlett, A. Wellstead, & J. Craft (Eds.), *Policy work in Canada: Professional practices and analytical capacities* (pp. 183–206). Toronto: Toronto University Press.

Palier, B. (2010). *A long goodbye to Bismarck? The politics of welfare reform in continental Europe.* Amsterdam: Amsterdam University Press.

Pierson, P. (2000). Increasing returns, path dependence and the study of politics. *American Political Science Review, 94*(2), 251–267.

Raadschelders, J. C. N. (2011). The future of the study of public administration: Embedding research object and methodology in epistemology and ontology. *Public Administration Review, 6*(1), 916–924.

Reed, M. I. (2009). Critical realism: Philosophy, method, or philosophy in search of method? In D. A. Buchanan & A. Bryman (Eds.), *The Sage handbook of organizational research methods* (pp. 430–448). London: Sage.

Rochaix, L., & Wilford, D. (2005). State autonomy, policy paralysis: Paradoxes of institutions and culture in the French health care system. *Journal of Health Politics, Policy and Law, 31*(1), 97–119.

Rouban, L. (2007). Les élites politiques et administratives. In P. Perrineau & L. Rouban (Eds.), *La politique en France et en Europe.* Paris: Presses de Sciences Po.

Roy, D. A., Litvak, E., & Paccaud, F. (2010). *Des réseaux responsables de leurs populations: Moderniser la gestion et la gouvernance en santé.* Montréal: Le Point en administration de la santé et des services sociaux.

Savoie, D. J. (2003). *Strengthening the policy capacity of government.* Ottawa, Report to the Panel on the Role of Government, Research Paper Series, Vol. 1.

Sims, S., Hewitt, G., & Harris, R., (2015). Evidence of collaboration, pooling of resources, learning and role blurring in interprofessional healthcare teams: A realist synthesis. *Journal of Interprofessional Care, 29*(1), 20–25.

Suleiman, E. (2008). *Schizophrénies françaises*. Paris: Grasset.

Tabuteau, D. (2013). *Démocratie sanitaire: Les nouveaux défis de la politique de santé*. Paris: Odile Jacob.

Tan, J., Wen, H., & Awad, N. (2005). Health care and services delivery systems as complex adaptive systems. *Communications of the ACM, 48*(5), 36–44.

Thelen, K. (2004). *How institutions evolve: The political economy of skills in Germany, Britain, the United States, and Japan*. Cambridge: Cambridge University Press.

Van den Berge, C. F. (2017). Dynamics in the Dutch policy advisory system: Externalization, politicization and the legacy of pillarization. *Policy Science, 50*(1), 63–84.

Van Gestel, N., Denis, J.-L., Ferlie, E., & McDermott, A. M. (2018). Explaining the policy process underpinning public sector reform: The role of ideas, institutions, and timing. *Perspectives on Public Management and Governance, 1*(2), 87–101.

6

Governmentality as a Relevant Idea for the Study of Healthcare Networks: A Scoping Review

Jean-Sebastien Marchand, Dominique Tremblay
and Jean-Louis Denis

Introduction

Building a better understanding of the implementation of healthcare reforms is a challenging mandate. Healthcare managers also face the challenge of managing healthcare reforms in ways that enhance coordination of care across boundaries. Much is at stake in the search for conceptually framing such highly complex arrangements as public healthcare networks or multi-level organizations with hybrid power dynamics. This theory-practice gap in health management (Chinitz and Rodwin 2014)

J.-S. Marchand (✉) · D. Tremblay
University of Sherbrooke, Sherbrooke, QC, Canada
e-mail: jean-sebastien.marchand@enap.ca

Charles-Le Moyne - Saguenay-Lac-Saint-Jean Research Center
on Health Innovations (CR-CSIS), Longueuil, QC, Canada

D. Tremblay
e-mail: dominique.tremblay2@usherbrooke.ca

© The Author(s) 2020   **115**
P. Nugus et al. (eds.), *Transitions and Boundaries in the Coordination
and Reform of Health Services*, Organizational Behaviour in Healthcare,
https://doi.org/10.1007/978-3-030-26684-4_6

has led some academics to highlight a "lack of theory" to better understand healthcare networks governance and for implementing mandated reforms in healthcare systems to improve care coordination across professional and organizational boundaries (Turner et al. 2018; Westra et al. 2017). Theory is essential for appreciating shared experiences of knowledge strategy and leadership necessary to guide improved coordination in health care. Van Rensburg et al. (2016, p. 7) argue the "need to go beyond traditional governance models and their inherent conceptions of power [...] focusing on the study of governmentality".

As an initial working definition, governmentality can be considered the exercise of power in multiple ways in relation to one's conduct, whether that is a question of control or freedom (Rose 1999). In seeking to capture the complexity of power in relation to control and freedom, the notion of "governmentality" has attracted growing attention in the study of healthcare organizations over the past two decades. This is unsurprising, given that health care is a relatively complex set of organizational apparatuses and interests. The roots of the notion of governmentality lie primarily in Foucault's work on knowledge (Foucault 1969) and discipline (Foucault 1975), but have spread through conferences and courses he and others have designed, and research drawing on the subject of governmentality and the technologies of the self (Foucault 2001 [1978], 2001 [1988]; Waring et al. 2016, p. 123).

Network forms of healthcare organization have attracted particular attention as fertile ground for those who would invoke the notion of governmentality. However, this domain is relatively new, is complexified by multidisciplinarity, and displays some inconsistencies in the

J.-S. Marchand
Canadian Institutes of Health Research (CIHR), Ottawa, ON, Canada

Ecole Nationale d'Administration Publique (ENAP), Montreal, QC, Canada

J.-L. Denis
University of Montreal, Montreal, QC, Canada
e-mail: jean-louis.denis@umontreal.ca

University of Montreal Hospital Research Centre (CRCHUM),
Montreal, QC, Canada

use of the notion of governmentality. In this chapter, we examine the state of the science, undertaking a scoping review to shed light on the way governmentality is used in the study of healthcare networks. First, we present the conceptual background to governmentality and healthcare networks. Second, we describe the methodology employed in the scoping review. Third, we describe the results, and fourth, we discuss the implications and limitations of the review. We argue for the value of governmentality to better understand the governance of healthcare networks and the implementation of mandated reforms. Finally, we conclude by proposing future research directions to further clarify the notion to guide its application for change in the direction of improved coordination among the elements of a healthcare system.

Background

This article draws on two main constructs that need to be defined: governmentality and network. Governmentality is a precise word referring to an imprecise idea. Coined by Michel Foucault in the 1970s, the idea of governmentality is rich, complex, and has evolved from his earlier work on the establishment of new modes of governance and knowledge (Foucault 1975) to his later seminars, most of which were published posthumously. In his early work on the subject, Foucault defines governmentality as "the whole [that is] constituted by institutions, procedures, analysis and reflections [...] that allows the use of power, that has [the] population as its main target, political economy as its major form of knowledge, and security apparatuses as its essential technical instrument" (Foucault 2001 [1978], p. 655). Governmentality is thought to be deeply embedded in the self and human relations, Foucault later defining it as "the government of the self, by the self, as articulated in relation to others" (Foucault 2001 [1981], p. 1032). Later still, he suggests that the term refers to "practices by which it is possible to constitute, organize, instrumentalize individual strategies" and "individuals trying to control, determine, delimit other individuals' liberties" (Foucault 2001 [1984], p. 1547). Mapping out how the term is used ought to support its conceptual use as a guide for healthcare structuring and reform.

Engagement with the idea of governmentality is relatively new to healthcare. Early attempts are seen in the work of Johnson (1995), Hughes and

Griffiths (1999), Gilbert (2001), and Light (2001), who focus on transformations occurring in healthcare organizations of the National Health Service (NHS) in the UK. Though recently deemed "promising" (Ferlie et al. 2013, p. 246), its presence in healthcare literature has been relatively marginal. For instance, Rice (2014, p. 113), in a recent theoretical chapter on the different views of network governance in the literature, classifies the idea of governmentality as a subset of the institutionalist perspective. Certainly, the two have common foci, like power relationships within organizations and the institutional apparatus surrounding stakeholders, but governmentality has its own distinct conceptual system.

Following Isett et al. (2011, p. i161), we define **network** broadly, as a more or less precise group of goal-oriented interdependent but autonomous actors (individual or organizational) that produce a collective output (tangible or intangible). For **healthcare networks**, governmentality might take the form of the performance assessment tools that are at the heart of New Public Management reforms of healthcare systems (Ferlie et al. 2013, p. 5; van Gestel et al. 2018, p. 11). Governmentality appears to imply that governing is linked to techniques of examination (*examens*) that are objective in appearance (Foucault 1975). Such techniques, once introduced, gradually become accepted by members of the network as objective references to measure the conformity of the members. These *examens* can be the multiple performance assessment tools that were at the centre of New Public Management reforms (Ferlie and Pettigrew 1996). Governmentality also implies Bentham's concept of the *panopticon*, that is, the possibility for a member of the system to be observed at any time without being aware of it. Although there is no exact analogy for panopticism in healthcare networks, the increasing presence of information technology audit systems or patient reporting systems is often cited as a similar form of surveillance (Martin et al. 2013; Greenhalgh et al. 2009). These two techniques, *examen* and the *panopticon*, for Foucault, are what makes members of a system "docile bodies" (Foucault 1975). They enable a small number of rulers with few resources to govern a large number of people in decentralized positions. Networks as decentralized phenomena are highly complex entities (Provan and Kenis 2008; Kenis and Provan 2009). This transparent literature review provides a basis for future studies in order to fill this knowledge gap.

Accessing and Assessing Research Related to Governmentality

The transparent review conducted for this study belongs to a family that can broadly be considered "scoping reviews". Scoping reviews are useful to "examine the extent, range, and nature of research activity", "summarize and disseminate research findings", and "identify research gaps in the existing literature" (Arksey and O'Malley 2005, p. 21). They address exploratory research questions "by systematically searching, selecting and synthesizing existing knowledge" (Colquhoun et al. 2014, p. 1293). Scoping reviews are said to be most useful when "a body of literature has not yet been comprehensively reviewed, or exhibits a large, complex, or heterogeneous nature not amenable to a more precise systematic review" (Peters et al. 2015, p. 141). The state of the literature on governmentality and healthcare networks therefore appears well suited to this form of review, especially in light of pervasive challenges of healthcare coordination.

Identifying the Research Question

We avoided a "highly focused research question" (Arksey and O'Malley 2005), posing a general question, "What is known from the existing literature about the application of governmentality to healthcare networks?" We employed a broad definition of the term "network" in order to generate as comprehensive a body of literature as possible. Our question was then broken down into relevant keywords (see Table 6.1).

Table 6.1 Searches and results

Keyword 1 (Phenomenon of interest)	Keyword 2 (Sample)	Operator	Results (n)
Governmentality	healthcare	and	219
Governmentality	health care	and	388
Governmentality	network*	and	528
Governmentality	public administration	and	538
Total			1673

We agreed that any publication that applied the idea of governmentality to the study of a more or less defined healthcare network should be included in our review.

Identifying Relevant Studies

Databases were searched using combinations of keywords. The keyword "governmentality" was very useful to obtain a reasonable number of search results. As it refers to a specific idea, it is rarely used in reference to other subjects or as a synonym for something else. From the 50 databases available to us, we selected all generic databases, along with those conceptually related to health, administration, or social sciences ($n = 17$). This seemingly large number of databases is justified by the multidisciplinary profile of the review question, the concept of networks, and governmentality studies, including in the domains of health care, nursing, public administration, organization, education, politics, and sociology. This reasoning was supported by discussion with a librarian. We were also less concerned about the need to screen out duplicates and irrelevant studies than we were about missing relevant ones.

We ran four searches with the combinations of keywords shown in Table 6.1. We did not exactly followed the PICO framework, which requires account for: Problem/Patient/Population, Intervention/Indicator, Comparison and Outcome (see Schardt et al. 2007). Neither did we follow the alternative SPIDER framework, which involves accounting for Sample, Phenomenon of Interest, Design, Evaluation and Research type (see Cooke et al. 2012). This is because our review question was not clinical and did not exclusively involve qualitative evidence synthesis.

Study Selection

For the initial screening, we assessed the potential relevance of studies based on title and abstract, using the inclusion criteria shown in Fig. 6.1. Inclusion criteria were strongly related to the review question, but also required that the study be written in English and be a scientific work. We also added the criterion that studies be undertaken in industrialized countries, as the healthcare systems of lower-income countries

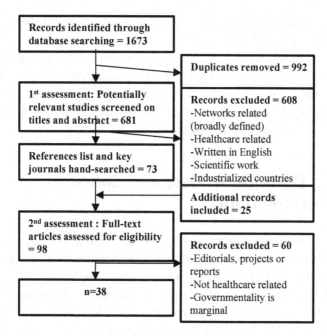

Fig. 6.1 Search strategy and results (flow diagram)

are significantly different (Mills 2014). We then searched the references of selected articles until saturation, adding these records to our database in *EndNote*, and checking for duplicates. As a final step, we searched key journals manually. We then undertook a second screening based on the full text of the articles, applying the same inclusion criteria, but adding post hoc exclusion criteria. The search and selection process is depicted in the flow diagram in Fig. 6.1, using the Preferred Reporting Items for Systematic Reviews and Meta-Analyses (PRISMA) approach (Moher et al. 2009; Tricco et al. 2018).

Charting the Data

We charted the information from the different articles on a spreadsheet containing independent fields for publication information, study objectives, study location, type of network studied, study design, data sources, and key finding. Discussion among the research team led to the addition of further categories, including study duration, definition of governmentality, and sources used to define governmentality. The final spreadsheet (see Table 6.3 in the Appendix) provided a useful means of comparing studies and organizing results. To discern themes, the first author coded each article's findings and compared and contrasted them across the articles, in a series of cycles, to determine the themes presented in the findings section below.

Scopes, Definitions, Use, and Concepts of Governmentality

As seen in the flow diagram in Fig. 6.1, the search strategy, conducted by the first author, resulted in an initial 1673 results from the databases, of which 992 were duplicates. The first screening by title and abstract excluded 608 records on the basis of relevance. The most common journals for the 73 remaining records were *Nursing Inquiry* ($n = 8$), *Social Science & Medicine* ($n = 6$), *Sociology of Health & Illness* ($n = 5$), *Journal of Advanced Nursing* ($n = 5$), and *Administrative Theory & Praxis* ($n = 5$). Hand-searching these journals and the references of the articles led to 25 additional records. The first author conducted a second full-text screening of the 98 retained records, 60 of which were excluded on the basis of relevance. Table 6.3 (Appendix) provides an overview of the 38 remaining studies that were used in our analysis.

Study Characteristics

Records were published between 1999 and 2016. If we divide these 18 years into three tiers, there were 10 studies in the first six years, 12 published between 2005 and 2010, and 16 published between 2011 and 2016. Of the 38 studies, 29 were empirical and 9 were conceptual. All empirical studies used qualitative methods. Only Lega et al. (2010) used quantitative secondary data (indexes, financial results) as evidence to support their conceptual study. Among empirical studies, the most common research designs were case studies ($n = 15$), discourse analysis

($n = 4$), and other qualitative studies (4). Data came mostly from interviews ($n = 26$), observations ($n = 14$), and documents ($n = 10$). With the exception of Moffatt et al. (2014), all studies ($n = 8$) with document data also used interviews and observation as data sources.

Countries

The majority of studies were conducted in Europe. If we include Larsen and Stone's (2015) comparative Denmark-US study, five studies were from non-European countries: Australia (Winch et al. 2002), Canada (Holton and Grandy 2016), New Zealand (Brunton and Pick 2014), and Singapore (Hau 2004). More than half the records ($n = 21$) involved studies conducted in the UK/NHS. Denmark ($n = 4$), Sweden ($n = 4$), and Australia ($n = 2$) follow the UK as the most studied settings. Other countries feature individual studies.

Definitions of Governmentality

All the studies in our sample cited Foucault as the father of governmentality. Only six studies (McGivern and Dopson 2010; Larsen and Stone 2015; Høgsgaard 2016; Heartfield 2005; Hasselbladh and Bejerot 2007; Dent 2006) proceed without explicitly defining the term. For others, definitions vary (see Table 6.2). Some authors use Foucault's original work, citing either his initial definition of 1978 (e.g. Kurunmäki and Miller 2011; Lega et al. 2010), his 1984 definition (e.g. Glasdam et al. 2015), or his 1988 definition (e.g. Hau 2004; Triantafillou 2007). Frequently, definitions from the classic works of so-called anglo-governmentalists are used. Short definitions are commonly encountered in this literature. "Governing at distance" from Miller and Rose (Miller and Rose 1990; Rose and Miller 1992) appears frequently (Hughes and Griffiths 1999; e.g. Hall 2012; Newman 2005), along with some references to McKinlay and Starkey (1998). "Conduct of conducts" (e.g. Gilbert 2005b; Waring 2007; Light 2001; Flynn 2002) was first used by Foucault in 1982 (Foucault 1982) to define the "exercise of power" and was popularized (without

Table 6.2 Various definitions of governmentality

Authors (year)	Definition
Foucault	
Foucault (2001 [1978], p. 655)	"The whole constituted by institutions, procedures, analysis and reflections […] that allows the use of power, that has population as his its main target, political economy as its major form of knowledge, and security apparatuses as its essential technical instrument"
Foucault (2001 [1981], p. 1032)	"The government of the self, by the self, as articulated in relation to others"
Foucault (2001 [1984], p. 1547).	"The whole range of practices that constitute, define, organize, and instrumentalize the strategies that individuals in their freedom can use in dealing with each other. Those who try to control, determine, and limit the freedom of others are themselves free individuals who have at their disposal certain instruments they can use to govern others"
Foucault (2001 [1988], p. 18)	"The meeting between technologies of power and technologies of the self"
Others	
Miller and Rose (1990, pp. 9, 14; 1992, p. 173)	"Governing at a distance"
Johnson (1995, p. 12)	"All those procedures, techniques, mechanisms, institutions and knowledges that, as an ensemble, empower political programmes"
McKinlay and Starkey (1998, p. 5)	"The cluster of apparatuses, practices and knowledge which operates at the macro level"
Dean (1999, p. 17)	"Conduct of conduct"
Gibbings and Taylor (2010, p. 35)	"Instilling a set of rules for the conduct of the self"

the plural form) by Dean (1999) as a legitimate definition for the "government". Gibbings and Taylor's (2010) recent definition was used by both Bludau (2014) and Holton and Grandy (2016). Some authors use multiple definitions (Martin et al. 2013; e.g. Fejes 2008; Ferlie and McGivern et al. 2012; Ferlie et al. 2013; Ferlie and McGivern 2014), and some forge definitions of their own (e.g. Brownlie and Howson 2006; Lynch 2004). We found no pattern linking a specific definition to a specific discipline of study. However, the chronological evolution of definitions tends to support Ferlie and McGivern's affirmation that, for anglo-governmentalists, "the tone appears less postmodern, culturally based, or discursive" (Ferlie and McGivern 2014, p. 7).

Use of Governmentality

Our search was based on explicit use or absence of the term "governmentality" in the papers. We found three broad usages of governmentality: epistemological, theoretical, and to describe a specific form of governance. A first set of studies uses the idea of governmentality as an epistemological approach. This way of thinking about organizations is adopted in various healthcare studies, often using the concept of power-knowledge and discourse analysis methods (e.g. Ceci 2004). Of the 38 records, only Gilbert (2005b) falls unambiguously into this category, using discourse analysis to explore the relationship between trust and managerialism in 14 organizations providing residential services for people with learning disabilities.

A second set of studies incorporates governmentality as a theoretical approach. These are mostly conceptual studies (e.g. Gilbert 2001; Light 2001; Winch et al. 2002), with the exception of the pioneering empirical work of Hughes and Griffiths (1999), who study the use of penalty clauses to understand Patient's Charter guarantees for waiting times in managerial and professional networks in the NHS Wales. In a case study conducted between 1993 and 1995, they found that the success of particular networks in legitimizing their translation of scientific knowledge depends on purposive action. The work of Ferlie and Crilly et al. (2012), Ferlie and McGivern (2014), and Ferlie et al. (2013) is a clear example of the theoretical approach to governmentality, using case study methodology to examine NHS networks through concepts of power-knowledge, subjectification, and technologies of governing.

A third set of studies, aligning with the sphere of practice, regards governmentality as a specific form of governance. Flynn (2002) produced one of the first such studies, a conceptual article on the assumptions underlying clinical governance in the NHS. He finds medical professional expertise to be an essential aspect of the management of health risks, but also concludes that regulation requires clinicians to engage in their own surveillance and "self-management". The first empirical work in the 38 records is by Sheaff et al. (2004), who look at the effects of clinical governance on professional self-regulation in England's semi-formal healthcare networks. They use multiple case studies to show how medical leaders have been strengthening professional discipline and *governmentality* in order to forestall further managerial encroachment into medical self-regulation. McGivern and Dopson (2010), in their study of knowledge objects in a biomedical network of the NHS, interpret efforts by the Department of Health to standardize the network's space of representation as an attempt to make that space more governable through a form of governmentality. Waring (2007) explores how "patient safety" reforms impact the regulation of medicine in the UK. The author states that: "regulatory practice doctors are engaging in new forms of self-surveillance that broadly correspond with the ambitions of policy and ultimately serve to negate the need for more or better management".

Key Concepts of Governmentality

Thus, our results show a variety of uses of the notion of governmentality, including visibility, knowledge, techniques, and practices and identities (Dean 2010, p. 33). "Visibility" refers to ways of "seeing and perceiving". Concepts like *surveillance* and *panopticism* fall into this dimension and are used to study transparency, accountability, or electronic reporting. For example, the concept of *surveillance* is used by Gilbert (2001) to analyse clinical supervision among healthcare professionals. "Knowledge" refers to distinctive ways of "thinking and questioning", as well as procedures for the production of knowledge. This dimension includes the related concepts of *power-knowledge* and *examen*. For example, *Power-knowledge* is used by Ferlie and Crilly et al. (2012) to analyse the evidence-based medicine movement in various NHS networks. "Techniques and practices" refer to ways of "acting, intervening and directing", relying on mechanisms and technologies, and frequently used concepts are *technologies of governing, discipline, docile bodies*, and *biopower*. For example, Triantafillou (2007) uses *technologies of governing* to explore the effects of benchmarking comparisons between hospitals in the Danish healthcare system. "Identity" refers to ways of "forming subjects, selves, persons, actors or agents". It can include concepts such as *subjectification* or *technologies of the self.* For instance, Fejes (2008) uses *technologies of the self* to analyse how reflection, commonly seen as a practice of freedom, can instead be used to govern and shape desirable nursing subjectivity in Swedish nursing homes. Governmentality has also been used to represent the complexity of decision-making arrangements in healthcare (Koppenjan and Klijn 2004, p. 4; Skelcher and Smith 2015).

Past and Future Contributions of Governmentality to Healthcare Networks

The starting point of this article was the lack of theory to guide the reform of public healthcare networks, especially in highly complex organizations. The findings above show new sorts of boundaries that characterize the literature on governmentality as it relates to health care—conceptual boundaries distinguishing epistemological, theoretical, and managerial levels of analysis. Healthcare researchers would do well to engage to a greater extent with the notion and ideas of governmentality. Indeed, the notion has been shown, in the findings of this chapter, to be an amenable tool to understand the complex interrelationships that need to be managed to improve healthcare coordination across professional and institutional boundaries. This discussion argues for the central role of theory in understanding reform efforts to improve healthcare work across boundaries and for the value of governmentality in the ensemble of available theories. The chapter also highlights four knowledge gaps that need to be addressed. Finally, we discuss research implications and recommendations for future studies. Governmentality provides fertile ground from which to generate concepts for studying healthcare networks. Records show successful use of governmentality to better understand (1) transformation of or change (and resistance) in networks (e.g. Light 2001; Hasselbladh and Bejerot 2007; Waring 2007); (2) governance of healthcare networks (e.g. Ferlie et al. 2013; Martin et al. 2013); (3) standardization or performance assessment (e.g. Triantafillou 2007; Bludau 2014); (4) governance of professions and professionals' activities (e.g. Gilbert 2001, 2005b; Sheaff et al. 2004), especially nursing (e.g. Fejes 2008; Heartfield 2005; Hau 2004; Winch et al. 2002); and (5) patient or public involvement (e.g. Dent 2006; Glasdam et al. 2015). Especially when it involves the key concepts of "identities" or "techniques and practices", governmentality as a theoretical approach proves useful to answer research questions such as "How can different health professional roles be coordinated?" or "How can highly professionalized organizations reach high standards of performance?" The gradual implementation of benchmarking comparisons with visible performance results, combined with a collective reflection on desirable professional values, is a useful starting point.

Governmentality also proves helpful in exploring the emergence of hybridity: hybrid structures (Kurunmäki and Miller 2011) and clinical, professional, or managerial hybrid roles (Evans 2003; Gilbert 2005b; Ferlie and McGivern et al. 2012; Ferlie et al. 2013; Ferlie and McGivern 2014; Hall 2012). Surprisingly, even in studies with a very explicit focus on healthcare networks, we rarely find clear descriptions of what exactly constitutes a network in terms of its structure or dimensions. Similarly, authors seldom pay much attention to a network's context or environment, despite these factors relevance in healthcare networks analysis (see Ferlie and Crilly et al. 2012; Martin et al. 2009; Provan and Brinton Milward 1995). Notably, hybrid networks have frequently been associated with turbulent environments (Martin et al. 2009, p. 772; Koppenjan and Klijn 2004, p. 4; Skelcher and Smith 2015, p. 446). Some studies superficially mentioned the issue of environmental turbulence (Evans 2003, p. 966; Dent 2006, p. 456; Light 2001, p. 1172), but none addressed it as a specific factor. Here, governmentality expresses its relevance to help the analysis of healthcare governance and change in healthcare systems. The concept can help answer questions such as "How can we strategically design and organize health services?" or "how can we improve the adaptability of healthcare organizations to changing environment?" Governmentality as a theoretical approach and the use of key concepts such as "visibility" and "knowledge" help to better understand boundary-work, in terms of the knowledge generated inside an organization (e.g. transparency, accountability) and between the organization and its environment (e.g. thinking, questioning, procedures for the production of knowledge). As public healthcare systems tend to be centralized and cyclically reformed, stable modes of governance appear of great importance. The enhanced capacity to "govern at a distance" is relevant to better understand how change can be implemented more or less uniformly, even with considerable hierarchical or geographical distance from the centre of the organization.

The review highlights four key knowledge gaps. First, most studies (33 of 38) were undertaken in European countries, with very sparse use of governmentality in work from the US, Canada, and the developing world. Second, there are very few studies involving non-government-led healthcare networks. Since "governmentality" refers directly to "government", and since it first flourished in countries like France and the UK were healthcare systems are government-led, this is no surprise. However, attempts by Larsen and Stone (2015) in Denmark and the USA or Brunton and Pick (2014) in New Zealand to apply governmentality in private networks provide additional insights. Third, while many studies focus on the micro-level (e.g. professionals, practitioners) and meso-level (e.g. middle managers), very few involve the macro-level and high-level managers or political actors. Newman (2005), who interviewed senior staff from government offices, reports interesting findings around the use of governmental discourse as a means of enhancing managerial power. Likewise, Kurunmäki and Miller (2011), who interviewed a small number of actors in senior policy roles, found promising insights linking regulatory interventions and organizational hybridity. Fourth, while empirical records show a rich range of research designs and data sources, we were surprised to find that there had been no attempt to explore governmentality using quantitative research methods, and we consider that exploratory attempts, while potentially awkward, would be of interest.

There are three general implications of our study. First, we recommend greater use of governmentality: as an epistemology, as a theoretical framework, or as a specific form of governance. Second, we suggest that studies employ an explicit definition of governmentality. Foucault did not bequeath a clear and unique definition of the word. The researcher must instead clearly state how they interpret "governmentality" and what the implications are of the use of this term, to avoid increasing confusion in the literature. We suggest the use of the 1984 definition, translated by Aranov and McGrawth (Foucault 1997) (see Table 6.2), which is one of the last definitions provided by Foucault and one that seems the clearest and most applicable to organizational and healthcare research. Third, key concepts related to governmentality, like "discipline", "technologies of governing", "power-knowledge", or "subjectification", are terms that can carry different meanings; these also require careful explanation.

Finally, we highlight two tendencies in this literature. First, we see a shift over time from a more marginal or pejorative use of the word, to a more mainstream or neutral use. Early studies related to healthcare organizations were often highly critical or postmodern (Johnson 1995; Hughes and Griffiths 1999; Flynn 2002; e.g. Ceci 2004; Sheaff et al. 2004). More recent studies tend to be neutral and seem uncomfortable with arguably pejorative-sounding phrases like "docile bodies" or "techniques of discipline". Second, sub-schools of thought may begin to emerge. For example, some state that "Anglo-governmentality" or "London governmentalist" has become a perspective of its own (Ferlie et al. 2013; Ferlie and McGivern 2014), since a great deal of work on governmentality has been conducted in the UK, relying greatly on British commentators of Foucault like Dean (1999), Rose and Miller (1992), or McKinlay and Starkey (1998). These two tendencies may indicate a maturation of the governmentality literature. They may also indicate the potential and adequacy of this theoretical *ensemble* to better understand healthcare organizations, their governance, and the implementation of mandated reforms.

Limitations

The main strength of this literature review is the broad spectrum of databases searched over a long period of time, and the inclusion of conceptual studies and books, all of which contribute to a more comprehensive view of the state of the science. Also, as previously discussed, the keyword "governmentality" refers to a specific idea, which limits biases related to the use of synonyms. Limitations of the review include the absence of comparative analysis of the studies, an endeavour that proved impossible given the range of subjects, methods, and designs. This heterogeneity also makes it very hard to assess the quality of the studies. Another limitation is the search for synonyms of the term "network", which might bear fruit in other studies. Finally, restricting the review to English-language publications may have limited the number of studies found.

Conclusion

Our objective in this article was to describe the state of the science on the use of governmentality in healthcare network studies. We conducted a scoping review to explore how the notion of governmentality has been applied to healthcare networks in the literature. The review enabled us to bring clarity to a subject that is multidisciplinary, relatively new, not yet mainstream, and complicated by certain inconsistencies in its use. Findings show a highly diverse set of studies, in terms of research object, type of network analysed, methods and data sources, and key findings. Studies from European countries, and especially NHS settings in the UK, dominate this literature. Definitions of "governmentality" are not always explicit and include many variations. Three broad usages are found, with governmentality serving as an epistemological approach, a theoretical approach, and a specific form of governance. Study findings reveal that the use of governmentality to study healthcare networks is helpful in capturing the complexity of these networks and in addressing questions about reforms that are needed to maximize the coordination of specialized actors in healthcare systems. We argue for the value of theory, more specifically governmentality, to better understand the governance of the boundaries within and across healthcare networks, and the implementation of mandated reforms.

In addressing the major implications of the research, listed above, we suggest three promising avenues for future research. First, there is a need to explore other settings, such as healthcare networks in non-European countries and networks in healthcare systems that are not government-owned. Second, most attention, in terms of study focus or interview subjects, has been on field-level professionals or middle managers. It would be valuable to acquire a more detailed picture of macro-level actors, such as senior managers or political actors. Third, existing studies show that governmentality holds promise for understanding the complexity of questions about governance, standardization, professions, hybridity, patient, or public involvement in health-care decision-making, reforms, and change. We began this article by quoting Van Rensburg et al. (2016) on the need to find new lenses to look at contemporary healthcare organizations. This scoping review shows that governmentality, its challenges notwithstanding, provides a fruitful and powerful lens through which to study healthcare networks and care coordination generally.

Appendix

See Table 6.3.

Table 6.3 Main works related to health care and governmentality

Author(s) (year)	Object of study	Network	Country, years[a]	Study design; data sources	Governmentality Defined (D); Foucault cited (F)			Use[b]	Key findings
					D	F	Definition		
Hughes and Griffiths (1999)	The use of penalty clauses to enforce Patient's Charter guarantees for waiting times	Managerial and professional networks	UK (Whales), 1993–5	Case study documents, observations and interviews (31) with contract staff	X	X	Action at distance	Theory	Success of particular networks in legitimizing their translations of scientific knowledge depends on purposive action
Gilbert (2001)	Surveillance, reflective practice, and clinical supervision	Healthcare practitioners	UK –	Conceptual	X	X	Intersection of practices of government with practices of ethical self-formation	Theory	The technologies of reflective practice and clinical supervision are modes of surveillance to discipline professionals' activity
Light (2001)	Managed competition in the transformation of healthcare organizations	NHS	UK –	Conceptual	X	X	Conduct of conduct	Gov.	The government structured healthcare markets, using managed competition as an instrument of governmentality
Flynn (2002)	The underlying assumptions of clinical governance	NHS	UK	Conceptual	X	X	Conduct of conduct	Gov.	Medical professional expertise helps to manage health risks. Its regulation requires clinicians' own surveillance and "self management"

(continued)

Table 6.3 (continued)

Author(s) (year)	Object of study	Network	Country, years[a]	Study design; data sources	Governmentality Defined (D); Foucault cited (F)			Use[b]	Key findings
					D	F	Definition		
Winch et al. (2002)	The evidence-based movement in nursing	Nurses and the nursing profession	Australia –	Conceptual	X	X	Foucault (1978, 1984)	Theory	Evidence-based nursing is a technology of government to direct practice at political and personal levels
Dent (2003)	The configuration of profession-al-management relations	Network of doctors and managers in a NHS hospital	UK, 1992–5	Case study, interviews, observation, and documents	X	X	Johnson (1995)	Theory	Reconfiguration of medical profession with clinical and managerial responsibilities
Evans (2003)	The policy and practice of multidisciplinary public health	NHS	UK –	Conceptual	X	X	Johnson (1995)	Gov./theory	Professions are part of the process of governmentality, and their autonomy is always contingent upon the wider political context
Hau (2004)	Nurses' practice of humanistic and holistic care, and professionalizing strategy	Local hospital	Singapore, the late 1990s	Qualitative study observations and interviews (14)	X	X	Foucault (1988)	Theory	Healthcare system regulates nurses to prioritize physical care over holistic care in order to achieve the turnover demanded by the hospital
Lynch (2004)	The behaviour of a large NHS trust	Individuals in the organization	UK, 2003–4	Conceptual	X	X	The management of a population on an aggregate level	Theory	Implementation of national targets is a disciplinary process of governmentality, to maintain the status quo of national governance

(continued)

Table 6.3 (continued)

Author(s) (year)	Object of study	Network	Country, years[a]	Study design; data sources	Governmentality Defined (D); Foucault cited (F)			Use[b]	Key findings
					D	F	Definition		
Sheaff et al. (2004)	Effects of clinical governance on professional self-regulation	Coronary heart disease and mental health networks	UK, 2000	Multiple case studies, interviews (49) with senior managers	X	X	The operation of power through such a discourse	Gov.	Medical leaders strengthen discipline and governmentality to forestall managerial encroachment upon medical self-regulation
Gilbert (2005b)	Relationship between trust and managerialism	Organizations (14) of services for people with learning disabilities	UK, 2001	Discourse analysis interviews (17) with managers	X	X	Conduct of conduct	Epis.	Tensions between trust and managerialism, and struggle for professional autonomy in the face of increasing managerial controls
Gilbert (2005a)	Relationship between trust, governmentality and professional activity	Organizations (14) of services for people with learning disabilities	UK, 2001	Discourse analysis interviews (17) with managers	X	X	How modern states have developed ways of managing populations without relying on coercion	Theory	Professional activity is constrained by material circumstances
Heartfield (2005)	Nursing practice and rationalization of hospital length of stay	Nurses in hospitals	Australia –	Ethnographic study observation, interviews, and documents	X		–	Theory	The monitoring and measurement of length of stay are used to govern nursing practice

(continued)

Table 6.3 (continued)

Author(s) (year)	Object of study	Network	Country, years[a]	Study design; data sources	Governmentality Defined (D); Foucault cited (F)			Use[b]	Key findings
					D	F	Definition		
Newman (2005)	Cultural processes and identification form network governance	NHS	UK, 2002–3	Qualitative study group discussions, interviews (23) with managers	X	X	Governing at a distance	Theory	Practitioners use governmental discourses to enhance managerial power, to pursue "local" goals or expand the social dimensions of public policy
Brownlie and Howson (2006)	Experiences of health practitioners in child immunization	Professionals involved in primary care	UK (Scotland), 1998–2001	Secondary analysis of existing data Interviews and focus group with healthcare practitioners	X	X	Processes through which the human body is managed and populations are governed	Gov.	(a) Target setting reinforces a hierarchical division of labour, (b) professionals resist, (c) trust as pervasive in the accounts of general practitioners
Dent (2006)	Patient and public involvement in the governance of healthcare	NHS	UK –	Conceptual		X	–	Gov.	Managerial ascendancy is offset by the governmentality role of the medical profession.
Hasselbladh and Bejerot (2007)	Institutional transformation of Swedish healthcare	Actors governing the Swedish healthcare system	Sweden –	Qualitative study Documents and interviews (15) with representatives		X	–	Theory	Technologies of agency are closely intertwined with appeals to common goods, the formation of new arenas and forms of expertise

(continued)

Table 6.3 (continued)

Author(s) (year)	Object of study	Network	Country, years[a]	Study design; data sources	Governmentality Defined (D); Foucault cited (F)			Use[b]	Key findings
					D	F	Definition		
Triantafillou (2007)	Benchmarking in public administration	Danish hospital system	Denmark –	Conceptual	X	X	Foucault (1988)	Theory	Through comparison, hospitals act like subjects, initiate action-oriented analyses and launch organizational and procedural changes
Waring (2007)	"Patient safety" reforms and the regulation of medicine	A NHS District general hospital	UK, 2000–3	Case study observations and interviews (43) with hospital staff	X	X	Conduct of conduct	Gov.	Doctors resist managerial prerogatives by subverting and "capturing" components of reform
Fejes (2008)	Reflection and subjectivity in nursing practice	Swedish nursing homes	Sweden, 2006–7	Discourse analysis interviews (42) with managers, and other actors	X	X	Multiple	Theory	Reflection is not neutral or apolitical; it is a governing practice
Lega et al. (2010)	The process of federalism	Italian National Health System (INHS)	Italy, –	Conceptual, examples and secondary data (indexes, financial results, etc.)	X	X	Foucault (1978)	Gov.	Decentralization and recentralization are effective for the State to maintain control over healthcare system

(continued)

Table 6.3 (continued)

Author(s) (year)	Object of study	Network	Country, years[a]	Study design; data sources	Governmentality Defined (D); Foucault cited (F)			Use[b]	Key findings
					D	F	Definition		
McGivern and Dopson (2010)	Multidisciplinary network established to translate genetics science into practice	University Genetics Knowledge Park (UGKP) network in the NHS	UK, 2002–7	Mixed processual qualitative methods Documents, observations, and interviews (76) with stakeholders	X		–	Gov.	Objects are transformed through interaction and power of local communities, and knowledge formation in epistemic and governmental communities
Kurunmäki and Miller (2011)	The "modernising government" reform programme of the Health Act 1999	Actors leading the reform process locally	UK, 2000–2	Case study Observations and interviews with stakeholders	X	X	Foucault (1978)	Theory	Hybrid organizational practices that emerge out of regulatory interventions are a distinctive feature of management control
Broer et al. (2012)	How actors are governed	Dutch quality improvement collaborative of mental healthcare	Netherlands, 2007–9	Ethnographic study Interviews (7+) with programme leaders and observations	X	X	Multiple; techniques and procedures for directing human behaviour	Theory	Improvements have to be visible. Three governance techniques: autonomy, panoptic of the projects, and measurement
Ferlie and Crilly et al. (2012)	Organizing in the English cancer services field	NHS networks	UK, 2001–8	Multiple case studies (8) Documents, observation, and interviews (228)	X	X	Multiple	Theory	Evidence-based-medicine movement as a power-knowledge nexus; subjectify clinical managerial hybrids as local governing agents

(continued)

Table 6.3 (continued)

Author(s) (year)	Object of study	Network	Country, years[a]	Study design; data sources	Governmentality Defined (D); Foucault cited (F) D	F	Definition	Use[b]	Key findings
Hall (2012)	Organizational power relations in healthcare reforms	Professionals in women's health clinic	Sweden, 2007–9	Case study Documents, observations, and interviews (10)	X	X	The disciplining techniques of the self; governing at distance	Theory	Technology of government is a form of recentralization, organizational steering, and an emancipatory endeavour of subjugated groups in the healthcare hierarchy
Nyberg (2012)	Political interventions and the local conduct of governing an individual's body	Individuals in Swedish hospitals	Sweden –	Case study observations and interviews (40) with actors	X	X	Foucault (1981, 1988)	Theory	Governmental standards are incompatible with each other, and this complexity allows for local strategies in managing the sickness absence process
Ferlie et al. (2013)	Managed networks in healthcare systems	NHS networks	UK	Multiple case studies (8), documents, observation, and interviews	X	X	Multiple	Theory	Many. Networks often display hybrid forms with a coexistence of different modes of governance
Martin et al. (2013)	Governance efforts to improve quality and safety	Healthcare professionals in hospitals	UK, 2011	Multiple case studies (3), Observations and interviews (44) with senior and middle managers	X	X	Multiple	Theory	The interaction of panopticism and governmentality creates spaces where behaviour change is achieved through novel forms of intra- and inter-professional interaction

(continued)

Table 6.3 (continued)

Author(s) (year)	Object of study	Network	Country, years[a]	Study design; data sources	Governmentality Defined (D); Foucault cited (F)		Definition	Use[b]	Key findings
					D	F			
Bludau (2014)	The role of standardized medical protocols in nurses professional identity	Professional environment of hospitals and healthcare systems	Czech Republic, 2008–11	Case study, interviews (55) and observations, nurses' narratives	X	X	Instilling a set of rules for the conduct of the self	Gov.	Protocols are tools instituted by the governing body and internalized by nurses to assess their quality of work
Brunton and Pick (2014)	Management of contracting for a diagnostic laboratory health service	Various actors in the healthcare system	New Zealand, 2006–9	Case study. Media data	X	X	How relationship between individuals and their social institutions and communities is guided	Theory	As politicians governed at distance, discourse of cultural "norms" of enterprise emerged
Ferlie and McGivern (2014)	Post-hierarchical UK healthcare settings	NHS networks	UK	Multiple case studies (2) Documents, observation, and interviews (228)	X	X	Multiple	Theory	The State and segments of the medical profession form a loose ensemble; professionals retain scope for colonizing these new arenas
Moffatt et al. (2014)	The construction of productivity in contemporary NHS discourse	NHS	UK, 2016–12	Discourse analysis documents	X	X	Conduct at a distance	Theory	NHS command/control principles failed to engage professionals and were obstructed by them

(continued)

Table 6.3 (continued)

Author(s) (year)	Object of study	Network	Country, years[a]	Study design; data sources	Governmentality Defined (D); Foucault cited (F)			Use[b]	Key findings
					D	F	Definition		
Brottveit et al. (2015)	How the Child Welfare Reform affects the work of professionals	New Child Welfare network	Norway, 2011–2	Qualitative Interviews (7) with project members		X	How subjects are formed by power in direct and indirect ways	Theory	Professional self-work is crucial as a mechanism for managing government control
Glasdam et al. (2015)	Patients' participation in decision-making in meetings	Healthcare professionals and clinic patients	Denmark, –	Case studies (2) Interviews (28) with professionals and patients	X	X	Foucault, 1984	Theory	Participation of patients can be regarded as a tacit governmentality strategy
Larsen and Stone (2015)	Ideas and political forces of free choice reforms	Danish health care system and US Medicare	USA and Denmark –	Conceptual/ comparative case studies Documents	X		–	Theory	Policy makers use neoliberal reforms to make a sector more governable
Høgsgaard (2016)	The Coherent and Holistic Patient perspective (CHP)	Healthcare professionals in a Danish hospital	Denmark –	Action-research project Interviews (36) and qualitative data	X		–	Theory	Professionals are exposed to management through different strategies of governing
Holton and Grandy (2016)	Voiced inner dialogue of healthcare middle managers	Horizon Health Network of New Brunswick	Canada, 2010–1	Interpretivist study Interviews (32) with middle managers	X	X	Instilling a set of rules for the conduct of the self	Gov.	Governmentality can foster silence and impede reflection. It informs the subjectivity of managers in pursuit of intended outcomes

[a]Country of origin and years span of study (if available)

[b]Epis. (epistemological approach); Theory (theoretical approach); Gov. (Governmental approach)

References

Arksey, H., & O'Malley, L. (2005). Scoping studies: Towards a methodological framework. *International Journal of Social Research Methodology, 8*(1), 19–32.

Bludau, H. (2014). The power of protocol: Professional identity development and governmentality in post-socialist health care. *Czech Sociological Review, 50*(6), 875–896.

Broer, T., Nieboer, A. P., & Bal, R. (2012). Governing mental health care: How power is exerted in and through a quality improvement collaborative. *Public Administration, 90*(3), 800–815.

Brottveit, G., Fransson, E., & Kroken, R. (2015). "A fine balance"—How child welfare workers manage organizational changes within the Norwegian Welfare State. *Society, Health & Vulnerability, 6*(1), 1–13.

Brownlie, J., & Howson, A. (2006). 'Between the demands of truth and government': Health practitioners, trust and immunisation work. *Social Science and Medicine, 62*(2), 433–443.

Brunton, M., & Pick, D. (2014). The contest for a community diagnostic laboratory contract in New Zealand: The influence of neo-liberalism in the public health sector. *International Journal of Healthcare Management, 7*(1), 45–52.

Ceci, C. (2004). Nursing, knowledge and power: A case analysis. *Social Science and Medicine, 59*(9), 1879–1889.

Chinitz, D. P., & Rodwin, V. G. (2014). On Health Policy and Management (HPAM): Mind the theory-policy-practice gap. *International Journal of Health Policy and Management, 3*(7), 361–363. https://doi.org/10.15171/ijhpm.2014.122.

Colquhoun, H. L., Levac, D., O'Brien, K. K., Straus, S., Tricco, A. C., Perrier, L., et al. (2014). Scoping reviews: Time for clarity in definition, methods, and reporting. *Journal of Clinical Epidemiology, 67*(12), 1291–1294.

Cooke, A., Smith, D., & Booth, A. (2012). Beyond PICO: The SPIDER tool for qualitative evidence synthesis. *Qualitative Health Research, 22*(10), 1435–1443.

Dean, M. (1999). *Governmentality: Power and rule in modern society*. London: Sage.

Dean, M. (2010). *Governmentality: Power and rule in modern society* (2nd ed.). London: Sage.

Dent, M. (2003). Managing doctors and saving a hospital: Irony, rhetoric and actor networks. *Organization, 10*(1), 107–127.

Dent, M. (2006). Patient choice and medicine in health care. *Public Management Review, 8*(3), 449–462.

Evans, D. (2003). 'Taking public health out of the ghetto': The policy and practice of multi-disciplinary public health in the United Kingdom. *Social Science and Medicine, 57*(6), 959.

Fejes, A. (2008). Governing nursing through reflection: A discourse analysis of reflective practices. *Journal of Advanced Nursing, 64*(3), 243–250.

Ferlie, E. B., Crilly, T., Jashapara, A., & Peckham, A. (2012). Knowledge mobilisation in healthcare: A critical review of health sector and generic management literature. *Social Science and Medicine, 74*(8), 1297–1304.

Ferlie, E. B., Fitzgerald, L., McGivern, G., Dopson, S., & Bennett, C. (2013). *Making wicked problems governable? The case of managed networks in health care.* Oxford: Oxford University Press.

Ferlie, E. B., & McGivern, G. (2014). Bringing Anglo-governmentality into public management scholarship: The case of evidence-based medicine in UK health care. *Journal of Public Administration Research and Theory, 24*(1), 59–83.

Ferlie, E. B., McGivern, G., & FitzGerald, L. (2012). A new mode of organizing in health care? Governmentality and managed networks in cancer services in England. *Social Science and Medicine, 74*(3), 340–347.

Ferlie, E. B., & Pettigrew, A. M. (1996). Managing through networks: Some issues and implications for the NHS. *British Journal of Management, 7*(s1), s81–s99.

Flynn, R. (2002). Clinical governance and governmentality. *Health, Risk & Society, 4*(2), 155–173.

Foucault, M. (1969). *L'archéologie du savoir.* Paris: Gallimard.

Foucault, M. (1975). *Surveiller et punir: Naissance de la prison.* Paris: Gallimard.

Foucault, M. (1982). The subject and power. In H. L. Dreyfus & P. Rabinow (Eds.), *Michel Foucault: Beyond structuralism and hermeneutics* (pp. 208–226). Chicago: The University of Chicago Press.

Foucault, M. (1997). The ethics of the concern of the self as a practice of freedom. In P. Rabinow (Ed.), *Ethics: Subjectivity and truth (Essential works of Foucault, 1954–1984, Vol. 1)* (pp. 281–301). Allen Lane, London: Penguin Press.

Foucault, M. (2001 [1978]). La "gouvernementalité". In D. Defert & F. Ewald (Eds.), *Dits et écrits II. 1976–1988* (pp. 635–657). Paris: Gallimard.

Foucault, M. (2001 [1981]). Subjectivité et vérité. In D. Defert & F. Ewald (Eds.), *Dits et écrits II. 1976–1988* (pp. 1032–1037). Paris: Gallimard.

Foucault, M. (2001 [1984]). L'éthique du souci de soi comme pratique de la liberté. In D. Defert & F. Ewald (Eds.), *Dits et écrits II. 1976–1988* (pp. 1527–1548). Paris: Gallimard.

Foucault, M. (2001 [1988]). Technologies of the self. In L. H. Martin, H. Gutman, & P. H. Hutton (Eds.), *Technologies of the self: A seminar with Michel Foucault* (pp. 16–49). Amherst: University of Massachusetts Press.

Gibbings, S., & Taylor, J. (2010). From rags to riches, the policing of fashion and identity: Governmentality and "what not to wear". *vis-à-vis: Explorations in Anthropology, 10*(1), 31–47.

Gilbert, T. P. (2001). Reflective practice and clinical supervision: Meticulous rituals of the confessional. *Journal of Advanced Nursing, 36*(2), 199–205.

Gilbert, T. P. (2005a). Impersonal trust and professional authority: Exploring the dynamics. *Journal of Advanced Nursing, 49*(6), 568–577.

Gilbert, T. P. (2005b). Trust and managerialism: Exploring discourses of care. *Journal of Advanced Nursing, 52*(4), 454–463.

Glasdam, S., Oeye, C., & Thrysoee, L. (2015). Patients' participation in decision-making in the medical field—'Projectification' of patients in a neoliberal framed healthcare system. *Nursing Philosophy, 16*(4), 226–238.

Greenhalgh, T., Potts, H. W., Wong, G., Bark, P., & Swinglehurst, D. (2009). Tensions and paradoxes in electronic patient record research: A systematic literature review using the meta-narrative method. *Milbank Quarterly, 87*(4), 729–788.

Hall, P. (2012). Quality improvement reforms, technologies of government, and organizational politics. *Administrative Theory & Praxis, 34*(4), 578–601.

Hasselbladh, H., & Bejerot, E. (2007). Webs of knowledge and circuits of communication: Constructing rationalized agency in Swedish health care. *Organization, 14*(2), 175–200.

Hau, W. W. (2004). Caring holistically within new managerialism. *Nursing Inquiry, 11*(1), 2–13.

Heartfield, M. (2005). Regulating hospital use: Length of stay, beds and whiteboards. *Nursing Inquiry, 12*(1), 21–26.

Høgsgaard, D. (2016). A Coherent and Holistic Patient perspective is an unreflective taken-for-granted talk in integrated care. *International Journal of Integrated Care, 16*(6), 1–2.

Holton, J. A., & Grandy, G. (2016). Voiced inner dialogue as relational reflection-on-action: The case of middle managers in health care. *Management Learning, 47*(4), 369–390.

Hughes, D., & Griffiths, L. (1999). On penalties and the Patient's Charter: Centralism v de-centralised governance in the NHS. *Sociology of Health & Illness, 21*(1), 71.

Isett, K. R., Mergel, I. A., LeRoux, K., Mischen, P. A., & Karl Rethemeyer, R. (2011). Networks in public administration scholarship: Understanding where we are and where we need to go. *Journal of Public Administration Research and Theory, 20*(s1), i157–i173.

Johnson, T. (1995). Governmentality and the institutionalization of expertise. In T. Johnson, G. Larkin, & M. Saks (Eds.), *Health professions and the state in Europe* (pp. 7–24). London: Routhledge.

Kenis, P., & Provan, K. G. (2009). Towards an exogenous theory of public network performance. *Public Administration, 87*(3), 440–456.

Koppenjan, J., & Klijn, E.-H. (2004). *Managing uncertainties in networks: A network approach to problem solving and decision making.* New York, NY: Routledge.

Kurunmäki, L., & Miller, P. (2011). Regulatory hybrids: Partnerships, budgeting and modernising government. *Management Accounting Research, 22*(4), 220–241.

Larsen, L. T., & Stone, D. (2015). Governing health care through free choice: Neoliberal reforms in Denmark and the United States. *Journal of Health Politics, Policy and Law, 40*(5), 941–970.

Lega, F., Sargiacomo, M., & Ianni, L. (2010). The rise of governmentality in the Italian National Health System: Physiology or pathology of a decentralized and (ongoing) federalist system? *Health Services Management Research, 23*(4), 172–180.

Light, D. W. (2001). Managed competition, governmentality and institutional response in the United Kingdom. *Social Science and Medicine, 52*(8), 1167–1181.

Lynch, J. (2004). Foucault on targets. *Journal of Health Organization and Management, 18*(2–3), 128–135.

Martin, G. P., Currie, G., & Finn, R. (2009). Leadership, service reform, and public-service networks: The case of cancer-genetics pilots in the English NHS. *Journal of Public Administration Research and Theory, 19*(4), 769–794.

Martin, G. P., Leslie, M., Minion, J., Willars, J., & Dixon-Woods, M. (2013). Between surveillance and subjectification: Professionals and the governance of quality and patient safety in english hospitals. *Social Science and Medicine, 99*(1), 80–88.

McGivern, G., & Dopson, S. (2010). Inter-epistemic power and transforming knowledge objects in a biomedical network. *Organization Studies, 31*(12), 1667–1686.

McKinlay, A., & Starkey, K. (Eds.). (1998). *Foucault, management and organization theory: From panopticon to technologies of self.* London: Sage.

Miller, P., & Rose, N. (1990). Governing economic life. *Economy and Society, 19*(1), 1–31.

Mills, A. (2014). Health care systems in low- and middle-income countries. *New England Journal of Medicine, 370*(6), 552–557.

Moffatt, F., Martin, P., & Timmons, S. (2014). Constructing notions of healthcare productivity: The call for a new professionalism? *Sociology of Health & Illness, 36*(5), 686–702.

Moher, D., Liberati, A., Tetzlaff, J., Altman, D. G., & Prisma Group. (2009). Preferred reporting items for systematic reviews and meta-analyses: The PRISMA statement. *PLOS Medicine, 6*(7), e1000097.

Newman, J. (2005). Enter the transformational leader: Network governance and the micro-politics of modernization. *Sociology, 39*(4), 717–734.

Nyberg, D. (2012). 'You need to be healthy to be ill': Constructing sickness and framing the body in Swedish healthcare. *Organization Studies, 33*(12), 1671–1692.

Peters, Micah D. J., Godfrey, C. M., Khalil, H., McInerney, P., Parker, D., & Soares, C. B. (2015). Guidance for conducting systematic scoping reviews. *International Journal of Evidence-Based Healthcare, 13*(3), 141–146.

Provan, K. G., & Brinton Milward, H. (1995). A preliminary theory of inter-organizational network effectiveness: A comparative study of four community mental health systems. *Administrative Science Quarterly, 40*(1), 1–33.

Provan, K. G., & Kenis, P. (2008). Modes of network governance: Structure, management, and effectiveness. *Journal of Public Administration Research and Theory, 18*(2), 229–252.

Rice, D. (2014). Governing through networks: A systemic approach. In R. Keast, M. Mandell, & R. Agranoff (Eds.), *Network theory in the public sector: Building new theoretical frameworks* (pp. 103–117). New York and London: Routledge.

Rose, N. (1999). *Powers of freedom: Reframing political thought* (321 p.). Cambridge: Cambridge University Press.

Rose, N., & Miller, P. (1992). Political power beyond the state: Problematics of government. *British Journal of Sociology, 43*(2), 173–205.

Schardt, C., Adams, M. B., Owens, T., Keitz, S., & Fontelo, P. (2007). Utilization of the PICO framework to improve searching PubMed for clinical questions. *BMC Medical Informatics and Decision Making, 7*(1), 16–21.

Sheaff, R., Marshall, M., Rogers, A., Roland, M., Sibbald, B., & Pickard, S. (2004). Governmentality by network in English primary healthcare. *Social Policy & Administration, 38*(1), 89–103.

Skelcher, C., & Smith, S. R. (2015). Theorizing hybridity: Institutional logics, complex organizations, and actor identities: The case of nonprofits. *Public Administration, 93*(2), 433–448.

Triantafillou, P. (2007). Benchmarking in the public sector: A critical conceptual framework. *Public Administration, 85*(3), 829–846.

Tricco, A. C., Lillie, E., Zarin, W., O'Brien, K. K., Colquhoun, H., Levac, D., et al. (2018). PRISMA extension for scoping reviews (PRISMA-ScR): checklist and explanation. *Annals of Internal Medicine, 169*(7), 467–473.

Turner, S., Vasilakis, C., Utley, M., Foster, P., Kotecha, A., & Fulop, N. J. (2018). Analysing barriers to service improvement using a multi-level theory of innovation: The case of glaucoma outpatient clinics. *Sociology of Health & Illness, 40*(4), 654–669. https://doi.org/10.1111/1467-9566.12670.

van Gestel, N., Denis, J.-L., Ferlie, E. B., & Mcdermott, Aoife M. (2018). Explaining the policy process underpinning public sector reform: The role of ideas, institutions, and timing. *Perspectives on Public Management and Governance, 1*(2), 87–101.

van Rensburg, A., Janse, A. R., Fourie, P., & Bracke, P. (2016). Power and integrated health care: Shifting from governance to governmentality. *International Journal of Integrated Care, 16*(3), 1–11.

Waring, J. (2007). Adaptive regulation or governmentality: Patient safety and the changing regulation of medicine. *Sociology of Health & Illness, 29*(2), 163–179.

Waring, J., Latif, A., Boyd, M., Barber, N., & Elliott, R. (2016). Pastoral power in the community pharmacy: A Foucauldian analysis of services to promote patient adherence to new medicine use. *Social Science and Medicine, 148*, 123–130.

Westra, D., Angeli, F., Carree, M., & Ruwaard, D. (2017). Understanding competition between healthcare providers: Introducing an intermediary inter-organizational perspective. *Health Policy, 121*(2), 149–157.

Winch, S., Creedy, D., & Chaboyer, A. W. (2002). Governing nursing conduct: the rise of evidence-based practice. *Nursing Inquiry, 9*(3), 156–161.

7

Public Health Policy to Tackle Social Health Inequalities: A Balancing Act Between Competing Institutional Logics

Gro Kvåle, Charlotte Kiland and Dag Olaf Torjesen

Introduction

One major trend in healthcare systems over the last decades has been the shift from a focus on curative health services and the dominant medical-treatment model to a stronger emphasis on multiple and complex health problems, health promotion, and disease prevention (Degeling 1995, p. 289; Adler et al. 2008; Antonovsky 1996; Eriksson and Lindström 2008). In public health, these trends have materialized

G. Kvåle (✉) · C. Kiland · D. O. Torjesen
Department of Political Science and Management,
University of Agder, Kristiansand, Norway
e-mail: gro.kvale@uia.no

C. Kiland
e-mail: charlotte.kiland@uia.no

D. O. Torjesen
e-mail: dag.o.torjesen@uia.no

© The Author(s) 2020
P. Nugus et al. (eds.), *Transitions and Boundaries in the Coordination and Reform of Health Services*, Organizational Behaviour in Healthcare,
https://doi.org/10.1007/978-3-030-26684-4_7

in efforts to integrate health issues within a broader set of social and political areas, sectors, and organizations. This broader perspective of public health as an aspect of several categories of public policy has been on the global health agenda since 1986, when the World Health Organization (WHO) launched the "Ottawa Charter" and what has become known as "The New Public Health" (Degeling 1995, p. 289). In this view, often referred to as the "Health in all policies" principle (HIAP), policies to promote and improve public health should be seen as a broad governmental responsibility rather than of the health sector alone (Beland and Katapaly 2018). However, this shift to HIAP is not without difficulties. One of its main challenges is to bring a broad spectrum of actors and organizations from different sectors together in the common pursuit of public health. Another challenge is that such strategies and processes must coexist with those underpinning the organizations' "business as usual" obligations (Head and Alford 2015). Accordingly, research has turned to focusing on multi-level governance systems, cooperation, and coordination across the boundaries of government, policy, and frontline practice (Romøren et al. 2011; Torjesen et al. 2016).

Furthermore, in 2008 the WHO formally linked HIAP and social inequalities in health (WHO 2008). This link saw health inequalities as a gradient through the population, where moving up the social scale is accompanied by a stepwise improvement in health (Dahl et al. 2014, p. 69). Although Norway was the first country to adopt specific public health legislation based on the fundamental principle that social health inequalities should be eliminated, it is well documented that, paradoxically, inequalities in health are still increasing in Norway (van der Wel et al. 2016). We have therefore chosen Norway as a case to examine how government's management of health issues—beyond the health sector, health organizations, and health services—manifests itself in public health policy and the social gradient. In this chapter, we aim to answer two research questions: (1) What is the character of policy measures and organizing principles put in place to tackle health inequalities? and (2) How do the challenges associated with the chosen approaches within the national public health policy arena manifest? In the following section, we present our theoretical point of departure: two opposing approaches to health and public health governance and management. We then elaborate on our chosen case and describe our research design and empirical material. After the empirical analysis, we discuss our findings in terms of public health governance and management promoting the reduction of public health inequalities

Logics in Governance of Public Health

The concepts of healthcare and public health—the appropriate problem definitions, goals and governance, management and organizational solutions—can be approached in different ways. These can be considered to constitute opposing institutional logics, i.e., "a set of material practices and symbolic constructions—which constitute its organizing principles, and which are available to organizations and individuals to elaborate" (Friedland and Alford 1991, p. 248). One fundamental difference between the approaches lies in whether the individual or society is at the core. We label logics concerning public health as *individualist* and *collectivist*, respectively (Kiland et al. 2015).

The Individualist Logic

One approach to health status is that it is a product of individual choice (Ayo 2011). As such, public health is the aggregate of individual choices, and the role of public policy is to influence health-related behavior in more or less subtle ways (Vallgårda 2001). "Empowerment" and "self-technologies" are central concepts within this logic, and the empowered citizen is encouraged and made able to take responsibility for and control over his or her own life (Andersen 2003). Health issues are a matter between the individual and the general practitioner (GP) other specialized agents who, by empowering the individual, target specific risks and diagnoses. Self-technologies (Foucault 1982) are methods for governing people in such ways that they obtain self-control and manage themselves. Yet, they do so in a way that reflects the expectations of society by means of, for example, education or incentives and "nudging" (Thaler and Sunstein 2008; Selinger and Whyte 2011). The self-empowered individual thereby becomes responsible for both his or her own health *and* for the public health by making healthy choices and accepting the challenge of limited resources in the health sector.

By focusing on the relationship between individual behavior and individual health conditions in terms of risk, diagnosis, and disease, public health is therefore limited to a matter of medical science, rather than collective wellbeing. Consequently, social inequality is not a particularly central nor relevant concern for public health policy in the individualist approach. The implication is that socioeconomic inequality should be handled instead by educating, counseling, and motivating the socially and economically disadvantaged to make better health choices. Public health *services* are also reduced and limited to individual counseling, recommendations, and treatments. Such services are seen as tasks with a low level of interdependency that promote a high degree of organizational specialization (see, e.g., Donaldson 2001) and as single task agencies within the health sector, distanced, and isolated from other policy areas and services.

The Collectivist Logic

An alternative approach to public health sees health as a common good that should be distributed equally, and when it is not, sees poor health and social inequalities as products of the structures of society (Coburn 2000; Smith-Nonini 2006). Thus, social determinants are at the core of the collectivist notion of public health, which takes for granted that tackling and reducing inequalities is a political responsibility. Governing public health, then, is a matter of how public actors handle and shape these processes. The social determinants of health inequalities fit the definition of a "wicked problem"—typically a modern and complex problem in social or policy planning (Head and Alford 2015). Such a wicked problem is inherently resistant to a clear definition and an agreed-upon, preferred solution. Furthermore, due to complex interdependencies, the effort to solve one aspect of a wicked problem may reveal or create other problems.

In the collectivist logic, the concept of public health has been broadened to include not only disease prevention and health promotion, but also a wide range of services across sectors. Thus, the inter-sectoral character of public health becomes even more pronounced (Axelsson and Axelsson 2006). Traditional hierarchical coordination has to be replaced by a more or less voluntary cooperation between "loosely coupled" organizations, which may not be part of a common management hierarchy. Such inter-organizational relationships, and the governance of processes where multiple interdependent actors contribute to the delivery of public services, have been described as New Public Governance (NPG) (Osborne 2006). In public health, the HIAP principle represents the NPG idea of non-hierarchical coordination. Accordingly, HIAP encourages integration and coordination *vertically*, i.e., between authorities at national, regional, and local levels, such as specialist and primary health care, and *horizontally* across, for example, the health, welfare, transport, and education sectors (Axelsson and Axelsson 2006; Hagen et al. 2018). The distinction between individualist and the collectivist logics in public health policies, and their accompanying government and management implications of specialization and integration, respectively, provides the main analytical tool in our investigation into the problem descriptions, the formulation of goals, and the choice of solutions in current Norwegian public health policy.

Understanding the Logics of Public Health

Despite ranking among the most equal societies in the world (Wilkinson and Pickett 2010), empirical studies document substantial inequalities in health in Norway (The Norwegian Directorate of Health and Social Affairs 2005; Eikemo et al. 2008; Huijts and Eikemo 2009; Raphael 2012; Dahl et al. 2014). Since the gap between socioeconomic groups is increasing and has been documented in relation to several health indicators, including life expectancy, infant mortality, and mental health (Raphael 2012; Dahl et al. 2014), Norway has been referred to as a "public health puzzle" (Bambra 2011). Therefore, despite the fact that Norway, along with other Nordic countries, has been quite active in developing public health policy and, most importantly, was the first country to pass a Public Health Act (PHA) in 2011, the obvious problem of increasing social health inequalities makes Norway an informative historical case study for understanding the logics, challenges, and complexities of public health policy, governance, and services. Our empirical approach is thus to study how Norwegian public health policy initiatives have addressed the challenges of social inequalities in health over the last decade. We do this by investigating how problems are defined and goals and priorities are explicated in the national policy on public health and by studying what measures have been introduced to reduce social inequalities in health.

The empirical analysis relies on the complete list of 10 policy documents constituting the Norwegian public health policy in the period 2003–2017. We chose this relatively long time frame to study policy changes. In this period, public health policy received increased political attention. The policy documents—laws, white papers (WP), and other reports outlined as general public health programs—are important and reliable data sources for tracing the ideas and goals of political parties or coalitions at the national level, and thus of political ambitions within public health policy. Furthermore, political documents usually meet the criteria of authenticity and credibility, because they are expressions of formulated government policies, serve as guiding principles and tools for government action, and reflect government ideology and intentions regarding the choice of policy instruments and measures to deal with policies related to health inequalities (Fosse 2011, pp. 262–263).

In the qualitative content analysis, we have traced the explicit and implicit values of the policies presented, which are closely linked to the explicit analytical tools chosen for the study (Yin 2004; Kohlbacher 2006; Flick 2009). To this extent, the approach was relatively deductive for a qualitative approach. In the qualitative content analysis of the policy documents, we concentrated on detecting and categorizing descriptions of problems, challenges, goals, and measures. The same procedure was applied to detect measures or solutions that have been recommended or chosen to address the problems and priorities. Each of the three coauthors independently read the documents systematically and at the same level of detail to identify the presence of meaningful patterns and to increase the reliability of the coding (Polit and Beck 2004). The coding procedure was done by labeling ideas regarding public health and health inequalities, including discrepancies and inconsistencies between and within the different national policy documents.

National Public Health Agendas from 2003 to 2017

In 2003, the Norwegian government introduced the WP no. 16 (2002–2003): "Prescription for a Healthier Norway" (Ministry of Health and Care Services 2003). At a press conference in January 2003, when the report was launched, the health minister proclaimed that the people of Norway should become "custodians" of their own health. The message was clear: "[…] you are your own health minister" (www.aftenposten.no/helse/Bli-din-egen-helseminister-6336973.html). Even though social inequality in health is mentioned several times in the document the focus is limited, and no suggestions are outlined for primary prevention. Instead, WP 16 specifies several factors influencing public health: tobacco, drugs, diet, physical activity, and social environment (p. 13). The document also introduced the so-called Green Prescription Scheme (ibid., p. 92), arguing that GPs should motivate and write referrals allowing patients to access support for healthy individual lifestyle changes. This includes increasing their physical activity, receiving nutritional guidance, and getting help to quit smoking. Another measure to guide and regulate individual behavior was the complete ban on smoking in all indoor public spaces, with the Norwegian Tobacco Act (Ministry of Health and Care Services 2004) being adopted in 2004. In fact, Norway was the first country to ratify the WHO Framework Convention on Tobacco Control (FCTC), which came into force in 2005.

In 2005, the Norwegian government and health authorities specified the presence of health inequalities as a major cause for concern and an important political challenge, foreshadowing a collectivist logic. As a result, the government assigned the Norwegian Directorate of Health a mission to develop a competence center on social inequalities in health. The

Norwegian Directorate of Health (2005) submitted a report called "The Challenge of the Gradient" focusing on the increasing health inequalities in Norway and their associations to socioeconomic status. Presented as a master plan to reduce health inequalities in Norway, the report related the factors shaping and maintaining social inequalities in health to a number of political-administrative sectors and tasks, both in and out of the health sector. Thus, the development of a national cross-sectoral coordination strategy was underlined and defined as the most important maneuver to reduce social inequalities in health (ibid., pp. 9, 29).

In 2007, the report was followed by WP no. 20 (2006–2007), "A National Strategy for Reducing Inequalities in Health in Norway" (Ministry of Health and Care Services 2007). This report highlighted three important characteristics: (1) Inequalities in health were considered the biggest threat to public health; (2) the principle of "proportional universalism" (Marmot 2005) targeted the "gradient" rather than disadvantaged groups themselves; and (3) the broad cross-sectoral coordination strategy was still considered important. Major concerns were the standard of living and quality of life (ibid., p. 66), as well as the causes of social health inequalities and social determinants of health, including income level, life employment, work environment, and social inclusion. Such language heralded a potential return to more overtly collectivist discourse.

As WP 20 emphasized the importance of developing cross-sectoral instruments, planning instruments such as municipal master plans ended up becoming the major cross-sectoral mechanisms in the strategy for decreasing social health inequalities (ibid., p. 79). In fact, in 2009, the revised Planning and Building Act (Ministry of Local Government and Regional Development 2008) embedded public health issues and strategies in an overall social, cross-sectoral community perspective on preventive public health, based on regional and local planning to increase social sustainability in health. Such municipal master plans were considered vital tools in defining future challenges and local priorities in all political areas to promote public health (Aarsæther et al. 2012, p. 76; Amdam and Veggeland 2011, p. 37). Nevertheless, this legislation implied a change in planning policy, from traditional physical area planning to overall societal planning, in order to introduce a broad public health perspective that included all sectors and policies. Since social inequality in health was on the agenda, the integration of public health into the Planning and Building Act was a step away from the more individualist health behavior-oriented trend of previous policy documents (WP no. 16, 2002–2003; Stenvoll et al. 2005; Vallgårda 2001, 2007, 2010).

In 2012, the Public Health Act, PHA, (Ministry of Health and Care Services 2011) was implemented and coordinated with the Planning and Building Act of 2009. The PHA which was founded on the HIAP approach (Grimm et al. 2013) described reducing social inequalities in health as a fundamental collectivist principle to be addressed:

> The Public Health Act shall contribute to a societal development that promotes public health, [thereby] neutralizing social health inequalities. (Chapter 1, §1)

According to the PHA, Chapter 2, §5, municipalities are expected to monitor social inequalities in health and the main social determinants of such inequalities. Municipalities are also expected to take coordinated action by incorporating a public health perspective into all master plans and sector plans at the local level. The PHA also recommends the creation of the position of Public Health Coordinator (PHC) in the municipalities.

Simultaneously, this collectivist view of social health inequalities is accompanied by a relaunch of the individual approach in the PHA. For example, in Chapter 2, §7, the PHA are defined as:

> The local government shall contribute with information, counseling and guidance concerning what the individual can do by herself or himself to promote health and prevent illness.

As a result, Healthy Lifestyle Centers (HLC) in all municipalities were promoted to institutionalize the individualist elements of the policy (The Norwegian Directorate of Health 2014).

Later, in 2013, the WP no. 34 (2012–2013) "The Public Health Report. Good Health – Common Responsibility" (Ministry of Health and Care Services 2013) was issued, which reinforced the focus on the individual:

Each of us has a considerable responsibility for our own health and empowerment of our own life … Society is responsible for organizing and preparing for equal opportunities, for giving people opportunities to exploit their own resources and for the possibility to use freedom of choice. (ibid., 8)

Much of this policy can be interpreted as a revival of the health behavior perspective in the WP no. 16 (2002–2003) "Prescription for a Healthier Norway," and the implementation of the Norwegian Tobacco Act in 2004. The importance of HLC at the local and regional level is again emphasized as an instrument in promoting public health, followed by revised and more detailed national guidelines for establishing such agencies (WP no. 34, 2012–2013, p. 13).

The most recent WP on public health, WP no. 19 (2014–2015), "The Public Health Report: Mastery and Opportunities," (Ministry of Health and Care Services 2015) continues and renews strategies to help people make wise lifestyle choices by "creating opportunities." For example, this WP announced, "The National Program for Local Public Health Work" (2017–2027) (Directorate of Health 2017) to facilitate, prioritize, and fund the local implementation of such policies, directed at children and youth, mental health, quality of life, and substance abuse. The program focused explicitly on specific diagnoses and populations, and a more singular, targeted, and specialized focus in public health policy in the project's organization and financing. This indicates a possible reorientation of the public health policy away from the gradient and cross-sectoral coordinated action. However, this policy's focus also indicates that these current policy measures are designed to match the PHA's emphasis on local authorities' responsibility to examine their own public health problems and to supposedly empower the municipalities to handle these issues.

Interweaving Logics of Public Health

At the turn of the twenty-first century, Norwegian public health policy was dominated by the individualist logic, focusing on the health risks of the individual citizen, and granting GPs a central role in empowering their patients to take responsibility for their own health. Another indication of the individualist logic is the strategy of establishing and organizing HLC as a specialized agency and services directed at working with individual health problems and risks. However, the challenge of social determinants of health was only put on the national public health agenda in 2007, committing Norway to dedicating a national and universal strategy to the gradient issue (WP no. 20 [2006–2007] "National Strategy to Reduce Social Inequalities in Health"). This strategy resulted in a planning regime based on the HIAP principle and cross-sectoral planning, indicating a turn toward the collectivist logic, as did the requirement that municipal planning processes monitor, analyze, and consider their citizens' health and social conditions. However, this policy did not represent a paradigmatic shift, nor a fundamental change in the approach to public health. This was because the individualist logic was relaunched with the PHA in 2012, followed by new WPs in 2013 and in 2015, and finally the National Program for Public Health Work in 2017. In other words, the universal strategy to reduce social health inequalities, focusing on equity and the gradient, has been downplayed to the benefit of a more fragmented and targeted strategy.

As a result, the two public health logics exist side by side as layers of policy initiatives, creating complex, hybrid, and ambiguous public health policies. The question is whether these different ideas and measures result in a public health policy that is either confusing, competing, or complementary. Considering the potential complementarity, it is important to remember that for the individual, the possibility of taking care of one's own health is a matter of personal autonomy. Thus, measures aimed at helping individual citizens to do so should be welcomed in as long as it does not replace the government's responsibility to regulate the collective preconditions for public health. That is, if such an individualist logic dominates public health governance and management, social inequalities will not be reduced. Finding the right balance between logics is, however, challenging.

Furthermore, because of these coexisting logics, it may appear unclear and confusing to understand what the major public health challenge really is. While the harmful health effects of smoking, alcohol abuse, and obesity are undisputed, they cannot explain the existence of social inequalities. There is some evidence that income and level of education affect, for example, individual smoking and nutrition habits, and thereby ill health and mortality (Van der Wel et al. 2016). However, such evidence only reveals that several factors work together to produce both individual and public health problems and social inequalities in health. Therefore, the knowledge base on how these factors work together is still weak and contested. Furthermore, the lack of specific technologies on how to reduce health inequalities renders "the gradient" a typically complex and wicked problem (Head and Alford 2015). Moreover, the individualist and collectivist logics could also be seen as competing, or even contradictory.

Considering that the national public health policy's aim to reduce health inequality is in line with the ideas of the Nordic welfare state, it seems paradoxical that public health policy should emphasize the individual's responsibility for her or his own health as a public health strategy. This paradox is made more apparent by the argument that the side effects of the individualist logic will inevitably lead to increasing inequalities in health (Ayo 2011, p. 104). Indeed, it seems inconsistent to define individual responsibility as a solution when inequalities are in fact produced within the health governance system itself. In other words, the logics are not only contradictory, but goals, measures, governance, and management stemming from the two logics are incompatible and paradoxical.

Because the responsibility for carrying out public health policies in Norway is currently decentralized, it is up to the local authorities to interpret the ambiguity of the national public health policy. Research on the implementation of public health policy indicates that specialized and isolated organizational measures imbued with individualist logic, like the HLC (Kiland et al. 2015), are the easiest to adopt at the local level. Yet, Hagen et al. (2018) found that municipalities that had created the position of PHC were *less* successful at focusing on social inequalities. This irony can be understood in light of the tensions the PHC might face, between different tasks, interests, understandings, and knowledge inherent in government (Williams 2012), and particularly the tension between the individualist and collectivist logics in public health policy. Hence, the influence that these PHC wield is limited within the local management and governance system because genuine cross-sectoral coordination and integration require attention from political and administrative leaders (Auschra 2018, pp. 6–7).

To be successfully addressed, public health issues need an organizational allocation at the strategic management and leadership levels of the organizations responsible for implementing the policy (Beland and Katapaly 2018). In other words, in order to tackle the social gradient, first of all there has to be an awareness across political and organizational levels and sectors, of how public health should be a public responsibility, and not primarily the responsibility of the individual citizen. Arguably, the coalescence of individual and collectivist experiments we documented is exacerbated under "neo-liberalism." The prevailing neoliberal philosophy has broadly held that elements of socioeconomic and sociopolitical life only have value if their value can be determined within the market economy (Simonet 2011). By such a view, it is unsurprising that the individualist logic has resurged in public health policy. The balance may possibly be so skewed that defenders of health as a public good need to be especially vigilant to protect the conditions of public health and promote collective awareness, articulation, and action across political, social, institutional and economic boundaries.

References

Aarsæther, N., Falleth, E., Nyseth, T., & Kristiansen, R. (Eds.). (2012). *Utfordringer for norsk planlegging: Kunnskap, bærekraft, demokrati* [Challenges in Norwegian planning: Knowledge, sustainability, democracy]. Oslo: Cappelen Damm.

Adler, P. S., Kwon, S.-W., & Heckscher, C. (2008). Professional work: The emergence of collaborative community. *Organization Science, 19*(2), 359–376.

Andersen, N. Å. (2003). *Borgerens kontraktliggørelse* [Contract with the citizen]. Copenhagen: Hans Reitzel Forlag.

Antonovsky, A. (1996). The salugenic model as theory to guide health promotion. *Health Promotion International, 11*(1), 11–18.

Amdam, J., & Veggeland, N. (2011). *Teorier om samfunnsstyring og planlegging* [Theories on social steering and planning]. Oslo: The University Press.

Auschra, C. (2018). Barriers to the integration of care in inter-organisational settings: A literature review. *International Journal of Integrated Care, 18*(1): 5, 1–14.

Axelsson, R., & Axelsson, S. B. (2006). Integration and collaboration in public health—A conceptual framework. *International Journal of Health Planning and Management, 21*(1), 75–88.

Ayo, N. (2011). Understanding health promotion in a neoliberal climate and the making of health conscious citizens. *Critical Public Health, 22*(1), 99–105.

Bambra, C. (2011). Health inequalities and welfare state regimes: Theoretical insights on a public health 'puzzle'. *Journal of Epidemiology and Community Health, 65*(9), 740–745.

Beland, D., & Katapaly, T. R. (2018). Shaping policy change in population health: Policy entrepreneurs, ideas, and institutions. *International Journal of Health Policy and Management, 7*(5), 369–373.

Coburn, D. (2000). Income inequality, social cohesion and the health status of populations: The role of neo-liberalism. *Social Science and Medicine, 51*(1), 135–146.

Dahl, E., Bergsli, H., & Van der Wel, K. A. (2014). *Sosial ulikhet i helse: en norsk kunnskapsoversikt* [Social inequality in health: A Norwegian knowledge overview]. Oslo: Oslo and Akershus University College.

Degeling, P. (1995). The significance of 'sectors' in calls for urban public health intersectoralism: An Australian perspective. *Policy and Politics, 23*(4), 289–301.

Directorate of Health and Social Affairs. (2005). *Plan for å redusere sosial ulikhet i helse. Gradientutfordringen* [Plan of action to reduce social inequalities in health. The challenge of the gradient] (Report No. 1245).

Directorate of Health. (2014). Samfunnsutvikling for god folkehelse. Rapport om status og råd for videreutvikling av folkehelsearbeidet i Norge [Societal development for good public health. Report on the status and advice on development of public health work in Norway] (Report No. 2203).

Directorate of Health. (2017). Nasjonalt program for lokalt folkehelsearbeid 2017–2027 (National Program for Local Health Work 2017–2027).

Donaldson, L. (2001). *The contingency theory of organizations*. Thousand Oaks: Sage.

Eikemo, T. A., Huisman, M., Bambra, C., & Kunst, A. E. (2008). Health inequalities according to educational level in different welfare regimes: A comparison of 23 European countries. *Sociology of Health and Illness, 30*(4), 565–582.

Eriksson, M., & Lindström, B. (2008). A salutogenic interpretation of the Ottawa Charter. *Health Promotion International, 23*(2), 190–199.

Flick, U. (2009). *An introduction to qualitative research*. London: Sage.

Fosse, E. (2011). Different welfare states—Different policies? An analysis of the substance of national health promotion policies in three European countries. *International Journal of Health Services, 2*, 255–272.

Foucault, M. (1982). How power is exercised. In H. L. Dreyfus & P. Rabinow (Eds.), *Michel Foucault: Beyond structuralism and hermeneutics: With an afterword by Michel Foucault* (pp. 216–226). New York: The Harvester Press.

Friedland, R., & Alford, R. R. (1991). Bringing society back in: Symbols, practices and institutional contradictions. In W. W Powell & P. J. DiMaggio (Eds.), *The new institutionalism in organizational analysis* (pp. 232–263). Chicago: University of Chicago Press.

Grimm, M. J., Helgesen, M. K., & Fosse, E. (2013). Reducing social inequities in health in Norway: Concerted action at state and local levels? *Health Policy, 113*, 228–235.

Hagen, S., Øvergård, K. I., Helgesen, M., Fosse, E., & Torp, S. (2018). Health promotion at local level in Norway: The use of public health coordinators and health overviews to promote fair distribution among social groups. *International Journal of Health Policy and Management, 7*(9), 807–817.

Head, B. W., & Alford, J. (2015). Wicked problems: Implications for public management. *Administration and Society, 47*(6), 711–739.

Huijts, T., & Eikemo, T. A. (2009). Causality, social selectivity or artefacts? Why socioeconomic inequalities in health are not smallest in the Nordic countries. *European Journal of Public Health, 19*(5), 452–453.

Kiland, C., Kvåle, G., & Torjesen, D. O. (2015). The ideas and implementation of public health policies: The Norwegian case. In A. R. Pedersen, L. Fitzgerald, E. Ferlie, & S. B. Waldorff (Eds.), *Managing change: From health policy to practice* (pp. 9–25). Basingstoke: Palgrave Macmillan.

Kohlbacher, F. (2006). The use of qualitative content analysis in case study research. *Forum Qualitative Sozialforschung/Forum: Qualitative Social Research, 7*(1), Art 21.

Marmot, M. (2005). Social determinants of health inequalities. *Lancet, 365*, 1099–1104.

Ministry of Health and Care Services. (2003). White Paper no. 16 (2002–2003) Resept for et sunnere Norge [Prescription for a healthier Norway].

Ministry of Health and Care Services. (2004). The protection against harm caused by tobacco act.

Ministry of Health and Care Services. (2007). White Paper no. 20 (2006–2007) Nasjonal strategi for å redusere sosiale ulikheter i helse [National strategy for decreasing social inequalities in health].

Ministry of Local Government and Regional Development. (2008). The planning and building act.

Ministry of Health and Care Services. (2011). The public health act.

Ministry of Health and Care Services. (2013). White Paper no. 34 (2012–2013) Folkehelsemeldingen. God helse – felles ansvar. 2008 [The public health report. Good health—Common responsibility].

Ministry of Health and Care Services. (2015). White Paper no. 19 (2014–2015) Folekehelsemeldingen. Mestring og muligheter [The public health report—Mastery and opportunities].

Osborne, S. P. (2006). The new public governance? *Public Management Review, 8*(3), 377–387.

Polit, D. F., & Beck, C. T. (2004). *Nursing research: Principles and methods.* Philadelphia, PA: Lippincott Williams & Wilkins.

Raphael, D. (Ed.). (2012). *Tackling health inequalities: Lessons from international experiences.* Toronto: Canadian Scholars' Press Inc.

Romøren, T. I., Torjesen, D. O., & Landmark, B. (2011). Promoting coordination in Norwegian health care. *International Journal of Integrated Care, 11,* 2011–2027.

Selinger, E., & Whyte, K. (2011). Is there a right way to Nudge? The practice and ethics of choice architecture. *Sociology Compass, 5*(10), 923–935.

Simonet, D. (2011). The new public management theory and the reform of European health care systems: An international comparative perspective. *International Journal of Public Administration, 34*(12), 815–826. https://doi.org/10.1080/01900692.2011.603401.

Smith-Nonini, S. (2006). Conceiving the health commons: Operationalizing a right to health. *Social Analysis, 50*(3), 233–245.

Stenvoll, D., Elvebakken, K. T., & Malterud, K. (2005). Blir norsk forebyggingspolitikk mer individorientert? *Tidsskrift for Den norske lægeforening, 5,* 603–605 [Is Norwegian preventive health policy becoming more oriented toward the individual? The Journal of the Norwegian Doctors Association].

Thaler, R. H., & Sunstein, C. R. (2008). *Nudge: Improving decisions about health, wealth, and happiness.* New York: Penguin Books.

Torjesen, D. O., Kvåle, G., & Kiland, C. (2016). The quest for promoting integrated care in the Scandinavian countries—Recent reforms, possibilities and problems. In R. Pinheiro, L. Geschwind, F. O. Ramirez, & K. Vrangbæk (Eds.), *Towards a comparative institutionalism: Forms, dynamics and logics across the organizational fields of health care and higher education. Research in the sociology of organizations* (Vol. 45, pp. 195–213). Bingley: Emerald Books.

Vallgårda, S. (2001). Governing people's lives. Strategies for improving the health of the nations in England, Denmark, Norway and Sweden. *European Journal of Public Health, 4,* 386–392.

Vallgårda, S. (2007). Review article: Public health policies—A Scandinavian model? *Scandinavian Journal of Public Health, 35,* 205–211.

Vallgårda, S. (2010). Addressing individual behaviors and living conditions: Four Nordic public health policies. *Scandinavian Journal of Public Health, 39,* 6–10.

Van der Wel, K. A., Dahl, E., & Bergsli, H. (2016a). The Norwegian policy to reduce health inequalities: Key challenges. *Nordic Welfare Research, 1,* 19–29.

Van der Wel, K. A., Dahl, E., & Bergsli, H. (2016b). The Norwegian policy to reduce health inequalities: Key challenges. *Nordisk välfärdsforskning | Nordic Welfare Research, 1*(1), 19–29.

Wilkinson, R., & Pickett, K. (2010). *The spirit level: Why equality is better for everyone.* London: Penguin Books Ltd.

Williams, P. (2012). *Collaboration in public policy and practice: Perspectives on boundary spanners.* Bristol: The Policy Press.

World Health Organization. (2008). Closing the gap in a generation: Health equity through action on the social determinants of health. *Commission on Social Determinants of Health.* http://www.who.int/social_determinants/final_report/csdh_finalreport_2008.pdf.

Yin, R. K. (2004). *Case study research* (3rd ed.). London: Sage.

8

Beyond Hybridity in Organized Professionalism: A Case Study of Medical Curriculum Change

Simon Moralee and Simon Bailey

Introduction

Hybridity in public service organizations refers to the combination of professional and managerial discourses within roles and individuals, for example, a manager with a nursing background (Currie 2006). It is commonly understood to have emerged in Western capitalist democracies from around the 1970s onwards and is associated with the changing role of the state in public service management and the corresponding rise of a variegated set of managerial principles and practices. This broad movement is often described under the rubric of "new public management" (NPM), and latterly "post" NPM (Ferlie et al. 1996;

S. Moralee (✉)
University of Manchester, Manchester, UK
e-mail: simon.moralee@manchester.ac.uk

S. Bailey
Center for Health Services Studies, University of Kent, Canterbury, UK
e-mail: simon.bailey@manchester.ac.uk

© The Author(s) 2020
P. Nugus et al. (eds.), *Transitions and Boundaries in the Coordination and Reform of Health Services*, Organizational Behaviour in Healthcare,
https://doi.org/10.1007/978-3-030-26684-4_8

Hoggett 1996; Hood 1991; Jun 2009). The central tenet of hybridity is that this combination—the professional and the managerial—gives rise to boundaries and resulting tensions between conflicting ways of knowing, practising and organizing. This is particularly apparent when viewed in the light of histories of professional dominance in domains such as health care and the changing fortunes that the rise of managerialism in public service appears to herald for them. This conflict gives rise to a range of individual and collective strategies and scenarios, from resistance to enrolment, encapsulated in descriptions of individual struggles: "reluctant but resourceful" (Currie 2006), "willing" and "incidental" (McGivern et al. 2015) and "agnostic" and "ambivalent" hybrids (Bresnen et al. 2017), and collective phenomena such as "organised professionalism" (Noordegraaf 2011) and "negotiated orders" (Bishop and Waring 2016).

There is clearly conceptual value in hybridity and the rich empirical rendering of contemporary public services that it affords. However, we wish to question the continued relevance of the concept by offering an analysis of a scenario we tentatively refer to as "beyond hybridity". Our analysis builds upon a qualitative examination of a curriculum programme which sought to introduce management and leadership skills to medical training at all levels, from undergraduate medical school to practising physicians.

The central claim of our argument is that the conflict which defines the notion of hybridity does not accurately portray the identities, knowledge and practices of our cohort. Instead, we demonstrate the capacity of individuals to internalize and resolve the boundaries and conflicts between professional and managerial ways of knowing, doing and being. In a way similar to engaging in a process of "identity work" (Watson 2008), individuals navigate these dynamics to reconcile professional identity with conflicting organizational and coordinative structures. Our case is built upon an analysis of the conditions which have shaped this capacity, through which we construct a conceptual framework for moving "beyond" hybridity in accounts of professional and managerial work in public service.

Previous literature has demonstrated the temporary settlements between competing discourses that can be created through hybrid work

(Bishop and Waring 2016; Iedema et al. 2004; Martin et al. 2015). We develop this stage further, highlighting the organizational and individual conditions that establish the possibility of an enduring resolution of conflicts. We conclude with a discussion of the conceptual and practical implications of our argument for future understanding of professional resistance and enrolment in public service management and the continued remaking of public service professionalism.

Professionalism, Managerialism and Hybridization

The concept of professionalism has been much discussed in terms of its traits, characteristics and functions (Carr-Saunders and Wilson 1933; Millerson 1964; Parsons 1951); its special status as a community of common experience and therefore different from other occupations (Freidson 2001; Abbott 1988; Goode 1957), and as a means of labour market closure and dominance (Larson 1977; Ferlie et al. 1996). The very act of classifying professionalism as something unique and special is intended to create positional legitimacy and credibility (Bourdieu 1994; as cited by Schinkel and Noordegraaf 2011). Formal recognition of a profession involves an "uncritical acceptance of a concept laden with distinctive profit and symbolic value particular to a specific social space" (Schinkel and Noordegraaf 2011, p. 80).

In turn, Freidson (2001) and Abbott (1988) both allude to "professionalization projects" whose purpose is to serve distinctive organizational, social and ideological objectives within different societies, in particular, to secure jurisdictional power within its domain of practice. This makes professionalism the "dominant occupational mode and organizational form for institutionalizing the provision and evaluation of expert services in modern capitalist societies", using "highly specialized knowledge and skill in such a way as to maximize the [profession's] stability, portability, generality and legitimacy across a wide range of relatively secure and cohesive jurisdictional domains" (Reed 1996, p. 583). It is argued that political and economic events of the past forty years, under the badge of managerialism (Hood 1991; Flynn 2007), have resulted in a degree of deprofessionalization (Leicht and Fennell 2001) and proletarianization (Freidson 1984). This means that relative autonomy and freedom from state intervention is weakened. Consequently, professionals have become more dependent on selling their labour in return for subsistence (Braverman 1974), resulting in the "content, control and location of [their] work being managed by outsiders" (Leicht and Fennell 2001, p. 8).

Despite the changing context of professional control, Freidson (1984, p. 7) contended early on that there is little evidence to suggest a "steadily shrinking jurisdiction" of professional knowledge and skills; instead, professionals have re-engineered and re-stratified their roles and behaviours (Waring and Currie 2009). Such re-constitution of roles has created hybrid approaches of "organized anarchy" or "professional bureaucracies" to maintain some form of control over their work (Freidson 1984, 2001). Individual freedom to act may become inhibited, but collective professional influence is maintained (Freidson 1984, 2001). The maintenance of such influence creates an intra-professional tension between elites and masses—with state recognition and protection, increased specialization and prominence and influence for elites.

In support of such a view, Currie et al. (2012) argue that medical professionals have shaped institutional arrangements to privilege their own jurisdictional claims and retain powerful positions (Battilana 2011), thus shaping "the change trajectory to ensure continued professional dominance" (Currie et al. 2012, p. 958). Furthermore, McGivern et al. (2015) conceptualize individuals taking on roles within these new organizational forms as "incidental" or "willing" hybrids, whose work represents, protects and maintains professionalism's foundation or alternatively challenges and disrupts traditional professionalism.

The picture that emerges is that despite the periodic marginalization of professions, they have shown considerable capacity to adapt to external controls through the creation of informal organizations. Ackroyd (1996) draws on case studies from the manufacturing industry and public services, in which professions worked with other middle-class groups (such as employers, managers and supervisors) at times, subordinating themselves to organizational controls, while maintaining a monopoly over key knowledge and employees. Hanlon (1998) discussed a type of "hybrid" professionalism that requires managerial and entrepreneurial skills in order to respond to emerging views where experts were no longer simply "trusted" and where their autonomy was now considered a "luxury". Hanlon (1998) goes on to discuss how such "professionalism-as-enterprise" created a fissure between more commercially minded professionals and those who stood by a social service logic. This, of course, could also be considered as evidence of hybridization within professions, adjusting to change by adopting new practices, or actively shaping practice and design of the organizational field as a means of maintaining some control over professional development (Muzio and Kirkpatrick 2011).

In support, Evetts' (2005) research describes two different types of discourse regarding professionalism that epitomize such professionalism-as-enterprise: "organizational", where managers aim to control, and "occupational", where professional groups maintain their collegial authority. The ways in which the two discourses are used by numerous stakeholders, such as the state, the professions and managers within organizations, may help to elucidate how professionalism becomes an instrument of occupational change and social control (Evetts 2005).

The evolving "new model professional" (Ackroyd 1996) has adapted in different ways to a world where commercial and service industries are more prevalent than manufacturing ones. These new kinds of professionals cooperate with managerial and organizational demands to ensure their survival, even thriving in environments where their uniqueness, innovation and expertise are valued as an economic premium (Reed 1996; Suddaby 2010). As Reed (1996, p. 586) suggests "[t]his pushes [them] towards an organic or network type of organizational form in which a logic of decentralized flexibility and autonomy ... move[s] them away from the administrative structures typically associated with both the liberal and organizational professions". Professionals are shaped by the institutions of which they are a part, but they may also exert pressure to enact institutional change. Professionalism, managerialism, bureaucracy and other structures are neither opposing nor mutually exclusive, but rather coevolve within institutions and their boundaries (Muzio et al. 2013).

Therefore, managerialism, with its increasing levels of bureaucracy, standardization, assessment and performance review, has now cemented itself alongside professionalism, shifting away from its long-established notions of partnership, collegiality, discretion and trust to create a hybrid form of professionalism. Such notions emerge as processes through various stages of education and professional identity formation, as reflected in the following case.

Understanding Hybridity in Medical Curricula

The *Enhancing Engagement in Medical Leadership* (EEML) project was a national status change initiative that took place between 2005–2010. The EEML project introduced "leadership" skills and knowledge through the undergraduate medical curriculum in the form of the *Medical Leadership Competency Framework* (MLCF) (NHS Institute for Innovation and Improvement [NHSI] and Academy of Medical Royal Colleges [AoMRC] 2010). The EEML project intends to give effect to the MLCF by providing doctors with leadership competences, to become more active participants in the planning, delivery and reform of health services, as indicated in Fig. 8.1.

The EEML project seeks to promote leadership skills through multiple levels of training, from undergraduate to continuing practice, in order to improve "organizational performance" (AoMRC and NHSI 2010). A formal and continuous leadership course among medical trainees had not been attempted before in the NHS. Such formal, collaborative working between the medical profession and with the direct involvement of senior NHS stakeholders and organizations on an educational initiative was also relatively novel in the UK. No previous studies have explored the role of such formal educational initiatives to intervene in regard to role positioning and negotiation, especially in regard to change in a mature institutional field. There is also very little in the existing literature that has explored the way medical professionals are expected to develop leadership and management skills and knowledge through the curriculum. An especially valuable opportunity exists to examine such an intervention by way

of a competency framework, given that competency frameworks are becoming increasingly prominent internationally (see Frank 2005, for one example).

The EEML project provides a qualitative case that allows for a rich understanding of phenomena and for theory-building (Yin 2014; Martin et al. 2012; Martin and Finn 2011) when applied to change processes that are taking or have taken place. An exploratory case study is valuable for examining the influence on social processes of the institutional context (Hartley 2004, p. 325), as is the case of the position of the medical profession in relation to changes in the NHS. Embracing a "naturalistic design" (Lincoln and Guba 1985), qualitative research methods were adopted, primarily focussed on interventions in the lives of participants through semi-structured interviews after the programme had finished. Participants were chosen from the EEML project team and steering group, comprising the individuals who conceived, designed and managed the implementation and development of the programme.

In choosing these participants, key person interviews of members of two groups were carried out. The first group was the project team, who were responsible for operationalizing the project and who worked under the remit of the second group, the project steering group. Membership of both groups was clear, making the two groups discrete, bounded entities for research, although two individuals were members of both groups. By focussing on these two groups, accounts, stories and histories could be compared, notably around the impact of the project on roles and identities. Membership across both groups accounted for no more than 50 people and from that sample, 25 individuals were initially approached, on the basis of maximum sampling variation. Of these, 21 responded, with 22 eventually being interviewed (Table 8.1). These participants were selected according to availability and ability to represent a variety of perspectives across the two groups. Interviews were carried out between October and December 2012, with one final interview in July 2013.

This study also employed analysis of historical documents and interviews. The use of documentation in case study research can offer rich, alternative insights into events that occurred as part of the case under examination. Defined as materials that are preserved and available for analysis and are relevant to the concerns of the research (Bryman 2008), the benefit of documentation is that it offers another account of the stories and narratives that arise from interviews that help in confirming or contrasting the various accounts of how the change was enacted. The following table (Table 8.2) outlines the documents consulted within the study. These documents were considered to be the key artefacts for considering actions and decisions taken, which would incorporate the approach and practices of individuals.

Table 8.1 Research participants' ($n = 22$) membership of EEML project team and steering group

	Project team ($n = 13$)	Steering group ($n = 9$)
Background	Administrator/manager (2), senior managerial (4), medical (4), academic/managerial, senior managerial[a], academic/managerial[a]	Medical (9)
Gender	Female (7), Male (6)	Female (1), Male (8)
Ethnicity	White British (11), White Other (2)	White British (9)

[a]They were also members of the steering group

Table 8.2 Documentary data collected between 2005 and 2010 ($n = 85$)

Type of written project material	No.	Approx. page count	Detail
Project initiation and background/project plan	11	148	Project summaries, scoping reports, project plans, communications strategy, terms of reference from 2005–2009. This also included a key internal briefing paper, which recorded the project timelines/actions
Project plan—team minutes and notes of actions [2006 = 3; 2007 = 17; 2008 = 14; 2009 = 10; 2010 = 5]	49	433	Meeting notes and actions, 2006–2010
Project plan—steering group minutes	10	130	Minutes from 2006 to 2009
Project plan—progress reports	15	195	Reports from 2006 to 2008
Total number	85	906	

Semi-structured interviews were conducted and audio-recorded by the first author. He listened to the interviews several times to consider which themes were covered and to allow for reflection on the notes taken immediately after the interviews had occurred. Following transcription and entry into NVivo 10 (QSR International 2012), key concepts were identified and coded by the first author (Barbour 2008). "Provisional coding" occurred, which involved an openness to new codes potentially emerging, in the context of evolving theoretical assumptions (Layder 1998, p. 55). Then began a precise process of open coding (Bryman 2008) to yield types of a priori and in vivo codes (Barbour 2008) and the thorough identification of themes across all 22 interviews. A sample of the coding frame is in Table 8.3.

In Table 8.3, codes from theoretical, methodological and emergent concepts can all be identified, and links drawn to other relevant codes. In seeking out codes, a number of variables or elements

Table 8.3 Coding frame or "template"

Level 1 Node	Level 2 Node	Level 3 Node	Definition	Linked to… (code/concept)	Source of code
Actions	Individually	Contribution (contributing)	Anything said in response to what the project would have looked like without their involvement		Interview guide/a priori
Actions	Individually	Practice (practising)	A specific action or practice by the research participant; strategy; mechanism, approach, style –whether they do it or not, e.g. talk, demonstrate, show, attend or not meetings, do a specific task	Agency Intentionality	Interview guide/a priori Strauss (1987), Taylor and Gibbs (2010) Social position
Actions	Individually	Representation (representing)	Required to act for/by others for a purpose; membership of/on the Steering Group, a voice/perspective for a particular stakeholder, e.g. patients		
Actions	Individually	Role	What the individual's (their organization's) purpose was in getting involved in the project, perceived or actual—related to but distinct from "practice" ALSO job, title, position	Practices Buy-in Behaviours Legitimacy Representation Motivation	Interview Guide/a priori/research question Lofland et al. (2006), Taylor and Gibbs (2010), social position

were considered, such as a participant's role in the project, his or her position or role, membership in a particular group or professional body, job and work experience, as well as experience and involvement in change projects. In coding the data and drawing on constructs from the research design and literature review, codes were grouped together to become themes.

It was from this thematic coding that analysis of the data could be drawn together into related notions to create meta-themes—for example, actions, from which pertinent concepts could be elaborated. This also meant that some codes were reviewed and compared for similarities and differences to others, or for other distinctions and patterns, resulting in some being left outside the core data for analysis. The focus of the interview data analysis was on the meta-category of "actions" incorporating the notion of practices and roles, to try to better understand the impact of the EEML project on roles and identities, particularly those relating to professional and managerial roles. The documents were then analysed in relation to those themes, looking for contrasting and comparative themes. Please note that pseudonyms are used to preserve anonymity.

Influences on Clinician-Managerial Identity

Social and Organizational Influences on Professional Identity

"Social and organizational influences on professional identities" was the first of two themes discerned in the analysis. The "traditional story" of medical involvement in management, be it medical professional views towards government policy initiatives or day-to-day operations with managers in healthcare organizations, talks of attempts to control on one side and efforts to resist on the other (Allen 1995; Marnoch 1996; Willcocks 1998; Degeling et al. 2003):

> *And I think there was a lot of struggle going on about maintaining status quo and people's reluctance to change, personal and organisational ... It was*

acknowledgement that doctors couldn't sit outside the tent any longer ... It was much more around a recognition [that] we need doctors to be very much in the driving seat ... recognising that doctors had an absolute[ly] essential role to play, and a responsibility actually.... [It was] always recognised that this could be working so much better if you didn't sideline and exclude probably one of the, if not the most, influential professional grouping within the system. (Jane [pseudonym], former senior manager, Project Team [PT])

One of the reasons that the profession may have been unsure as to where or how to position itself, and hence be seen to be reluctant or resistant, that one participant proposed, was uncertainty as to the merit of involvement in medical management. Such participation was seen to lack credibility among professional peers. This participant then describes how there was the beginning of a shift in professional attitudes towards the need for formal leadership training:

We had the Darzi fellows. We had the schemes that the Health Foundation had for supporting people to go abroad. There's the Harkness fellowships. A lot of things have happened since then that have made it perfectly reasonable for doctors to be engaged in management, improvement issues.... It just took time and also of course the changes in the health service. Really, once Griffiths [1983 NHS Management Inquiry] had got into action, it was almost inevitable that you could either put your head in the sand, which was a really daft thing to do, or you could start to see that high-quality health care needed all of these things. (Margaret, doctor, Steering Group [SG])

Other participants corroborated a sense of a change in professional priorities towards greater engagement from within the profession itself and, in some cases, enthusiasm from medical school and junior doctor feedback for the development of leadership skills:

... The world has, in every specialty, changed beyond belief.... Someone in their second or third year at medical school probably is seeing this framework as part of their curriculum – is starting to think, actually this is very interesting almost irrespective of what might happen. (Amanda, manager, PT)

This specific shift in professional attitudes among the newer generation of doctors appears to be one of the contributing factors towards an impetus for formal changes within the profession. Furthermore, the participant conveys potentially increased acceptance of formal educational interventions in relation to the negotiation of professional and managerial roles, identity and work. Although the medical profession is experiencing ongoing change, and negative attitudes towards management persist, many participants felt a growing sense of optimism about the role doctors can play in the reform agenda. This optimism was particularly apparent among trainee doctors, but was generally understood within the wider profession, according to participants. In many respects, this typifies the sense that professional thinking continues to evolve, while seeking to maintain its previous position in a particular field (Abbott 1988; Freidson 1986).

Participants perceived increased momentum—clearly demonstrated also by key policy documents—for formalizing intervention to encourage reflection on the relationship between professional and managerial roles. Combined interest among doctors, medical educators and medical leaders came to provide a cultural structure—as a particular environmental condition—to support such education (Fig. 8.2):

... Compared to the decade before, the thought that you would get all of the colleges and faculties, being not only comfortable but actually wanting to be involved in the process to codify the skills associated with medical leadership was a really good thing. (David, doctor, SG)

While the above conditions represent social and organizational factors for change, they do not inform us as to how the project was able to successfully integrate leadership development into medical education with the publication of the *MLCF* in 2008, nor the impact of this project on the cohort's ability to move beyond hybridity.

Individual Influences

As with many change initiative or projects, the addition of leadership and management training to medical curricula happened as a result of a number of factors: individuals adopting recognized practices, routines and actions; drawing on their positions, networks and relationships;

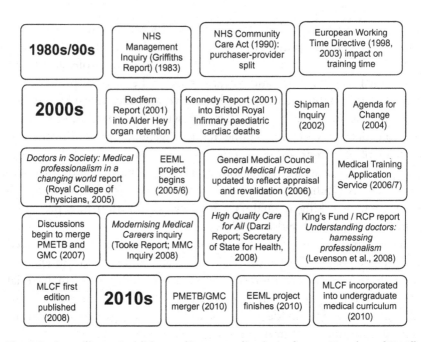

Fig. 8.2 Prevailing Conditions (Conceptualisation from Moralee [2016]). Moralee, S. J. C. (2016). *Practising change in strongly institutionalized environments: using system capital, being system centric.* Ph.D. thesis (Accessed 17 July 2019)

and aligning these around the social and organizational factors for change outlined above. The project team and steering group met iteratively with medical education stakeholders between 2005 and 2010. This included meetings with those responsible for curriculum development within the General Medical Council (GMC), Postgraduate Medical Education and Training Board (PMETB), individual Medical Royal Colleges, local area deaneries (all organizations which are responsible for specialty syllabi and medical training) and university medical schools. Meetings were also held with reference groups, providing opportunities for the project team to present ideas and receive feedback on how leadership and management training could be integrated into medical education.

Much of the initial collaboration took place internally. One of the key partnerships was between the two main project organizations:

the Academy of Medical Royal Colleges (AoMRC) and the NHS Institute for Innovation and Improvement (NHSI). The project would operate in joint ownership of the delivery and publication of any outputs, as can be seen with the *above-mentioned Medical Leadership Competency Framework (MLCF)*, even if the work was carried out by one partner or the other. Much of this relationship was built on the existence of a prior relationship, as it enabled a certain freedom in which to manage the project:

> *We had so much autonomy, ... [it] came from [senior manager of the EEML project] trusting me ... the steering group pretty rapidly trusting us ... So, without a doubt there was that autonomy ... I think some of it is around personal relationships, personal friendships.... Keith [pseudonym] and I have known each other for a number of years ... and a sort of confidence in me and then a confidence in the team.* (Patrick, academic/senior manager, PT/SG)

This demonstrates the relevance of good internal working and prior relationships as a foundation for negotiating roles and identity. Such relationships were seen to build support and legitimacy for the changes from organizations, such as the Academy of Medical Royal Colleges, which was represented by many of the key stakeholders responsible for curricula. Managing relationships "inside" the project environment, comprising the project team and steering group, was a core practice that underpinned the project. However, managing relationships outside of that environment was equally important, notably building wider awareness and support for the project, its purpose and products.

> *... At that meeting with the thirty or so Deans of Medical School, Andrew [pseudonym] would kick it off by saying how important it is that young doctors of tomorrow, you know, have good management leadership... "It's critical isn't it?" and he'd see half the group nodding. And so from the start we put out that message that this is really important. And then ... it was me, but it could have [been] one of my other colleagues ... doing our little spiel around what we were doing. And then concluding that we'd like to come and meet each of the Deans or their representative. With Andrew then summing up at the end saying, "This is so important you know and this project needs to know what you're already doing in this area because that will inform the finish.* (Patrick, academic/senior manager, PT/SG)

The steering group and project team consisted of individuals who had a combination of knowledge, expertise and credibility to add legitimacy to working with the medical profession:

> *The steering group was chaired by Margaret, influential, very powerful, incredibly well networked, and a real gift to the project, because within the medical world at that time who Margaret didn't know could be counted on one set of fingers.* (Keith, academic, PT/SG)

Steering group members acted as both governors of the project but also enablers and influencers for access to discuss specific aspects of the project with other stakeholders, such as medical colleges. Such a role for steering group members was to aid project awareness, buy-in and facilitation within the profession:

> *I had been around the postgraduate educational world for quite a long time, had a track record, and can get along with most folk, those sorts of things all help without a doubt.* (Tim, doctor, SG)

This idea of using the legitimacy and authority of relationships and contacts with influential stakeholder groups was not only the case for steering group members, but also for some of the project team:

> *I think the advantage of having me was the network and the ability to say we'll get this through [organization]. And so, I was able to discuss how to do this with people at [organization] and it was harder for [organization] to reject me; they could have rejected some guy they didn't know … But then as is the way of things generally in medicine, it's often about network and contacts. So, I think I was probably the right person.* (Alan, doctor, PT)

The negotiation of this educational project to promote reflection on role hybridity was evidently an exercise in hybridization itself. Overt networking and relationship-building began to break down barriers and bring about some consensus around leadership and management in the curriculum. Such consensus centred on the project's purpose, strategy and focus of attention, as well as the expected professional identities and values:

And this big group would be made up of doctors in training, medical manag-
ers, tutors from secondary and primary care – all specialties. Often some good
discussions [were held] around, 'Well, surely a doctor should do what the chief
executive said', to the doctor saying, 'Well actually we have got dual loyalties,
one is to the NHS, the organisation, but also to the [General Medical Council
– GMC] and the ethics the GMC had.' And that was never a sticking point
... but it did identify the ethics for which the profession has to go forward.
(Claire, doctor, PT)

The above quotation illustrates how the views of stakeholders started to
evolve, eliciting an understanding of what type of competency framework might impact on, or reflect, hybrid role negotiation. Indeed,
much of the iteration involved medical professionals in these reference
groups producing materials and case studies that were relevant and
grounded in practice.

The approach described above through these various excerpts matches
that described in the Project Plan (AoMRC and NHSI 2006) around
making the process of engagement meaningful and collaborative. What
this argument also demonstrates is how such an iterative, collaborative
approach to engagement was undertaken by participants and linked to
the core project purpose of implementing leadership and management
into medical curricula. This approach drew on individual motivations,
peer relationships, networks and influence to understand stakeholder
perspectives (Suchman 1995). Supported by a research evidence base,
experience and expertise of the project team and steering group, it
resulted in a more seamless view of organized medical professionalism
beyond conflicted notions of hybridity.

Implication—Beyond Hybridity—
Of Organized Professionalism

Using qualitative data gathered from participants in an educational
change programme, and drawing on contemporaneous historical documentary evidence, we have presented an account of a shift in attitudes
towards roles and identities that came about as a result of a series of

emergent and interlocking phenomena (Fig. 8.2) which over time accumulated into a transformative change. We have contributed an educational perspective to the literature on professional and managerial identities and roles in medicine, showing that the conduct and outcomes of an educational project can manifest or prompt a shift in attitudes towards distinct but reconciled hybrid roles. We divide the phenomena that were evident in our findings into four broad themes—social/professional, organizational, individual/relational and material/epistemic—which together establish a set of conditions for the possible resolution of the embodied conflict between professional and managerial discourses commonly known as "hybridity".

Social/Professional Conditions

This set of conditions refers to those which professionals experienced over a period of time. This includes the perceived credibility of more managerial approaches to running health care and letting go of the "old ways" of doing things, which harks back to the triumvirate approach of managing hospitals in the 1940s (Harrison et al. 1992). Over time, there was a concurrent shift in professional attitudes towards the acceptance and internalization of management and leadership knowledge. For example, the "newer" generation of doctors seemingly appreciated leadership and management "skills" development as an inherent part of doctors' work (GMC 2006a [2013]), and there was evidence of a wider realization of the requirements of the NHS reform agenda of the 2000s from the wider profession.

Organizational Conditions

As the findings detail, the project had support from medical schools, a key partnership between the Academy of Medical Royal Colleges and the NHS Institute for Innovation and Improvement, in addition to dedicated resourcing and the credibility of project team and steering group members. Such "formal" recognition of a programme to introduce leadership and management skills development into medical curricula emphasizes the role of regulative institutionalization, helping to legitimize the professional identity of the doctor as both clinician and leader (Scott 2014). Furthermore, GMC recognition via *Good Medical Practice* (GMC 2006a [2013]) and *Management for Doctors* (GMC 2006b) and specifically of the *MLCF* in *Tomorrow's Doctors* (GMC 2009) helped further to endorse leadership and management as an essential part of the doctor's role. Recently, *Outcomes for Graduates* (GMC 2018) details how quality improvement and leadership are regarded as core elements of professional values and behaviours.

Individual/Relational Conditions

The findings confirm the importance of professional and social networks and capital, built through existing relationships as well as new alliances. Many of the project team and steering group members adopted dedicated boundary-spanning roles between managerial/professional groups (Kislov et al. 2017). There were courting and subsequent buy-in of key stakeholders and opinion leaders at contrasting strategic and operational levels within the various professional associations and regulatory bodies. Many of the stakeholders and opinion leaders had come to adopt managerial/leadership roles within their respective colleges and organizations.

Material/Epistemic Conditions

The project and its participants adopted a "bottom-up" and pragmatic approach to the formulation of the competency framework, "sounding out" individuals and testing ideas. An example of such ideas is the iterative development of the competency framework, through the reference groups. Participants embraced a flexible and adaptive agenda, which was open to modification, aiming for a "compass point" rather than a fixed ideal; and educational materials on leadership and management skills and behaviours were developed from practice-based scenarios and were written by medical professionals.

A limitation of the study is that it did not sample doctors outside of this educational intervention, to sample broader trends in perceptions of role and identity, or patient or community representatives. These perspectives ought to be included in future research. Looking across the proposed conditions that shape perspectives on the relationship between professional and managerial identities, it appears that there is an important effect of generational shifts at the social and professional level. This shift demonstrates the dynamic interaction of history and biography, with junior doctors entering a fundamentally different world than had their senior peers a generation earlier. Junior doctors were working to reconcile the "received wisdom" of their profession with the "immediate struggles" they encounter in the contemporary organization of care. This suggests that Freidson's (1970, 2001) influential account of the effects of reform upon professional jurisdictional shifts requires some modification, because over time it appears that the maintenance of status and power comes at a gradual and accumulative cost to confidence and clarity over their identities. Exposure to explicit opportunities to reflect on roles and identities involves a process of adaptation and internalization through which conflicts become resolved in a manner that supports the further reformation of the profession through organizational values and role-based distinctions (cf. Waring 2007). Moreover, doctors working on the programme came to see their management and leadership knowledge and skills as an inherent part of their medical practice. Medical participants also perceived such a shift among doctors generally.

Role and identity shifts across role-based and organizational boundaries have potentially important implications for our understandings of professional enrolment and resistance. If we are moving beyond a conflicted hybridity in individuals and organizations, then such shifts in perception might represent a collective internalization of social and political discourses upon which more radical shifts could develop.

For individuals, the process of shifting identities and roles implies a kind of plateauing in what is commonly understood to be the ongoing "flux" of identity work (Clarke et al. 2009). Such flux could be seen as positive—the resolution of inner conflict caused by the narrowing of differing identities to more of a shared experience of identity. We may be seeing the start of a shared language for use when embarking upon change/improvement initiatives, and a firmer adoption of "leaderism" rather than "managerialism" (O'Reilly and Reed 2011). Collectively, the development of a shared language may help in "refreezing" professional identity, which is never a stable entity, but becomes more stabilized around such discourses of leadership. However, the need will arise to examine what newly stabilized "leaderist" identities mean for individuals in their day-to-day work, because work is shaped by professional/role identity. Such newly constituted professional work is itself likely to shift through learning, which is iterative and dependent on context as well as timing. This means that reform (such as implementing leadership/management into the medical curriculum) can introduce new language, which becomes embedded in shared identities and perceptions of role.

Beyond work and learning, change agency is challenging in strongly institutionalized environments (e.g. the medical profession). However, contradiction itself might be the key to such institutional reform (Seo and Creed 2002). Arguments about individual and collective conditions for change support the notion of a kind of embedded institutional entrepreneurship afforded to individuals with appropriate capital endowments. This may then alter the balance towards those stakeholders who imbue themselves with the notion of "leaderism".

References

Abbott, A. (1988). *The system of professions: An essay on the division of expert labor*. London: University of Chicago Press.

Academy of Medical Royal Colleges and NHS Institute for Innovation and Improvement. (2006, August 9). *Enhancing engagement in medical leadership—Project plan*.

Ackroyd, S. (1996). Organization contra organizations: Professions and organizational change in the United Kingdom. *Organization Studies, 17*(4), 599–621.

Allen, D. (1995). Doctors in management or the revenge of the conquered: The role of management development for doctors. *Journal of Management in Medicine, 9*, 44–50.

Barbour, R. (2008). *Introducing qualitative research: A student's guide to the craft of doing qualitative research.* London: Sage.

Battilana, J. (2011). The enabling role of social position in diverging from the institutional status quo: Evidence from the UK National Health Service. *Organization Science, 22*(4), 817–834.

Bishop, S., & Waring, J. (2016). Becoming hybrid: The negotiated order on the front line of public–private partnerships. *Human Relations, 69*(10), 1937–1958. https://doi.org/10.1177/0018726716630389.

Bourdieu, P. (1994). *Raisons pratiques. Sur la théorie de l'action.* Paris: Seuil.

Braverman, H. (1974). *Labor and monopoly capital: The degradation of work in the twentieth century.* New York: Monthly Review Press.

Bresnen, M., Hodgson, D., Bailey, S., Hyde, P., & Hassard, J. (2017). *Managing modern healthcare: Knowledge, networks, practice.* Abingdon: Routledge.

Bryman, A. (2008). *Social research methods* (3rd ed.). Oxford: Oxford University Press.

Carr-Saunders, A. M., & Wilson, P. A. (1933). *The professions* (1st ed.). Oxford: The Clarendon Press.

Clarke, C., Brown, A., & Hope Hailey, V. (2009). Working identities? Antagonistic discursive resources and managerial identity. *Human Relations, 62,* 323–352.

Currie, G. (2006). Reluctant but resourceful middle managers: The case of nurses in the NHS. *Journal of Nursing Management, 14,* 5–12.

Currie, G., Lockett, A., Finn, R., Martin, G., & Waring, J. (2012). Institutional work to maintain professional power: Recreating the model of medical professionalism. *Organization Studies, 33*(7), 937–962.

Degeling, P., Maxwell, S., Kennedy, J., & Coyle, B. (2003). Medicine, management, and modernisation: A "danse macabre"? *British Medical Journal, 326,* 649–652.

European Working Time Directive (European Commission). (2003). *Working conditions—Working time directive,* 2003/88/EC. Available from: http://ec.europa.eu/social/main.jsp?catId=706&langId=en&intPageId=205. Accessed 8 Jan 2016.

Evetts, J. (2005, October 19). *The management of professionalism: A contemporary paradox.* Paper presented at Changing teacher roles, identities and professionalism, King's College, London. Available from: www.tlrp.org/themes/seminar/gewirtz/papers/.../paper%20-%20evetts.doc. Accessed 15 Aug 2014.

Ferlie, E., Ashburner, L., Fitzgerald, L., & Pettigrew, A. (1996). *The new public management in action.* Oxford: Oxford University Press.

Flynn, N. (2007). *Public sector management.* London: Sage.

Frank, J. R. (2005). *The CanMEDS 2005 physician competency framework*. Ontario: The Royal College of Physicians and Surgeons of Canada.

Freidson, E. (1970). *Professional dominance: The social structure of medical care*. Chicago: Aldine.

Freidson, E. (1984). The changing nature of professional control. *Annual Review of Sociology, 10*, 1–20.

Freidson, E. (1986). *Professional powers: A study of the institutionalization of formal knowledge*. Chicago: University of Chicago Press.

Freidson, E. (2001). *Professionalism: The third logic*. Cambridge: Polity Press.

General Medical Council. (2006a [2013], March). *Good medical practice: guidance for doctors*. London: General Medical Council. Available from: https://www.gmc-uk.org/ethical-guidance/ethical-guidance-for-doctors/good-medical-practice. Accessed 2 Oct 2018.

General Medical Council. (2006b). *Management for doctors*. London: General Medical Council.

General Medical Council. (2009). *Tomorrow's doctors*. London: General Medical Council.

General Medical Council. (2018). *Outcomes for graduates*. Available from: https://www.gmc-uk.org/education/standards-guidance-and-curricula/standards-and-outcomes/outcomes-for-graduates. Accessed 2 Oct 2018.

Goode, W. J. (1957). Community within a community: The Professions. *American Sociological Review, 22*, 194–200.

Hanlon, G. (1998). Professionalism as enterprise: Service class politics and the redefinition of professionalism. *Sociology, 32*(1), 43–63.

Harrison, S., Hunter, D. J., Marnoch, G., & Pollitt, C. (1992). *Just managing: Power and culture in the National Health Service*. London: Macmillan International Higher Education.

Hartley, J. (2004). Case study research. In C. Cassell & G. Symon (Eds.), *Essential guide to qualitative methods in organizational research* (pp. 323–333). London: Sage.

Hoggett, P. (1996). New modes of control in the public service. *Public Administration, 74*, 9–32.

Hood, C. (1991). A public management for all seasons. *Public Administration, 69*, 3–19.

Iedema, R., Degeling, P., Braithwaite, J., & White, L. (2004). "It's an interesting conversation I'm hearing": The doctor as manager. *Organization Studies, 25*(1), 15–33.

Jun, J. S. (2009). The limits of post-new public management and beyond. *Public Administration Review, 69*(1), 161–165.

Kennedy, I. (2001). *Learning from Bristol: The report of the public inquiry into children's heart surgery at the Bristol Royal Infirmary 1984–1995*. CM 5207, Final Report: The Inquiry into the management of care of children receiving complex heart surgery at the Bristol Royal Infirmary.

Kislov, R., Hyde, P., & McDonald, R. (2017). New game, old rules? Mechanisms and consequences of legitimation in boundary spanning activities. *Organization Studies, 38*, 1421–1444.

Larson, M. S. (1977). *The rise of professionalism: A sociological analysis*. Berkeley, CA: University of California Press.

Layder, D. (1998). *Sociological practice: Linking theory and social research*. London: Sage.

Leicht, K. T., & Fennell, M. L. (2001). *Professional work: A sociological approach*. Oxford: Blackwell.

Levenson, R., Dewar, S., & Shepherd, S. (2008). *Understanding doctors: Harnessing professionalism*. London: King's Fund and Royal College of Physicians.

Lincoln, Y. S., & Guba, E. G. (1985). *Naturalistic inquiry*. London: Sage.

Lofland, J., Snow, D., Anderson, L., & Lofland, L. H. (2006). *Analyzing social settings: A guide to qualitative observation and analysis*. Belmont, CA: Wadsworth/Thomson Learning.

Marnoch, G. (1996). *Doctors and management in the NHS*. Maidenhead: Open University Press.

Martin, G. P., Armstrong, N., Aveling, E.-L., Herbert, G., & Dixon-Woods, M. (2015). Professionalism redundant, reshaped or reinvigorated? Realizing the "third logic" in contemporary health care. *Journal of Health and Social Behaviour, 56*(3), 378–397.

Martin, G. P., & Finn, R. (2011). Patients as team members: Opportunities, challenges and paradoxes of including patients in multi-professional health-care teams. *Sociology of Health & Illness, 33*(7), 1050–1065.

Martin, G. P., Weaver, S., Currie, G., Finn, R., & Mcdonald, R. (2012). Innovation sustainability in challenging health-care contexts: Embedding clinically led change in routine practice. *Health Services Management Research, 25*, 190–199.

McGivern, G., Currie, G., Ferlie, E., Fitzgerald, L., & Waring, J. (2015). Hybrid manager-professionals' identity work: The maintenance and hybridization of medical professionalism in managerial contexts. *Public Administration, 93*(2), 412–432.

Millerson, G. (1964). *The qualifying associations: A study in professionalization*. London: Routledge & Kegan Paul.

MMC Inquiry. (2008). *Aspiring to excellence: Final report of the independent inquiry into modernising medical careers* (Tooke Report). London: Universities UK.

Muzio, D., Brock, D. M., & Suddaby, R. (2013). Professions and institutional change: Towards an institutionalist sociology of the professions. *Journal of Management Studies, 50*(5), 699–721.

Muzio, D., & Kirkpatrick, I. (2011). Introduction: Professions and organizations—A conceptual framework. *Current Sociology, 59*(4), 389–405.

National Health Service and Community Care Act. (1990). Available from: http://www.legislation.gov.uk/ukpga/1990/19/contents. Accessed 29 Mar 2016.

NHS Institute for Innovation and Improvement and Academy of Medical Royal Colleges. (2010). *Medical Leadership Competency Framework: Enhancing engagement in medical leadership* (3rd ed.). Retrieved from: https://www.leadershipacademy.nhs.uk/wp-content/uploads/2012/11/NHSLeadership-Leadership-Framework-Medical-Leadership-Competency-Framework-3rd-ed.pdf.

Noordegraaf, M. (2011). Risky business: How professionals and professional fields (must) deal with organizational issues. *Organization Studies, 32*(10), 1349–1371.

O'Reilly, D., & Reed, M. (2011). The grit in the oyster: Professionalism, managerialism and leaderism as discourses of UK public services modernization. *Organization Studies, 32,* 1079–1101.

Parsons, T. (1951). *The social system.* London: Tavistock.

QSR International Pty Ltd. (2012). *NVivo qualitative data analysis software: Version 10.* Burlington, MA: QSR International Pty Ltd.

Reed, M. I. (1996). Expert power and control in late modernity: An empirical review and theoretical synthesis. *Organization Studies, 17*(4), 573–597.

Royal College of Physicians. (2005, December). *Doctors in society: Medical professionalism in a changing world.* Report of a Working Party. London: RCP.

Royal Liverpool Children's Inquiry (Redfern Report). (2001). Summary and Recommendations. London: TSO. Available from: https://www.gov.uk/government/uploads/system/uploads/attachment_data/file/250914/0012_i.pdf. Accessed 4 Feb 2015.

Schinkel, W., & Noordegraaf, M. (2011). Professionalism as symbolic capital: Materials for a Bourdieusian theory of professionalism. *Comparative Sociology, 10,* 67–96.

Scott, W. R. (2014). *Institutions and organizations: Ideas, interests, and identities.* Thousand Oaks, CA: Sage.

Secretary of State for Health. (2008, June). *High quality care for all: NHS next stage review final report* (Department of Health/Darzi Report), CM 7432. TSO: Norwich.

Seo, M.-G., & Creed, W. D. (2002). Institutional contradictions, praxis, and institutional change: A dialectical perspective. *Academy of Management Review, 27*(2), 222–247.

Shipman Inquiry. (2002, July). *Shipman: The first report: Volume 1: Death disguised.* Manchester: COI Communications.

Strauss, A. L. (1987). *Qualitative analysis for social scientists.* New York, NY, US: Cambridge University Press.

Suchman, M. C. (1995). Managing legitimacy: Strategic and institutional approaches. *Academy of Management Review, 20*, 571–610.

Suddaby, R. (2010). Challenges for institutional theory. *Journal of Management Inquiry, 19*(1), 14–20.

Taylor, C., & Gibbs, G. R. (2010). What is qualitative data analysis (QDA)? *Online QDA Web Site.* Available from: http://onlineqda.hud.ac.uk/Intro_QDA/what_is_qda.php. Accessed 22 Oct 2018.

Waring, J. (2007). Adaptive regulation or governmentality: Patient safety and the changing regulation of medicine. *Sociology of Health & Illness, 29*(2), 163–179. https://doi.org/10.1111/j.1467-9566.2007.00527.x.

Waring, J., & Currie, G. (2009). Managing expert knowledge: Organizational challenges and managerial futures for the UK medical profession. *Organization Studies, 30*(7), 755–778.

Watson, T. J. (2008). Managing identity: Identity work, personal predicaments and structural circumstances. *Organization, 15*(1), 121–143.

Willcocks, S. (1998). The development of clinical management at an NHS Trust hospital: A case study example. *Journal of Management in Medicine, 12*, 168–177.

Yin, R. K. (2014). *Case study research design and methods* (5th ed.). Thousand Oaks, CA: Sage.

Part III

Leadership as Boundary-Spanning Between Strategy, Identity, Knowledge and Change

Part III draws together conceptual and applied dimensions of boundary work, with chapters that collectively deal with the impact of identity and learning on intentional strategy and change in health services and systems. The opening chapter by Gutberg and colleagues, from Canada, posits middle managers as central players in strategic processes, who are nonetheless bound or enabled by system-level structures and processes. Liz Wiggins, based on research in the National Health Service of the UK, applies an action research methodology to explain how the notion of "tempered tenacity" enables leadership and resilience in health services. In a comparative study across Sweden, Canada, Australia and the UK, Kislov and colleagues then demonstrate the association between types of knowledge and evidence that are regarded as legitimate with prospects for health system and service reform. Finally, Lennox and colleagues, from the UK, show how overt mechanisms and "tools" can explicitly direct attention to particular priorities and thereby foster sustainability of reforms.

9

Scoping the Contribution of Middle Managers to the Strategic Change Process in Healthcare Organizations

Jennifer Gutberg, Whitney Berta, Tyrone A. Perreira and G. Ross Baker

Introduction

Research on both implementation and change management literatures endorses the centrality of leadership at all organizational levels to facilitate meaningful change (McKnight 2013; Nadler and Tushman 1990). While the need for senior leadership and a strong vision when creating

J. Gutberg (✉) · W. Berta · T. A. Perreira · G. R. Baker
Institute of Health Policy, Management and Evaluation,
University of Toronto, Toronto, ON, Canada
e-mail: jennifer.gutberg@mail.utoronto.ca

W. Berta
e-mail: whit.berta@utoronto.ca

T. A. Perreira
e-mail: ty.perreira@utoronto.ca

G. R. Baker
e-mail: ross.baker@utoronto.ca

© The Author(s) 2020
P. Nugus et al. (eds.), *Transitions and Boundaries in the Coordination and Reform of Health Services*, Organizational Behaviour in Healthcare,
https://doi.org/10.1007/978-3-030-26684-4_9

change has been well established, the persistent challenge of sustaining strategic change initiatives (Harvey et al. 2014; Narine and Persaud 2003; Wachter 2010) suggests that senior leadership may be a necessary but insufficient condition to enact and sustain organizational change (Gutberg and Berta 2017). This view is supported by literature that has found that failed organizational strategic efforts (e.g., quality improvement, patient safety) (Wachter 2010) arise from frequent and sometimes insurmountable resistance, and a lack of engagement from frontline clinicians. These findings underscore that traditional leadership roles are in fact insufficient to enact meaningful change (Harvey et al. 2014; Narine and Persaud 2003).

Recently, the importance of leadership at the level of middle management (MM) in strategic change initiatives has been highlighted in the change management literature (Balogun 2003; Floyd and Wooldridge 1997; Pappas and Wooldridge 2007; Wooldridge et al. 2008). Engagement of middle managers has been linked to success of strategic initiatives aimed at large-scale change, and in further sustaining these changes long-term (Willis et al. 2016). However, the strategic role of MM has been given less attention in the healthcare literature, with most work focused on MM's role in implementation (Birken et al. 2012; Muller et al. 2011). This chapter aims to better understand current evidence regarding MM's contribution to change strategy in the healthcare context, particularly exploring how MM have been involved in the full spectrum of the strategic change process, from formulation through to implementation and sustainability.

Though a more substantial body of research has already been established on MM in the strategic change process in sectors outside of health care (Wooldridge et al. 2008), far less research exists on this group's relevance in healthcare contexts. This distinction is significant as MM in healthcare organizations, and large centralized hospitals in particular, often have to work within highly hierarchical structures siloed by professional group (e.g., doctors, nurses, allied health professionals). Moreover, given the increased focus in health care on team- and clinical microsystem-level functioning, leadership is becoming increasingly distributed across the organization (Denis et al. 2012). Thus, by necessity, MM will need to play an increasingly significant role in organizational functioning.

Objectives

Following the work of Arksey and O'Malley, this chapter presents a scoping review designed to map out and synthesize the existing literature on the contribution and involvement of MM in the strategic change processes of healthcare organizations (Arksey and O'Malley 2005). A scoping review was determined as the most appropriate review type not only for its ability to synthesize information, but also because of the heterogeneous nature of the literature surrounding MM (discussed in detail in the Methods section). In the light of these aims, the review is framed by the following research question: What is the contribution of middle managers to the strategic change processes of healthcare organizations?

Understanding How Middle Managers Contribute to Strategic Change Processes

Search Strategy

Comprehensive literature searches were conducted in Ovid (MEDLINE and Healthstar, ultimately yielding identical results), CINAHL, ABI/Inform (ProQuest), and Business Source Premier (EBSCOhost). The grey literature was searched and reference lists of included studies were scanned. All searches were conducted on 15 December 2017, and the search strategy, including selection of databases and specific search terms, was developed in consultation with an expert librarian (VL).

Parameters of Search

The searches used a combination of medical subject headings (MeSH) as well as free text terms. Search terms included in all databases were as follows: strategy; management; mid-manager/mid-management; hospital; healthcare facility; organizational change. Variations on the following terms related to strategic management (where "strategy" is adjacent within two words) were also included: planning; development process; formulation; implementation; execution; delivery; change. Database searches were limited to English language results and were further limited to full-text scholarly/peer-reviewed articles. Within these peer-reviewed articles, all study types including empirical (quantitative, qualitative, or mixed method), theoretical, and review articles were included. There was no conceptual justification to limit the date of the results so all results meeting the aforementioned criteria were included regardless of date of publication.

Inclusion and Exclusion Criteria

Beyond the limitations listed above regarding pre-screening removal of abstracts, the following criteria for inclusion and exclusion were used to screen abstracts:

Inclusion Criteria:

- Empirical or theoretical article [any study type]
- Setting: Health service organizations
- In particular, specific to healthcare/health service organizations providing *direct patient care*
- Participants: Specific reference to mid-level managers*
- Context/Intervention: Study relates to strategic change processes (e.g., strategy development/strategic planning, implementation of strategic intervention, etc.)
- Must, therefore, reference strategic or organizational change.

Exclusion Criteria:

- Setting: Sectors other than healthcare, or health-related organizations not providing direct patient care excluded (e.g., pharmaceutical companies, medical R&D companies, medical device and technology organizations)
- Participants: Articles referring to "management" or "leadership" broadly, not distinguishing between levels of management

- Context/Intervention: Articles that discuss mid-level managers roles, behaviours, or perceptions with no explicit link to organizational strategy or strategic activities
- Non-English language articles
- Non-peer-reviewed/scholarly journal articles.

Screening for "Mid-level Managers"

As indicated above, mid-level managers were screened. Limiting the search to this population was an important and expected challenge in screening abstracts. Indeed, one of the driving motivations for conducting this review was the lack of empirical definition and clarity surrounding who precisely is a "middle manager". The literature was highly inconsistent in its identification of and reference to this group and as a result, some flexibility had to be employed in enforcing this criterion. For the abstract screening process, articles that referenced "middle" or "mid-level" managers were easily identified for inclusion, but those that referenced "multi-level management/leadership" were also included in the hope that the findings section of the full-text would distinguish between these groups. When in doubt as to whether the title and abstract would otherwise warrant inclusion, a very brief scan of the full-text was undertaken to determine whether the article warranted inclusion for more detailed review. Lastly, the literature had no consensus on who encompasses the "middle" layer of management and how many layers of supervision above or below this level are required to meet these criteria. As a result, any reference to managers that were neither senior leadership nor frontline employees was considered appropriate.

Outcome of Search

The vast majority of results were found in the ABI/Inform database (1983 results), with remaining databases yielding fewer results (CINAHL = 4 results; Ovid = 2 results; Business Source Premier = 4 results), for a total of 1993 results. Six duplications were found and removed, resulting in a total of 1987 abstracts to be screened. As is demonstrated in Appendix A,

1907 abstracts were removed; six were removed due to not being schol-arly/peer-reviewed articles, and eight were removed for being non-English articles. The remainder either did not meet inclusion criteria or were not relevant to, or did not address the primary research question. The search resulted in 80 articles included for full-text screening. All abstracts were screened by one reviewer (JG); though this may enter the possibility of bias into the search, it is not an uncommon approach to screening for scoping reviews (Pham et al. 2014). Given the subject matter expertise of the reviewer and the consistent approach to the search, it is a reasona-ble methodological decision to conduct the screening (and charting) pro-cesses single-handedly.

Data Charting

Prior to charting data from the full-text review, a preliminary screen of the full-text results was conducted. Criteria for final inclusion were the same as for abstract inclusion. However, at this stage, MM had to reflect a meaningful component of and relevance to the article, in particular for studies captured that reflected the broad process of strategy imple-mentation, where "the support of managers" is listed as an enabling factor without further context. From this screening of the 80 articles initially included, 20 were removed; one was identified as a duplicate (both duplicate abstracts were included; however, one was labelled with anonymous authorship, explaining how it was not filtered out earlier); and three others were removed, because they could not be accessed through university nor affiliate library access. The remaining articles were removed due to lack of fit with initial inclusion/exclusion criteria regarding the identification of mid-level managers. Such abstracts were often vague in identifying participants or the population of interest. Some of these remaining articles were also removed because of insignifi-cant focus of article on the relevant topic. Sixty articles from the screen-ing, plus one article known from the first author's prior work ($n = 61$), were ultimately included as the final set for data charting.

We did not intend to assess quality of included studies. Many arti-cles that met inclusion criteria (e.g., focus on strategic change process and specific reference to mid-level managers) were focused on the effectiveness, or implementation success, of a given strategy, which alluded to the involvement of MM, without explicating their role. Because the guiding research question concerns understanding the specific contributions of MM to strategy, a formal assessment of the outcomes of each study is beyond the scope of this review (Arksey and O'Malley 2005).

The Engagement of Middle Managers in Strategic Change Processes

The results of the scoping review are synthesized below, first examining study characteristics, and then through themes generated from a qualitative descriptive thematic analysis of results.

Study Characteristics

Articles were published between 1987 and 2017, which aligns with the emergence of seminal strategy articles 10 or so years prior to this time (Miles et al. 1978; Mintzberg and Waters 1985; Porter 1991; Wernerfelt 1984). Table 9.1 reflects the remaining characteristics that were charted from the full-text readings (see Appendix B).

Before addressing the thematic findings, this section will concentrate on defining the group of "middle managers" captured in this review. As the heterogeneity of this group was highlighted in the search strategy above, it is helpful to frame the context of the analytical results with this understanding at the outset.

Defining the Population

As discussed above, there is a significant gap in the literature regarding the identification of MM. The following quotation appropriately captures the challenge in defining the group:

Middle managers are more difficult to distinguish, as the boundaries between levels of hierarchy are often blurred. The exercise is further complicated in organisations with organic structures where demarcation may be ambiguous. As a result few writers have attempted to define the role. Middle line management is often described in terms of what it is not. (McConville 2006, p. 639)

Furthermore, these authors also go on to provide a more damning definition of MM, as a place *"where nobody really wants to be (Dopson et al. 1992), being either a staging post on the road from supervisor to executive or an equally undesirable cul-de-sac for those whose careers will progress no further"* (McConville 2006). In spite of this apparently negative perspective, the definitional and negatively judgmental challenges are very much accounted for in both the design of this scoping review as well as the results. Indeed, this review took an extremely broad definition of MM, i.e., as long as they do not represent frontline employees, nor the senior *organizational* leadership. Examples in this review range from undefined middle managers (Applebaum and Wohl 2000; Junior et al. 2012; Kreindler et al. 2014; O'Shannassy 2014; Woollard et al. 2003), to "unit-level" managers (Chaston 1994; Dainty and Sinclair 2017; Dannapfel et al. 2014), to clinical directors (Corbridge 1995; Van der Wees et al. 2014), as well as idiosyncratically defined middle managers, i.e., where the authors intentionally set bounded criteria, possibly guided by the organization(s) in question being studied (McConville 2006; Pappas and Wooldridge 2007).

Thematic Analysis

Results were categorized by themes articulated as the three key questions that the studies addressed:

- *What are the Critical Activities that MM Engage in Throughout the Strategic Change Process?*
- *What are MM's Needed Skills and Capabilities to Influence the Strategic Change Process in Healthcare Organizations?*

- *What are the Contextual Barriers and Facilitators related to MM and Strategic Change?*

Each of these questions addresses a discrete component of the guiding research question, capturing differing important elements of the contribution of MM.

What are the Critical Activities that MM Engage in Throughout the Strategic Change Process?

Two sub-themes emerged related to this area: communication to senior management above and to supervised employees below; and MM as the "doers" of strategy.

Communication was one of the most frequently reported activities related to the strategic role of MM. It is important to note that communication as an activity can be considered an overarching behaviour across multiple themes identified in this review. However, in this context, communication is used to specifically refer to the "communicator" *role*, which demonstrates how different communication strategies for different targets affect the strategic change process (Woollard et al. 2003). In this vein, two sub-themes of communication are emphasized: downward and upward communication.

Downward Communication

This refers to the tactics employed by MM to disseminate messages to employees around organizational strategy, interventions, implementation activities, etc. These communication tactics drive implementation of strategic interventions forward by clarifying expectations around performance and providing timely feedback on performance (Broad 2006). Such timely feedback allows for continued adaptation of employees' responses to the intervention. Birken et al. (2012) devised a theoretical model of the role of MM in the implementation of innovations related to evidence-based care. Although the authors focus on broad activities that MMs engage into advance innovation implementations, the model addresses a number of elements that directly relate to communication, including diffusing and synthesizing information, and selling the innovation implementation. These behaviours point to an important role for MM in facilitating innovation (and, if considered more broadly, perhaps strategic) implementation.

Downward communication is also central to managing relationships with subordinates in order to develop open working environments and strong interpersonal relationships with employees (Shanley 2007). Such strong interpersonal relationships can be useful in facilitating the acceptance of new strategic interventions and ultimately reducing employee uncertainty, the latter of which has been identified as a factor impacting the success of organizational change (Bordia et al. 2004; Herzig and Jimmieson 2006).

Upward Communication

This relates to the strategic communication employed by MM both to generate information to and receive information from senior leadership. Both upward and downward communications share a fundamental tenet, whereby MM have to "sell" their ideas (Currie 2006; O'Shannassy 2014). Specifically, MM need to sell such strategic ideas, both for the benefit of the organization and the benefit of their own career advancement; senior managers reported the importance of MM selling issues for personal recognition and to gain trust from senior leadership. Sharing of ideas with senior management also reflects middle managers' own filtering of ideas and insights from the frontline to organizational leadership.

Though these findings address the beneficial outcomes of effective communication, they also highlight detrimental outcomes. Where MM are ineffective communicators, the strategic process encounters significant barriers. One study focused on how high-performance management strategies might increase operational and service efficiency in ambulance services (Woollard et al. 2003). MM were considered the main barrier to change because they were the least well informed of all staff on matters relating to performance management, owing to their ineffective and "manipulative" communication with staff. Similar results were found in a

Swedish hospital study of first-line managers' "communicative actions", where more controlling communicative actions reduced dialogue and resulted in a "dismissive and evasive" atmosphere (Grill et al. 2011).

MM as the "Doers" of Strategy: This section refers to the activities typically expected of MM, which ultimately contribute to a strategy's successful implementation. That is, beyond simply *communicating* strategy up and down in their organizations, MM must also engage in the "hands-on" processes that facilitate strategic implementation. These activities include coordinating and delegating employee tasks (Juan-Gabriel and Cepeda-Carrión 2010), analyzing strategic issues using data such as performance indicators (O'Shannassy 2014), defining activities or roles of subordinates (Belasen et al. 2016). Quite simply, such actions refer to the operational, day-to-day tactics that must take place within MM's jurisdiction in order for strategy to become realized and embedded in operational processes. Another important component of "doing" strategy is following through on it, whereby the initiative, its implementation, and its performance indicators are all appraised and adapted as needed (Fleiszer et al. 2015; Junior et al. 2012). For example, a study regarding the long-term sustainability of a programme for nursing best practice guidelines identified a number of key factors to sustainability, one of which was the process-related factor they coined the "reflection-and-course-correction" strategy (Fleiszer et al. 2015). Supported by complementary leadership working in conjunction across all levels of the department, the "reflect-and-course-correct" approach entails "*iterations over time of leaders' deliberate efforts to learn from program experiences and, in response, to try to implement continued improvements to the program*" (Fleiszer et al. 2015).

What are MM's Needed Skills and Capabilities to Influence the Strategic Change Process in Healthcare Organizations?

The following sub-themes are presented: commitment to the strategic initiative, alignment of MM with organizational strategy, and skill-building capacity.

Commitment to the strategic initiative was one of the most frequently re-occurring concepts to emerge in the literature (Ayton et al. 2017;

Fleiszer et al. 2015; Lifvergren et al. 2010; Shanley 2007; Van der Wees et al. 2014; Zhang et al. 2012). Although "commitment" to an initiative could be considered more as an attitude or emotion than a behaviour, the implication from the literature is that commitment manifests in managerial behaviour. Not only do MM need to internalize commitment for the change, but their commitment should also be reflected in creating meaningful and tangible opportunities for staff to engage with the change (Ayton et al. 2017). Specifically, MM have an opportunity to demonstrate their commitment to the initiative by providing resources for employees to feasibly accomplish strategy implementation activities, including via training opportunities, and protecting staff time for the strategic initiative (Ayton et al. 2017; Van der Wees et al. 2014). An example of this can be found in the 2010 realist evaluation of a "high commitment management" strategy implemented in an urban hospital in Ghana, which found impacts of high commitment on hospital performance and employee empowerment and engagement (Marchal et al. 2010).

A related component of commitment is the *alignment of MM with the organizational strategy*. With regard to aligning the organization and employees to the strategic vision, Zhang notes:

> One of the reasons that most companies fail to implement their strategy is the insufficient involvement of the people who actually implement the strategy… As corporate staff begins to deploy initiatives to deliver strategic objectives, midlevel managers might disparage those initiatives. (Zhang et al. 2012)

Zhang's quote reflects what might be considered a Catch-22 for MM: on the one hand, they are expected to align themselves with the organizational strategy, but on the other, when senior leadership fails to foster commitment, MM are unable to understand what it is they are aligning themselves with.

Skill-Building Capacity

A consistent gap reported in the literature is MM's limited efficacy in change management, created by inadequate training and formal learning opportunities (Buchanan et al. 1999; Dainty and Sinclair 2017;

Dannapfel et al. 2014; Liang et al. 2012; Mosadeghrad 2013a; Shanley 2007). One qualitative study found that there was no formal experience required to move into the MM role; rather, there existed an expectation of "on-the-job" learning (Shanley 2007). This led to MM feeling unprepared and lacking external support to succeed in their roles. Moreover, a mixed methods study published in 2012, investigating the required competencies of MM in Australia, identified that one of the six core competencies, "leading and managing change", was almost never listed in an analysis of formal position descriptions (Liang et al. 2012). Relatedly, Buchanan and colleagues found that change management skills were sorely lacking in MM (1999), both in terms of standard capabilities, such as relationship management and political skill, as well as skills required for managing complexity (Applebaum and Wohl 2000; McDaniel 2007).

What are the Contextual Barriers and Facilitators related to MM and Strategic Change?

Two sub-themes emerged relating to the contextual barriers and facilitators that affect MM's ability to engage in the strategic change process: being *stuck in the middle*, and *empowerment* from senior leadership.

Being stuck in the middle (the "Panini Press" effect): Though MM have been described as having a "semi-autonomous" role (Currie 2006), they ultimately remain at the mercy of their context—namely, being stuck between the constraints of senior management and the needs of employees (Eicher 2006). The following two quotes, captured by two separate qualitative studies, reflect the perceptions around MM:

> [The middle] manager's role was like the Panini effect ... like a hot press, and both sides... are pressing at the same time ... I think they get a little "squished." (Dainty and Sinclair 2017)

> If anyone is the jam in the sandwich, it is [MM]. (Currie 1999)

Examples of similar tensions experienced by MM in this review abounded. A case study of three UK health authorities found that MM were forced to deal with simultaneous competing priorities in a limited time span from senior leadership, who, because of requirements for extra funding, was in a perennial state of applying to, and therefore, needing to carry out, new pilot projects (Marshall 1999). Another example is the added resource constraints within which MM must operate (Forbes and Prime 1999; Junior et al. 2012; McConville 2006). In such cases, MM perceived that senior leadership had ultimate control over resources, which limited their capacity to incentivize employees with financial or other gains. From the employee side, MM also had to balance focus between their own strategic interests (or those of their superiors) and urgent issues of employees (McConville 2006).

Sometimes MM were left to implement what they perceive to be illogical strategies because senior leadership did not effectively communicate the strategy (Herzig and Jimmieson 2006; Mosadeghrad 2013a; Zhang et al. 2012). If strategy was not communicated correctly from "up high", as a result of uncertainty around the project, MM in turn became less effective in managing employees' uncertainty, which negatively impacted the implementation process and effectiveness (Dannapfel et al. 2014). In contrast, one case study of the creation and dissemination of a quality improvement strategy found that involvement of all levels of management in the entire process resulted in a successful strategy implementation with support for the initiative across the entire organization (Telford et al. 1992).

Empowerment

These findings emphasize numerous instances where MM do not have perceived or actual control over their environment and were therefore unable to autonomously perform their roles. This suggests that it is important to consider the role of empowerment, which factored prominently in a number of studies reported here (Trebble et al. 2014). Interestingly, the vast majority of articles—with exceptions (Marchal et al. 2010)—referenced empowerment in a context where it was noticeably absent (Hancock et al. 2005). For example, one case study of a UK NHS Healthcare Trust found severe discrepancies between senior and mid-level managers' perceptions of MM empowerment (Procter et al. 1999). In spite of a strategic initiative aimed at embedding greater empowerment into the organizational structure, MM continued to feel "disempowered" by senior leadership's constraints and competing priorities. This article and others with similar results (Hancock et al. 2005) highlight a broader finding of the review: too much centrality of decision-making and failure to communicate the entire strategic change process tended to result in disempowered employees and managers (Mosadeghrad 2013b; Parkes et al. 2007).

Current and Future Contributions of Middle Managers to Strategic Change Processes

This review synthesizes the existing literature on MM and their current—and potential—contributions to the strategic change process in healthcare organizations. The results demonstrate that MM are often able to meaningfully influence the strategic change process, from planning through implementation and, particularly, longevity. Strategic communication activities directed to senior leadership and frontline staff, as well as effective execution and implementation, are key areas where MM can influence the strategic change process. As well, MM have an important role in evaluating or sustaining strategic change for example through "reflect and course correct" processes, which have been linked to improve sustainment of strategy implementation.

Furthermore, the results suggest the importance of context, and of understanding the environments in which MM operate. These contextual barriers and facilitators can be directly linked to the critical activities in which MM must engage to ensure effective strategy formulation, implementation and longevity. MM need to engage in activities of selling up, offering competing suggestions and doing boundary-spanning work; but these behaviours would only be feasible in a context where senior leadership enables MM to act. Among the contextual factors identified, the core contextual aspect appears to be centralization, where high centrality of decision-making and a failure to communicate the entire strategic change process can result in disempowered employees and managers (Mosadeghrad 2013b; Parkes et al. 2007). Thus, organizational change efforts—and, indeed, organizational structures in and of themselves—may benefit from leveraging shared and distributed approaches to leadership in order to enact strategic change effectively. These leadership approaches posit that informal leaders are critical to the functioning of complex organizations and systems and consider leadership as an interactive adaptive process, often emergent in nature (Bolden 2011; Gronn 2002; Uhl-Bien et al. 2007). Such leadership operates through dynamic interactions, exists multiple organizational levels and appears as a shared process (McKee et al. 2013; Northouse 2015). The structures and processes of distributed leadership offer a valuable framework for the activities of MM and their roles in the strategic process, given that distributed leadership is predicated on leadership practice within the existing and embedded context (Spillane et al. 2004). For middle managers, enacting change requires balancing and responding to the inherent tensions involved in responding to a strategic change initiative from senior leadership, while simultaneously trying to empower frontline staff to take ownership of the strategic initiative.

MM also have the opportunity to contribute to strategic planning through offering alternative models, theories or information to senior leadership based on their local, contextual knowledge. However, MM require the necessary conditions to meaningfully contribute or they may become barriers to the strategic change process. Senior leadership should actively involve MM as early in the planning process as feasible to engender the required commitment and alignment between the organizational vision and frontline context and practices. Early communication also allows managers more time to disseminate the strategic change messages to employees and facilitate the necessary internal learning and sense-making processes; or, as described by McDaniel (2007), the role of managers becomes "shift[ing] from controlling what is going on to making sense of a world characterized by an unpredictable dynamic" (p. 37).

Moreover, where senior management retains excessive levels of control, MM do not have the opportunity to feel empowered, nor engage in entrepreneurial boundary-spanning activities. Lastly, in order to be truly effective, MM require both formal training at the outset of their jobs, particularly in change management skills, as well as a clearer understanding of the strategic implications of their role so that change management work is not considered "out of scope".

Limitations

As previously addressed, the search strategy for this scoping review was undertaken by one author (JG), which may have implications on the assessment of fit with the included, and excluded, articles and the application of the criteria, as well as broader generalizations. Moreover, given that the review amalgamates various levels of MM into a collective whole, the results do not speak to differences among types of managers, where it might be expected that differences would exist between administrative versus clinician managers, and within that, among physicians, nurses, and other health professionals. As well, for feasibility purposes, this review intentionally limited the inclusion of related categories of strategic "players", such as change agents and clinician champions, who are known to be significant contributors to organizational strategy. It is likely that MM would either interact or perhaps overlap with these roles; understanding the synergies between them would be important for future research.

Conclusion

Ultimately, these results point to a meaningful contribution of MM to the strategic process; however, such a contribution requires support and commitment on the part of organizational leaders to facilitate the development of this role. Indeed, many of the referenced articles identified the need to foster empowerment, commitment and autonomy in MM. From a practical perspective, it appears that we know what needs to be done even if the resources or will of organizational leaders do not allow for it at the moment. Researchers should look to better understand and empirically assess how the involvement of MM in strategic activities tangibly impacts organizational performance. Given the shift in thinking around leadership, these models of disempowered managers are likely to be unsustainable in health care. That is, with the popularization of concepts such as distributed leadership (Denis et al. 2012), complex adaptive systems (Junior et al. 2012; McDaniel 2007), and increasing breakdowns of functional silos and formal layers of responsibility (Buchanan et al. 1999; McKee et al. 2013; Trastek et al. 2014), the value of MM in a broader role is only likely to expand, if only we empower them to communicate up and down, and to enact strategic change initiatives accordingly.

Appendix A: PRISMA Flow Chart

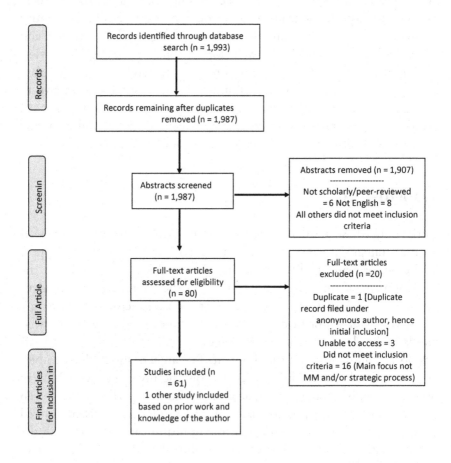

Appendix B: Table 9.1. Study Characteristics

Table 9.1 Study characteristics of included articles (alphabetical by first author)

Authors	Year	Setting	Methodology
Abernethy MA, Lillis AM	2001	Public Hospital	Quantitative
Applebaum SH, Wohl L	2000	Theoretical	Mixed methods
Ayton DR, Barker AL, Morello RT, et al.	2017	Hospitals (6 hospitals participating in a cluster randomized controlled trial)	Qualitative
Beech N	2000	3 cases, one healthcare organization not specific [others non-health sector]	Quantitative
Belasen A, Belasen AR	2016	Theoretical	Quantitative
Birken SA, Lee S-YD, Weiner BJ	2012	Theoretical	
Broad ML	2006	Theoretical	
Buchanan D, Claydon T, Doyle M	1999	Organization development and change forum	Qualitative
Chaston I	1994	NHS Trust	
Corbridge C	1995	Theoretical	Qualitative
Currie G, Procter S	2001	NHS hospital trust	Qualitative
Currie G	2006	Theoretical	Qualitative
Currie G	1999	NHS hospital trust	Qualitative
Dainty KN, Sinclair D	2017	Large, urban, academic health sciences centre	Qualitative
Dannapfel P, Poksinska B, Thomas K	2014	3 cases: county council, National Health Service Institute for Innovation (NHSI), Odense University Hospital	Qualitative
Dent M	2003	UK NHS	Mixed methods
Eicher JP	2006	Theoretical	Qualitative
Eriksson A, Holden RJ, Williamsson A, Dellve L	2016	Hospital	
Fleiszer AR, Semenic SE, Ritchie JA, Richer M-C, Jean-Louis D	2015	Large, urban, multisite acute care centre	Qualitative
Forbes T, Prime N	1999	Multiple hospital settings in NHS	

(continued)

Table 9.1 (continued)

Authors	Year	Setting	Methodology
Grill C, Ahlborg G, Lindgren EC	2011	Hospitals	Qualitative
Ham C	2003	Theoretical	
Hancock H, Campbell S, Bignell P, Kilgour J	2005	NHS Trust	Qualitative
Harris D, Hillier LM, Keat N	2007	Comprehensive Advanced Palliative Care Education (CAPCE) (Educational intervention)	Mixed methods
Herzig SE, Jimmieson NL	2006	Organizations that had recently undergone a significant change event	Qualitative
Hovlid E, Bukve O, Haug K, Aslaksen AB, von Plessen C	2012	District general hospital	[Not specified]
Juan-Gabriel C-N, Cepeda-Carrión G	2010	Hospital-in-home unit	Qualitative
Junior VM, Pascucci L, Murphy JP	2012	Hospitals	Qualitative
Kreindler SA, Larson BK, Wu FM, et al.	2014	4 ACOs	Qualitative
Leban W, Zulauf C	2004	Six organizations from varied industries (including health care not specified)	Quantitative
Liang Z, Howard P, Koh L	2012	Community health service organizations	Mixed methods
Lifvergren S, Gremyr I, Hellström A, Chakhunashvili A, Bergman B	2010	Skaraborg Hospital Group (SkaS)	Qualitative
Marchal B, Dedzo M, Kegels G	2010	Urban hospital	Qualitative
Marshall MN	1999	Three health authorities: rural, inner city, suburban	Qualitative
Martin N, Gregor S, Hart D	2005	Mixed public sector organizations	Qualitative
McDaniel RR, Jr.	2007	Theoretical	
Mosadeghrad, AM	2013	Theoretical	
Nilsson K, Furåker C	2012	Swedish hospitals	Qualitative
Nuti S, Seghieri C, Vainieri M	2013	[Not specified]	Qualitative
Nutt PC	1987	Multiple organizations	Qualitative

(continued)

Table 9.1 (continued)

Authors	Year	Setting	Methodology
Nyström ME, Höög E, Rickard G, Weinehall L, Ivarsson A	2013	Health and social services in Sweden	Qualitative
O'Shannassy T	2014	Health sector	Mixed methods
Olsson J, Elg M, Lindblad S	2007	Primary healthcare centres and hospitals	Quantitative
Øvretveit J, Andreen-Sachs M, Carlsson J, et al.	2012	Public health system organizations	Qualitative
Pappas JM, Wooldridge B	2007	Urban hospital	Quantitative
Parkes C, Scully J, West M, Dawson J	2007	Hospital and primary care trusts	Qualitative
Popovich K, Popovich M	2000	Hospital	Quantitative
Procter S, Currie G, Orme H	1999	City Community Healthcare Trust (CCHT)	Qualitative
Richards B, Howard P	2004	Hospital	Qualitative
Sandoff M, Widell G	2015	Large university hospital (and non health-sector)	Qualitative
Scroggins WA	2006	Hospital	Qualitative
Shanley C	2007	Residential aged care industry	Qualitative
Shetach A	2010	Theoretical	Qualitative
Sorensen R, Paull G, Magann L, Davis J	2013	Major public metropolitan referral hospital	Qualitative
Telford B, Cropper S, Ackermann F	1992	Acute joint 'unit' of 5 hospitals	Qualitative
McConville T	2006	NHS Trust (other non-health sector)	Qualitative
Thomas AM	1993	Hospital	[Not specified]
Trebble TM, Heyworth N, Clarke N, Powell T, Hockey PM	2014	NHS Trust	Qualitative
Van der Wees PJ, Friedberg MW, Guzman EA, Ayanian JZ, Rodriguez HP	2014	Six community health centres	Mixed methods
Woollard M, Lewis D, Brooks S	2003	Ambulance services	Qualitative
Zhang S, Bamford D, Moxham C, Dehe B	2012	National Health Service (NHS) Community Health Services (CHS) organization	Qualitative

References

Applebaum, S. H., & Wohl, L. (2000). Transformation or change: Some prescriptions for health care organizations. *Managing Service Quality, 10*(5), 279–298.

Arksey, H., & O'Malley, L. (2005). Scoping studies: Towards a methodological framework. *International Journal of Social Research Methodology, 8*(1), 19–32.

Ayton, D. R., Barker, A. L., Morello, R. T., Brand, C. A., Talevski, J., Landgren, F. S., et al. (2017). Barriers and enablers to the implementation of the 6-PACK falls prevention program: A pre-implementation study in hospitals participating in a cluster randomised controlled trial. *PLoS One, 12*(2). http://dx.doi.org/10.1371/journal.pone.0171932.

Balogun, J. (2003). From blaming the middle to harnessing its potential: Creating change intermediaries. *British Journal of Management, 14*(1), 69–83. https://doi.org/10.1111/1467-8551.00266.

Belasen, A., Belasen, A., Belasen, A. R., & Belasen, A. R. (2016). Value in the middle: Cultivating middle managers in healthcare organizations. *Journal of Management Development, 35*(9), 1149–1162.

Birken, S., Lee, S.-Y., & Weiner, B. (2012). Uncovering middle managers' role in healthcare innovation implementation. *Implementation Science, 7*(1), 28.

Bolden, R. (2011). Distributed leadership in organizations: A review of theory and research. *International Journal of Management Reviews, 13*(3), 251–269.

Bordia, P., Hobman, E., Jones, E., Gallois, C., & Callan, V. J. (2004). Uncertainty during organizational change: Types, consequences, and management strategies. *Journal of Business and Psychology, 18*(4), 507–532. https://doi.org/10.1023/B:JOBU.0000028449.99127.f7.

Broad, M. L. (2006). Improving performance in complex organizations. *Industrial and Commercial Training, 38*(6), 322–329. https://doi.org/10.1108/00197850610685833.

Buchanan, D., Claydon, T., & Doyle, M. (1999). Organisation development and change: The legacy of the nineties. *Human Resource Management Journal, 9*(2), 20–37.

Chaston, I. (1994). Assessing strategic behaviour within the acute sector of the National Health Service. *Journal of Management in Medicine, 8*(5), 58.

Corbridge, C. (1995). Pandora's box: Clinical directorates and the NHS. *Journal of Management in Medicine, 9*(6), 16.

Currie, G. (1999). The influence of middle managers in the business planning process: A case study in the UK NHS. *British Journal of Management, 10*(2), 141–155.

Currie, G. (2006). Reluctant but resourceful middle managers: The case of nurses in the NHS. *Journal of Nursing Management, 14*(1), 5–12. https://doi.org/10.1111/j.1365-2934.2005.00613.x.

Dainty, K. N., & Sinclair, D. (2017). A critical qualitative study of the position of middle managers in health care quality improvement. *Journal of Nursing Care Quality, 32*(2), 172–179. https://doi.org/10.1097/ncq.0000000000000224.

Dannapfel, P., Poksinska, B., & Thomas, K. (2014). Dissemination strategy for lean thinking in health care. *International Journal of Health Care Quality Assurance, 27*(5), 391–404.

Denis, J.-L., Langley, A., & Sergi, V. (2012). Leadership in the plural. *Academy of Management Annals, 6*(1), 211–283.

Dopson, S., Risk, A., & Stewart, R. (1992). The changing role of the middle manager in the United Kingdom. *International Studies of Management & Organization, 22*(1), 40–53.

Eicher, J. P. (2006). Making strategy happen. *Performance Improvement, 45*(10), 31–37, 48.

Fleiszer, A. R., Semenic, S. E., Ritchie, J. A., Richer, M. C., & Denis, J. L. (2015). An organizational perspective on the long-term sustainability of a nursing best practice guidelines program: A case study. *BMC Health Services Research, 15,* 535. https://doi.org/10.1186/s12913-015-1192-6.

Floyd, S. W., & Wooldridge, B. (1997). Middle management's strategic influence and organizational performance. *Journal of Management Studies, 34*(3), 465–485.

Forbes, T., & Prime, N. (1999). Changing domains in the management process radiographers as managers in the NHS. *Journal of Management in Medicine, 13*(2), 105–113.

Grill, C., Ahlborg, G., & Lindgren, E. C. (2011). Valuation and handling of dialogue in leadership. *Journal of Health Organization and Management, 25*(1), 34–54. https://doi.org/10.1108/14777261111116815.

Gronn, P. (2002). Distributed leadership as a unit of analysis. *The Leadership Quarterly, 13*(4), 423–451. https://doi.org/10.1016/S1048-9843(02)00120-0.

Gutberg, J., & Berta, W. (2017). Understanding middle managers' influence in implementing patient safety culture. *BMC Health Services Research, 17*(1), 582. https://doi.org/10.1186/s12913-017-2533-4.

Hancock, H., Campbell, S., Bignell, P., & Kilgour, J. (2005). The impact of leading empowered organisations (LEO) on leadership development in nursing. *International Journal of Health Care Quality Assurance, 18*(2/3), 179–192.

Harvey, G., Jas, P., Walshe, K., & Skelcher, C. (2014). Analysing organisational context: Case studies on the contribution of absorptive capacity theory to understanding inter-organisational variation in performance improvement. *BMJ Quality & Safety, 24*(1), 48–55. bmjqs- 2014-002928.

Herzig, S. E., & Jimmieson, N. L. (2006). Middle managers' uncertainty management during organizational change. *Leadership & Organization Development Journal, 27*(8), 628–645. https://doi.org/10.1108/014377 30610709264.

Juan-Gabriel, C.-N., & Cepeda-Carrión, G. (2010). How to implement a knowledge management program in hospital-in-the-home units. *Leadership in Health Services, 23*(1), 46–56. https://doi.org/10.1108/17511871011013760.

Junior, V. M., Pascucci, L., & Murphy, J. P. (2012). Implementing strategies in complex systems: Lessons from Brazilian hospitals. *Brazilian Administration Review, 9,* 19–37.

Kreindler, S. A., Larson, B. K., Wu, F. M., Gbemudu, J. N., Carluzzo, K. L., Struthers, A., et al. (2014). The rules of engagement: Physician engagement strategies in intergroup contexts. *Journal of Health Organization and Management, 28*(1), 41–61. http://dx.doi.org/10.1108/JHOM-02-2013-0024.

Liang, Z., Howard, P., & Koh, L. (2012). Hey boss, are you sure they are the managers you are looking for? Managerial competency requirements for level II & III managers in community health services. *GSTF International Journal on Bioinformatics & Biotechnology (JBio), 2*(1), 87–92.

Lifvergren, S., Gremyr, I., Hellström, A., Chakhunashvili, A., & Bergman, B. (2010). Lessons from Sweden's first large-scale implementation of Six Sigma in healthcare. *Operations Management Research, 3*(3–4), 117–128. https://doi.org/10.1007/s12063-010-0038-y.

Marchal, B., Dedzo, M., & Kegels, G. (2010). Turning around an ailing district hospital: A realist evaluation of strategic changes at Ho Municipal Hospital (Ghana). *BMC Public Health, 10*(1), 787. https://doi.org/10.1186/1471-2458-10-787.

Marshall, M. N. (1999). Improving quality in general practice: Qualitative case study of barriers faced by health authorities. *BMJ: British Medical Journal, 319*(7203), 164. https://doi.org/10.1136/bmj.319.7203.164.

McConville, T. (2006). Devolved HRM responsibilities, middle-managers and role dissonance. *Personnel Review, 35*(6), 637–653.

McDaniel, R. R., Jr. (2007). Management strategies for complex adaptive systems: Sensemaking, learning, and improvisation. *Performance Improvement Quarterly, 20*(2), 21–41.

McKee, L., Charles, K., Dixon-Woods, M., Willars, J., & Martin, G. (2013). 'New' and distributed leadership in quality and safety in health care, or 'old' and hierarchical? An interview study with strategic stakeholders. *Journal of Health Services Research & Policy, 18*(2, suppl.), 11–19. https://doi.org/10.1177/1355819613484460.

McKnight, L. L. (2013). Transformational leadership in the context of punctuated change. *Journal of Leadership, Accountability and Ethics, 10*(2), 103–112.

Miles, R. E., Snow, C. C., Meyer, A. D., & Coleman, H. J. (1978). Organizational strategy, structure, and process. *Academy of Management Review, 3*(3), 546–562.

Mintzberg, H., & Waters, J. A. (1985). Of strategies, deliberate and emergent. *Strategic Management Journal, 6*(3), 257–272.

Mosadeghrad, A. M. (2013a). Obstacles to TQM success in health care systems. *International Journal of Health Care Quality Assurance, 26*(2), 147–173.

Mosadeghrad, A. M. (2013b). Healthcare service quality: Towards a broad definition. *International Journal of Health Care Quality Assurance, 26*(3), 203–219. https://doi.org/10.1108/09526861311311409.

Muller, A., McCauley, K., Harrington, P., Jablonski, J., & Strauss, R. (2011). Evidence-based practice implementation strategy: The central role of the clinical nurse specialist. *Nursing Administration Quarterly, 35*(2), 140–151.

Nadler, D. A., & Tushman, M. L. (1990). Beyond the charismatic leader: Leadership and organizational change. *California Management Review, 32*(2), 77–97.

Narine, L., & Persaud, D. D. (2003). Gaining and maintaining commitment to large-scale change in healthcare organizations. *Health Services Management Research, 16*(3), 179–187. https://doi.org/10.1258/095148403322167933.

Northouse, P. G. (2015). *Leadership: Theory and practice.* Thousand Oaks: Sage.

O'Shannassy, T. (2014). Investigating the role of middle managers in strategy-making process: An Australian mixed method study. *Journal of Management and Organization, 20*(2), 187–205. https://doi.org/10.1017/jmo.2014.29.

Pappas, J. M., & Wooldridge, B. (2007). Middle managers' divergent strategic activity: An investigation of multiple measures of network centrality. *Journal of Management Studies, 44*(3), 323–341. https://doi.org/10.1111/j.1467-6486.2007.00681.x.

Parkes, C., Scully, J., West, M., & Dawson, J. (2007). "High commitment" strategies. *Employee Relations, 29*(3), 306–318. https://doi.org/10.1108/01425450710741775.

Pham, M. T., Rajić, A., Greig, J. D., Sargeant, J. M., Papadopoulos, A., & McEwen, S. A. (2014). A scoping review of scoping reviews: Advancing the approach and enhancing the consistency. *Research Synthesis Methods, 5*(4), 371–385. https://doi.org/10.1002/jrsm.1123.

Porter, M. E. (1991). *How competitive forces shape strategy.* Boston, MA: Harvard Business School Press.

Procter, S., Currie, G., & Orme, H. (1999). The empowerment of middle managers in a community health trust: Structure, responsibility and culture. *Personnel Review, 28*(3), 242–257.

Shanley, C. (2007). Managing change through management development: An industry case study. *The Journal of Management Development, 26*(10), 962–979. https://doi.org/10.1108/02621710710833414.

Spillane, J. P., Halverson, R., & Diamond, J. B. (2004). Towards a theory of leadership practice: A distributed perspective. *Journal of Curriculum Studies, 36*(1), 3–34.

Telford, B., Cropper, S., & Ackermann, F. (1992). Quality assurance and improvement: The role of strategy making. *International Journal of Health Care Quality Assurance, 5*(3), 5.

Trastek, V. F., Hamilton, N. W., & Niles, E. E. (2014). *Leadership models in health care—A case for servant leadership.* Paper presented at the Mayo Clinic Proceedings.

Trebble, T. M., Heyworth, N., Clarke, N., Powell, T., & Hockey, P. M. (2014). Managing hospital doctors and their practice: What can we learn about human resource management from non-healthcare organisations? *BMC Health Services Research, 14*(1), 1–11. http://dx.doi.org/10.1186/s12913-014-0566-5.

Uhl-Bien, M., Marion, R., & McKelvey, B. (2007). Complexity leadership theory: Shifting leadership from the industrial age to the knowledge era. *The Leadership Quarterly, 18*(4), 298–318. https://doi.org/10.1016/j.leaqua.2007.04.002.

Van der Wees, P. J., Friedberg, M. W., Guzman, E. A., Ayanian, J. Z., & Rodriguez, H. P. (2014). Comparing the implementation of team approaches for improving diabetes care in community health centers. *BMC Health Services Research, 14*(1), 608. http://dx.doi.org/10.1186/s12913-014-0608-z.

Wachter, R. M. (2010). Patient safety at ten: Unmistakable progress. *Troubling Gaps: Health Affairs, 29*(1), 165–173. https://doi.org/10.1377/hlthaff.2009.0785.

Wernerfelt, B. (1984). A resource-based view of the firm. *Strategic Management Journal, 5*(2), 171–180.

Willis, C. D., Saul, J., Bevan, H., Scheirer, M. A., Best, A., Greenhalgh, T., et al. (2016). Sustaining organizational culture change in health systems. *Journal of Health Organization and Management, 30*(1), 2–30. https://doi.org/10.1108/jhom-07-2014-0117.

Wooldridge, B., Schmid, T., & Floyd, S. W. (2008). The middle management perspective on strategy process: Contributions, synthesis, and future research. *Journal of Management, 34*(6), 1190–1221. https://doi.org/10.1177/0149206308324326.

Woollard, M., Lewis, D., & Brooks, S. (2003). Strategic change in the ambulance service: Barriers and success strategies for the implementation of high-performance management systems. *Strategic Change, 12*(3), 165.

Zhang, S., Bamford, D., Moxham, C., & Dehe, B. (2012). Strategy deployment systems within the UK healthcare sector: A case study. *International Journal of Productivity and Performance Management, 61*(8), 863–880. https://doi.org/10.1108/17410401211277129.

10

Tempered Tenacity: The Leadership Required to Work Across Boundaries

Liz Wiggins

The Health Context: The Need for Leading Across Boundaries

The challenges facing the English healthcare system have been thoroughly documented by Fitzgerald and McDermott (2017). Financial austerity has further widened the gap between demand for care and available funding (Lafond et al. 2016; Charlesworth et al. 2017). Trusts are autonomous organizational units within England's NHS, serving a geographical area or specialized function, established in 1990 with the intention of improving efficiencies by encouraging competition. (The NHS is structured differently in Scotland, Wales, and Northern Ireland as health is devolved to national governments.)

L. Wiggins (✉)
Ashridge Executive Education, Hult International Business School, Berkhamsted, UK
e-mail: liz.wiggins@ashridge.hult.edu

© The Author(s) 2020
P. Nugus et al. (eds.), *Transitions and Boundaries in the Coordination and Reform of Health Services*, Organizational Behaviour in Healthcare, https://doi.org/10.1007/978-3-030-26684-4_10

In England, there are 137 acute trusts, 17 specialist trusts, 56 mental health trusts, 35 community trusts, 10 ambulance trusts, and over 5000 GP practices in England (Keough 2017). NHS organizations are now being told to collaborate (Ham and Alderwick 2015). The introduction of sustainability and transformation plans (STPs) in 2016 has increased the need for, and urgency of, working across organizational and geographical boundaries. Indeed, the intention behind the 44 STPs is to reduce fragmentation—to move from "fortresses to systems", to quote the King's Fund report.

The figures above draw attention to the veritable patchwork quilt of organizational boundaries that constitutes the English NHS. Yet, boundaries do not just exist between institutions. There are also structural and functional divides between teams, departments, and the hierarchical levels expressed visibly in organizational charts and written into accountabilities and governance procedures. Psychosocial perspectives suggest divisions between us and them emerge in behaviours and attitudes, because of where people see themselves sitting in the system (Oshry 1998) and as a result of psychodynamic patterns such as splitting, an internal process which leads to a polarization of good and bad (Bion 2004). Furthermore, in the health service, professional cultures and subcultures (Schein 2010) create important sources of identity and belonging, yet also reinforce patterns of behaviour that differentiate and divide, amplifying boundaries (Wiggins et al. 2018). From a political perspective, divides may also emerge around different leadership styles, corporate priorities, and approaches to change (Baddley and James 1987).

It has long been recognized that individuals working at the "skin" of an organization (Katz and Kahn 1966, p. 192) can face role conflict, with boundary spanners "responsible for receiving, processing and transmitting information across varying permeable boundaries" (Mehra and Schenkel 2008, p. 140). However, in this chapter, the interest goes beyond receiving, processing, and transmitting information to *leading* across boundaries where the work is to diminish or even disappear boundaries.

The Context for This Research

This chapter emerged from Action Research (AR) undertaken with leaders who had been participants on a master's-level development programme for senior health leaders in the UK, designed and delivered by the author and colleagues, and funded by The Health Foundation (www.health.org.uk). The programme, established in 2009, is marketed as GenerationQ, but known academically as the Ashridge Masters in Leadership (Quality Improvement). It has been attended by over 140 senior clinical, managerial, and policy leaders whom it seeks to equip to lead the improvement of healthcare delivery. The programme has, from the beginning, been informed by different perspectives about how to effect change in healthcare organizations, embracing both technical quality improvement disciplines such as Lean, Theory of Constraints and Six Sigma, as well as more relational approaches from organization development (Wiggins and Smallwood 2018).

Literature on Leadership and Boundaries

In this section, we draw first on a range of interlinked theories that suggest that viewing organizations through different metaphors has implications for how leaders think about their role and the rigidity with which they understand boundaries. We then draw on the organizational change literature examining how more emergent approaches to change encourage leaders to make small gestures, to build relationships, and to create the conditions for dialogue. Such leadership acts are congruent with seeing boundaries as socially constructed rather than inherently rigid and fixed.

Machine Thinking Versus Complexity Thinking: Implications for Leadership

Looking at organizations through different metaphors gives a "means of enhancing our capacity for creative yet disciplined thought ... that allows us to grasp and deal with the many-sided character of organizational life" (Morgan 1986, p. 17). Seeing organizations as if they were machines is a metaphor with origins in early production lines, Newtonian physics, and a belief in causal linear relationships (Zohar 1997). It is the dominant discourse, unconsciously underpinning the way the NHS, and, indeed, many Western organizations are organized and led (Binney et al. 2012). Examples of machine thinking include the division of organizations into departments, with job specifications and protocols; the importance of standardization and efficiency; an assumption that control is possible through hierarchy with people viewed as parts of the machine, as cogs who should do what has been specified. Change through this lens is planned and directive, frequently involving fixing the parts through restructuring or replacing the largest cog, i.e. the CEO (Wiggins and Hunter 2016). It is a view that encourages seeing boundaries within and across organizations as rigid and immutable—another part of the machinery to be fixed.

The leadership action expected at such hard divides tends to be negotiation through service contracts, performance management, or target setting. In specifying what each side expects and promises, this arguably reinforces boundaries through amplifying a sense of them and us. It ignores the potential for nonlinear interaction at the boundary interface where there is inherent unpredictability and messiness because of difference. It discounts the possibility that what may be needed is a more emergent approach to change that allows for innovation and creativity rather than control, for more to-ing and fro-ing, and for building trust and relationship through conversation (Shaw 2002).

Essentially, machine thinking casts leaders in the role of superheroes, as transformational leaders who should know the answer to any organizational problem and who are in control (Binney et al. 2012). Many of the leaders we work with talk of the overwhelming burden of responsibility that comes from believing that such omniscience and omnipotence is expected of them as leaders. They talk of the pressures to "know" or have the answer, even when there is no clear solution. It is a short step to experiencing imposter syndrome (Clance and Imes 1978) and feeling lonely and isolated.

A further vicious cycle is enacted because the heroic model of leadership does not just set unrealistic expectations for the leader.

It encourages followers to be passive onlookers, thus amplifying the structural boundaries created by hierarchy. The temptation to conform to the heroic leader model thus carries an inherent risk of isolation. "If you treat others as the audience for your performance, then they will applaud from time to time – or throw rotten eggs – but they are unlikely to get up on stage to help you" (Binney et al. 2012, p. 34).

In contrast, seeing organizations through the lens of complexity thinking focuses on the local, micro-interactions between people and sees organizing as "an ongoing self-referencing process of gestures and responses between people" (Stacey 2012, p. 18), rather than spatial entities which have an existence separate from the people who populate them. Complexity science suggests that stable states consist of patterned dynamic movement, which can "tip" into new states on the basis of small, perhaps un-noticed, variations. Furthermore, complex systems have the capacity for emergence—for entirely new properties to be created, which cannot be predicted from pre-existing conditions (Midgley 2008). From this perspective, organizations might be thought of as networks of "complex responsive processes" (Stacey 2012) in which people create the patterns and relative stabilities that are recognizable as "organisations" in constant interaction with each other and their perceived circumstances. From this perspective, boundaries and borders between or within organizations are themselves social constructions (Weick 1995), comprised of different patterns of interaction between people where such differences may be noticed and labelled as different, as "other".

The same argument holds for the recognizable patterns of interaction, "of the way things are done round here" that constitute what are often referred to as cultures or subcultures (Wiggins and Smallwood 2018, p. 22). Subcultures, in the sense of distinct and sustained patterns of interaction, may exist between professional groups, between layers in the hierarchy, between departments where there are perceived to be different ways of doing things and different norms about what can or cannot be done. Boundaries may thus be perceived to define and divide: they are socially constructed markers of difference. This way of understanding the world allows for the nature of patterns and boundaries to be constructed as flexible and permeable rather than fixed and immutable. By not reifying them, there are a number of significant implications for leaders. Shifting such patterns and working across socially constructed boundaries may seem more do-able. The focus of action becomes building relationships through processes of gestures and responses (Shaw 2002) and change becomes emergent rather than highly directed (Wiggins and Hunter 2016). Leaders need to develop the capability to "see many shades of grey, see many patterns and connections, accept uncertainty as the norm" (Petrie 2014, p. 13). Consequently, leaders are in charge but not in control of what happens at the boundary (Stacey 2012). The gestures they make—be they physical actions, decisions, spoken words or non-verbal movements—are important whilst acknowledging that those gestures may not always have the impact intended as meaning is socially constructed (Weick 1995). Leaders therefore need to develop the ability to also reflect on the gestures they have made, to be curious about the responses they have received, to learn and, if necessary, to ask, "what is needed right now?" (Fig. 10.1).

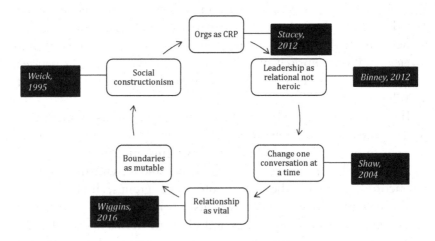

Fig. 10.1 Implications of complexity thinking for leading across boundaries

Acting: The Power of Small Gestures

In the change literature, there is a growing emphasis on change taking place through small, rather than grand gestures. From a complexity perspective, change is constructed as taking place one conversation at a time (Shaw 2002). When organizations are constructed as complex responsive processes, such gestures or moves are like the ripples on a pond. A core principle of complex responsive processes is that small differences can be amplified and become transformative patterns, or what Gladwell (2000) describes as tipping points. This explains how "small differences can escalate into major, completely unpredictable changes" (Stacey 2012, p. 291) in complex systems.

Change approaches rooted in a range of academic traditions also advocate the power of small moves. This includes, for instance, plan–do–check–act (PDSA) cycles in the improvement sciences (Langley et al. 2009), the notion of nudges from behavioural economics (Thaler and Sunstein 2009), and short-term wins within the mainstream change literature (Kotter 1996). Sometimes the rationale for this is political and motivational rather than theoretical. A series of small wins is "less likely to engage the organizational immune system against deep change" (Frost and Egri 1991, p. 242), and again, "small wins reduce large problems to a manageable size. Big unwieldy problems produce anxiety which limits people's capacity to think and act creatively" (Meyerson and Scully 1995, p. 595).

Looking at change through "small wins" is helpful motivationally, in terms of encouraging leaders' beliefs about what is possible at the boundary, and what is needed. However, it arguably downplays and undertheorizes the impact of power relations invested in the status quo. From a political perspective, it could be seen as representing a certain naivety, being an innocent sheep rather than a wise owl (Baddley and James 1987). Vanstone (2010) thus draws attention to the balancing act required for leaders attempting to shift cultures, to work across divides, and to bring in new ways of working. Aligning too closely to the current culture risks collusion. Yet, if the gestures made remain too small and out of sight, they risk being ineffective and overwhelmed.

On the other hand, being perceived as too challenging risks being side-lined, ignored, rejected, and even ejected. Meyerson and Scully (1995) describe this dynamic for internal change agents as being tempered rad-icals, a term explored further in the discussion section. Despite what we know about complexity approaches, most empirical literature on change and leadership continues to focus at a directive, managerialist, and broad-system level. Complexity-informed approaches, empha-sizing local dynamism mostly appear as conceptual accounts, with an under-representation in empirical research. The aim of this chapter is to illuminate the increasing canon of ideas on enacted forms of organiza-tional life through an empirical study of NHS leaders' discourses relat-ing to change and leadership.

Examining Leadership in Organizational Contexts

The teaching philosophy and underlying methodological approach in the GenerationQ programme, and this chapter, is informed by Action Research (AR) (Ladkin 2007; Reason and Bradbury 2008). Action Research differs significantly from mainstream research in a number of ways: it is reflexive in that it acknowledges that the research process will affect what is being researched, and that researchers will be affected by the research. Participant researchers notice and think about the organiza-tional changes they are engaged in whilst in the process of enacting them and, in so doing, reflect on and modify their practice on the ground. In this respect, it is also a form of learning in which participant research-ers make sense of and "theorise" about their own work as they are doing it. The intention is to help bring about positive impact, as defined by participants themselves. As such, the research itself is a collaborative endeavour conducted *with* people rather than *on* them, to give rise to "actionable knowledge" (Coghlan 2011) through disciplined cycles of action and reflection, which have parallels with quality improvement PDSA cycles (Langley et al. 2009). The ontological position of AR mir-rors that of Stacey's (2010) complex responsive process approach in that it conceptualizes people as "agents" who are capable of articulating their own sense of their worlds.

The themes in this chapter initially emerged from reading assignments and master's theses written by senior NHS leaders participating in GenerationQ. Twenty-five alumni from the programme then participated in AR specifically focused on their experience of working across a variety of boundaries. Two research questions are the focus for this chapter:

> *RQ1: What mental models of organization and leadership do leaders find helpful in enabling them to work well across boundaries?*

> *RQ2: How do leaders describe, and make sense of, what they actually do in order to work well across boundaries?*

First-person AR took the form of leaders' journaling about their experiences, writing assignments, and completing a set of inquiry questions, prior to meeting twice as a whole group. Meeting together was an opportunity for second-person AR where stories were shared and leaders collectively made sense of emerging themes for the whole as well as identified insights and learning for themselves. Some individuals then wrote their stories, anonymizing people and places for reasons of confidentiality, as part of third-person AR. The ideas raised in the writing were compared and contrasted, after close and repeated reading, in order to produce the themes outlined in the findings below. Typical representations of the central themes are represented as excerpts. Some of these stories have been published in book form for the practitioner rather than academic community (Wiggins et al. 2018).

The Boundary Work of Leaders

Mental Models of Organizations and Leading

As the machine model of organizations dominates Western thinking about organizations (Binney et al. 2012; Morgan 1986, Zohar 1997), it is no surprise that this is how the majority of the senior UK National Health Service (NHS) leaders saw organizations at the beginning of their involvement with the GenerationQ leadership programme.

In the first extract, a leader reflects on the way machine thinking is ingrained in clinicians during training.

> *I was trained as a diagnostician: I would gather the evidence (symptoms), decide what was the cause (diagnose) and implement a change as a remedy (prescribe). Therefore as the medical leader, I assumed that I could identify mechanistically the fault with the system and put in a fix.* (NHS leader 1)

Another leader reflects on the way machine thinking can unwittingly create a barrier between leaders and followers:

> *There often seems to be a lot of apathy, 'jobs worth', and abrogation of responsibility once anything extends beyond individuals' immediate sphere but this is in keeping with the dehumanisation of individuals when considered as a machine part, and encouraged by the mentality that orders come from above and they are just there to do what they are told.* (NHS leader 2)

In the third extract, a clinician recounts the experience of arriving as the new clinical director.

> *When I introduced myself to people, they would reply with phrases such as "Ah! You're here to sort us out'...Without realizing it, I was in the 'command and control' model of leadership. As I took more and more control, I elicited a vicious circle where colleagues took less responsibility and placed more dependence on my decision-making.* (NHS leader 3)

These illustrate some shadow sides of machine thinking which can impede working across hierarchical and role boundaries within organizations, let alone across them. However, we should not pretend that understanding organizations through the lens of complexity thinking is immediately welcomed. As one participant wrote:

I felt disturbed by the idea of complexity thinking. It seemed to beg the question "why bother?" If the organisation only exists within the personal interactions of individuals, what is the role of the leader? (NHS leader 4)

Nevertheless, over time, participants begin to experiment with complexity thinking about leading and often describe feeling liberated. Complexity thinking can take the spotlight away from them, becoming less about the person in charge and more about how the collective is jointly engaged in conversation and action. To quote another participant:

The ideas (about complexity thinking) were like a revelation, a soothing balm for a struggling leader's soul – I did not have to be perfect; maybe I was good enough already….The notion that leadership happens between people, and that the vital ingredient is the quality of the relationship between leaders and those who depend on them made so much sense to me. (NHS leader 5)

The findings thus support our initial expectations that machine thinking has significant shadow sides for leaders' understanding of their role and amplifies differences across hierarchical and institutional boundaries. In contrast, complexity thinking, whilst initially discombobulating, can give a sense of liberation allowing a focus on relationships and behavioural gestures which, as we argue below, allows for a different, more relational approach to leading across boundaries and to seeing them as mutable.

Behavioural Gestures and Moves

In this section, we summarize leaders' accounts of what they noticed themselves doing, informed by a complexity perspective, thus addressing the second research question:

RQ2: How do leaders describe, and make sense of, what they actually do in order to work well across boundaries?

In their accounts, boundaries take different forms depending on individuals' local contexts, but there is consistency in the descriptions of the bridging moves required. Leaders talk of making multiple small but significant moves to shift and build relationships; to reach out to understand others more; to encourage inquiry and dialogue rather than debate and assertion (Isaacs 1999); to demonstrate empathy and see the world from others' viewpoints.

> *I discovered that the gesture of having a conversation itself, without an agenda or intended outcome in mind, … was enabling issues to be raised that had not been spoken of before.* (NHS Leader 1)

Thus, writes a physician (*NHS Leader 1*) whose role was to create one division from two tribes, the surgeons and the physicians.

Many describe the energy and tenacity required to keep going, especially if the impact of their gestures can seem elusive or difficult to gauge. They speak of drawing on theory to help them make sense of what is going on. One writes,

> *I have found knowledge of theory helps me be more resilient, to realize that I am not unique, nor alone in my experience, to understand why things might happen as they do.* (NHS leader 5)

A further theme emerging is the need to consider carefully when to challenge and how to offer an alternative view or behave counter to the norm. Participants describe the need to speak up in ways that others can hear without rejecting the idea or them personally. There were frequent mentions of the need to understand and navigate organizational politics, to be a wise owl rather than a truculent donkey or naïve sheep (Baddley and James 1987)

Moments of Judgement

A common theme throughout all the accounts is the notion of choice, not just about which gesture or move to make but also about timing. In some cases, leaders made a deliberate move after significant reflection. In other cases, gestures were more spontaneous in response to something emerging "in the moment". Congruent with a complexity perspective, such moves are made, recognizing that the response cannot be predicted, so that a level of uncertainty is always present. The leader may feel in the moment, or indeed afterwards, that a move was noteworthy or high stakes, whilst others may interpret the same gesture differently, in terms of significance. For instance, a medical director, new to a trust, saw a surgeon wearing a watch. He privately asked the surgeon to support his "bare below the elbows" campaign and thought no more of this. Several weeks later, a senior nurse told the medical director that she and other nurses had noticed the surgeon had changed his behaviour. The medical director's original personal gesture to a colleague thus came to carry greater organizational significance as it was interpreted by nurses on the ward as showing that doctors were no longer untouchable, shifting their views of the perceived sanctity of professional boundaries.

Nevertheless, working across boundaries, challenging stuck cultural patterns, and offering new ways of seeing a situation are not without risk of ridicule or retribution. The accounts reflect concerns about being brave and the need to take calculated risks, without being foolhardy or politically naïve. For instance, in one account, a clinician director used the metaphor of his cycling helmet to describe his own attitude to risk. He did not want to disrupt the relationship he was building with the new CEO but when writing about a senior nurse suspended he affirmed;

I decided that I should write to the CEO not as one of a collection of consultants but from me, as an individual in a respected leadership position.... (I thought I should) leave the helmet behind, take a risk and do what felt to be the right thing. (NHS leader 8)

In another case, a clinical director made a more spontaneous physical gesture, literally blocking the door during a board meeting to stop the CEO from leaving until a promised, but frequently postponed, decision was made.

During the second-person AR, when participants met together to discuss their experiences, a number of key phrases emerged.

These included the differences between walking the line and toeing the line, and the need to be 10% braver. There was widespread recognition that challenging existing norms too much can invite rejection, whilst overly colluding with the status quo risks no shift at all. There is thus a balance required; leaders need to dare to act and do differently in the interests of working across boundaries, shifting local cultures, and creating new ways of working, but must do so with care. This amalgam of thought, action, feeling, reflection and care, of small moves done consistently and persistently over time, we describe as tempered tenacity.

Conceptualizing Tempered Tenacity

These senior leaders' accounts suggest that a complexity-informed approach to thinking about organizations and leadership (Stacey 2012) frees leaders of the felt need to be in control and, rather than reifying borders, allows them to see the borders as socially constructed and mutable. The focus of this chapter, and the study on which it is based, does not preclude the influence of large-scale structures, such as laws, professional regulations, society-wide gender dynamics, organizational norms, and financial incentives. Such structures influence individual behaviour and decision-making. However, empirically, this chapter addresses the paucity of attention that has been paid to the dynamism of choices and actions by individuals, in local contexts, especially individual leaders, in influencing others' work across boundaries. In terms of complex responsive processes, change is viewed as happening one conversation at a time (Shaw 2002), with a focus on making small but often significant moves that build relationships and trust, creating an interlinked and nested set of benefits that aids working well across multiple boundaries.

There is recognition in the accounts that from both a practical and theoretical perspective, the significance of a gesture cannot be known in the moment (Stacey 2012) and depends on the meaning constructed by others. An emphasis on small moves encourages leaders to pick battles carefully, allowing them to take advantage of unexpected opportunities, whilst recognizing they have finite amounts of energy, resources and power. Weick (1995) argues that the real power of small wins as a strategy for social change comes in the capacity to gather and label *retrospectively* a series of relatively innocuous small wins into a bigger "package" that would have been too threatening to be *prospectively* adopted.

How might we describe and theorize these ways of thinking, behaving and feeling, which seem to have helped these participants to lead across boundaries? Any concept needs to be considered in terms of the frequent references to persistence and resilience, to holding on and staying true to a belief that different ways of working were needed and possible. Despite setbacks, there was, throughout the accounts, a sense of energy, even moral imperative, to create something different. It is striking that in many of the accounts, leaders had been making moves over a considerable period of time as they seek to shift the local culture so these are not stories of quick fixes. To include this quality alongside the findings related to leaders' mental models and behavioural moves, we propose the notion of tempered tenacity.

Meyerson and Scully write,

> Temperedness reflects the way (individuals) have been toughened by challenges, angered by what they see as injustices or ineffectiveness and inclined to seek moderation in their interactions with members closer to the centre of organizational values and orientations. (1995, p. 585)

A view that is tempered is one that has been modified and nuanced. The leaders in this study continued to notice the relevance of seeing organizations as machines, but also learnt to view them through the lens of complexity science, which we refer to as multi-level pluralism (Wiggins and Marshall 2018). In the language of physics, "tempered" describes a metal being made tougher by alternately heating it up and then cooling it down. Similarly, in the leaders' accounts, they talk of both challenges and setbacks, as well as significant progress. But "tempered" also refers to having a temper. Here, too, the leaders talk of their anger at what they see as injustices or inadequacies and voice their annoyance at boundaries impeding what is needed to work in a more collaborative way for patients. Yet, being "even tempered" also means having composure and being thoughtful about how and when to act, so the anger needs to be tempered, controlled, channelled wisely. Herein lie

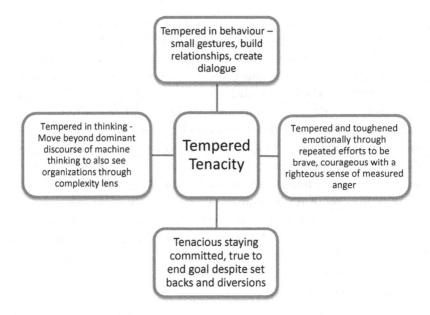

Fig. 10.2 Tempered tenacity

some of the subtleties and relational skills required when challenging and shifting the dominant culture. Leaders need to learn the balancing act between over challenge and collusion, between walking the line and toeing the line. Yet, unlike the internal change agents in Meyerson and Scully's study, these leaders did not identify themselves as radicals.

The energy and tenacity required to keep going, especially if the impact of your gestures can seem elusive or difficulty to gauge, can be draining. Personal resilience is therefore vital. Leaders mention the value that comes from having other, like-minded leaders to talk to—good colleagues, a coach, co-members of an action learning set (Fig. 10.2).

Conclusion and Critique

This chapter uniquely articulated how an individual leader's small moves can shape the way organizations function, including the way health care is delivered, by influencing those with whom they work and deliver services. One might ask: How should such research be evaluated and what might be its limitations? Although AR is beginning to find a foothold within healthcare research (Coleman and Wiggins 2017), AR is not an objective process, and its findings are not generalizable in the conventional scientific sense but like all researchers, we asked critical questions about the rigour of practice and the trustworthiness of research outcomes (Reason and Bradbury 2008). In AR, this is done through exercising awareness and transparency about choices, and paying attention to the extent to which key dimensions, such as collaboration and actionable knowledge, have been realized.

There are clear signs that "actionable knowledge" has emerged from our research (Waller et al. 2015). At the same time, we recognize that the leaders participating in this research will have been shaped by the particular experience of being on a leadership programme where their learning was supported and encouraged through reading about complexity thinking, writing reflective assignments, paying attention to the detail of how they were leading in their own contexts, and participating in first- and second-person AR. Arguably, it is the very uniqueness of their experience participating in a master's programme that gives a rare insiders' view into the lived experience of leading well across boundaries in the NHS. Generally, senior leaders are too busy to share their thinking and feelings in such depth and with such personal disclosure. This is perhaps what gives this AR its particular contribution to academic knowledge, as well as its practical use to those participating.

The findings also suggest that how leaders think should be as much of interest to practical people, whether leaders themselves, politicians, policy makers, commissioners, or leadership developers. Implications of our research include the need to find ways of helping leaders examine their underlying assumptions and mental models about organizations, leadership, and the nature of boundaries and to learn to see themselves and their work with new eyes.

In summary, this research suggests that tempered tenacity is a core leadership capability for leaders who want to work well across boundaries, to create more collaboration and fewer fortresses (Ham et al. 2015) in the interests of providing better quality and efficient care for patients. Further research is required to explore the usefulness of tempered tenacity more broadly, including its relationship to system-wide influences and structures, and the relationships among the various elements of the concept.

Acknowledgements The author would like to acknowledge, with thanks, the contribution to this chapter made by her two colleagues and thought partners, Janet Smallwood and Brian Marshall. Thanks also to Peter Nugus and Donetta Marie Hines for their wise and helpful editorial suggestions.

References

Baddley, S., & James, K. (1987). Owl, fox, sheep and donkey: Political skills for managers. *Management Education and Development, 18*(1), 3–19.

Binney, G., Wiles, G., & Williams, C. (2012). *Living leadership: A practical guide for everyday heroes.* Harlow: Financial Times/Prentice Hall.

Bion, W. R. (2004). *Experiences in groups and other chapters.* New York, NY: Brunner-Routledge (Originally published by Tavistock Press in 1961).

Charlesworth, A., Thorlby, R., Roberts, A., & Gershlick, B. (2017). *Election briefing: NHS and social care funding: Three unavoidable challenges.* London: The Health Foundation.

Clance, P. R., & Imes, S. A. (1978). The imposter phenomenon in high achieving women: Dynamics and therapeutic intervention. *Psychotherapy: Theory, Research and Practice, 15*(3), 241–247.

Coghlan, D. (2011). Action research: Exploring perspectives on a philosophy of practical knowing. *Academy of Management Annals, 5*(1), 53–87.

Coleman, G., & Wiggins, L. (2017). Bringing humanity into view: Action research with Qatar's ambulance service. *Journal of Health Organization and Management, 31*(5).

Fitzgerald, L., & McDermott, A. M. (2017). *Challenging perspectives on organizational change in healthcare.* Abingdon, Oxon: Routledge.

Frost, P. J., & Egri, C. P. (1991). The political process of innovation. In B. Staw & L. L. Cummings (Eds.), *Research in organizational behaviour* (Vol. 13, pp. 229–295). Greenwich, CT: JAI Press.

Gladwell, M. (2000). *Tipping points: How little things can make a big difference.* Boston, MA: Little, Brown, and Company.

Ham, C, & Alderwick, H. (2015). *Sustainability and transformation plans explained.* https://www.kingsfund.org.uk/topics/integrated-care/sustaina-bility-transformation-plansexplained?gclid=EAIaIQobChMIg9X0wtjF-1wIVBd0bCh1TUglgEAAYASAAEgK1LvD_BwE. Downloaded 22 Nov 2017.

Isaacs, W. (1999). *Dialogue and the art of thinking together.* New York: Bantam Doubleday Dell Publishing Group.

Katz, D., & Kahn, R. L. (1966). *The social psychology of organizations.* New York, NY: Wiley.

Keough, B. (2017, November 1). Key note address. In *BMJ Conference Liverpool.*

Kotter, J. (1996). *Leading change.* Harvard Business School Press.

Ladkin, D. (2007). Action research. In C. Seale, G. Gobo, J. Gubrium, & D. Silverman (Eds.), *Qualitative research practice* (pp. 478–490). London: Sage.

Lafond, S., Charlesworth, A., & Roberts, A. (2016). *A perfect storm: An impossible climate for NHS providers' finances? An analysis of NHS finances and factors associated with financial performance.* London: The Health Foundation.

Langley, G. J., Moen, R., Nolan, K., Nolan, T. W., Norman, C. L., & Provost, L. P. (2009). *The improvement guide: A practical approach to enhancing organizational performance.* London: Wiley.

Mehra, A., & Schenkel, M. T. (2008). The price chameleons pay: Self-monitoring, boundary spanning and role conflict in the workplace. *British Journal of Management, 19,* 138–144.

Meyerson, D. E., & Scully, M. A. (1995). Tempered radicalism and the politics of ambivalence and change. *Organization Science, 6*(5), 585–600.

Midgley, G. (2008). Systems thinking, complexity and the philosophy of science. *Emergence: Complexity and Organization, 10*(4), 55.

Morgan, G. (1986). *Images of organization.* London: Sage.

Oshry, B. (1998). *Seeing systems: Unlocking the mysteries of organizational life.* Oakland, CA: Berrett-Koehler Publishers, Inc.

Petrie, N. (2014). Vertical leadership development—Part 1. *Developing leaders for a complex world.* Greensboro, NC: Center for Creative Leadership.

Reason, P., & Bradbury, H. (Eds.). (2008). *The Sage handbook of action research: Participative inquiry and practice* (2nd ed.). London: Sage.

Schein, E. (2010). *Organizational culture and leadership* (4th ed.). San Francisco, CA: Jossey-Bass.

Shaw, P. (2002). *Changing conversations in organizations: A complexity approach to change (Complexity and emergence in organizations).* London: Routledge.

Stacey, R. (2010). *Strategic management and organisational dynamics: The challenge of complexity* (6th ed.). London: Financial Times/Prentice Hall.

Stacey, R. (2012). *The tools and techniques of leadership and management: Meeting the challenge of complexity*. London: Routledge.

Thaler, R., & Sunstein, C. (2009). *Nudge: Improving decisions about health, wealth and happiness*. London: Penguin.

Vanstone, C. (2010). *An introduction to appreciative inquiry: Change, performance and engagement*. Ashridge: Ashridge Consulting.

Waller, L, Marshall, B., Smallwood, J., & Wiggins, L. (2015). *GenerationQ: The organizational and personal impact of the programme*. Ashridge Research Report.

Weick, K. (1995). *Sensemaking in organizations*. Thousand Oaks, CA: Sage.

Wiggins, L., & Hunter, H. (2016). *Relational change: The art of changing organizations*. London: Bloomsbury.

Wiggins, L., & Marshall, B. (2018). Multi-level pluralism: A pragmatic approach to choosing change and improvement methods. In A. McDermott, M. J. Kitchener, & M. Exworthy (Eds.), *Managing improvement in healthcare: Attaining, sustaining and spreading quality*. Cham, Switzerland: Palgrave.

Wiggins, L., & Smallwood, J. (2018). An OD approach to leadership development: Questions and consequences. *Journal of Management Development, 37*(8), 613–623.

Wiggins, L., Smallwood, J., & Marshall, B. (2018). *Leaders shifting local cultures in healthcare: Hope behind the headlines*. Farringdon, Oxon: Libri Publishing.

Zohar, D. (1997). *Rewiring the corporate Brain: Using the new science to rethink how we structure and lead organizations*. San Francisco, CA: Berrett-Koehler Publishers, Inc.

11

The Chain of Codified Knowledge: Organisational Enactment of Evidence-Based Health Care in Four High-Income Countries

Roman Kislov, Paul Wilson, Greta Cummings, Anna Ehrenberg, Wendy Gifford, Janet Kelly, Alison Kitson, Lena Pettersson, Lars Wallin and Gill Harvey

Introduction

Evidence-based health care is a paradigm-shifting doctrine based on the premise that professional clinical practice should integrate clinical experience with the best available evidence about the effectiveness of

---

The reworked and expanded version of this chapter was published by Wiley Periodicals, Inc. on behalf of The American Society for Public Administration as: Kislov, R., Wilson, P., Cummings, G., Ehrenberg, A., Gifford, W., Kelly, J., Kitson, A., Pettersson, L., Wallin, L., and Harvey, G. (2019). From research evidence to "evidence by proxy"? Organisational enactment of evidence-based health care in four high-income countries. *Public Administration Review, 79*(5), 684–698. https://doi.org/10.1111/puar.13056.

R. Kislov (✉) · P. Wilson
Alliance Manchester Business School, University of Manchester, Manchester, UK
e-mail: roman.kislov@manchester.ac.uk

P. Wilson
e-mail: paul.wilson@manchester.ac.uk

© The Author(s) 2020
P. Nugus et al. (eds.), *Transitions and Boundaries in the Coordination and Reform of Health Services*, Organizational Behaviour in Healthcare, https://doi.org/10.1007/978-3-030-26684-4_11

the interventions used (Ferlie et al. 2009; Rousseau and Gunia 2016; Sackett et al. 1996). It is usually taken for granted that "the best available evidence" is represented by the findings of rigorous scientific research which, in turn, directly inform the development of recommendations for practice in the form of clinical guidelines (Harrison 1998; Knaapen 2013; Timmermans and Kolker 2004). We challenge this assumption and examine the role played in the enactment of evidence-based health care by other forms of codified knowledge, i.e. knowledge that is formal, systematic and expressible in language or

G. Cummings
University of Alberta, Edmonton, AB, Canada
e-mail: gretac@ualberta.ca

A. Ehrenberg · L. Pettersson · L. Wallin
School of Education, Health and Social Studies, Dalarna University,
Borlänge, Sweden
e-mail: aeh@du.se

L. Pettersson
e-mail: lpt@du.se

L. Wallin
e-mail: lwa@du.se

W. Gifford
School of Nursing, University of Ottawa, Ottawa, ON, Canada
e-mail: wgifford@uottawa.ca

J. Kelly · G. Harvey
Adelaide Nursing School, University of Adelaide, Adelaide, SA, Australia
e-mail: janet.kelly@adelaide.edu.au

G. Harvey
e-mail: gillian.harvey@adelaide.edu.au

A. Kitson
Adelaide College of Nursing and Health Sciences, Flinders University,
Adelaide, SA, Australia
e-mail: alison.kitson@flinders.edu.au

numbers, making it easy to store, transfer and use across space (Turner et al. 2014). This chapter suggests that *evidence by proxy*, which we define as codified non-research knowledge that is, nonetheless, resonant with research evidence, could be a way towards more coordinated and patient-centred care. However, uncritical over-reliance on evidence by proxy may lead to the detachment of front-line clinicians from fundamental competencies of evidence-based practice, with the latter becoming a prerogative of experts represented by senior clinicians and designated facilitators.

Evolution of Evidence-Based Health Care

Expansion of the Notion of "Evidence"

Analysis of the literature on the evolution of evidence-based practice guides us towards a number of observations. First and foremost, there is a tendency towards expanding the notion of "evidence". Such expansion is associated with a common criticism of the evidence-based movement as "a restrictive interpretation of the scientific approach to clinical practice" (Fava 2017, p. 3). On the one hand, there are renewed calls to shift away from objectivist hierarchies of research evidence (privileging randomised controlled trials and systematic reviews) to methodological pluralism, where the value is placed on the appropriateness of research to support decision-making (Holmes et al. 2006).

On the other hand, there is a growing understanding of the importance that non-research forms of evidence play in actual practice, characterised by the existence of competing bodies of knowledge amenable to multiple interpretations (Dopson et al. 2002). Many authors highlight the competition between research evidence, represented by clinical guidelines as the cornerstone of evidence-based health care (Harrison 1998; Timmermans and Kolker 2004) and tacit knowledge, including stakeholder concerns, practitioner—and patient—judgement and contextual awareness (Dopson et al. 2003; Mackey and Bassendowski 2017; Rousseau and Gunia 2016; Rycroft-Malone et al. 2004). It is now generally accepted that codified research evidence informs, and is informed by, multiple forms of tacit knowledge and skills (Gabbay and le May 2011; Knaapen 2013), making the latter ineliminable from evidence-based practice.

Institutionalisation of Evidence-Based Practice

Evidence-based health care has entered a mature phase of its lifecycle, gradually morphing from an innovative approach to practising medicine into a new orthodoxy, widely adopted by healthcare organisations and institutionalised in their practices as "business as usual" (Dopson et al. 2003; Ferlie et al. 2009). This maturation has been enabled by a number of interconnected processes unfolding at several levels. As far as the *production of evidence* is concerned, the international elite of senior academics/clinicians sift through the primary research evidence and control the development of clinical guidelines, which has been interpreted as a form of professional stratification (Dopson et al. 2003; Knaapen 2013; Timmermans and Kolker 2004). Other contributions highlight the shift of influence away from clinical practitioners towards epidemiologists, information scientists, systematic reviewers and health economists (Fava 2017; Ferlie and McGivern 2014; Harrison 1998).

In terms of the *implementation of evidence,* the growing popularity of "decision supports", such as checklists, protocols and assessment routines, has contributed to the greater codification of decisions and practices at the organisational level (Rousseau and Gunia 2016). At the same time, there has been growing attention to creating local capacity for engagement with evidence (Ferlie et al. 2009; Kislov et al. 2014). In particular, the diffusion of evidence can be enabled by a favourable historical and cultural context (Fitzgerald et al. 2002), distributed change leadership (Buchanan et al. 2007) and functional mechanisms to bridge professional and organisational boundaries (Kislov 2014). A new cadre of professionals, whose remit explicitly involves the implementation of evidence-based practice, has emerged, including designated facilitators and knowledge brokers (Harvey and Kitson 2015; Kislov et al. 2016).

Spread of Evidence-Based Practice Across Disciplines and Countries

Although evidence-based practice emerged as a professionally driven movement within medicine, it has now spread to other clinical areas, such as nursing and allied health professions (Mackey and Bassendowski 2017; Satterfield et al. 2009), as well as to other domains of the public sector (Ferlie et al. 2016). There is an ongoing debate about the advantages and disadvantages of this development. Evidence-based nursing, for example, has been criticised for marginalising tacit forms of knowledge in an attempt to increase professional legitimacy in the competitive health occupational marketplace (Mackey and Bassendowski 2017; Rycroft-Malone et al. 2004). At the same time, it has been argued that the relative scarcity of trial evidence (Dopson et al. 2002; Mackey and Bassendowski 2017), has prompted evidence-based nursing to push beyond evidence-based medicine in qualitative research and to integrate patients' experiences into practice decisions (Satterfield et al. 2009).

This spread of evidence-based practice has an international dimension which can partly be explained by the international nature of elite clinical networks responsible for the production of clinical guidelines (Ferlie and McGivern 2014; Knaapen 2013). It is also enabled by the international ideology of New Public Management, which aims to cut costs and improve quality through managerial, rather than professional means, including transparent measurement of performance against centrally set standards and targets (Ferlie and McGivern 2014; Hasselbladh and Bejerot 2007). Of the sampled nations in this study, the New Public Management has been expressed most overtly in the UK and Australia (Ferlie et al. 2016). In the UK context, for example, the appropriation of the evidence-based movement by the New Public Management agenda is apparent in the development of top-down, formalised and prescriptive policy frameworks. Such formal frameworks have come to rely on the disciplinary power of audit and benchmarking, along with the establishment of government agencies responsible for producing clinical guidelines and for commissioning, regulating and monitoring evidence-based health care (Ferlie et al. 2009). Although exhibiting a lesser degree of overt embrace of New Public Management discourse, emphasis on nationwide intervention has still been prioritised by Sweden, as evident in their embrace of National Quality Registries (Fredriksson et al. 2014).

Gaps in Our Understanding of Knowledge and Evidence

Recent contributions show that codified knowledge can inform managerial practice and service improvement by interacting with tacit knowledge and skills at different clinical and organisational levels (Ferlie et al. 2016; Turner et al. 2014). However, little research has focused on the composition of codified knowledge involved in the enactment of evidence-based health care, as well as the relationships between different forms of codified knowledge.

Extant research tends to characterise the enactment of evidence-based practice either as a macro-level international movement, with the main focus on the production of research evidence and its conversion into clinical guidelines, or by exploring the careers of individual evidence-based innovations (and of specific methods deployed to increase their uptake) in different organisational contexts. In particular, while researchers have paid attention to the differences in evidence-based practice between primary and hospital care (Fitzgerald et al. 2002), less is known about the macro-level factors influencing its enactment in healthcare organisations (Ferlie et al. 2009).

Even less is known about the organisational structures and processes enabling the local institutionalisation of evidence-based practice as "business as usual". Such knowledge is vital for the ambitions of health reform, because it underpins interventions that maximise a combination of both distributed and shared knowledge across systemic and epistemic boundaries, and wisdom from the front line.

To address these research gaps, the study will be guided by the following research questions:

1. What forms of codified knowledge are seen as credible evidence?
2. What is their impact on evidence-based nursing?

3. How do the composition and impact of codified knowledge vary across different countries?

This study emerged from a broader research programme exploring leadership and facilitation roles in the implementation of evidence-based nursing across four high-income countries (UK, Australia, Canada and Sweden) (Harvey et al. 2019). Within each country case, up to two organisations were selected using the combination of convenience and purposeful sampling based on the following criteria: (1) self-declared adherence of the organisation's senior leadership to the implementation of evidence-based nursing; (2) adequate organisational performance as measured by outcome-based metrics; and (3) broad access to several levels within the organisational hierarchy granted to the research team.

In total, 55 research participants were purposefully recruited to represent different levels within the hierarchy (executive, middle and front line), roles (nursing managers and facilitators of evidence-based practice) and sectors of health care (acute and primary/community services). Semi-structured face-to-face or phone interviews conducted in English or Swedish in 2016–2017 served as the main method of data collection. The interviews included the elements of critical incident technique (Chell 2004), whereby the respondents were asked to provide concrete examples of implementing evidence-based practice. Informal conversations with research participants influenced the analysis.

The interviews were digitally recorded and transcribed verbatim. Swedish transcripts were (partially) translated into English, and all transcripts were analysed with the aid of NVivo. Matrix analysis was deployed to make comparisons across different countries, sectors and groups of respondents (Nadin and Cassell 2004). The first author read the transcripts and coded the data by comparing and contrasting units of meaning in the transcripts. All authors negotiated the higher-level interpretations in a cyclical fashion, in which occasional disagreements were resolved through negotiation. This iterative process of detecting patterns and developing explanations resulted in the articulation of the three main themes described in the following section.

The Credibility of Knowledge as Evidence

Forms of Codified Knowledge Seen as Credible Evidence

As shown in Table 11.1, our participants referred to several forms of codified knowledge as the "sources of evidence" used in their organisations.

Across the four countries, the use of original research was only reported by hybrid clinician-researchers, nurse educators and senior clinicians specialising in a particular area of nursing. Other respondents often dismissed original research as something that "doesn't help necessarily with the practical component of things" (NM4-CE).[1] Indeed, there was a general tendency among participants across different roles to emphasise performance targets, local data and, in particular, organisational policies and procedures as having more credibility than the direct use of evidence-based clinical guidelines:

> I would imagine my staff, the way they would probably get the evidence is through our policies and procedures—would be 90 percent of how they get their evidence... (NM1-A)

Figure 11.1 shows the chain of codified knowledge through which multiple forms of knowledge are interconnected. This chain is dominated by top-down knowledge flows, whereby national, regional or organisational standards inform the development of organisational policies and procedures. Such standards are implemented through continuous processes of clinical audit and quality improvement. They also determine particular forms of outcome data that are routinely collected and analysed. Another top-down element of the chain is the selection and adaptation of clinical guidelines for the local policies and procedures. This is usually undertaken by selected groups of senior clinicians with a significant contribution from experts specialising in a given clinical area and without necessarily seeking input from a range of front-line health professionals:

Table 11.1 Forms of codified knowledge used in the enactment of evidence-based practice

Form of knowledge	Description	Quote
Research articles	A primary source of research evidence which reports and/or reviews the results of original research assesses its contribution to the body of knowledge, including implications for practice, and is published in a peer-reviewed scholarly journal	*I have tried putting articles regarding current topics in the staff room, for example... and then discussing these with the staff. Some are interested but others not (CF1-S)*
Clinical guidelines	Recommendations summarising current best practice based on a systematic review of research evidence in a specific clinical area, usually produced by the professional associations or governmental bodies at the national or international level	*...If we take NICE guidelines... we make sure that, as a consultant group, we look at that together. With guidelines, there are always some risks... And so we've discussed what the risks are potentially. And then obviously, we integrate that into our practice... (CN4-UK)*
Policies and procedures	Principles, rules and protocols formulated or adopted by an organisation to ensure that a point of view held by its governing body informs the day-to-day organisational operations and is translated into an outcome compatible with that view	*We have a policy for everything, literally. There's policies for infection control, there's policies for ANTT<aseptic non touch technique>, there's policies for clinical things, there's policies for fire safety, everything that we do in the Trust there is a policy that outlines what we do (NM2-UK)*

(continued)

Table 11.1 (continued)

Form of knowledge	Description	Quote
Performance standards	Minimum levels of outcome-based performance used to set expectations for the healthcare organisations and professionals as well as for consumers and purchasers of health services, typically developed and used in professional certification and organisational accreditation	*We're taking this audit according to the best practice, so this is the national key performance indicators. These are the indicators nationally and they are not indicators for nothing, they have been tested to be the best practice. If you do this you will have better health outcomes, so that's probably what we talk about all the time (CF3-A)*
National Quality Registries (unique for the Swedish case)	Standardised and complete sets of systematically collected individualised data concerning patient problems, healthcare interventions and outcomes, used to monitor the quality of care	*…We work with… the Palliative Health Quality Registry. We use that registry and work together in the group to think critically around what we could have done better or how well we think we do. Every time a patient dies we look at the registry. It is a way of evaluating the care we have given. Particularly the nursing care given (NM1-S)*

(continued)

Table 11.1   (continued)

Form of knowledge	Description	Quote
Local data	Performance-related data collected in organisations or their units as a result of clinical audit, performance measurement, patient feedback and project evaluation and typically compared with policies, standards or registries	...You need to be able to capture data, to be able to measure data in a consistent way against the evidence-based practice and maybe the targets and the goals et cetera, and you need to be able to see that information on a regular and ongoing basis, to not only your leadership team, but to the front line so that they can see whether or not they're actually making a difference or not (NM4-CE)

...The people who are responsible for writing [the organisational policies and procedures] are mostly dependent on the [medical or surgical] specialities. So if it's something around insulin administration on the ward... the diabetes education nurses, along with the endocrinologist, would write it. (NM1-A)

In some cases, however, the top-down approach described above was complemented by the bottom-up direction of knowledge flows. Sometimes, a perceived practical problem or performance issue triggered the quality improvement interventions, thus granting credibility to the sphere of everyday practice. Grass roots-initiated clinical audits, for example, often resulted in the development of action plans and change packages, which were then incorporated into organisational policies and procedures:

...I see it going both ways – that there might be something that's important from leadership top down, but then, also, that staff identify [what] needs quality improvement or process improvement – so, from a grass-roots level, from bottom up. (CF3-CW)

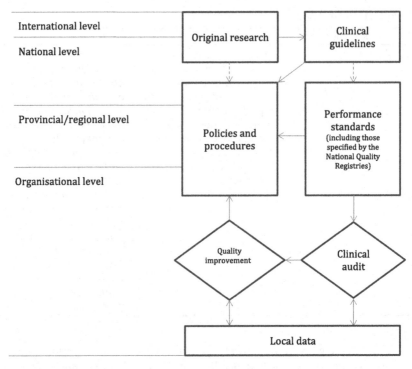

Fig. 11.1 The chain of codified knowledge (Adapted from Kislov et al. 2019)

The Impact of Codified Knowledge on Evidence-Based Nursing

The tendencies of coalescent top-down and bottom-up knowledge work, exemplified above, have a number of important consequences for day-to-day clinical practice. First, the existence of several levels of codification means that there are multiple loci of interaction between codified knowledge and everyday practice within organisations at both senior and front-line levels, including educational events, various team meetings and face-to-face interactions. However, such multiple inter-connected forms of codified knowledge can lead to overformalisation:

> ...Sometimes the priorities set by the organisation... may slightly differ from [what] is important for patients or families, in that the time that

the [registered nurse], say as an example, has to spend with the patient, [conflicts with] filling out documents... (CF3-CW)

Second, there is a risk of over-reliance on local organisational processes and structures related to the appraisal of evidence, production and renewal of local policies and procedures, and their dissemination across the organisation:

> ...[Frontline nurses] know that there's an expectation that they use evidence-based practice, but a lot of the time... it tends to be based on rote learning or... procedures that dictate the way things are done. I don't know whether they necessarily understand the evidence process that's gone into informing those procedures... (CF2-A)

In other words, there is a risk that valorisation of local knowledge and experience leads to misunderstanding of how research comes about, and its roots in and potential relationship with front-line clinical practice. The value of local knowledge and experience is further evident in the view that locally collected information is occasionally seen as no less credible than evidence from the research:

> I don't know about evidence, but I can say that since we've used that [tool] I've had a reduction in falls with harm... (NM1-UK)

Finally, dependence of the chain of codified knowledge on the input of professionals with a specialist expertise around evidence-based practice, data analysis, and quality improvement can further increase the gulf between the "experts" and the "rank-and-file".

> ...I and my closest managerial colleagues use PDSA[2] at a smaller scale... I might use it when I bring things out into the field, but it is not something [frontline] staff use on their own. (NM3-S)

> [The frontline ward staff] are relying on us being the expert ... to have done the research. (CF2-UK)

Across the four countries we sampled, nurses with specialist expertise in a particular clinical area (known as specialist nurses in the UK and Sweden, advanced practice consultants in Canada and clinical practice consultants in Australia) were universally seen as influential in the integration of formal and informal knowledge. However, the configurations of designated facilitator roles involved in the circulation of codified knowledge varied across our four case studies. We describe such variations, and other country-level differences, in the following section.

Variability in the Circulation of Codified Knowledge Across the Four Countries

Table 11.2 shows the relative strength of the key empirical themes across the four countries.

First, the cases differ markedly in the degree of formalisation and reliance on locally adopted standards and policies to the detriment of clinical guidelines. The UK and Australian cases provide an extreme example:

> …From a patient to staff member to ward manager to Exec Board, everybody's aware of those standards and how to maintain them… (EF1-UK)

> So everything that we do has a policy and procedure assigned to it… (CF5-A)

By contrast, although references to local policies and procedures *(beslutsunderlag)* are prominent in the Swedish case, they do not necessarily marginalise system-wide clinical guidelines. For example, *vårdhandboken* (the healthcare handbook)—a web-based compendium of simplified clinical guidelines, which is produced nationally and specifically targets nurses—was often mentioned, unprompted, among the sources of codified knowledge:

> …With nurses and other staff, it might be appropriate to use [the] *vårdhandboken*… or where there are Swedish guidelines for risk of fall available… (CF1-S)

Table 11.2 Variability in the strength of key empirical themes across the four countries

Theme	UK case	Australian case	Canadian case	Swedish case
Marginalisation of clinical guidelines in actual practice	+++	+++	++	+
Perceived overformalisation of practice	+++	+++	++	++
Development of bottom-up flows of codified knowledge	+++	+	++	+
Influence of regional and provincial policies on organisational processes	+	+++	++	+++
Development of designated facilitator roles to support the implementation of evidence-based practice	++	+	+++	+++
Designated roles with expertise in facilitation involved in the chain of codified knowledge	Quality improvement specialists, data analysts	Clinical nurse educators	Clinical practice team and clinical practice coaches (Eastern Canada), clinical nurse educators, research librarians and knowledge management professionals (Western Canada)	Regional and local facilitators, knowledge management professionals

Second, there were national differences in the prevalence and variety of designated facilitator roles. The role of professionals whose remit explicitly involves the facilitation of evidence-based practice was more prominent in codifying the chain of knowledge in the Swedish case and especially prominent in the Canadian case. In these cases, the multi-level infrastructure of peer-to-peer facilitator roles operated outside the lines of formal supervision and performance management. Such boundary-spanning was evident in the virtual (telephone-based and online) "clinical practice teams" and face-to-face "clinical practice coaches" (in Eastern Canada), and the regional and local facilitators (*verksamhetsutvecklare* and *vårdutvecklare* respectively) in Sweden:

> I would really rely on the reports generated by the clinical practice coach to provide a summary of what their observations are, what their interventions are, [and] what gaps in opportunities are observed for individual and group level learning and training... (NM5-CE)

Finally, the development of bottom-up knowledge flows appeared to be variable, with the following quotes exemplifying the marked difference between the UK and Australian cases:

> ...Rather than [imposition of procedures] top-down, it's staff looking at the solution that will work on their ward (EF1-UK)

> Unfortunately, even if I want to say [that knowledge derives] from the bottom up, it's really from the top down... We usually try to bottom up, but then it depends on individual conversion; whereas if it's top down, then it becomes more systematic and... you really make a quicker difference... (CF3-A)

A positive association of quality improvement with the development of bottom-up knowledge flows was reported in the UK case, denoting knowledge from the front line as credible. For one UK participant, for example, "the quality improvement culture really does stand out" (CN4-UK).

Another factor influencing the bottom-up/top-down ratio is the level at which the policies and procedures adopted by the organisation tend to be produced. Australian and Swedish participants, for instance, placed greater emphasis on the direct top-down importation of provincial and regional policies and procedures than did Canadian and, in particular, UK participants:

> [Provincial health authority] have put out some procedures, [regional hospital network] has put out some procedures... How about if we want to get another thing, how do we do this? ...If it's not in the procedure, you're not allowed to do that, so you're really limited as a nurse... (CF3-A)

Thus, policies and procedures that were imposed onto local settings were seen to risk stifling bottom-up knowledge flows.

Evidence-by-Proxy in the Chain of Codified Knowledge

Previous research has highlighted the importance of multiple forms of tacit knowledge and skills in the enactment of evidence-based practice (Dopson et al. 2002; Gabbay and le May 2011). Researchers have rarely questioned the dominance of research evidence as the main form of codified knowledge. The contribution of this study is to outline the central role in health service reform of codified non-research knowledge that is, at best, informed by research evidence partly or indirectly, but is nevertheless perceived as credible evidence. We call this knowledge *evidence by proxy.*

Different forms of evidence by proxy are interconnected in the *chain of codified knowledge*, manifesting in multiple interfaces, where codified knowledge interacts with front-line practice. Although this chain does contain evidence from original research and clinical guidelines, the majority of front-line healthcare staff are likely to rely on performance standards, organisational policies and procedures, and locally collected data as the most frequently consulted forms of codified knowledge. Our study demonstrates that the marginalisation of research evidence is underpinned by a reliance on evidence by proxy and the consequences of its various forms. Mechanisms of generating non-research evidence can in turn be interpreted as an organisational response to the triple pressure of adhering to the evidence-based paradigm as a new orthodoxy (Dopson et al. 2003), coping with the volume of research evidence which has become unmanageable (Greenhalgh et al. 2014) and managing external performance management expectations (Ferlie and McGivern 2014).

While the direction of knowledge flows in the chain of codified knowledge remains predominantly top-down, our findings demonstrate the potential of system-wide, formal knowledge to integrate locally collected forms of data. The implication for policy and practice is that, through bottom-up channels, supported at the organisational level, knowledge from front-line practice can trigger the processes of quality improvement and clinical audit. Eventually such local knowledge can lead to the modification of organisational policies and standards, thus ensuring that the chain of knowledge always, rather than occasionally and accidentally, takes its optimal form—that of a circle. Our findings suggest that an uncritical incorporation of local data can further marginalise the role of research evidence in the enactment of evidence-based practice. This may undermine the credibility that could otherwise be granted to measurable evidence of local improvement, even in the absence of corroboration by rigorous research.

Professional Stratification and Detachment of Rank-and-File Nurses from Clinical Guidelines

The study outlined in this chapter provides further implications about the activation of the chain of codified knowledge. The functioning of the chain of codified knowledge relies on the input of several specialist and hybrid groups. This goes beyond previously described stratification between the selected elite of international experts responsible for the production of clinical guidelines and the rest of the profession (Dopson et al. 2003; Knaapen 2013; Timmermans and Kolker 2004), and also the emergence of "grey sciences", such as systematic reviewing or health economics (Ferlie and McGivern 2014). In fact, institutionalisation of evidence-based practice involves extending stratification towards the middle of the professional hierarchy—and thereby towards the middle of the chain of codified knowledge. After all, senior clinicians with specialist expertise in a particular domain become instrumental for the transformation of clinical guidelines into organisational policies and procedures. The embedding of evidence-based practice is also accompanied by the growing involvement of groups whose main area of expertise is the implementation of codified knowledge through evidence retrieval (librarians), collection and analysis of local data (quality improvement specialists and data analysts), formal education (clinical educators) and supportive facilitation (designated facilitators).

It should come as no surprise, then, that front-line clinical staff may find limited credibility in and become detached from the basic sciences (Fava 2017). They may also become detached from evidence-based clinical guidelines, relying on shortcuts created or translated by specialist and hybrid groups. Our findings show that trust in experts is still apparent in the implementation of evidence-based practice, even though its basis might now be shifting from reliance on experts' clinical judgement towards the faith in these experts' ability to retrieve, appraise, synthesise, translate and apply research evidence. Furthermore, the evidence-based model, due to its emphasis on procedural transparency, does not, in principle, preclude the scrutiny of the elites involved in the process of evidence production by "rank-and-file" clinicians (Knaapen 2013), However, we found that the chain of codified knowledge—originating in the sphere of practice and resonant with research evidence—was rarely questioned by front-line or middle management.

The Influence of Macro-Level Context on the Chain of Codified Knowledge

Our findings reveal how the organisational enactment of evidence-based practice in general and the dynamics of knowledge codification in particular are affected by macro-level context. First, the prioritisation of evidence by proxy and the marginalisation of clinical guidelines are likely to be more prominent in those countries, such as Australia and the UK, whose public sectors have historically been more engaged with the New Public Management logics of standardisation and performance measurement than in those countries, such as Sweden, that display many features of New Public Management but do not belong to the "core" New Public Management group (Ferlie et al. 2016).

Second, the particular forms of codified knowledge and methods of its implementation that appear in any particular setting may be predetermined by the unique features of its historical and technological context. The system of designated facilitator roles in Canada, for example, could be the direct consequence of the pioneering role of Canadian health services researchers in working with policymakers to develop and embed the techniques and practices of knowledge mobilisation (Cooper and Levin 2010). Similarly, the widespread use of National Quality Registries as evidence by proxy in Sweden might be explicable by the unique and long history of governmental support for this "meta-intervention" seen as vital for facilitating evidence-based practice (Fredriksson et al. 2014).

Finally, our findings suggest that there may be two generic archetypes in relation to the preferred ways of maintaining the chain of codified knowledge. The first archetype is characterised by the emphasis on the disciplinary power of standards and audit with less investment in the development of designated facilitator roles. Conversely, the second archetype prioritises the "soft power" of designated facilitator roles with less emphasis on performance standards. Inverse relationship between the reliance on standards and the reliance on designated facilitator roles merits further investigation.

A limitation of this study is that participants may not be representative of their nations. Furthermore, there is a risk of over-generalising about particular nations based on relatively specific and small samples. First, the case and the participants were purposively sampled, which means that they were expected to reflect national patterning on a topic—health system interventions—that involves national jurisdiction covering the whole nation. Second, the point of this chapter was less to argue about central characteristics of the nations of the UK, Sweden, Australia and Canada, and more to represent variations of a particular way to understand the relationship between knowledge work and health system reform.

Conclusion

The tendencies described in this chapter reveal dual effects of codification on evidence-based practice. On the one hand, the legitimisation and mobilisation of contextual and local knowledge counterbalance a certain dogmatic authoritarianism, apparent in the more restrictive interpretations of the evidence-based paradigm (Fava 2017; Holmes et al. 2006). The chain of codified knowledge brings the evidence-based movement closer to addressing the implementation gap it faces (Dopson et al. 2003) and can enable bottom-up knowledge flows through incorporating clinical audit and quality improvement. At the same time, the chain of codified knowledge has its dark side. Over-reliance on evidence by proxy can be accompanied by a significant dilution of the initial evidence-based practice paradigm, excessive formalisation and detachment of front-line staff from the fundamental competencies and knowledge base of evidence-based decision-making. Should these tendencies continue, healthcare organisations may risk turning into "machine bureaucracies" which operate on an incomplete and impoverished knowledge base, can only integrate knowledge at the top of the hierarchy and learn predominantly through the slow process of formalisation (Lam 2000).

To conclude, the study presented in this chapter offers a number of practical implications for change agency in healthcare reform. First, the stratification of clinical professionals in relation to different elements in the chain of codified knowledge underscores the importance of multi-level change interventions, deploying different tools, techniques and forms of codified knowledge to engage with front line and "elite" professionals. Second, moving from over-reliance on evidence by proxy towards embracing the basic principle of "the conscientious, explicit, and judicious use of current best evidence in making decisions about the care of individual patients" (Sackett et al. 1996) would require making the development of fundamental competencies of evidence-based practice a key component of continuing professional education. Finally, executive and senior clinical leaders need to span the boundaries of formal policy and everyday practice, taking a central strategic role in the enactment of evidence-based practice. Such a role would seek to balance external regulatory requirements with internal processes and infrastructure for creating an evidence-based culture and encouraging and supporting critical thinking at the level of front-line practice, with the ultimate aim that patients of their organisations receive care that is optimally coordinated and that maximises their health.

Notes

1. The following abbreviations are used throughout this section to refer to research participants: CF—clinical facilitator; CN—consultant nurse; EF—executive facilitator; NM—nursing manager; A—Australia; CE—Canada East; CW—Canada West; S—Sweden; and UK—United Kingdom.
2. The PDSA (Plan-Do-Study-Act) cycles are widely used in service improvement and include developing a plan to test the change (*Plan*), carrying out the test (*Do*), observing and learning from the consequences (*Study*) and determining what modifications should be made to the test (*Act*).

References

Buchanan, D. A., Addicott, R., Fitzgerald, L., Ferlie, E., & Baeza, J. I. (2007). Nobody in charge: Distributed change agency in healthcare. *Human Relations, 60*(7), 1065–1090.

Chell, E. (2004). Critical incident technique. In C. Cassell & G. Symon (Eds.), *Essential guide to qualitative methods in organizational research* (pp. 45–60). London: Sage.

Cooper, A., & Levin, B. (2010). Some Canadian contributions to understanding knowledge mobilisation. *Evidence & Policy, 6*(3), 351–369.

Dopson, S., Fitzgerald, L., Ferlie, E., Gabbay, J., & Locock, L. (2002). No magic targets! Changing clinical practice to become more evidence based. *Health Care Management Review, 27*(3), 35–47.

Dopson, S., Locock, L., Gabbay, J., Ferlie, E., & Fitzgerald, L. (2003). Evidence-based medicine and the implementation gap. *Health, 7*(3), 311–330.

Fava, G. A. (2017). Evidence-based medicine was bound to fail: A report to Alvan Feinstein. *Journal of Clinical Epidemiology, 84*, 3–7.

Ferlie, E., Dopson, S., Fitzgerald, L., & Locock, L. (2009). Renewing policy to support evidence-based health care. *Public Administration, 87*(4), 837–852.

Ferlie, E., Ledger, J., Dopson, S., Fischer, M. D., Fitzgerald, L., McGivern, G., et al. (2016). The political economy of management knowledge: Management texts in English healthcare organizations. *Public Administration, 94*(1), 185–203.

Ferlie, E., & McGivern, G. (2014). Bringing Anglo-governmentality into public management scholarship: The case of evidence-based medicine in UK health care. *Journal of Public Administration Research and Theory, 24*(1), 59–83.

Fitzgerald, L., Ferlie, E., Wood, M., & Hawkins, C. (2002). Interlocking interactions: The diffusion of innovations in health care. *Human Relations, 55*(12), 1429–1449.

Fredriksson, M., Eldh, A. C., Vengberg, S., Dahlström, T., Halford, C., Wallin, L., et al. (2014). Local politico-administrative perspectives on quality improvement based on national registry data in Sweden: A qualitative study using the consolidated framework for implementation research. *Implementation Science, 9*, 189.

Gabbay, J., & le May, A. (2011). *Practice-based evidence for healthcare: Clinical mindlines*. Oxon: Routledge.

Greenhalgh, T., Howick, J., & Maskrey, N. (2014). Evidence based medicine: A movement in crisis? *British Medical Journal, 348*, g3725.

Harrison, S. (1998). The politics of evidence-based medicine in the United Kingdom. *Policy & Politics, 26*(1), 15–31.

Harvey, G., Gifford, W., Cummings, G., Kelly, J., Kislov, R., Kitson, A., et al. (2019). Mobilising evidence to improve nursing practice: A qualitative study of leadership roles and processes in four countries. *International Journal of Nursing Studies, 90*, 21–30.

Harvey, G., & Kitson, A. (Eds.). (2015). *Implementing evidence-based practice in healthcare: A facilitation guide*. London: Routledge.

Hasselbladh, H., & Bejerot, E. (2007). Webs of knowledge and circuits of communication: Constructing rationalized agency in Swedish health care. *Organization, 14*(2), 175–200.

Holmes, D., Murray, S. J., Perron, A., & Rail, G. (2006). Deconstructing the evidence-based discourse in health sciences: Truth, power and fascism. *International Journal of Evidence-Based Healthcare, 4*(3), 180–186.

Kislov, R. (2014). Boundary discontinuity in a constellation of interconnected practices. *Public Administration, 92*(2), 307–323.

Kislov, R., Hodgson, D., & Boaden, R. (2016). Professionals as knowledge brokers: The limits of authority in healthcare collaboration. *Public Administration, 94*(2), 472–489.

Kislov, R., Waterman, H., Harvey, G., & Boaden, R. (2014). Rethinking capacity building for knowledge mobilisation: Developing multilevel capabilities in healthcare organisations. *Implementation Science, 9*, 166.

Kislov, R., Wilson, P., Cummings, G., Ehrenberg, A., Gifford, W., Kelly, J., et al. (2019). From research evidence to "evidence by proxy"? Organizational enactment of evidence-based health care in four high-income countries. *Public Administration Review, 79*(5), 684–698. https://doi.org/10.1111/puar.13056.

Knaapen, L. (2013). Being 'evidence-based' in the absence of evidence: The management of non-evidence in guideline development. *Social Studies of Science, 43*(5), 681–706.

Lam, A. (2000). Tacit knowledge, organizational learning and societal Institutions: An integrated framework. *Organization Studies, 21*(3), 487–513.

Mackey, A., & Bassendowski, S. (2017). The history of evidence-based practice in nursing education and practice. *Journal of Professional Nursing, 33*(1), 51–55.

Nadin, S., & Cassell, C. (2004). Using data matrices. In C. Cassell & G. Symon (Eds.), *Essential guide to qualitative methods in organizational research* (pp. 271–287). London: Sage.

Rousseau, D. M., & Gunia, B. C. (2016). Evidence-based practice: The psychology of EBP implementation. *Annual Review of Psychology, 67*, 667–692.

Rycroft-Malone, J., Seers, K., Titchen, A., Harvey, G., Kitson, A., & McCormack, B. (2004). What counts as evidence in evidence-based practice? *Journal of Advanced Nursing, 47*(1), 81–90.

Sackett, D. L., Rosenberg, W. M. C., Gray, J. A. M., Haynes, R. B., & Richardson, W. S. (1996). Evidence based medicine: What it is and what it isn't. *British Medical Journal, 312*(7023), 71–72.

Satterfield, J. M., Spring, B., Brownson, R. C., Mullen, E. J., Newhouse, R. P., Walker, B. B., et al. (2009). Toward a transdisciplinary model of evidence-based practice. *Milbank Quarterly, 87*(2), 368–390.

Timmermans, S., & Kolker, E. S. (2004). Evidence-based medicine and the reconfiguration of medical knowledge. *Journal of Health and Social Behavior, 45*, 177–193.

Turner, S., Higginson, J., Oborne, C. A., Thomas, R. E., Ramsay, A. I. G., & Fulop, N. J. (2014). Codifying knowledge to improve patient safety: A qualitative study of practice-based interventions. *Social Science and Medicine, 113*, 169–176.

Part IV

Enacting Boundary Capabilities

This fourth and final part of the book moves the debate on boundaries forward by focusing on the capabilities of boundaries themselves. To commence, Sharp and colleagues, from the UK, expose the transformational capacity of "toolkits" as "boundary-objects-in-use," beyond the still-prevalent "pipeline" view of knowledge translation and mobilisation. Coté-Boileau and colleagues, undertake a realist evaluation in Québec, Canada, to show the transcendence of academic and service boundaries across the care continuum, as a model for cross-sectoral, non-linear and relational modes of system transformation. In the final chapter of the book, French and colleagues, from the UK, show how facilitated quality improvement (QI) activities can also foster local adaptation, and hence, improvement capability, by health professionals and staff at the frontlines of health services.

12

A Qualitative Exploration of Sustainability Processes for Improvement: The Role of Structured Sustainability Tools

Laura Lennox, Catherine E. French and Julie E. Reed

Introduction

Making change in complex health systems often results in unpredictable and unexpected challenges (Plsek et al. 2001). Health systems are made up of diverse programmes, actors, organisational practices and interventions which often represent different professional and organisational boundaries, and which are often dependent on each other for optimal care coordination (Plsek et al. 2001). Interactions among system stakeholders occur under constantly changing conditions replete with uncertainty and surprises (Dovers 1996; Fiksel 2007; Shigayeva and Coker 2015). Such

L. Lennox (✉) · C. E. French · J. E. Reed
National Institute for Health Research Collaboration for Leadership in
Applied Health Research and Care (NIHR CLAHRC) Northwest London,
Imperial College London, Chelsea and Westminster Hospital, London, UK
e-mail: l.lennox@imperial.ac.uk

L. Lennox
Department of Primary Care and Public Health,
Imperial College London, London, UK

© The Author(s) 2020
P. Nugus et al. (eds.), *Transitions and Boundaries in the Coordination
and Reform of Health Services*, Organizational Behaviour in Healthcare,
https://doi.org/10.1007/978-3-030-26684-4_12

unpredictability poses a significant challenge not only to successful implementation of interventions but also to the sustainability of changes within these environments (Greenhalgh et al. 2004; Stirman et al. 2012).

Healthcare organisations engage in a wide range of initiatives aimed at transforming and improving health and care services. Unfortunately, it is now well recognised that demonstrated success of an initiative does not ensure a programme's maintenance beyond its initial funding (Savaya et al. 2009; Williams et al. 2015). Despite significant resources invested in improvement initiatives, approximately only one-third of initiatives show evidence of sustainability and spread, and few maintain all aspects originally implemented (NHS Modernisation Agency 2004; Maher et al. 2010; Stirman et al. 2012). Many factors determine whether improvement efforts succeed or fail (Chaudoir et al. 2013). Factors such as dependence on external funding, unrealistic budgets, short-term grant funding, limited staff commitment, shifting organisational priorities and failure to change organisational culture have all been discussed in the literature as potential causes for initiative failure to be sustained (Goodman et al. 1993; Senge et al. 1999; Damschroder et al. 2009; Martin et al. 2012).

Initiatives that fail to sustain their improved outcomes or processes waste valuable human and monetary resources and contribute to unnecessary and inefficient variation across similar services (Shediac-Rizkallah and Bone 1998; Gruen et al. 2008). This has also been seen to cause staff, patients and the public to lose trust and enthusiasm for engaging in improvement programmes (Hovlid et al. 2012; Martin et al. 2012). Given the current economic climate, characterised by cost-cutting, healthcare organisations cannot afford to waste limited resources engaging in 'unsuccessful' improvement efforts (Healthcare Improvement Scotland 2013). Rising healthcare demands and competition for scarce resources have resulted in more healthcare managers and planners

C. E. French
Guy's and St Thomas' NHS Foundation Trust, London, UK
e-mail: catherine.french@gstt.nhs.uk

J. E. Reed
e-mail: julie.reed02@imperial.ac.uk

wanting to ensure the long-term impact of their investments (Stirman et al. 2012; Chambers et al. 2013). This has resulted in a growing interest in understanding how sustainability of initiatives can be influenced (Stirman et al. 2012; Chambers et al. 2013).

Prospective Exploration of Sustainability

Sustainability threats present across multiple stages of initiative planning, implementation and follow-up to influence sustainability outcomes over time (Shediac-Rizkallah and Bone 1998). While many studies on sustainability of improvement initiatives have been conducted, the majority of these studies investigate sustainability retrospectively (only after the end of the initial funding period) (Pluye et al. 2004; Savaya et al. 2009). This linear perspective on sustainability 'does not take account of the recursive or reflexive character of sustainability and learning or of the continuous adjustments that shape the sustainability process' (Pluye et al. 2004). To fully comprehend the process of achieving sustainability, a prospective approach is needed (Scheirer and Dearing 2011). This is because a prospective approach enables the influences on the sustainability of initiatives being played out in real times and places to be observed.

The concept of sustainability as a 'process' rather than an 'outcome' has been represented by some as a system's resilience or ability to respond to and recover from changes made within the environment (Dovers 1996; Fiksel 2007; Shigayeva and Coker 2015). Viewing sustainability as process incorporates concepts of 'adaptation, self-organization and learning' (Shigayeva and Coker 2015). This lens allows sustainability to be viewed as a change process that can be influenced by individuals throughout initiatives by continuing to develop and adapt in response to the needs of the system (Folke et al. 2002; Fiksel 2003; Shigayeva and Coker 2015). It also allows for guidance to improve initiative design and characteristics necessary to sustain particular interventions (Johnson et al. 2004). This has led many to recognise that in order to achieve sustainable improvement, actions and planning for sustainability must start during initiative implementation, long before the programme's funding ends (Pluye et al. 2004; Maher et al. 2010; Scheirer and Dearing 2011).

Studying sustainability throughout initiatives is complex as there is little consensus in the literature on what needs to be sustained and what constitutes 'achieving sustainability' (Shediac-Rizkallah and Bone 1998; Martin et al. 2012). The terms used in sustainability research prove a significant challenge because of multiple definitions, descriptions and meanings of sustainability. Sustainability of improvements is claimed to be a priority for most improvement initiatives, but the concept of what will be sustained is diverse (Altman et al. 1991; Shediac-Rizkallah and Bone 1998; Martin et al. 2012). This may include: continuation of the *health benefits* from an initiative. Others claim it takes the form of the continuation of *initiative activities*, or even the *capacity built* in the workforce or community (Shediac-Rizkallah and Bone 1998). More recently, the ability to adapt and continuously improve has also been recognised as a potential definition of sustainability (Moore et al. 2017). For the purposes of this work, 'sustainability' will refer to the general continuation and maintenance of a desirable feature of an improvement initiative and its associated outcomes, until such time when they are replaced with new evidence or more favourable interventions or processes.

The study of sustainability in ongoing improvement initiatives requires the analysis of sustainability 'by proxy'—that is, with identification of particular capabilities or characteristics hypothesised to be precursors of sustainability (Shigayeva and Coker 2015). To aid this analysis in practice, various models, frameworks and tools have been proposed (Glasgow et al. 1999; WHO 2004; Sirkin et al. 2005; Bowman et al. 2008; Feldstein and Glasgow 2008; Gruen et al. 2008; Chambers et al. 2013; Schell et al. 2013). Such sustainability tools attempt to render sustainability less complicated by breaking the concept down into manageable factors or constructs (Shediac-Rizkallah and Bone 1998; Bowman et al. 2008; Wiek et al. 2012).

Influencing Sustainability with a Structured Tool

To influence the sustainability process, improvement teams must have the ability to manage processes and respond to initiative needs; to collaborate across professional and institutional boundaries with stakeholders to build relationships; to make informed decision about sustainability risks; and to plan actions to mitigate challenges (Shediac-Rizkallah and Bone 1998; Mancini and Marek 2004; Gruen et al. 2008; Maher et al. 2010; Lennox et al. 2017). Specific sustainability tools, such as a structured guide of principles to follow, have been proposed as a way to support these needs. Evidence for the use of sustainability tools currently relies on individual study findings which have reported anecdotal benefits of use. These hypothesised benefits include: improved understanding of the barriers and risks to sustainability; facilitation of the development of vision and mission for programs; building group consensus and initiative ownership; improving involvement of stakeholders; and providing an overview of the initiative that may not otherwise be monitored (Sarriot et al. 2004; Doyle et al. 2013; Calhoun et al. 2014). Considerable efforts are invested in the development and application of these tools. Therefore, there is a need to explore the role of sustainability tools in achieving these benefits and understand how using a structured sustainability tool may influence the sustainability process in improvement initiatives. Unfortunately, few sustainability tools have been studied in healthcare practice. This means that we have little evidence on if or how they may influence initiative processes and outcomes (Schouten et al. 2008; Stirman et al. 2012). The aim of this chapter is to understand the processes by which improvement teams influence sustainability in improvement initiatives using a structured sustainability tool.

Understanding Efforts Towards Sustainable Quality Improvement

This study will investigate the application of one sustainability tool: The Long Term Success Tool. The 'Long Term Success Tool' (LTST) was developed at The National Institute for Health Research Collaboration for Leadership in Applied Health Research and Care for Northwest London (CLAHRC NWL) in 2015 (Lennox et al. 2017). The tool was informed by literature and was developed with stakeholders and end-users to provide an evidence-based user-friendly approach, for improvement teams to consider sustainability of their initiatives. The LTST aims to: 'support those implementing improvements reflect on 12 key factors to identify risks and prompt actions to increase chances of sustainability over time'. The tool includes a framework that identifies and describes factors for sustainability and a questionnaire to assess the factors. The factors assessed within the tool are: *Commitment to the improvement; Involvement; Skills and capabilities; Leadership; Team functioning; Resources in place; Evidence of benefits; Progress monitored for feedback and learning; Robust and adaptable processes; Alignment with organisational culture and priorities; Support for improvement;* and *Alignment with external political and financial environment* (Lennox et al. 2017).

As part of the broader project from which the study in this chapter derives, the 12 factors were rated on a 5-point Likert scale (from Very good to Very poor), as well as 'no opinion' and 'don't know' options. Each question includes an opportunity for free text comments for each factor. Improvement team members answer 12 questions within the tool individually and anonymously. As part of the larger project, individual scores were collated to produce team reports which include descriptive statistics, visual charts as well as comment lists for each factor. Because this chapter is intended to discern patterns of influence on sustainability of improvement initiatives, only qualitative data will be reported in this chapter.

Context and Cases

The LTST was applied within three diverse Quality Improvement (QI) Programmes across the UK throughout this work. A brief description of each programme is presented below. The use of three cases allows for the comparison of the tool across different contexts and settings. Programme 1 is a London-based five-year funded research programme supporting front-line care teams to implement evidence-based practice to ensure resonance across the research-practice boundary. The programme funds improvement initiatives that cover a diverse range of health topics and disease areas. The initiatives are undertaken across diverse healthcare settings, including primary, secondary and community care. Initiatives run for approximately 18–24 months with the aim to have established improvements that will sustain beyond this period.

Programme 2 is a government-led initiative that involves supporting and implementing local, unscheduled care improvement teams in hospitals, to enhance coordination in the hospitals' care pathways, to deliver optimal patient care, as well as meet a four-hour Accident and Emergency Department targets across Scotland. This programme engages and supports healthcare teams to overcome challenges and provides targeted investment to support implementation with the use of local improvement teams. The programme delivers learning and improvement workshops where innovation and best practices are shared with improvement teams and QI skills are developed.

Programme 3 was set up in partnership between a health education network and an academic institution in Oxford, in the United Kingdom (UK). It aimed to promote continuous learning to support innovation adoption throughout the National Health Service (NHS). All programme participants were managers and clinicians from NHS organisations. The programme aimed to support participants to develop the tools and skills necessary to efficaciously introduce clinical innovations within their organisations. Participants of the programme designed and implemented an innovation project within their healthcare workplace settings. Table 12.1 describes the application of the tool across each programme.

We conducted a longitudinal mixed methods study. Data were collected across the three Quality Improvement (QI) Programmes in the UK from January 2015 to July 2017.

The LTST was used by the programmes at varying time intervals throughout the duration of their initiatives. Use ranged from two to six times throughout the study period. Tool responses were collected on a paper questionnaire form, online Qualtrics survey or on the CLAHRC NWL Web Improvement System for Healthcare (WISH) (Curcin et al. 2014). The first author observed improvement teams to identify how teams discuss sustainability within their projects, and how the tool was used in practice. Observation took both participant and non-participant forms and was conducted a sample of team meetings and workshops and involved discussion of perceived outcomes of the LTST us.

Table 12.1 Description of use and application of the LTST

Application	Programme 1 (P1)	Programme 2 (P2)	Programme 3 (P3)
Rationale for use	To identify issues to sustainability to aid in planning	Identifying areas for progress and needs of the project	Diagnosis for progress
Timing of use	Quarterly	Improvement workshops	Module sessions and in workplace
# of Improvement teams	11	19	26
Data collection	Paper or Online tool	Paper	Paper or Online survey
Data input	Team members (often project manager)	Facilitator	Project lead/ Project manager
Report generation	Online system	Facilitator	Facilitator
Feedback and discussion of reports	Team meetings and reviews	Workshops	Module sessions and in workplace

Semi-structured interviews were also conducted to gain in-depth understanding of perceived sustainability processes and actions. A purposive sampling strategy was used to recruit interviewees from across improvement teams. Participants were selected based on their role within diverse improvement projects and their level of knowledge of the project. This approach aimed to maximise the diversity of perspectives gained from the interviews (Onwuegbuzie and Leech 2007). Two researchers, the first author and two other CLAHRC NWL researchers, conducted the interviews in either a face-to-face format, via Skype or via telephone.

All interviews were professionally transcribed, and the observing researcher typed observational notes into electronic files. All transcripts, LTST reports and uploaded observation field notes were imported into qualitative research software NVivo 10 for analysis (QSR International Pty Ltd. 2016). Qualitative comments and actions made within the transcripts were analysed cyclically to explore contextual issues underpinning scores and discern thematic findings across programmes.

An iterative and inductive process guided the thematic analysis, in which data excerpts were compared and contrasted to provide increasingly abstract themes, which are illustrated in the following sections (Ritchie 1994; Braun and Clarke 2006; Vaismoradi et al. 2013). The research team collaboratively developed a preliminary coding structure, drawing on a framework of sustainability constructs as coding nodes, with themes on processes and actions inductively derived (Lennox et al. 2018). The coding structure was iteratively developed, integrated and refined as further data were added to the dataset (Elo and Kyngäs 2008). Findings are reported using narrative summaries and example quotes with explicit links to the original written texts.

Sustainable Improvement Through the Long Term Success Tool

During the study period, data were collected from 56 improvement teams across the three programmes. In total, 658 LTST responses were collected with over 2350 qualitative comments. Interviews were conducted with 34 improvement team members, and 37 hours of observation were undertaken.

Processes and Mechanisms to Sustain Improvement

The use of the LTST throughout initiatives supported three processes highlighted in the sustainability literature: *collaboration, decision- making* and *action planning* (Dovers 1996; Shediac-Rizkallah and Bone 1998; Mancini and Marek 2004; Fiksel 2007; Gruen et al. 2008; Dauphinee et al. 2011; Shigayeva and Coker 2015). We explored how the processes were supported by the tool and identified eight underlying mechanisms: *Identifying and engaging stakeholders; gathering team perspectives; giving people a voice; raising awareness; Identifying risks and needs; providing direction or focus; proposing actions; and taking action.* Each of these processes and mechanisms is discussed below.

1. Collaboration: Building Networks and Relationships

In order for QI initiatives to sustain they require collaboration between diverse stakeholders such as professionals and managers from different disciplines and patients and carers (Shediac-Rizkallah and Bone 1998; Mancini and Marek 2004; Gruen et al. 2008). Collaboration between these diverse groups allows shared understanding of the problem to be established and aids in the creation of responsive and effective interventions (Leffers and Mitchell 2011). Unfortunately, gaining commitment and continued involvement from diverse groups in health care can be challenging. Professional and personal boundaries between groups often have to be considered as these groups often have competing ideas and priorities (Wenger 1998; Lamont and Molnár 2002). The use of the tool across all sites appeared to promote and encourage collaboration among improvement teams. In this regard, we identified four mechanisms: *identifying and engaging stakeholders; gathering team perspectives; giving people the space to express opinions; and raising awareness.*

I. Identifying and Engaging Stakeholders:

Bringing together multiple stakeholders and working in collaboration were related to having the ability to reveal important links and interdependencies which would have otherwise remained hidden. The process of engaging colleagues was seen as an important practice taken on by multiple teams to maintain interest and support from stakeholders. Participants expressed how the use of the tool allowed them to speak to their colleagues about the project and provided them with the opportunity to engage members of their team who were less involved. Some participants commented that engaging colleagues to complete the tool was itself a challenge. Many participants were convening projects on their own. So, establishing who was on their 'team' proved difficult. These difficulties were seen to highlight the need for further engagement planning.

I think for us, it definitely gave us food for thought about how we get a wider reach… When we sat and looked around before filling it in, it did make me think: a) do you have two local improvement teams in each area? – because we don't have two local teams in each table completing this form. So, what do we need to do about that; how do we… make sure that we're engaging the right people? (P2_I34_Project R)

II. Gathering Team Perspectives:

The ability of the tool to provide a platform for users to share their views of the project was also highlighted as a mechanism influencing the degree of collaboration. In some cases, discussing results created a forum for teams to come together and recognise shared experiences which, in turn, fostered a sense of team cohesiveness and support. A number of participants recognised the importance of receiving feedback on the initiative from their colleagues and stakeholders. Such feedback was seen as crucial to understanding if the intervention was meeting needs and understanding what changes may be needed.

People have … learnt that it's OK to ask questions and to offer their knowledge, experience, advice into the mix and to not see it as a silo. (P1_I10_ Project Alpha)

It was a tool that really enabled us as a team to be more cohesive … because it really made us realise that they also feel the same. Like, oh, I'm not here on my own. (P1_I15_ Project Gamma)

III. Giving People the Space to Express Opinions:

The tool was also observed to be beneficial to teams as it permitted people to anonymously voice their unpopular or challenging opinions, and share concerns. Participants commented that the tool allowed some less confident team members to voice concerns without being criticised, which contributed to the openness of conversations.

It's the anonymity of it as well, which is the fact that, obviously, as a team member I'm quite outspoken, but there's a lot of people who aren't, and the fact that there is nobody that can interfere with your thoughts when you're completing that form is really important. (P1_I15_Project Gamma)

IV. Raising Awareness:

Many participants reported that awareness of their projects was limited, making building partnerships around the work challenging. The tool was highlighted as a mechanism to aid awareness-raising, because it gave participants something tangible with which to initiate interactions and discussions about the initiatives and share their work more broadly.

It's quite difficult for them to raise their projects or to go and talk to people, just to cold call about the project, but the tool was a vehicle that they could hang a conversation on about their projects. (P3_I27_Programme Lead)

2. Supporting Decision-Making

Managing processes, adapting to needs and responding to system changes have been seen as essential to sustaining improvements (Dovers 1996; Fiksel 2007; Dauphinee et al. 2011; Shigayeva and Coker 2015). Having a mechanism to assess and judge sustainability risks and plan actions may aid this process (Johnson et al. 2004; Doyle et al. 2013). The tool supported decision-making by allowing for the *identification of risks and needs* and *providing focus or direction* for improvement efforts.

V. Identifying Risks and Needs:

Participants recognised the importance of identifying potential risks to sustainability in order to understand how best to avoid pitfalls. The tool played a key role in identifying such risks and aiding teams to consider how best to address them to mitigate risks throughout initiative journeys. Comments made concerning lack of support from staff and unrealistic expectations helped teams to understand embedded influences on sustainability.

> *The tool of itself obviously is not a solution for fixing your risks or for avoiding your risks, but…[the tool] helped me to reflect about them. I could plan before the risk happened.* (P3_I28_Project 26)

> *Whilst the organisation emphasizes the need to improve, there is some reluctance amongst some staff to support new initiatives.* (P2_Project H_LTS report 2)

VI. **Providing Direction or Focus:**

The sustainability of improvement initiatives depends on interrelated and wide-ranging factors (Shediac-Rizkallah and Bone 1998; Scheirer 2005; Gruen et al. 2008). The tool was seen as a way of providing focus among team members and strategically planning for risks factors. It provided a structure to account for sustainability and highlighted the importance of maintaining attention to sustainability risks throughout the project.

> *Are you focusing enough on this thing that you always knew you had to do, that maybe you've lost sight of a little bit? I think that's extremely valuable, because it's easy to get caught up in something and forget about other things that are important.* (P1_I1_Project Beta)

3. **Action Planning**

Using the LTST allowed teams to understand where action was considered crucial for the success of the project. Planning actions support the sustainability of initiatives by reshaping behaviours and activities, changing and adapting interventions and reorganising relationships (May and Finch 2009; Finch et al. 2013). The development of such actions also benefits from being informed by multiple stakeholders at various organisational levels (Persaud 2014). The tool provided a mechanism for teams to: *suggest actions* and *take actions* to increase chances of making a lasting change.

VII.   Suggesting Actions:

The tool provided a way of collecting team perspectives on where action was needed and what particular actions would be beneficial to the initiative. Participants shared ideas on what actions may be necessary and also suggested potential solutions to problems.

VIII.   Taking Action:

I got ideas from them (LTST comments), because they would say, 'oh, they did something similar at such and such place, and we do this in clinic', and we find it quite successful. So, they'd give me ideas. (P1_I29_Project 18)

Participants also took particular actions that were shaped by particular suggestions. Such actions included designating tasks and responsibilities fairly to improve work distribution, using teaching to build the project into everyday practice and taking steps to improve patient engagement. These actions were seen as crucial to sustainability, because they allowed teams to proactively respond to challenges and address problems that may hinder the sustainability of the project in future.

The comments that were provided to me by my stakeholders, I've used them and responded accordingly, and based my actions from their response … because it's like having a customer. If you don't know what a customer needs you don't know what to provide the customer. (P3_I32_Project 24)

They did action a couple of things in regards to educating other staff. So, they had MDTs (multi-disciplinary teams) where they started to educate the other nurses [who] weren't involved in the project on what they were doing, and also junior doctor turnover. The consultant cardiologist would be teaching them anyways. So, he added in a slot where they'd talk about the bundle (a heart failure care bundle to optimise the care of heart failure patients) and tell them what you need to do. (P1_I21_Project Delta)

The Role of Structured Tools for Sustainable Improvement

The aim of this chapter was to discern the processes by which improvement teams influence sustainability in improvement initiatives using a structured sustainability tool, the LTST. The contribution of the chapter was to show that structured tools focused specifically on sustainability can aid sustainability by focusing on challenges, and optimising opportunities, for long-term survival as they present during a project's design and implementation. To this extent, such tools also complement participatory action research methods, which, through cycles of action, evaluation, modification and re-implementation, can help ensure that innovations are coherent with the reality of everyday practice in particular contexts. This work explored the role of a sustainability tool in supporting sustainability processes and investigated underlying mechanisms which contributed to these processes.

The LTST was used by 56 diverse improvement teams. We explored the tool's role in negotiating sustainability processes across three QI programmes. Our findings have shown that the LTST supported three high-level sustainability processes with eight mechanisms throughout the initiatives: *collaboration* (*identifying and engaging stakeholders, gathering team perspectives, giving people the space to express opinions* and *raising awareness*); *decision-making* (*identifying risks and needs*, and *providing direction or focus*); and *action planning* (*suggesting actions* and *taking action*).

Our findings are supported by other studies in the field which have also shown that overtly fostering collaboration among team members and their wider stakeholders; supporting decision-making by highlighting risks and needs of the initiatives; and prompting action planning to improve chances of sustainability throughout initiative journeys are important processes to sustain changes (Brinkerhoff and Goldsmith 1992; Mancini and Marek 2004; Leffers and Mitchell 2011; May et al. 2011; Scheirer and Dearing 2011; Iwelunmor et al. 2016). While our study corroborates much of the research evidence, we also contribute new empirical findings to the sustainability literature. Our work has demonstrated that a sustainability tool can play a role in enhancing and supporting sustainability processes in improvement initiatives. Initiative sustainability can be aided by forming networks and building collaboration between diverse stakeholders although fostering this collaboration can be labour-intensive to achieve (Shediac-Rizkallah and Bone 1998; Mancini and Marek 2004; Maher et al. 2010; Leffers and Mitchell 2011; Lennox et al. 2017). Professional and personal boundaries often have to be considered, given that these groups have competing priorities and perspectives (Wenger 1998; Lamont and Molnár 2002).

Bringing together different stakeholders in a QI initiative requires cooperation from all groups to reconcile or make sense of the 'social worlds' held by each (Gerson 1983; Star and Griesemer 1989). The LTST appears to provide a mechanism which supports collaboration by highlighting different perspectives held between team members and providing a forum for sharing diverse opinions. Specifically, the anonymity of the scores was highlighted as providing a safe place for people to voice difficult or controversial views. This becomes increasing important in health care where established hierarchies can discourage critical feedback (Sutcliffe et al. 2004).

Shared decision-making among stakeholders is also an important determinant for the sustainability of complex health programmes (Mancini and Marek 2004). This process often requires improvement teams to address multiple priorities and potentially conflicting agendas (Wheeler 2009). It is, therefore, essential that improvement teams have the ability to identify risks and respond to system needs to sustain changes over time (Dauphinee et al. 2011). Our findings indicate the LTST aided the sustainability process by enhancing knowledge of risks within ongoing initiatives and enabled participants to understand the views and concerns within their teams.

In order to enhance sustainability in practice, improvement teams must take action to respond, adapt and mitigate challenges and risks(Shediac-Rizkallah and Bone 1998; Maher et al. 2010; Lennox et al. 2017). The tool served as a reflective and thought-provoking mechanism connecting key perspectives within teams and directing attention to particular challenges and risks needing attention.

This resulted in specific actions being identified and taken that were directed, as opposed to being relatively random and based on the whims of one stakeholder, for example team members highlighted the reliance of the initiatives on particular staff members and therefore the wider team took action to designate tasks and responsibilities more widely and fairly.

This research provides not only valuable information on the processes involved in sustaining improvements, but also provides insight into how a sustainability tool can foster prospective sustainability planning and actions throughout initiative journeys. The tool enabled the ongoing tacit and collaborative working within teams and across stakeholders to be made visible. The value that the tool added shows the importance of studying sustainability prospectively as an ongoing process throughout initiatives. Prospective sustainability planning can allow those engaged in new initiatives to make connections, maintain focus and mitigate risks to enhance chances of achieving long-term success (Pluye et al. 2004).

Although our study aided in the exploration of prospective sustainability processes, impact on sustainability outcomes remains unknown. The findings suggest that having a tool to study sustainability throughout an initiatives' journey may aid in prospective sustainability actions and planning, but we do not know if this will ultimately increase initiative longevity. Generalisability of study findings is also a limitation. The tool was tested across three QI programmes with diverse initiatives, but it is unknown if similar results would be achieved in other healthcare contexts (i.e. programmes with little or no QI support).

We suggest that our study could support further research in this area by providing a basis for identifying similar or additional sustainability processes in other settings. We are also unsure of the extent to which other sustainability tools will support the identified processes. Further investigation and application of other tools in practice are required to understand if sustainability tools can all perform a general function of supporting sustainability processes. Future research in this field would also benefit from applying available tools to understand the application processes and assess the overall impact of their use (Scheirer and Dearing 2011).

Conclusion

This chapter conveyed how the LTST supported three processes for the sustainability of improvement initiatives. Given the complexity of boundary-work in contemporary health care, the optimal coordination of diverse health professionals and services demands greater insight into sustainability processes. The extent to which these processes occur in individual initiatives and how they impact sustainability outcomes is unknown. Future research should focus on how various stakeholders of a new initiative can adapt their initiatives in real times and places. Future research by the current team will involve a cross-site analysis in which programme-level findings will be examined, with the aim of discerning generalisable learning on challenges and facilitators to sustainability. Ultimately, this study indicates that sustainability tools may be useful to assessing teams' perceptions of sustainability to prompt planning and actions to increase chances of success. Sustainability is a challenging concept to explore but the use of a prospective tool may aid those undertaking improvement initiatives to identify risks and allow for prospective sustainability planning.

References

Altman, D. G., et al. (1991). Obstacles to and future goals of ten comprehensive community health promotion projects. *Journal of Community Health, 16*(6), 299–314. https://doi.org/10.1007/BF01324515.

Bowman, C. C., et al. (2008). Measuring persistence of implementation: QUERI series. *Implementation Science, 3*(21). https://doi.org/10.1186/1748-5908-3-21.

Braun, V., & Clarke, V. (2006). Using thematic analysis in psychology. *Qualitative Research in Psychology, 3,* 77–101.

Brinkerhoff, D. W., & Goldsmith, A. A. (1992). Promoting the sustainability of development institutions: A framework for strategy. *World Development, 20*(3), 369–383. https://doi.org/10.1016/0305-750X(92)90030-Y.

Calhoun, A., et al. (2014). Using the program sustainability assessment tool to assess and plan for sustainability. *Preventing Chronic Disease, 11*(Table 1), 130185. https://doi.org/10.5888/pcd11.130185.

Chambers, D. A., Glasgow, R. E., & Stange, K. C. (2013). The dynamic sustainability framework: Addressing the paradox of sustainment amid ongoing change. *Implementation Science: IS, 8*(1), 117. https://doi.org/10.1186/1748-5908-8-117.

Chaudoir, S. R., Dugan, A. G., & Barr, C. H. I. (2013). Measuring factors affecting implementation of health innovations: A systematic review of structural, organizational, provider, patient, and innovation level measures. *Implementation Science: IS, 8*(22), 1–20. https://doi.org/10.1186/1748-5908-8-22.

Curcin, V., et al. (2014). Model-driven approach to data collection and reporting for quality improvement. *Journal of Biomedical Informatics, 52*, 151–162.

Damschroder, L. J., et al. (2009). Fostering implementation of health services research findings into practice: A consolidated framework for advancing implementation science. *Implementation Science: IS, 4*, 50. https://doi.org/10.1186/1748-5908-4-50.

Dauphinee, W. D., et al. (2011). A framework for designing, implementing, and sustaining a national simulation network. *Simulation in Healthcare: Journal of the Society for Simulation in Healthcare, 6*(2), 94–100. https://doi.org/10.1097/SIH.0b013e31820695e8.

Dovers, S. R. (1996). Sustainability: Demands on policy. *Journal of Public Policy, 16*(3), 303–318. https://doi.org/10.1017/S0143814X00007789. Imperial College London Library.

Doyle, C., et al. (2013). Making change last: Applying the NHS institute for innovation and improvement sustainability model to healthcare improvement. *Implementation Science: IS, 8*(1), p. 127. https://doi.org/10.1186/1748-5908-8-127.

Elo, S., & Kyngäs, H. (2008). The qualitative content analysis process. *Journal of Advanced Nursing, 62*(1), 107–115. https://doi.org/10.1111/j.1365-2648.2007.04569.x.

Feldstein, A. C., & Glasgow, R. E. (2008). A practical, robust implementation for integrating research findings into practice. *The Joint Commission Journal on Quality and Patient Safety, 34*(4), 228–243.

Fiksel, J. (2003). Designing resilient, sustainable systems. *Environmental Science and Technology, 37*(23), 5330–5339. https://doi.org/10.1021/es0344819.

Fiksel, J. (2007). Sustainability and resilience: Toward a systems approach. *IEEE Engineering Management Review, 35*(3), 5. https://doi.org/10.1109/EMR.2007.4296420.

Finch, T. L., et al. (2013). *Improving the normalization of complex interventions* (pp. 1–8). https://doi.org/10.1186/1748-5908-8-43.

Folke, C., et al. (2002). Resilience and sustainable development: Building adaptive capacity in a world of transformations. *Ambio, 31*(5), 437–440. https://doi.org/citeulike-article-id:1524120.

Gerson, E. M. (1983). Scientific work and social worlds. *Knowledge, 4*(3), 357–377. https://doi.org/10.1177/107554708300400302.

Glasgow, R. E., Vogt, T. M., & Boles, S. M. (1999). Evaluating the public health impact of health promotion interventions: The RE-AIM framework. *American Journal of Public Health, 89*(9), 1322–1327.

Goodman, R. M., et al. (1993). Development of level of institutionalization scales for health promotion programs. *Health Education Quarterly, 20*(2), 161–178.

Greenhalgh, T., et al. (2004). *How to spread good ideas: A systematic review of the literature on diffusion, dissemination and sustainability of innovations in health service delivery and organisation.* London.

Gruen, R. L., et al. (2008). Sustainability science: An integrated approach for health-programme planning. *The Lancet, 372*(9649), 1579–1589. https://doi.org/10.1016/S0140-6736(08)61659-1. Elsevier Ltd.

Healthcare Improvement Scotland. (2013, July). Guide on spread and sustainability. *Change and Its Leadership: The Role of Positive Emotions, 39.*

Hovlid, E., et al. (2012). Sustainability of healthcare improvement: What can we learn from learning theory? *BMC Health Services Research, 12,* 235. https://doi.org/10.1186/1472-6963-12-235.

Iwelunmor, J., et al. (2016). Toward the sustainability of health interventions implemented in sub-Saharan Africa: A systematic review and conceptual framework. *Implementation Science: IS, 11*(1), 43. https://doi.org/10.1186/s13012-016-0392-8.

Johnson, K., et al. (2004). Building capacity and sustainable prevention innovations: A sustainability planning model. *Evaluation and Program Planning, 27*(2), 135–149. https://doi.org/10.1016/j.evalprogplan.2004.01.002.

Lamont, M., & Molnár, V. (2002). The study of boundaries in the social sciences. *Annual Review of Sociology, 28*(1), 167–195. https://doi.org/10.1146/annurev.soc.28.110601.141107.

Leffers, J., & Mitchell, E. (2011). Conceptual model for partnership and sustainability in global health. *Public Health Nursing, 21*(1), 91–102. Copyright (C) 2011 Blackwell Publishing Ltd.: Blackwell Publishing Inc.

Lennox, L., et al. (2017). What makes a sustainability tool valuable, practical, and useful in real world healthcare practice? A qualitative study on the development of the long term success tool in Northwest London. *British Medical Journal Open, 7*(e014417), 1–13. https://doi.org/10.1136/bmjopen-2016-014417.

Lennox, L., Maher, L., & Reed, J. (2018). Navigating the sustainability landscape: A systematic review of sustainability approaches in healthcare. *Implementation Science, 13*(1), 1–17. https://doi.org/10.1186/s13012-017-0707-4.

Maher, L., Gustafson, D., & Evans, A. (2010). *Sustainability model and guide.* Coventry, UK: NHS Institute for Innovation and Improvement.

Mancini, J. A., & Marek, L. I. (2004). Sustaining community-based programs for families: Conceptualization and measurement. *Family Relations, 53*(4), 339–347.

Martin, G. P., et al. (2012). Innovation sustainability in challenging health-care contexts: Embedding clinically led change in routine practice. *Health Services Management Research, 25,* 190–199. https://doi.org/10.1177/0951484812474246.

May, C., & Finch, T. (2009). Implementing, embedding, and integrating practices: An outline of normalization process theory. *Sociology, 43*(3), 535–554. https://doi.org/10.1177/0038038509103208.

May, C. R., et al. (2011). Evaluating complex interventions and health technologies using normalization process theory: Development of a simplified approach and web-enabled toolkit. *BMC Health Services Research.* C.R. May, Faculty of Health Sciences, University of Southampton, UK, 11, p. 245.

Moore, J. E., et al. (2017). Developing a comprehensive definition of sustainability. *Implementation Science, 12*(1), 110. https://doi.org/10.1186/s13012-017-0637-1.

NHS Modernisation Agency. (2004). *Complexity of sustaining healthcare improvements: What have we learned so far: Research into Practice report 13.*

Onwuegbuzie, A. J., & Leech, N. L. (2007). Sampling designs in qualitative research: Making the sampling process more public. *The Qualitative Report, 12*(2), 19–20. https://doi.org/10.1007/s11135-006-9000-3.

Persaud, D. (2014). Enhancing learning, innovation, adaptation, and sustainability in health care organizations: The ELIAS performance management framework. *Health Care Manag (Frederick).* (C) 2014 Wolters Kluwer Health|Lippincott Williams & Wilkins: Author Affiliation: School of Health Administration, Dalhousie University, Halifax, Canada, pp. 183–204.

Plsek, P. E., Wilson, T., & Greenhalgh, T. (2001). Complexity science: The challenge of complexity in health care. *British Medical Journal, 323*(7315), 625–628. https://doi.org/10.1136/bmj.323.7315.746.

Pluye, P., Potvin, L., & Denis, J.-L. (2004). Making public health programs last: Conceptualizing sustainability. *Evaluation and Program Planning, 27*(2), 121–133. https://doi.org/10.1016/j.evalprogplan.2004.01.001.

QSR International Pty Ltd. (2016). *NVivo qualitative data analysis software* (11th ed.). Melbourne, Australia: QSR International Pty Ltd.

Ritchie, J. S. (1994). *Qualitative data analysis for applied policy research* (R.G. Burgess, Ed.). London: Routledge.

Sarriot, E. G., et al. (2004). A methodological approach and framework for sustainability assessment in NGO-implemented primary health care programs. *International Journal of Health Planning and Management, 19,* 23–41.

Savaya, R., Elsworth, G., & Rogers, P. (2009). Projected sustainability of innovative social programs. *Evaluation Review, 33*(2), 189–205. https://doi.org/10.1177/0193841X08322860.

Scheirer, M. A. (2005). Is sustainability possible? A review and commentary on empirical studies of program sustainability. *American Journal of Evaluation, 26*(3), 320–347. https://doi.org/10.1177/1098214005278752.

Scheirer, M. A., & Dearing, J. W. (2011). An agenda for research on the sustainability of public health programs. *American Journal of Public Health, 101*(11), 2059–2067. https://doi.org/10.2105/AJPH.2011.300193.

Schell, S. F., et al. (2013). Public health program capacity for sustainability: A new framework. *Implementation Science, 8*(1), 15. https://doi.org/10.1186/1748-5908-8-15.

Schouten, L. M. T., et al. (2008). Evidence for the impact of quality improvement collaboratives: Systematic review. *BMJ (Clinical Research Ed.), 336*(7659), 1491–1494.

Senge, P., et al. (1999). *The dance of change: The challenges of sustaining momentum in learning organizations.* London: Nicholas Brealey.

Shediac-Rizkallah, M. C., & Bone, L. R. (1998). Planning for the sustainability of community-based health programs: Conceptual frameworks and future directions for research, practice and policy. *Health Education Research, 13*(1), 87–108.

Shigayeva, A., & Coker, R. J. (2015). Communicable disease control programmes and health systems: An analytical approach to sustainability. *Health Policy and Planning, 30*(3), 368–385. https://doi.org/10.1093/heapol/czu005.

Sirkin, H. L., Keenan, P., & Jackson, A. (2005, October). The hard side of change management. *Harvard Business Review, 10,* 109–118.

Star, S. L., & Griesemer, J. R. (1989). Institutional ecology, 'translations' and boundary objects: Amateurs and professionals in Berkeley's Museum of vertebrate zoology, 1907–39. *Social Studies of Science, 19*(3), 387–420. https://doi.org/10.1177/030631289019003001.

Stirman, S. W., et al. (2012). The sustainability of new programs and innovations: A review of the empirical literature and recommendations for future research. *Implementation Science, 7*(1), 17. BioMed Central Ltd. https://doi.org/10.1186/1748-5908-7-17.

Sutcliffe, K. M., Lewton, E., & Rosenthal, M. M. (2004). Communication failures: An Insidious contributor to medical mishaps. *Academic Medicine, 79*(2), 186–194. https://doi.org/10.1097/00001888-200402000-00019.

Vaismoradi, M., Turunen, H., & Bondas, T. (2013). Content analysis and thematic analysis: Implications for conducting a qualitative descriptive study. *Nursing Health Sciences, 15*(3), 398–405.

Wenger, E. (1998). Communities of practice: Learning as a social system. *Systems Thinker, 9*(5), 2–3. https://doi.org/10.2277/0521663636.

Wheeler, S. (2009). Using research. *Business Information Review, 26*(2), 112–120. https://doi.org/10.1177/0266382109104412.

WHO. (2004). *Guidelines for Conducting an Evaluation of the Sustainability of CDTI Projects, African Programme for Onchocerciasis Control.*

Wiek, A., et al. (2012). From complex systems analysis to transformational change: A comparative appraisal of sustainability science projects. *Sustainability Science, 7*(Suppl. 1), 5–24. https://doi.org/10.1007/s11625-011-0148-y.

Williams, L., et al. (2015, August). A cluster-randomised quality improvement study to improve two inpatient stroke quality indicators. *BMJ Quality & Safety, 25*(4), 257–264. https://doi.org/10.1136/bmjqs-2015-004188.

13

The Means Not the End: Stakeholder Views of Toolkits Developed from Healthcare Research

Charlotte A. Sharp, William G. Dixon, Ruth J. Boaden and Caroline M. Sanders

Introduction

The purpose of this chapter is to articulate the factors influencing the development of toolkits to mobilise knowledge from healthcare research according to the perspectives and experiences of key stakeholders. The epistemological approach taken views knowledge as arising cumulatively

C. A. Sharp (✉) · R. J. Boaden
Alliance Manchester Business School,
The University of Manchester, Manchester, UK
e-mail: charlotte.sharp@manchester.ac.uk

R. J. Boaden
e-mail: ruth.boaden@manchester.ac.uk

W. G. Dixon
Centre for Epidemiology Versus Arthritis,
School of Biological Science, Faculty of Biology, Medicine and Health,
The University of Manchester, Manchester, UK
e-mail: will.dixon@manchester.ac.uk

© The Author(s) 2020
P. Nugus et al. (eds.), *Transitions and Boundaries in the Coordination and Reform of Health Services*, Organizational Behaviour in Healthcare,
https://doi.org/10.1007/978-3-030-26684-4_13

(Crilly et al. 2010) and from a combination of organisational context and the interactions between and within those using it (Greenhalgh and Wieringa 2011). We will begin by offering an explanation for the rise in the development of "products" from healthcare research and justify the focus on "toolkits". We engage boundary object theory (Star and Griesemer 1989) as a theoretical lens to inform the interpretation of qualitative data. Our findings indicate that research "products" such as toolkits might (or might not) live up to their hope of spanning the boundary between the different disciplines or communities of practice (CoPs) in healthcare research and practice (Wenger 1998).

The analysis first unveils some less-frequently identified boundaries between different actors in the field of healthcare research. We then explore the ways in which toolkits have the properties of boundary objects across these boundaries in the development and mobilisation of knowledge, at times in unexpected ways. Finally, we examine the implications of our findings to suggest how healthcare researchers, funders, practitioners, research subjects and other stakeholders might change their current ways of working to improve the impact of toolkits and other "non-academic" products from healthcare research.

Knowledge Mobilisation

Getting research evidence into healthcare practice is said to involve the crossing of two "translational gaps", going from "bench-to-bedside" and "implementing these products and approaches into clinical practice" (Cooksey 2006, pp. 12, 35). Despite the language used to demarcate precisely particular phases and actors, this messy and complex process does not follow the traditional "pipeline" approach of research dissemination (Green 2008) and is highly dependent upon a number of different, interrelated factors (Ward et al. 2009). Acknowledgement of this complexity (Ferlie et al. 2012) leads to the view that the process of

C. M. Sanders
NIHR Centre for Primary Care, Faculty of Biology, Medicine and Health, The University of Manchester, Manchester, UK
e-mail: caroline.sanders@manchester.ac.uk

getting research into action may best be regarded as knowledge mobilisation: "how research- based knowledge is accessed, applied and embedded" (Crilly et al. 2010, p. 11). Collaborative knowledge creation, also known as "mode 2" knowledge production (Nowotny et al. 2001); participatory research (Cornwall and Jewkes 1995); engaged scholarship (Van de Ven and Johnson 2006); co-design (Bate and Robert 2007) and integrated knowledge translation (Straus et al. 2013), may increase the potential for knowledge mobilisation (Rycroft-Malone et al. 2016) by involving stakeholders throughout the research process and empowering them to enact findings in practice (Marshall et al. 2014).

The traditional organisational separation between healthcare providers and academia and the different institutional drivers for these organisations (Macleod et al. 2014) promote a transactional approach to healthcare research. In the main, academics continue to "create" knowledge for "use" by practitioners (Davies et al. 2008), adhering to the "pipeline" view (Green 2008). Such a view assumes that knowledge is sufficient in itself to enable research findings to be implemented in practice. Notable examples of organisations that include formal collaborations between academia and healthcare providers worldwide include the Veteran's Association in the United States (US) (Atkins et al. 2017) and the United Kingdom's (UK) National Institute for Health Research Collaborations for Leadership in Applied Health Research and Care (NIHR CLAHRCs), both of which have a focus on translating research into practice. These pockets of innovative practice are, however, far from the norm. Despite their relative success in mobilising knowledge, both institutions acknowledge that challenges persist, notwithstanding their claims of integrated practice (Atkins et al. 2017; Rycroft-Malone et al. 2015).

Toolkits

The formal policy context provides well-intentioned incentives for the demonstration, or "performance", of knowledge mobilisation. Healthcare researchers are increasingly obliged to demonstrate that they have considered knowledge mobilisation during grant applications (Tetroe et al. 2008), in addition to more "traditional" dissemination via academic papers. The push for dissemination to "extend beyond publication" (Wilson et al. 2010) is due, in part, to the increasing emphasis on demonstrating research "impact" (Greenhalgh et al. 2016). In the UK, for example, university funding is based largely upon the Research Excellence Framework, which introduced impact case studies in 2014, designed to demonstrate the impact of research beyond academia (Research England 2019). Outputs other than academic papers now have currency within academia, contributing to the rise in the development of "products" of healthcare research, such as toolkits (Yamada et al. 2015) and actionable tools (Cooke et al. 2017) that aim to support actively the implementation of research findings. This study uses toolkits as an exemplar of a non-academic product to explore the factors influencing their development and potential engagement, drawn from an analysis of the perspectives and experiences of key stakeholders.

Barac et al. (2014, p. 124) define toolkits as a "packaging of multiple resources that codify explicit knowledge, such as templates, pocket-cards, guidelines, algorithms and summaries, and that are geared to knowledge sharing, educate, and/or facilitate behaviour change". They may be used as a simple and flexible means of promoting evidence-based practice (Yamada et al. 2015). Despite a steady increase in their production in the last twenty years (Davis et al. 2017), awareness of toolkits within the NHS remains low (Lee et al. 2014), and the only published literature review of their value in implementation concluded that there is little evidence regarding their impact (Yamada et al. 2015).

Davis et al.'s (2017) qualitative study explored the desires of end-users and the factors that might support frontline engagement with toolkits. This was the only publication identified which addresses stakeholder perspectives on toolkits. The authors put forward characteristics of effective toolkits, which comprised one of four key themes, including the requirements to: specify the target audience, be tested out and shown to be effective, be presented in multiple formats and be easy to navigate and brief (Davis et al. 2017), the last point being mirrored by Powell et al. (2015). Whilst Davis et al. (2017) contribute useful learning to the scant commentary upon and synthesis of evidence on toolkits, they include only the perspective of end-users and do not consider the factors influencing the toolkits' development. We attempt to add to the existing literature, addressing this gap in our knowledge and understanding by including a broader range of stakeholders and drawing upon and applying existing theory to our analysis.

Boundary Objects

The prevailing sociocultural differences between healthcare research and practice are reinforced by the organisational separation between universities and healthcare organisations, which the rare exceptions noted above have tried to overcome (Atkins et al. 2017; Rycroft-Malone et al. 2015). There are numerous, less explicit boundaries within such organisations (Kislov et al. 2011). This chapter will focus on three boundaries between researchers and other actors within the broader field of applied healthcare research, namely researchers and practitioners, research funders and researchers, and researchers and research subjects. When different disciplines, or CoPs (Lave and Wenger 1991), attempt to transfer knowledge across the boundaries, between them, boundary spanners such as brokers, interactions and objects may be employed (Kislov et al. 2011).

Boundary objects are created with the intention of "serv[ing] as bridges between intersecting cultural and social worlds" (Nicolini et al. 2012, p. 614). We explore stakeholder views on whether or how toolkits have the properties of boundary objects in mediating the boundaries outlined above. The concept of boundary objects was first outlined by Star and Griesemer, who described them as being:

> ...both plastic enough to adapt to local needs and the constraints of the several parties employing them, yet robust enough to maintain a common identity across sites. They are weakly structured in common use, and become more strongly structured in individual use. (Star and Griesemer 1989, p. 393)

Wenger identifies them as including "artefacts, documents, terms, concepts ... around which communities of practice can organise their interconnections" (Wenger 1998). One of the key facets of Star's original notion of a boundary object was that of interpretive flexibility (Star 2010), denoting their varied meanings to different people. The concept has been subject to a number of interpretations and significant debate regarding its application, as elaborated upon in Trompette and Vinck's review (2009) and by Star herself (2010).

Carlile's highly cited work outlined how boundary objects might help to *transform* knowledge (Carlile 2002, 2004). Levina and Vaast (2005) extended this further, proposing that "designated-boundary objects" are developed with the express aim of spanning boundaries. In order to fulfil this aim and be transformed into a "boundary object-in-use", it must be useful locally; have a common identity, or symbolic structure, that is recognisable to more than one field; and be integrated into everyday practice (Levina and Vaast 2005) (see Table 13.1).

Whilst designated boundary objects may be developed with the intention of spanning boundaries, objects which unintentionally reinforce boundaries (Oswick and Robertson 2009; Swan et al. 2007) can act as negative boundary objects (Allen 2014). Swan et al. (2007) propose that boundary objects may play a symbolic role across particular boundaries, bridging these gaps in less instrumental ways than other commentators have suggested.

We propose that toolkits from healthcare research may be viewed as boundary objects. As packages of resources that users may select and apply to their local context, toolkits, we suggest, may fulfil Star's criterion of having a variable structure. They have the potential for interpretive flexibility by virtue of being understandable by a number of groups, including healthcare researchers, practitioners and funders. They may help to transport invisible structures by advising on how to go about the practical implementation of specific practices (Star and Griesemer 1989). We will use this theoretical lens to explore how toolkits are viewed and how decision-makers might optimise their potential for transforming knowledge into practice (Carlile 2004), taking them from designated boundary objects to boundary objects-in-use (Levina and Vaast 2005).

Table 13.1 Designated boundary objects versus boundary objects-in-use (adapted from Levina and Vaast 2005, p. 342)

Designated boundary objects	Boundary objects-in-use
Artefacts assigned the role of boundary spanning across different fields, due to inherent features including design and properties	Artefacts that span boundaries and are used in practice across different fields, with a common vision. These artefacts do not need to have been designated as a boundary object and may fulfil this function spontaneously

Understanding Stakeholder Perspective on Toolkits

This chapter draws on a qualitative study of the perspectives and experiences of key stakeholders, which aimed to understand the factors influencing the development of toolkits intended to mobilise knowledge from healthcare research. Purposive sampling was employed; the initial participants were academics working on projects from a commissioned call from the UK's main healthcare funding agency, the National Institute for Health Research (2016), an approach employed in similar studies (Goering et al. 2010). Four of the seven original projects within this call planned to develop a toolkit. So, this group included individuals who did or did not intend to develop a toolkit, therefore representing an ideal initial sample (Stake 2005). Subsequent snowball sampling (Carter and Henderson 2005) led to the inclusion of individuals from a broad range of roles in the organisational hierarchy, disciplines, subject expertise in knowledge mobilisation and experience in using or developing toolkits. A particular strength of this sample is that stakeholders from every stage of the research process were targeted, including those funding, developing and using toolkits, and from a number of locations across the UK.

Semi-structured interviews were conducted to gain a deep understanding of participants' experiences, feelings, opinions and knowledge of toolkits in healthcare research (Patton 2002). 20/23 individuals who were invited to be interviewed accepted. Interviews were recorded and transcribed; data were coded and analysed using Quirkos software. All interviews, coding and analysis were performed by Charlotte A. Sharp (CAS). Interviews were coded as soon as possible after they took place, informing the topic guide for subsequent interviews. Thematic analysis was performed iteratively, using techniques based on Grounded Theory (Donovan and Sanders 2005). As more data were generated, line-by-line inductive coding was refined into broader themes. Once sensitisation to "boundary objects" theory had occurred, some of the data were readily mapped to components of that theory, whilst also allowing inductive development of themes beyond the notion of boundary objects themselves. These themes were further refined in three-weekly discussions with the research team and by returning to the literature.

Because some research participants were fellow academics and because of her professional background in medicine, it was important for CAS to practice reflexivity and to consider her background and perspectives within the research process (Mays and Pope 2000). Peer—interviewing may break down some of the barriers to discussing difficult issues in depth because of a "shared understanding" between interviewer and interviewee (Chew-Graham et al. 2002). However, peers may unwittingly conspire to reduce the depth and quality of the data collected (Chew-Graham et al. 2002). CAS's position as a relative newcomer to social sciences academia was used to justify asking more probing questions on issues which might otherwise have been taken for granted, mediating this risk. Reflexivity, through field notes and discussion, was also practised throughout the study in meetings with the wider research team.

Emergent themes were presented to a focus group at the end of the study period. The focus group comprised those attending an "Action Learning Set" from the commissioned call described above (National Institute for Health Research 2016). This provided a platform on which a collective discussion (Fitzpatrick and Boulton 1994) on both the acceptability of the themes and new insights was held. Three of those invited to the focus group declined, but they had already been interviewed. Ethical approval was granted by the University of Manchester's Research Ethics Committee (AMBS-2016-030).

Structures and Processes of Knowledge Mobilisation in Health Care

Participants

Twenty-eight (28) individuals in total participated: in semi-structured interviews ($n = 20$) and a focus group ($n = 11$), with three participants contributing to both. Senior academics with subject expertise in knowledge mobilisation, principal investigators and more junior "researchers" (research associates and research fellows) were included. They came from a number of disciplines (sociology, psychology, medicine, anthropology), had a range of subject expertise in knowledge mobilisation (from none to being experts) and had experience in using or developing toolkits (Table 13.2). Research funders came from organisations funding healthcare research. Our "practitioners" group included individuals in managerial roles with experience in using or developing toolkits (or both).

The analysis identified three major themes: perceptions of toolkits, the process of their development and their role as boundary objects, each with corresponding sub-themes (Fig. 13.1).

Many participants noted the ambiguity of the term "toolkit", which was reported to be a *"catch all"* (F2), *"trendy"* (PI5 and M2), *"buzzword"* (R2). There was broad agreement, however, that the term implied a collection of practical tools to aid the implementation of research findings.

Toolkits were felt to contain a variety of resources, including *"pathways for thinking"* (A6), activities, templates or tools, with the aim of *"taking people step by step and ... giving them practical tips"* (M1). Emphasis was placed on the need for users to be able to adapt and select which elements to employ. Some participants wanted them to focus on how to do something, rather than on what to do. Others preferred that they should contain prompts and questions to stimulate thoughtful use rather than simply being passively received. Participants, especially practitioners, were clear that toolkits would be used *"if they're meeting a need"* (M3). Most participants anticipated that toolkits would be hosted online, and that they might include a variety of media, including PDF files, videos and recordings.

Table 13.2 Participant characteristics and codes

Code	Role	Number
A	Senior academic with subject expertise in knowledge mobilisation	6
PI	Principal investigator	7
R	Researcher	9
F	Research funder	3
M	Practitioner	3

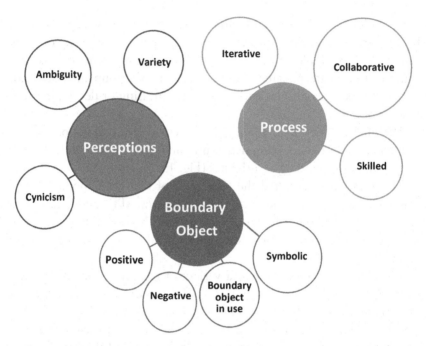

Fig. 13.1 Themes and sub-themes

The vast majority (16/20) of interview participants reported feeling cynical about toolkits, regardless of whether or not they planned to develop a toolkit themselves. One described how: "… *my heart slightly sank when we were asked to do a toolkit because I thought, 'Oh no, this is something people are a bit fed up with*'" (M2). Some were concerned that producing a toolkit "*feels like a quite reductionist way of thinking about something incredibly complex*" (A3), "*seems a bit naïve*" (R1) and is "*just not that simple*" (PI3). Participants reported that toolkits might not always be an appropriate output, and that this varied, depending on the project.

Cynicism stemmed from the view that "*the NHS is awash with toolkits developed by academics*" (A6), with the proliferation of toolkits leading to a self-fulfilling cycle of production. Many participants perceived that funders expected toolkits as an output from their research, describing them as a "*tick-box*" exercise (R1, F2, M3, PI6) on application forms and a *"convention of a grant"* (A6). This was due to toolkits having become the *"default option"* (M1) for non-academic outputs. In contrast to the perceptions of researchers, funders were clear that whilst *"more imaginative dissemination strategies"* (F2) were desired, toolkits were neither mandated nor suggested as possible outputs, and they indeed commented that their presence on applications forms elicited a *"groan"* (F2). Participants reported that, at times, little thought was given to toolkit content, and that applicants felt obliged to pursue them:

> *You get to the end of the project and you're knackered, but you've planned to do a toolkit, so here's the flipping toolkit.* (M1)

Process

Collaboration between healthcare researchers and end-users of toolkits was felt to be the optimum approach to their development. Participants felt that, ideally, stakeholders should be embedded from the beginning of a project, reporting that toolkits which are developed as *"a sort of add-on at the end"* (F2) were less likely to succeed. The work of developing the aesthetic side of toolkits was seen as skilled, and some participants strongly believed that uptake would be enhanced by collaborating with design teams to *"provide tailored marketing products for the research findings"* (F3) and making toolkits *"more tactile and more engaging with other bits of peoples' brains"* (A3). Collaborating with organisations that would "host" the toolkit (assuming it were online) was also suggested as a way to enhance its potential use and sustainability.

The process of toolkit creation was described as iterative, resulting in anxiety for researchers: *"I think that the toolkit perhaps won't look like what I thought it might look like previously ... um, but not that I had a terribly clear idea at the beginning of what it might look like"* (PI2). Anxiety was also created by academics rescinding control of their project to the collaborative process, particularly those with a strong co-design element.

Boundary objects

Participants reported specific examples of toolkits that were regarded as having been successful in bridging the gap between research and practice, fulfilling their potential role as a positive, boundary object-in-use. The following comments provide examples of a toolkit helping to get knowledge into practice: *"it's been very widely used, and well received"* (PI6). And *"genuinely, I do think the [XX] toolkit has been phenomenally useful for those people trying to learn about [XX]"* (PI5). Participants described how a toolkit could help to mediate the relationship between healthcare researchers and practitioners: "[it creates] *the possibility of engaging once again in a kind of continuing dialogue with the people on whose behalf we do this work"* (A6).

The focus group discussion provided evidence of participants using the process of developing a toolkit as an output from their research *"as a sort of bargaining chip"* (R6) to enhance access to research participants and as a symbol to mediate relationships with them.

> R4: *It's aiding the research. It's aiding the process.*
> R8: *Yes.*
> R4: *Whether the toolkit is actually useful in the end…*
>   R8: *Yes. I think that's the question.*
> R4: *… it's a process of … yeah, it's a point to galvanise us around, to forge the relationships and to puzzle over the problems.*

Although toolkits were often viewed as having the potential to be boundary objects, participants were keen to emphasise that toolkits would need to form part of a *"broader strategy"* (A2) of knowledge mobilisation, without which their potential impact might remain unfulfilled. Participants from all fields highlighted the need for action to be taken in response to a toolkit:

> *"But the bottom line is still, develop your toolkit by all means, and then tell us what you're going to do with it"* (F3); *"… even if you produce a toolkit you need to have someone at the other end that … knows how to go about implementing it".* (M3)

Participants warned against the prospect of toolkits being seen as an end in themselves. The concern was that if toolkits were "*seen as the causal agent*" (A5), "*you feel reassured by the fact you can see it in your office rather than actually using it in your work*" (A2). Participants from all backgrounds voiced concerns that a toolkit could "*be something that just sits on the shelf*" (A3) and that "*there's a danger ... then [that] no one ever looks at them, just like they don't look at papers*" (A6). Thus, the sense of security offered by having a toolkit was, paradoxically, felt to have the potential to act as a barrier to implementing change, turning them into potentially negative boundary objects. Finally, the creation of toolkits was seen by a minority as "*reinforcing the transactional nature of research*" (R1), perpetuating the "pipeline approach" of knowledge being produced in one place and simply passed down for use elsewhere.

Toolkits as Boundary Objects

Our study of multiple stakeholder groups found that the term toolkit was interpreted in a variety of ways. Ideas of knowledge mobilisation have advanced to take account of contested and dynamic realities, motivations, contexts and circumstances, yet are likely still to manifest in practical terms as a simple "pipeline" from the active designers and producers to obedient users. The contribution of this chapter is to articulate stakeholder expectations that toolkits are only worthwhile if they, or the processes that deliver them, maximise the agency of users, who would use them as and when they would benefit their everyday work.

Our findings about the various interpretations of the notion of a "toolkit" build on previous research on toolkits that focused on codification of practices and the perception of toolkits as outputs (Davis et al. 2017; Barac et al. 2014). The present research showed the dynamics and factors that shape applied use and contextual relevance, as toolkits come alive in the real-time processes of spanning various boundaries of knowledge mobilisation. Potential unintended consequences of toolkit application (Linstead et al. 2014) might be mitigated by such acknowledgement of processes and contexts of application and building collaborative relationships and cultures across stakeholder boundaries.

Toolkits at the Boundary Between Researcher and Practitioner

Respondents in this study provided clear examples of toolkits acting as boundary objects between healthcare researchers and practitioners, explaining that this occurs when users can select and adapt specific aspects and apply these to their local context, thus demonstrating interpretive flexibility (Star 2010; Star and Griesemer 1989). Designated boundary objects may become boundary objects-in-use only if they are "useful" locally and have a common identity across fields (Levina and Vaast 2005). We use our empirical findings, first, to propose an explanation for toolkits getting stuck as designated boundary objects and, second, to identify factors which, if addressed, may help move toolkits into more productive boundary objects-in-use.

Cynicism about toolkits was a strong theme in our study and one which emerged early. We propose that this common sentiment, found in all stakeholder groups, may represent frustration that toolkits fail to serve consistently as boundary objects-in-use, in turn obstructing the transformation of toolkits from their state as designated boundary objects. If those involved in commissioning and developing them are so wary of them, how can they be expected to ensure that their design and execution are optimised and to expend valuable time and resources on promoting their use by busy practitioners?

Participants in our study identified three factors which may help to transform toolkits from their role as designated boundary objects into boundary objects-in-use. First, they reported that toolkits are more likely to be used if they meet a pre-established need. Second, they reported that collaboration with stakeholders and those skilled in developing such products would enhance their use. If successful, this co-design could help to ensure that toolkits have a symbolic structure that is recognisable to both CoPs, "acquir[ing] a common identity in joint practices" (Levina and Vaast 2005, p. 342). Third, participants felt that in order to increase their potential use, toolkits should be developed as part of a broader strategy of knowledge mobilisation rather than being seen as ends in themselves. Facilitation of implementation, in particular via face-to-face interaction, is an important feature of successful implementation of toolkits (Davis et al. 2017; Sapsed and Salter 2004) and the transition of boundary objects into the "in-use" category (Kitson et al. 2008; Levina and Vaast 2005). The present study drew strength from engaging a wider variety of stakeholders than previous studies, showing common requirements that the processes of toolkit implementation needed to resonate with everyday work contexts.

Our empirical data suggest that toolkits can function as negative boundary objects, impeding application, such as through the reinforcement of boundaries between particular CoPs (Allen 2014; Oswick and Robertson 2009; Rycroft-Malone et al. 2016; Swan et al. 2007). First, toolkits were perceived to reinforce the transactional nature of research, perpetuating the pipeline approach and highlighting the differences between the CoPs at play. Second, respondents expressed concern that if toolkits were seen as ends in themselves, this might represent a barrier to change (Oswick and Robertson 2009), that having a copy on the shelf, albeit unused, might lead to a false sense of security, giving its owner the feeling that they were doing more than they were in practice.

Toolkits at the Boundary Between Researcher and Research Subject

Boundary objects may have symbolic uses in addition to their more widely recognised instrumental uses (Swan et al. 2007). This was evident in regard to the boundary between researchers and their research participants. Participants of our study who were researchers reported that they used the prospect of creating a toolkit to bridge the divide between themselves and their research participants, using it as a "bargaining chip", providing resources for practical use in exchange for better access to and relationships with them. If researchers realised toolkits' potential to enhance the research process as a symbolic boundary object through building relationships with research subjects, along with their potential to act as boundary objects across the more heavily cited boundary between themselves and healthcare practitioners, some of the cynicism about them might be countered.

Toolkits at the Boundary Between Researcher and Funder

Some participants reported that their motivation for developing toolkits was due to a perceived desire for them by funders. The mismatch between performed development of toolkits and demand by users can result in research waste (Macleod et al. 2014; Toews et al. 2016). Applicants use a proposed toolkit as a symbolic boundary object in an attempt to negotiate successful grant application, unveiling a further boundary within the academic world between researchers and research funders. Paradoxically, this perceived desire was not matched by the reported desires of funders in our study. Funders wanted more than a mere statement of intent and found it off-putting if they felt that applicants were paying lip service to toolkits. Researchers misconceived that simply including a toolkit on a proposal could enhance their prospects of success. We propose that the use of toolkits as a symbolic boundary object, in this case, illuminates a potential false assumption that has clear practical implications; namely, better dialogue is needed between these two groups in order to avoid toolkits being proposed and created without careful thought or planning, further fuelling the cynicism directed towards them and resulting in research waste.

Implications

Our empirical data and analysis have implications for practice on a number of different levels. Whilst reform of the institutions that give rise to the boundaries in operation in our study is beyond the reach of both the individuals and organisations involved, collaborative endeavours are attempting some kind of reform even if the effect might be limited (Kislov et al. 2018). In regard to the boundary between healthcare researchers and practitioners, the key pragmatic message regarding knowledge mobilisation is that toolkits should not be seen as ends in themselves and should instead form one part of a broader knowledge mobilisation strategy (Kislov et al. 2018; Macleod et al. 2014).

The fact that most healthcare research is publicly funded confers upon funders and researchers a moral obligation to mobilise research findings, with any failure to do so constituting a waste of resources and human effort. Our findings identified an assumption at the boundary between these groups, with the development of toolkits being used symbolically by researchers in an attempt to gain funding. Closer collaboration between researchers and their funders may mitigate the risk of toolkits being propagated merely to fulfil a perceived, but not necessarily "real", desire from funders, instead fulfilling the objective of mobilising knowledge. Taking this one step further, funders might collaborate with and support researchers during the toolkit development process itself.

We identified that researchers use the development of toolkits to secure and improve access to research participants. Encouraging and building upon this use of toolkits as a symbolic boundary object may result in the development of toolkits that are more relevant and applicable to end-users (Bate and Robert 2007; Cornwall and Jewkes 1995; Nowotny et al. 2001; Rycroft-Malone et al. 2016; Straus et al. 2013; Van de Ven and Johnson 2006). Secondly, collaboration between these groups might pave the way for more effective collective work in future. Finally, those considering developing a toolkit would do well to critique the notion itself. Asking why a particular toolkit should be developed and what is expected of it might lead the end-product closer to fulfilling its presumed aim of mobilising research in ways that best support practice.

Conclusion

Our study, which included a broad range of stakeholders, adds to the scant extant literature on toolkits. This is important because as long as the impact agenda is pursued and the incentive structures within higher education persist in their current state, the development of toolkits is likely to continue. In conceptualising toolkits as boundary objects, we identified them as having multiple potential roles across multiple boundaries. At the boundary between researcher and practitioner, we explored these potential roles as designated boundary objects and boundary objects-in-use, as well as negative boundary objects, reinforcing boundaries. We examined their use as symbolic boundary objects to illuminate the less identified boundaries between healthcare researchers and their research participants, and their funders, respectively. The lens of knowledge mobilisation enabled an interrogation of toolkit development and use, highlighting areas for potential improvement. Researchers, funders, healthcare practitioners and other stakeholders involved in mobilising knowledge from healthcare research might consider these factors when commissioning and designing "non-academic" products such as toolkits, to optimise their well-intended potential for improving healthcare practice.

Acknowledgement This study is funded by the National Institute for Health Research (NIHR) Collaboration for Leadership in Applied Health Research and Care (NIHR CLAHRC) Greater Manchester. The views expressed are those of the author(s) and not necessarily those of the NIHR or the Department of Health and Social Care.

References

Allen, D. (2014). Lost in translation? 'Evidence' and the articulation of institutional logics in integrated care pathways: From positive to negative boundary object? *Sociology of Health & Illness, 36*(6), 807–822.

Atkins, D., Kilbourne, A. M., & Shulkin, D. (2017). Moving from discovery to system-wide change: The role of research in a learning health care system: Experience from three decades of health systems research in the Veterans Health Administration. *Annual Review of Public Health, 38*(1), 467–487.

Barac, R., Stein, S., Bruce, B., & Barwick, M. (2014). Scoping review of toolkits as a knowledge translation strategy in health. *BMC Medical Informatics and Decision Making, 14,* 121.

Bate, P., & Robert, G. (2007). *Bringing user experience to healthcare improvement: The concepts, methods and practices of experience-based design.* Abingdon, UK: Radcliffe Publishing.

Carlile, P. R. (2002). A pragmatic view of knowledge and boundaries: Boundary objects in new product development. *Organization Science, 13*(4), 442–455.

Carlile, P. R. (2004). Transferring, translating, and transforming: An integrative framework for managing knowledge across boundaries. *Organization Science, 15*(5), 555–568.

Carter, S., & Henderson, L. (2005). Approaches to qualitative data collection in social science. In A. Bowling & S. Ebrahim (Eds.), *Handbook of health research methods: Investigation, measurement and analysis* (pp. 215–230). Maidenhead: Open University Press.

Chew-Graham, C. A., May, C. R., & Perry, M. S. (2002). Qualitative research and the problem of judgement: Lessons from interviewing fellow professionals. *Family Practice, 19*(3), 285–289.

Cooke, J., Langley, J., Wolstenholme, D., & Hampshaw, S. (2017). "Seeing" the difference: The importance of visibility and action as a mark of "authenticity" in co-production; comment on "collaboration and co-production of knowledge in healthcare: Opportunities and challenges". *International Journal of Health Policy and Management, 6*(6), 345–348.

Cooksey, D. (2006). *A review of UK health research funding*. London: The Stationery Office.

Cornwall, A., & Jewkes, R. (1995). What is participatory research? *Social Science and Medicine, 41*(12), 1667–1676.

Crilly, T., Jashapara, A., & Ferlie, E. (2010). *Research utilisation and knowledge mobilisation: A scoping review of the literature*. City: National Institute for Health Research Service Delivery and Organisation programme.

Davies, H., Nutley, S., & Walter, I. (2008). Why "knowledge transfer" is misconceived for applied social research. *Journal of Health Services Research & Policy, 13*(3), 188–190.

Davis, M. M., Howk, S., Spurlock, M., McGinnis, P. B., Cohen, D. J., & Fagnan, L. J. (2017). A qualitative study of clinic and community member perspectives on intervention toolkits: "Unless the toolkit is used it won't help solve the problem". *BMC Health Services Research, 17*(1), 497.

Donovan, J., & Sanders, C. (2005). Key issues in the analysis of qualitative data in health services research. In A. Bowling & S. Ebrahim (Eds.), *Handbook of health research methods* (pp. 515–532). Maidenhead: Oxford University Press.

Ferlie, E., Crilly, T., Jashapara, A., & Peckham, A. (2012). Knowledge mobilisation in healthcare: A critical review of health sector and generic management literature. *Social Science and Medicine, 74*(8), 1297–1304.

Fitzpatrick, R., & Boulton, M. (1994). Qualitative methods for assessing health care. *Quality in Health Care, 3*(2), 107.

Goering, P., Ross, S., Jacobson, N., & Butterill, D. (2010). Developing a guide to support the knowledge translation component of the grant application process. *Evidence & Policy: A Journal of Research, Debate and Practice, 6*(1), 91–102.

Green, L. W. (2008). Making research relevant: If it is an evidence-based practice, where's the practice-based evidence? *Family Practice, 25*(1_suppl.), i20–i24.

Greenhalgh, T., Raftery, J., Hanney, S., & Glover, M. (2016). Research impact: A narrative review. *BMC Medicine, 14*(1), 1–16.

Greenhalgh, T., & Wieringa, S. (2011). Is it time to drop the 'knowledge translation' metaphor? A critical literature review. *Journal of the Royal Society of Medicine, 104*(12), 501–509.

Kislov, R., Harvey, G., & Walshe, K. (2011). Collaborations for leadership in applied health research and care: Lessons from the theory of communities of practice. *Implementation Science, 6,* 64.

Kislov, R., Wilson, P. M., Knowles, S., & Boaden, R. (2018). Learning from the emergence of NIHR Collaborations for Leadership in Applied Health Research and Care (CLAHRCs): A systematic review of evaluations. *Implementation Science, 13*(1), 111.

Kitson, A. L., Rycroft-Malone, J., Harvey, G., McCormack, B., Seers, K., & Titchen, A. (2008). Evaluating the successful implementation of evidence into practice using the PARiHS framework: Theoretical and practical challenges. *Implementation Science, 3*(1), 1–12.

Lave, J., & Wenger, E. (1991). *Situated learning: Legitimate peripheral participation.* Cambridge: Cambridge University Press.

Lee, L., Cresswell, K., Slee, A., Slight, S. P., Coleman, J., & Sheikh, A. (2014). Using stakeholder perspectives to develop an ePrescribing toolkit for NHS Hospitals: A questionnaire study. *Journal of the Royal Society of Medicine Open, 5*(10), 1–9.

Levina, N., & Vaast, E. (2005). The emergence of boundary spanning competence in practice: Implications for implementation and use of information systems. *MIS Quarterly, 29*(2), 335–363.

Linstead, S., Maréchal, G., & Griffin, R. W. (2014). Theorizing and researching the dark side of organization. *Organization Studies, 35*(2), 165–188.

Macleod, M. R., Michie, S., Roberts, I., Dirnagl, U., Chalmers, I., Ioannidis, J. P., et al. (2014). Biomedical research: Increasing value, reducing waste. *The Lancet, 383*(9912), 101–104.

Marshall, M., Pagel, C., French, C., Utley, M., Allwood, D., Fulop, N., et al. (2014). Moving improvement research closer to practice: The researcher-in-residence model. *BMJ Quality & Safety, 23*(10), 801–805.

Mays, N., & Pope, C. (2000). Qualitative research in health care: Assessing quality in qualitative research. *British Medical Journal, 320*(7226), 50–52.

National Institute for Health Research. (2016). Commissioning brief 14/156—New research on use and usefulness of patient experience data. City.

Nicolini, D., Mengis, J., & Swan, J. (2012). Understanding the role of objects in cross-disciplinary collaboration. *Organization Science, 23*(3), 612–629.

Nowotny, H., Scott, P., Gibbons, M., & Scott, P. B. (2001). *Re-thinking science: Knowledge and the public in an age of uncertainty.* Buenos Aires: SciELO Argentina.

Oswick, C., & Robertson, M. (2009). Boundary objects reconsidered: From bridges and anchors to barricades and mazes. *Journal of Change Management, 9*(2), 179–193.

Patton, M. Q. (2002). *Qualitative research & evaluation methods.* London: Sage.

Powell, L., Ellis, T., & Mawson, S. (2015). *What makes a successful telehealth implementation toolkit: A qualitative study exploring the usability and perceived value of the "ready, steady go" telehealth toolkit* [Online]. NIHR CLAHRC Yorkshire and Humber. https://drive.google.com/ file/d/0B3-SF4FxenwJaWxjR0R4Z2tGX1E/view. Accessed 22 Sep 2019.

Research England. (2019). *REF 2021: Guidance on submissions (2019/01)* [Online]. Bristol: Research Excellent Framework. https://www.ref.ac.uk/ publications/guidance-on-submissions-201901/. Accessed 22 Sep 2019.

Rycroft-Malone, J., Burton, C., Wilkinson, J. E., Harvey, G., McCormack, B., Baker, R., et al. (2015). Collective action for knowledge mobilisation: A realist evaluation of the collaborations for leadership in applied health research and care. *Health Services and Delivery Research, 3*(44). https://doi. org/10.3310/hsdr03440.

Rycroft-Malone, J., Burton, C. R., Bucknall, T., Graham, I. D., Hutchinson, A. M., & Stacey, D. (2016). Collaboration and co-production of knowledge in healthcare: Opportunities and challenges. *International Journal of Health Policy and Management, 5*(4), 221–223.

Sapsed, J., & Salter, A. (2004). Postcards from the edge: Local communities, global programs and boundary objects. *Organization Studies, 25*(9), 1515–1534.

Stake, R. (2005). Case studies. In N. Denzin & Y. Lincoln (Eds.), *Handbook of qualitative research* (pp. 443–466). London: Sage.

Star, S. L. (2010). This is not a boundary object: Reflections on the origin of a concept. *Science, Technology and Human Values, 35*(5), 601–617.

Star, S. L., & Griesemer, J. R. (1989). Institutional ecology, translations' and boundary objects: Amateurs and professionals in Berkeley's Museum of Vertebrate Zoology, 1907–39. *Social Studies of Science, 19*(3), 387–420.

Straus, S. E., Tetroe, J., & Graham, I. D. (2013). Introduction knowledge translation: What it is and what it isn't. *Knowledge translation in health care* (pp. 1–13). Chichester: Wiley.

Swan, J., Bresnen, M., Newell, S., & Robertson, M. (2007). The object of knowledge: The role of objects in biomedical innovation. *Human Relations, 60*(12), 1809–1837.

Tetroe, J. M., Graham, I. D., Foy, R., Robinson, N., Eccles, M. P., Wensing, M., et al. (2008). Health research funding agencies' support and promotion of knowledge translation: An international study. *Milbank Quarterly, 86*(1), 125–155.

Toews, I., Glenton, C., Lewin, S., Berg, R. C., Noyes, J., Booth, A., et al. (2016). Extent, awareness and perception of dissemination bias in qualitative research: An explorative survey. *PLoS One, 11*(8), e0159290.

Trompette, P., & Vinck, D. (2009). Revisiting the notion of boundary object. *Revue d'anthropologie des connaissances, 3*(1), 3–25.

Van de Ven, A. H., & Johnson, P. E. (2006). Knowledge for theory and practice. *Academy of Management Review, 31*(4), 802–821.

Ward, V., House, A., & Hamer, S. (2009). Developing a framework for transferring knowledge into action: A thematic analysis of the literature. *Journal of Health Services Research & Policy, 14*(3), 156–164.

Wenger, E. (1998). *Communities of practice: Learning, meaning, and identity*. Cambridge: Cambridge University Press.

Wilson, P. M., Petticrew, M., Calnan, M. W., & Nazareth, I. (2010). Does dissemination extend beyond publication: A survey of a cross section of public funded research in the UK. *Implementation Science, 5*, 61.

Yamada, J., Shorkey, A., Barwick, M., Widger, K., & Stevens, B. J. (2015). The effectiveness of toolkits as knowledge translation strategies for integrating evidence into clinical care: A systematic review. *BMJ Open, 5*(4), e006808.

14

Building Transformative Capacities by Expanding the Academic Mission Across the Care Continuum: A Realist Evaluation

Élizabeth Côté-Boileau, Marie-Andrée Paquette and Jean-Louis Denis

Introduction

Evidence increasingly supports the potential of Academic Health Centres (AHCs) to accelerate healthcare integration and quality improvement by developing capacities for innovation, interprofessional teamwork and translational research (Lieff and Yammarino 2017;

É. Côté-Boileau (✉)
Faculty of Medicine and Health Sciences Research,
University of Sherbrooke, Longueuil, QC, Canada
e-mail: elizabeth.cote-boileau@usherbrooke.ca

Doctoral Award Fellow, Fonds de recherche Québec - Santé,
Montreal , QC, Canada

Health Standards Organization, Ottawa, Canada

É. Côté-Boileau · M.-A. Paquette
Charles-Le Moyne – Saguenay– Lac-Saint-Jean Research Center
on Health Innovations, Longueuil, QC, Canada

© The Author(s) 2020
P. Nugus et al. (eds.), *Transitions and Boundaries in the Coordination and Reform of Health Services*, Organizational Behaviour in Healthcare,
https://doi.org/10.1007/978-3-030-26684-4_14

317

Blackburn 2009; Dzau et al. 2010; Lander 2016; Wartman 2015; Coleman et al. 2017). AHCs are unique hybrid models that integrate clinical, scientific and managerial functions (Wartman 2015). The apparently positive effects generated by AHCs have justified significant and increasing financial support from governments in Canada, the United States, Europe and Australia (French et al. 2014); AHCs thus face significant pressure to bring about change within and across healthcare organizations (Lander 2016).

Spreading the tripartite (clinical, scientific and managerial) academic mission across the care continuum represents an important new challenge for AHCs. Lander (2016) conceives AHCs as boundary-spanning organizations that blend logics of science and care, and bridge professional, hierarchical and territorial divides (Kilpatrick et al. 2012; Brimacombe 2010; Huby et al. 2014; Håland et al. 2015; Washington et al. 2016; Datté and Barlow 2017). Recent literature on AHCs identifies a number of potentially actionable levers to integrate the academic mission within and between healthcare organizations. These include accountability systems that clarify the distribution of roles and responsibilities (Blackburn 2009); a multidisciplinary workforce supported by non-hierarchical relationships between clinical, scientific and managerial actors (Ferlie et al. 2005; Hsiao et al. 2018; Coleman et al. 2017; Dzau et al. 2010; Lander 2016; King et al. 2016); alignment of clinical, scientific and managerial missions through incentives and performance targets (Misso et al. 2016); translational activities to increase the impact of research in shaping healthcare services (Lavis et al. 2003, 2006; Mitton et al. 2007; Straus et al. 2011; Van de Ven and Johnson

J.-L. Denis
Health Administration Department, School of Public Health,
University of Montreal, Quebec, Canada
e-mail: jean-louis.denis@umontreal.ca

University of Montreal Hospital, Research Center, Quebec, Canada

Canada Research Chair (Tier I) holder on Health system design and adaptation (Canadian Institutes of Health Research), Montreal, Canada

2006); formalized feedback mechanisms that enable continuous reflection and improvement (Bowen and Martens 2005; Cousins and Simons 1996; Crilly et al. 2013; Kramer and Wells 2005; Mitchell et al. 2009; Wilkinson et al. 2012); and distributed governance alongside inclusive and democratic processes (Denis 2015; Denis and van Gestel 2016). While these insights from the literature provide a deeper understanding of how AHCs might work to integrate the academic mission across boundaries, little attention has been paid to the organizational capacities required to support this integration. Empirical research is needed to understand how capacities are activated through the process of integrating the academic mission across various levels of care.

Denis (2015) refers to the capacities mobilized through large-scale health system change as transformative capacities, defined as "*a set of resources, levers and practices mobilized at the three levels of governance of healthcare systems (macro, meso, micro) to bring about change*" (Denis 2015, p. 1). We argue that a focus on the emergence of transformative capacities may reveal the daily work undertaken by actors at policy (macro), organizational (meso) and clinical (micro) levels through the integration of the academic mission across the care continuum (Ferlie and Shortell 2001; Best et al. 2012). This paper aims to understand how organizational actors mobilize transformative capacities through the process of integrating the academic mission across the care continuum.

Theoretical Framework

Institutional work is defined as "*the intentional action of individuals and organizations to create, maintain and disrupt institutions*" (Lawrence and Suddaby 2006, p. 15 in Lawrence et al. 2013, p. 1024). According to Denis (2015), this concept applies to the study of transformative capacities as it helps to understand the resources and practices activated by organizational actors in times of public sector reform. In this paper, we will use a typology of institutional work recently developed in an empirical study of healthcare reform in Quebec as our conceptual model (Cloutier et al. 2015; Denis 2015). Cloutier et al. (2015) identify four types of institutional work (see Fig. 14.1): (1) structural work focuses

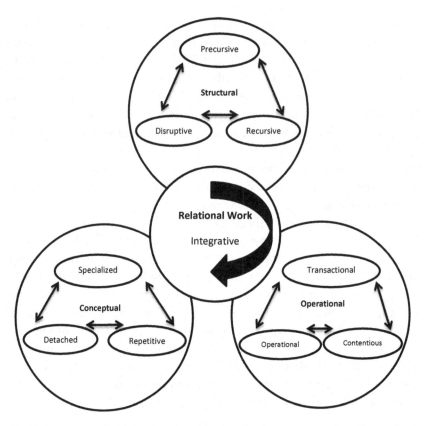

Fig. 14.1 Forms of institutional work in the enactment of policy reform (Cloutier et al. 2015, p. 10)

on aligning organizational design and incentives (including resource allocation channels) with the new organizational mandate; (2) conceptual work involves development of a common vision and shared understanding among internal and external actors; (3) operational work refers to the organization's ability to identify and test projects that embody the new vision and mandate, and assess whether organizational aspirations are realistic; and (4) relational work focuses on the development of trust and shared knowledge between actors involved in the implementation of the new vision and mandate. Relational work is central to mobilizing and integrating the three other types of work. Our empirical study explores manifestations of institutional work following the adoption of a specific mandate to integrate the academic mission across the continuum of care in a given territory.

Realistic Evaluation of Institutional Work Across the Care Continuum

Setting

The setting for the study is an integrated academic health and social services centre in the province of Quebec, Canada. This model of organization was created in the 2015 health system reform in Quebec, which saw the province's 182 healthcare establishments merged into 34 organizations. Regional health authorities (RHAs) were abolished, thereby instituting a two-tier governance system involving the Ministry of Health and Social Services and 22 integrated structures: 13 integrated health and social services centres (IHSSC) and nine integrated academic health and social services centres (IAHSSC). Twelve additional organizations remained independent, including AHCs and several specialized centres. IAHSSCs differ from IHSSCs in that their territory includes "... *a designated academic health and social services institute; and excludes academic health centres*" (MSSS 2015). The Ministry allowed one exception to this model: the organization we will refer to as "IAHSSC A" integrates an AHC within its governance structure, providing a unique opportunity to study empirically the integration of the academic mission beyond the AHC.

The creation of IAHSSC A was based on the premise that embedding an AHC within its governance would extend the benefits of the academic mission in improving quality and overall system performance. Shortly after the 2015 reform, IAHSSC A adopted "*integration of the academic mission across the care continuum*" as a strategic priority across domains (from physical health to social services), levels of care (from primary to super-specialized care), and territories (urban and rural). A first step was to reformulate the academic mission from the three traditional components of research, education and patient care to six: (1)

research, (2) education, (3) knowledge transfer, (4) development of evidence-based practice, (5) health technology assessment (HTA) and (6) dissemination.

Leadership at IAHSSC A recognized that this transformation would involve significant efforts to transcend boundaries between healthcare domains, services and settings, and commissioned our research team, including all three authors of this paper, to support their early work in this direction. Stakeholders from IAHSSC A participated in designing and validating each step of the research process.

Design

Our research objective was to provide a better understanding of *why* and *how* complex organizational processes generate mechanisms of change in a given social context (Yin 2013; Reed 2009). We conducted an embedded qualitative single case study of IAHSSC A, a unique structure (Yin 2013), within the context of a major provincial healthcare reform. Our research question is explored through three sub-cases embedded within IAHSSC A. Based on a variation sample, the selected sub-cases involve three *care and service pathways* in specific healthcare domains that integrate the entire delivery structure from primary to super-specialized care. In terms of selection criteria (Gerring 2006), each sub-case (1) constitutes a defined care and service pathway, (2) is associated with one of the three research centres in the region and (3) exhibits variable progress and experimentation with regard to the academic mission. The study was approved by the institution's ethics review board on 16 March 2016.

Data Collection and Analysis

Data collection involved document review and semi-structured interviews with key stakeholders. Data were collected and analysed by the first author. Documents included 88 peer-reviewed articles, 40 papers from the grey literature, 8 internal documents provided by the organization, and 137 newspaper articles. Semi-structured interviews were conducted with key informants to document the processes involved in integrating the academic mission. Participants were selected through intentional sampling and solicited for interviews (Kuper et al. 2008). We interviewed 27 informants: 19 senior leaders of the academic mission and 8 organizational leaders responsible for care and service pathways (sub-cases). Interviews lasting 60–90 minutes were conducted by two members of the research team in tandem between 5 April 2017, and 20 July 2017. All interviews were recorded and transcribed.

Each form of data was analysed separately and then collectively. Transcribed texts and documents were thematically analysed through careful and repeated reading. Units of meaning were discerned as codes and continually refined into more abstract themes that are conveyed in the findings and exemplified in data excerpts.

Realist Evaluation Research Process

The study employed a realist evaluation, a methodological approach allowing a relatively deep understanding of the complex organizational

Table 14.1 The realistic evaluation process (Adapted from Frykman et al. 2017, p. 68)

Research phases	Description of research phases	Data collected
Phase 1: generate a programme theory	The research team generated a programme theory about the development of transformative capacities through the expansion of the academic mission across the care continuum	Document analysis
Phase 2: develop hypotheses	The programme theory embedded 25 CIMO configurations, which were analysed using our theoretical framework (Cloutier et al. 2015)	Semi-structured interviews
Phase 3: test the hypotheses	Preliminary CIMO configurations were tested and validated with research team members and stakeholders at IAHSSC A	Testing and validation were accomplished through group meetings
Phase 4: refine the programme theory	Refinement of the programme theory resulted in 6 final CIMO configurations	No additional data collected

dynamics involved in large-scale health system transformation (Greenhalgh et al. 2009; Best et al. 2012). The core idea is to "*elucidate the mechanisms by which an intervention triggers a response in the context of application*" (Frykman et al. 2017, p. 65). This enables us to trace the causal chain between context, intervention, mechanism and outcome (CIMO) involved in a change process, and develop middle-range theory around the phenomenon of interest (Frykman et al. 2017; Pawson and Tilley 1997). Context refers to the spatial, geographical, institutional and social circumstances in which the intervention or programme is enacted (Pawson and Tilley 1997). Interventions constitute concrete actions undertaken by actors to achieve their objectives. Mechanisms are defined as the choices and capacities of individuals that generate specific behavioural patterns (Pawson and Tilley 1997); mechanisms are generated by interventions embedded within specific contexts (de Souza 2013; Jagosh et al. 2015; Robert and Ridde 2013). Outcome refers to the joint product of interactions between context, intervention and mechanism and can be characterized as a state of (1) transformation, (2) invariance or (3) reinforcement (Pawson and Tilley 1997; de Souza 2013).

We based our research process on Frykman et al.'s (2017) four phases of realist evaluation: (1) generate a programme theory, (2) develop hypotheses, (3) test the hypotheses and (4) refine the programme theory (Frykman et al. 2017, p. 68) (see Table 14.1).

Processes and Products that Expand the Academic Mission of Academic Health Centres

CIMO Configurations

We identified 6 CIMO configurations (Table 14.2), involving 13 interventions, that provide potential explanations for how transformative capacities were mobilized by organizational actors through the integration of the academic mission across the care continuum (see Appendix A).

Table 14.2 CIMO configurations and institutional work

Contexts	Interventions	Mechanisms	Outcomes
Systemic restructuring through policy reform	Structural	Decreasing relational capacity	Decreased operational capacity
	Relational	Increasing relational capacity	Decreased conceptual capacity
New distributed governance structure	Structural	Decreasing structural capacity	Limited relational capacity
	Structural	Limiting relational capacity	Limited conceptual capacity
Structural integration of pre-existing structures	Operational	Increasing relational capacity	Increased structural capacity
Culmination of performance pressure	Conceptual	Increasing conceptual capacity	Increased conceptual capacity
	Operational	Increasing structural capacity	Increased conceptual capacity
	Relational	Limiting structural capacity	Limited operational capacity
Clinical governance restructuring	Structural	Decreasing relational capacity	Decreased structural capacity
	Structural	Increasing relational capacity	Increased operational capacity
Limited overall transformative capacities	Structural	Decreasing structural capacity	Increased conceptual capacity
	Conceptual	Limiting conceptual capacity	Increased structural capacity
	Relational	Increasing structural capacity	Increased operational capacity

CIMO 1: Betting on Restructuring; Unleashing Power Relations

Context: Respondents characterized the massive 2015 restructuring of the health system in Quebec as a new relational context. The creation of IAHSSC A based on the structural integration of local and regional levels created a distance, both human and geographic, between members of the organization. As stated by one participant:

> ... the installations are drowned in the vast magma that is IAHSSC A. As I tell you, no one in the structure is responsible for an installation in itself. It's another logic. We are in a logic of territory.

Interventions: The Board of Directors of IAHSSC A, including the Chief Executive Officer (CEO) and the two Deputy Chief Executive Officers (DCEOs) of IAHSSC A, decided to merge the IAHSSC and the AHC on the territory under a single-governance entity in order to accelerate integration of the academic mission across boundaries. A Strategic Committee responsible for supporting and monitoring the integration was created, and it included traditional actors (e.g. Dean of the Faculty of Medicine and Health Sciences) and non-traditional actors (e.g. Dean of the Faculty of Arts and Sciences) associated with the academic mission.

Mechanism: The structural integration of the AHC and IAHSSC brought a loss of relational landmarks, a lack of clarity regarding role distribution and accountability relationships and emphasized pre-existing power relationships between hierarchical, geographical and knowledge boundaries. As described by one respondent:

> There is a risk associated with the urban centre as a major pre-established academic hub. It clearly appears that other smaller rural territories, which have never had academic institutes on their territory, face the same expectations for the integration of the academic mission, while they are much less equipped to do so.

Nevertheless, the distribution of governance capacities to new actors involved in the integration of the academic mission was also seen to activate trust relationships between actors across geographic and domain boundaries.

Outcomes: Overall, the conflict dynamic that emerged from both the reinforcement of existing power relations and the development of new relationships generated only partial openness to the idea of being part of an integrated health academic organization, which jeopardized the operational capacity to integrate the academic mission.

CIMO 2: Navigating Distributed Governance and Structural Ambiguity

Context: In parallel with the new relational context introduced by the health system reform, a new structural context emerged around research activities in IAHSSC A.

Interventions: The Board of Directors created a new directorate responsible for research, with a mandate to design a shared governance template with the three research centres on the territory. In contrast to the research governance models of the other IHSSCs and IAHSSCs in Quebec, this new directorate had neither structural nor hierarchical authority over the three research centres. In parallel, IAHSSC A established a new Board of Directors for its research component.

Mechanisms: The creation of this new Research Directorate, supported by a distributed governance structure, created ambiguity around the distribution of roles and accountability relationships. Organizational actors expressed difficulty in understanding the directorate's mandate and how to differentiate it from the broader initiative of integrating the academic mission within the care continuum, as expressed here:

> I still find it difficult, even after two years, to find the right person to speak to, because understanding the organization of this directorate, its internal governance, is extremely complex.

Moreover, the creation of a new senior management board for the research mission, including the CEO, the two DCEOs and the Administrative Director of Research, appears to have centralized decision making at the strategic level, thereby limiting participation of organizational and clinical actors across boundaries.

Outcomes: A new distributed governance structure, coupled with centralized decision making at strategic level, limited the development of both relational and conceptual capacities among organizational actors.

CIMO 3: Capitalizing on Relationships to Accelerate Change

Context: Alongside the creation of a new structure for research, the Board of Directors chose to merge pre-existing governance structures responsible for the education component of the academic mission. Responsibility for education thus shifted from the Human Resources Directorate of the AHC (pre-reform) to the Human Resources, Communications and Legal Affairs Directorate (HRDCAJ) of the IAHSSC (post-reform).

Interventions: In 2016, the HRDCAJ, a strategic actor, developed and disseminated a new education policy for IAHSSC A.

Mechanisms: According to participants, the fact that the HRDCAJ was built on pre-existing structures allowed it to capitalize on and reinforce relational capacity to accelerate the formalization of collaborations between actors across boundaries:

> ... since it's the responsibility of all to participate in our education mission, especially through the supervision of trainees, we asked them to commit to their contribution in this aspect of our mission; and within a period of two years, we actualized our education policy.

Outcomes: The acceleration of positive relationships between organizational actors led to an increase in the structural capacity to support the integration of the academic mission.

CIMO 4: Managing the Tension Between Perceived Value and Operational Capacity

Context: Almost a year after its creation, IAHSSC A faced further major changes to its governance structure. Clinical governance restructuring, involving the appointment of more than 300 new clinical managers, appeared as a significant source of destabilization. This major transformation, combined with increasing performance and accountability requirements from the Ministry, put additional pressure on clinical stakeholders (especially managers) throughout the IAHSSC.

Interventions: The Board of Directors decided to include the academic mission as one of the six major components of its performance management system.

Mechanisms: While participants described this intervention as conceptually strong, they pointed to a lack of clear strategic direction, concrete resources and support for integrating the academic mission within their practices. In the context of high-performance-pressure, organizational actors came to perceive the academic mission as "additional workload" rather than added value. According to participants, smaller targeted operational projects to start the integration of the academic mission would have been helpful to disseminate "quick wins" throughout the IAHSSC. Facing this challenge, the Research Directorate shifted from a managerial approach to focus on collaborative leadership and knowledge brokering among actors from different fields and levels. This resulted in new relationships with high potential for promoting the academic mission, as stated by one Research Directorate member:

> Rather than trying to sell a vision and some projects, we'll rather look for what are the issues people need to deal with on a daily basis, and then use tools from our performance management system to support them.

Outcomes: Conceptual and operational capacities were conflicted regarding the integration of the academic mission.

CIMO 5: Crossing Boundaries: Reconciling the Good and the Messy

Context: As mentioned above, the clinical governance structure of IAHSSC A experienced further significant changes in 2016.

Interventions: The Board of Directors created a new strategic governance structure responsible for supporting and monitoring all clinical governance activities within the organization. In addition, administrator and clinical manager duos became co-leaders of each of the six care and service pathways.

Mechanisms: On the one hand, creation of the new structure responsible for clinical governance exacerbated structural ambiguity around role distribution and accountability relationships among hierarchical actors (e.g. administrative and clinical managers). One of the main challenges reported by participants was the difficulty of crossing knowledge boundaries between managerial and clinical actors. On the other hand, it triggered new and positive relationships between managerial-clinical leadership teams and knowledge brokers located in the

Research Directorate, who provided valuable guidance, as stated by one respondent:

> Anyway, for me, it's a winning strategy; now, I don't forget the knowledge brokers. I am able to communicate and share responsibilities with my clinical co-manager more efficiently.

Outcomes: While structural ambiguity was reinforced, the new form of distributed governance between clinician and managerial leaders accelerated operational capacity to integrate the academic mission.

CIMO 6: From Inertia to Improvement: Starting with Relationships

Context: By the beginning of 2017, senior IAHSSS A management acknowledged the significant difficulties involved in operationalizing the integration of the academic mission.

Interventions: The Board of Directors created a new governance structure responsible for integrating the academic mission. This was partly to clarify that the Research Directorate was responsible for the research component and not the integration of the entire academic mission. The intention was also to associate the academic mission with the concept of clinical relevance as a new organizational culture. Partnerships were rapidly initiated between the academic mission and clinical governance structures, both of which had arms-length relationships with the CEO of IAHSSC A.

Mechanisms: As this new structure was placed under the responsibility of a respected senior manager and redirected the academic mission towards an aim (clinical relevance) already valued throughout the IAHSSC, organizational stakeholders were generally enthusiastic and confident in its capacity to lead integration of the academic mission. However, this structure was implemented in addition by the Research Directorate, which had as well a mandate related to clinical relevance; and this brought increased ambiguity and confusion regarding the structures governing academic mission integration.

At first, we could see this structure as an upgrade of the academic mission in the organizational chart, because it became closer to the CEO. Nevertheless, the Research Directorate remained directly accountable to the CEO. So, it created some kind of triangulated governance structure that is still hard to [understand] at the moment.

At the same time, stakeholders specifically involved in the management of healthcare pathways did not share the enthusiasm of colleagues in clinical directorates, because they felt excluded from the formal consultative arrangements of the new directorate and, thus, from governance of the academic mission. Difficulties with ambiguity and differentiation of governance roles generated variable levels of commitment between managerial and clinical actors around the integration of the academic mission.

Outcomes: Recent structural changes have helped to evoke a formal commitment from the strategic level to strengthen the vision, support and relationships needed to achieve integration of the academic mission.

Transformative Capacities of Academic Health Centres

The contribution to organizational change theory of this chapter is to show how relational processes underpin conceptual capacities and operational capacities and thereby create organic, processual ways to transform organizations and systems. The results show that the structural, conceptual, operational and relational work involved in extending the academic mission is a heterogeneous, nonlinear and social process (Kerosuo 2004; Hwang and Colyvas 2011). Capacities evolve, interact with and influence each other through processes of organizational change. In line with Cloutier et al. (2015), our empirical data support the idea that relational work is at the heart of the transformative capacity development involved in integrating the academic mission across healthcare domains, levels of care and territories within IAHSSC A (Smets and Jarzabkowski 2013). This section discusses our emerging mid-range theory of the development, through health system reforms, of institutional work that represents transformative capacities.

Structural Work

We argue that the development of structural capacities (structural work) through health system reforms is triggered by perceptions of meaningful, rather than mandated, need for change. We further find that redrawing the organizational chart does not bring immediate changes in distribution of roles and responsibilities, shifts in power and accountability relationships, or organizational practices (Denis et al. 2001, 2012; Lusiani et al. 2016). The merger of heterogeneous actors under the same governance structure seems to reinforce organizational boundaries and differentiation mechanisms at the expense of relational integration and collaborative mechanisms (Mintzberg 2017). Our case study shows that the creation of new integrated governance structures in the context of system-wide turbulence seems to destabilize organizational identity and professional autonomy (Zietsma and Lawrence 2010). Moreover, the tacit distribution of power between actors triggered by structural integration can blur decision-making responsibility and paralyse operational capacities, contributing to inertia in the face of reforms (Delmestri 2006; Delbridge and Edwards 2008). Collaborative experimentation is seen in our empirical study to ease these tensions and accelerate the process through which new organizational structures manifest in new organizational teams. Redrawing the organizational chart does not bring immediate changes in organizational practice.

Structural capacities are fundamentally shaped by relational opportunities. The particular academic context, composed of constellations of actors across academic, managerial and clinical boundaries, tends both to complicate and to enrich relational opportunities. Relational interaction enables organizational actors to negotiate various perceptions of the need for change (conceptual work) mobilized by different sources of knowledge within the academic context, which, in turn, motivate the enactment of structural transformations. Our study challenges the logic behind restructuring as an approach to healthcare transformation, for we find that relational work is required to trigger negotiation of the organizational visions and priorities that will nourish and guide the translation of structural transformation into meaningful operational changes.

Operational Work

Our study shows that the development of operational capacities (operational work) is triggered and accelerated by inclusive and reflexive opportunities focused on *actual* work, rather than *expected* work. In the context of health system reform, pressure to accomplish the clinical and structural reorganization was found to heighten institutional instability and decrease opportunities for conceptual work that would help organizational actors see new ideas and practices as valuable, feasible and supportive of, rather than competing with, other institutional priorities (Battilana et al. 2009). Our empirical results show that despite stakeholders' positive perception of the academic mission, their willingness to invest in the effort was hampered by a lack of concrete improvement in quality of care and of operational guidance to enact the concept in daily practice (Glimmerveen 2015; Greenfield et al. 2010). Consequently, several participants identified the academic mission as more of a "burden" than an added value to their daily activities, jeopardizing rather than enabling the sense-making of change. When organizational actors do not clearly see the benefits or impact of changing their practices, the potential for operational translation of a new concept is reduced (Burns et al. 2011). We argue that this is because operational capacities are constantly reshaped by organizational actors' reflection on their experimentation, which emphasizes the need for efforts to focus on what people actually do rather than what they should be doing. What people accomplish on a daily basis is a strong indicator of what they perceive to be valuable and of the knowledge mobilized in assessing value.

Our study shows that the meaning attached to change differs between people and over time. Given the plurality and complexity of healthcare organizations, challenging this reality did not appear as a relevant investment of time and energy. However, we found that within the academic context, better alignment between visions and operations across boundaries can be fostered by inclusive spaces where organizational actors can collectively exchange and reflect on their experimentation with change (Hean et al. 2015; Hoge and Howenstine 1997; Moldogaziev and Resh 2016). We argue that operational capacities are strongly dependent on conceptual capacities, which are shaped by relational opportunities within and across boundaries.

Conceptual Work

We find that conceptual capacities (work) are triggered and accelerated by the promotion of an organizational vision that is dynamic and heterogeneous rather than static and standardized (Kitchener 2002; Waring et al. 2015). Our empirical results show that the academic mission is generally perceived as an "organizational culture of innovation". According to study participants, this culture needs to be embodied within values and daily practices of organizational actors across clinical, managerial and territorial boundaries. However, the meaning of this vision differed for actors within and across these boundaries, making it challenging for senior managers to monitor progress in the integration of the academic mission as it translates into practices and performance outcomes (Teulier and Rouleau 2013).

We consider that conceptual capacities must be supported by structures capable of guiding actors in collective learning and the application of new organizational values and practices, while not compromising organizational autonomy and creativity (Burns et al. 2011; Heikkilia and Gerlak 2013). Such a structural context fosters local interactions between actors across all levels of the organization, with the aim of generating relational mechanisms such as communication, experimentation and reflexivity (Lanham et al. 2013; Shaw et al. 2017). The main idea is to concentrate efforts on valuing the diversity of meanings around the mandated change rather than constraining transformative capacities through standardization. We found that interaction enables the emergence of shared beliefs and values and their translation into synergistic operational practices.

Our findings underline the importance of acknowledging that organizational visions need to adapt to the constant evolution of meaning around change within reform contexts. The development of conceptual capacities across organizational boundaries appears to be rooted in local and organic interactions.

Relational Work

Our study supports relational capacities as fundamental to mobilizing other transformative capacities among organizational actors. A shortfall in relational capacities can significantly jeopardize the activation of other capacities. Our empirical results show that, on the one hand, the acute destabilization of relationships induced by reforms has been a significant obstacle to the development of the academic mission within the organization. Early efforts failed to include actors from all hierarchical levels of the organization—notably delivery-level actors in care and service pathways—in strategic actions regarding the academic mission. On the other hand, the integration of the academic mission across levels of care and territories was fundamentally supported by the reconstruction of relationships and trust between organizational actors. Relational work not only develops mutual knowledge and trusting relationships, it can also mediate boundaries to create pathways of exchange that would not otherwise exist, and it can embed opportunities for interpreting, reflecting on and negotiating the meaning of change among various actors. Relational capacities must not be considered simply as informal assets within an organization in the context of transformation. Stakeholders must consider relational capacities as a highly context-sensitive, adaptable and powerful engine to bring about change in healthcare organizations (O'Flynn et al. 2013; Edwards 2017).

Conclusion

This study finds that the mobilization of transformative capacities through the integration of the academic mission across the care continuum in the context of large-scale health system transformation is not a rational process that produces expected outcomes. Rather, it appears as a dynamic process of co-construction, with unpredictable effects that emerge from the complex interplay between professional, hierarchical and territorial boundaries that characterize the academic context (Schneider 1987). Relational capacities appear to act as triggers for both meaningful perceived change and for the synergistic blurring of boundaries in academic healthcare organizations. This study, by empirically investigating the role of institutional work in public sector organizations, contributes to the field of organizational theory by deepening our understanding of the social mechanisms that underlie the relationship between organizational structure and human agency in highly institutionalized and rapidly changing organizational contexts. Further research could explore the particular role of relational work, developed through experimentation, in fostering alignment between actors across hierarchical boundaries during large-scale health system transformations.

Appendix A: Detailed CIMO Configurations

CIMO	Contexts	Interventions	Mechanisms	Outcomes
Betting on restructuring: unleashing power relations	Systemic restructuring through policy reform	Structural integration of pre-existing structures	Reinforcement of existing power relations across hierarchical, geographical and knowledge boundaries *(Decreased relational capacity)*	Partial openness to the idea of being part of an academic institution *REINFORCEMENT: Decreased operational capacity*
		Creation of new formal spaces for exchange across boundaries	Emergence of distributed and trusting relations across boundaries *(Increased relational capacity)*	Emergence of a shared and holistic vision of the academic mission *TRANSFORMATION: Increased conceptual capacity*
Navigating distributed governance and structural ambiguity	New distributed governance structure	Creation of a new management structure	Emergence of structural ambiguity towards distribution of roles and accountability relationships *(Decreased structural capacity)*	Limited leadership capacities of this new structure *INVARIANCE: Limited relational capacity*
		Creation of a new senior management board	Reinforcement of centralization in governance capacities *(Limited relational capacity)*	Exclusive opportunities to exchange, reflect on and appropriate the meaning of the academic mission *INVARIANCE: Limited conceptual capacity*

(continued)

CIMO	Contexts	Interventions	Mechanisms	Outcomes
Capitalizing on relationships to accelerate change	Structural integration of pre-existing management structures	Dissemination of a new organizational policy for education	Consolidation of pre-existing trust relationships (*Increased relational capacity*)	Accelerated capacities to create new formal coordination mechanisms across boundaries *REINFORCEMENT: Increased structural capacity*
	Culmination of performance pressures	Adoption of a new mandated integrated performance management system	Emergence of a positive organizational vision across boundaries (*Increased conceptual capacity*)	Emergence of a shared vision of the academic mission as a vector for an organizational culture of innovation *TRANSFORMATION: Increased conceptual capacity*
Managing the tension between perceived value and operational capacity		Lack of operational guidelines to translate organizational vision	Emergence of discrepancies between expectations and the availability of management support and resources (*Limited structural capacity*)	Prioritization of other operations that were structurally secured *REINFORCEMENT: Limited operational capacity*
		Shift in managerial approach towards reciprocity	Appreciative vision of new managerial support (*Increased conceptual capacity*)	Emergence of distributed leadership across management structures *TRANSFORMATION: Increased relational capacity*

(continued)

CIMO	Contexts	Interventions	Mechanisms	Outcomes
Crossing boundaries; reconciling the good and the messy	Clinical governance restructuration	Creation of a new clinico-administrative management structure	Emergence of structural ambiguity around the distribution of roles and accountability relationships between managerial and clinical actors (*Decreased structural capacity*)	Lack of structural integration of the academic mission within clinical governance capacities *INVARIANCE: Decreased structural capacity*
		Development of healthcare and services pathways	Emergence of positive relationships between clinical-administrative management teams (*Increased relational capacity*)	Increased utilization of knowledge transfer resources as one of the six components of the academic mission *TRANSFORMATION: Increased operational capacity*
From inertia to improvement; starting with relationships	Limited overall transformative capacities towards the integration of the academic mission	Restructuring of the senior management governance board	Reinforcement of structural ambiguity around the distribution of roles and accountability relationships (*Decreased structural capacity*)	Reinforcement of the academic mission as a strategic performance and improvement lever *TRANSFORMATION: Increased conceptual capacity*
		Reorientation of organizational vision towards clinical relevance	Emergence of discrepancies between new organizational vision and lack of operational guidance (*Limited conceptual capacity*)	Clarification of the alignment of the academic mission with more specific structures of the organizational design *TRANSFORMATION: Increased structural capacity*
		Development of new inclusive collaborative mechanisms within clinical-administrative structures	Emergence of steps towards structural integration within clinical governance (*Increased structural capacity*)	Development of a strategic framework for the integration of the academic mission within healthcare and service pathways *TRANSFORMATION: Increased operational capacity*

References

Battilana, J., Leca, B., & Boxenbaum, E. (2009). How actors change institutions: Towards a theory of institutional entrepreneurship. *Academy of Management Annals, 3,* 65–107.

Best, A., Greenhalgh, T., Lewis, S., Saul, J. E., Carroll, S., & Bitz, J. (2012). Large-system transformation in health care: A realist review. *The Milbank Quarterly, 90*(3), 421–456.

Blackburn, J. (2009). *Securing the future of Canada's Academic Health Sciences Centres: Environmental scan report.* Academic Health Sciences Centres, National Task Force = Centres des sciences de la santé universitaires, Groupe de travail national.

Bowen, S., & Martens, P. (2005). Demystifying knowledge translation: Learning from the community. *Journal of Health Services Research & Policy, 10*(4), 203–211.

Brimacombe, G. (2010). Three missions one future. Optimizing the performance of Canada's academic health sciences centres. *A report from the National Task Force on the future of Canada's academic health sciences centres.* Available at: ahscntf.org/docs/AHSCs/NTF%20Report/Final%20Report/05.30-NTF-EN-FINAL.pdf. Accessed 8 Nov 2013.

Burns, L., Bradley, E., & Weiner, B. (2011). *Shortell and Kaluzny's healthcare management: Organization design and behavior.* New York: Cengage Learning.

Cloutier, C., Denis, J. L., Langley, A., & Lamothe, L. (2015). *Agency at the managerial interface: Public sector reform as institutional work.* Journal of Public Administration Research and Theory. First published online June 1, 2015. https://doi.org/10.1093/jopart/muv009.

Coleman, D. L., Wardrop III, R. M., Levinson, W. S., Zeidel, M. L., & Parsons, P. E. (2017). Strategies for developing and recognizing faculty working in quality improvement and patient safety. *Academic Medicine, 92*(1), 52–57.

Cousins, J. B., & Simon, M. (1996). The nature and impact of policy-induced partnerships between research and practice communities. *Educational Evaluation and Policy Analysis, 18*(3), 199–218.

Crilly, T., Jashapara, A., Trenholm, S., Peckham, A., Currie, G., & Ferlie, E. (2013). *Knowledge mobilisation in healthcare organisations: Synthesising evidence and theory using perspectives of organisational form, resource based view of the firm and critical theory.* NIHR Health Services and Delivery Research programme.

Dattée, B., & Barlow, J. (2017). Multilevel organizational adaptation: Scale invariance in the Scottish healthcare system. *Organization Science, 28*(2), 301–319.

de Souza, D. E. (2013). Elaborating the context-mechanism-outcome configuration (CMOc) in realist evaluation: A critical realist perspective. *Evaluation, 19*(2), 141–154.

Delbridge, R., & Edwards, T. (2008). Challenging conventions: Roles and processes during nonisomorphic institutional change. *Human Relations, 61*(3), 299–325.

Delmestri, G. (2006). Streams of inconsistent institutional influences: Middle managers as carriers of multiple identities. *Human Relations, 59*(11), 1515–1541.

Denis, J.-L. (2015). *Taking stock of healthcare reforms: A research program on transformative capacity of healthcare systems in Canada.* Research proposal, Canadian Institutes of Health Research.

Denis, J.-L., Lamothe, L., & Langley, A. (2001). The dynamics of collective leadership and strategic change in pluralistic organizations. *Academy of Management Journal, 44*(4), 809–837.

Denis, J.-L., Langley, A., & Sergi, V. (2012). Leadership in the plural. *The Academy of Management Annals, 6*(1), 211–283.

Denis, J. L., & van Gestel, N. (2016). Medical doctors in healthcare leadership: Theoretical and practical challenges. *BMC Health Services Research, 16*(2), 158.

Dzau, V. J., Ackerly, D. C., Sutton-Wallace, P., Merson, M. H., Williams, R. S., Krishnan, K. R., et al. (2010). The role of academic health science systems in the transformation of medicine. *The Lancet, 375*(9718), 949–953.

Edwards, A. (Ed.). (2017). *Working relationally in and across practices: A cultural-historical approach to collaboration.* Cambridge: Cambridge University Press.

Ferlie, E., Fitzgerald, L., Wood, M., & Hawkins, C. (2005). The nonspread of innovations: The mediating role of professionals. *Academy of Management Journal, 48*(1), 117–134.

Ferlie, E. B., & Shortell, S. M. (2001). Improving the quality of health care in the United Kingdom and the United States: A framework for change. *The Milbank Quarterly, 79*(2), 281–315.

French, C. E., Ferlie, E., & Fulop, N. J. (2014). The international spread of Academic Health Science Centres: A scoping review and the case of policy transfer to England. *Health Policy, 117,* 382–391.

Frykman, M., von Thiele Schwarz, U., Muntlin Athlin, Å., Hasson, H., & Mazzocato, P. (2017). The work is never ending: Uncovering teamwork sustainability using realistic evaluation. *Journal of Health Organization and Management, 31*(1), 64–81.

Gerring, J. (2006). *Case study research: Principles and practices.* Cambridge, UK: Cambridge University Press.

Glimmerveen, L. (2015). Pursuing community ownership in local service design and delivery: Challenging the boundaries of professional long-term care? *International Journal of Integrated Care, 15*(5).

Greenfield, D., Pawsey, M., & Braithwaite, J. (2010). What motivates professionals to engage in the accreditation of healthcare organizations? *International Journal for Quality in Health Care, 23*(1), 8–14.

Greenhalgh, T., Humphrey, C., Hughes, J., Macfarlane, F., Butler, C., & Pawson, R. A. Y. (2009). How do you modernize a health service? A realist evaluation of whole-scale transformation in London. *The Milbank Quarterly, 87*(2), 391–416.

Håland, E., Røsstad, T., & Osmundsen, T. C. (2015). Care pathways as boundary objects between primary and secondary care: Experiences from Norwegian home care services. *Health, 19*(6), 635–651.

Hean, S., Willumsen, E., Ødegård, A., & Bjørkly, S. (2015). Using social innovation as a theoretical framework to guide future thinking on facilitating collaboration between mental health and criminal justice services. *International Journal of Forensic Mental Health, 14*(4), 280–289.

Heikkila, T., & Gerlak, A. K. (2013). Building a conceptual approach to collective learning: Lessons for public policy scholars. *Policy Studies Journal, 41*(3), 484–512.

Hoge, M. A., & Howenstine, R. A. (1997). Organizational development strategies for integrating mental health services. *Community Mental Health Journal, 33*(3), 175–187.

Hsiao, Y. L., Bass, E. B., Wu, A. W., Richardson, M. B., Deutschendorf, A., Brotman, D. J., et al. (2018). Implementation of a comprehensive program to improve coordination of care in an urban academic health care system. *Journal of Health Organization and Management, 32*(5), 638–657.

Huby, G., Harris, F. M., Powell, A. E., Kielman, T., Sheikh, A., Williams, S., et al. (2014). Beyond professional boundaries: Relationships and resources in health services' modernisation in England and Wales. *Sociology of Health & Illness, 36*(3), 400–415.

Hwang, H., & Colyvas, J. A. (2011). Problematizing actors and institutions in institutional work. *Journal of Management Inquiry, 20*(1), 62–66.

Jagosh, J., Bush, P. L., Salsberg, J., Macaulay, A. C., Greenhalgh, T., Wong, G., et al. (2015). A realist evaluation of community-based participatory research: Partnership synergy, trust building and related ripple effects. *BMC Public Health, 15*(1), 725.

Kerosuo, H. (2004). Examining boundaries in health care—Outline of a method for studying organizational boundaries in interaction. *Outlines. Critical Practice Studies, 6*(1), 35–60.

Kilpatrick, K., Lavoie-Tremblay, M., Ritchie, J. A., Lamothe, L., & Doran, D. (2012). Boundary work and the introduction of acute care nurse practitioners in healthcare teams. *Journal of Advanced Nursing, 68*(7), 1504–1515.

King, G., Thomson, N., Rothstein, M., Kingsnorth, S., & Parker, K. (2016). Integrating research, clinical care, and education in academic health science centers: An organizational model of collaborative workplace learning. *Journal of Health Organization and Management, 30*(7), 1140–1160.

Kitchener, M. (2002). Mobilizing the logic of managerialism in professional fields: The case of academic health centre mergers. *Organization Studies, 23*(3), 391–420.

Kramer, D. M., & Wells, R. P. (2005). Achieving buy-in: Building networks to facilitate knowledge transfer. *Science Communication, 26*(4), 428–444.

Kuper, A., Lingard, L., & Levinson, W. (2008). Critically appraising qualitative research. *BMJ, 337*(aug07_3), a1035.

Lander, B. (2016). Boundary-spanning in academic healthcare organisations. *Research Policy, 45*(8), 1524–1533.

Lanham, H. J., Leykum, L. K., Taylor, B. S., McCannon, C. J., Lindberg, C., & Lester, R. T. (2013). How complexity science can inform scale-up and spread in health care: Understanding the role of self-organization in variation across local contexts. *Social Science & Medicine, 93*, 194–202.

Lavis, J. N., Lomas, J., Hamid, M., & Sewankambo, N. K. (2006). Assessing country-level efforts to link research to action. *Bulletin of the World Health Organization, 84*(8), 620–628.

Lavis, J. N., Robertson, D., Woodside, J. M., McLeod, C. B., & Abelson, J. (2003). How can research organizations more effectively transfer research knowledge to decision makers? *The Milbank Quarterly, 81*(2), 221–248.

Lawrence, T. B., Leca, B., & Zilber, T. B. (2013). Institutional work: Current research, new directions and overlooked issues. *Organization Studies, 34*(8), 1023–1033.

Lawrence, T. B., & Suddaby, R. (2006). 1.6 institutions and institutional work. *The Sage Handbook of Organization Studies, 2*, 215–254.

Lieff, S. J., & Yammarino, F. J. (2017). How to lead the way through complexity, constraint, and uncertainty in Academic Health Science Centers. *Academic Medicine, 92*(5), 614–621.

Lusiani, M., Denis, J.-L., & Langley, A. (2016). Plural leadership in health care organizations. In *The Oxford handbook of health care management* (p. 210). Oxford, UK: Oxford University Press.

Ministère de la Santé et des Services sociaux. (2015). *Organizational profile.* Available at: http://www.msss.gouv.qc.ca/en/reseau/reorganisation/portrait. Consulted 27 Nov 2017.

Mintzberg, H. (2017). *Managing the myths of health care: Bridging the separations between care, cure, control, and community.* Oakland: Berrett-Koehler Publishers.

Misso, M. L., Ilic, D., Haines, T. P., Hutchinson, A. M., East, C. E., & Teede, H. J. (2016). Development, implementation and evaluation of a clinical research engagement and leadership capacity building program in a large Australian health care service. *BMC Medical Education, 16*(1), 13.

Mitchell, P., Pirkis, J., Hall, J., & Haas, M. (2009). Partnerships for knowledge exchange in health services research, policy and practice. *Journal of Health Services Research & Policy, 14*(2), 104–111.

Mitton, C., Adair, C. E., McKenzie, E., Patten, S. B., & Perry, B. W. (2007). Knowledge transfer and exchange: Review and synthesis of the literature. *The Milbank Quarterly, 85*(4), 729–768.

Moldogaziev, T. T., & Resh, W. G. (2016). A systems theory approach to innovation implementation: Why organizational location matters. *Journal of Public Administration Research and Theory, 26*(4), 677–692.

O'Flynn, J., Blackman, D., & Halligan, J. (Eds.). (2013). *Crossing boundaries in public management and policy: The international experience* (Vol. 15). London: Routledge.

Pawson, R., & Tilley, N. (1997). *Realistic evaluation.* London: Sage.

Reed, M. (2009). Critical realism: Philosophy, method, or philosophy in search of a method. In *The SAGE handbook of organizational research methods* (pp. 430–448). London: Sage.

Robert, É., & Ridde, V. (2013). L'approche réaliste pour l'évaluation de programmes et la revue systématique: de la théorie à la pratique. *Mesure et évaluation en éducation, 36*(3), 79–108.

Schneider, S. C. (1987). Managing boundaries in organizations. *Political Psychology, 8*(3), 379–393.

Shaw, J., Shaw, S., Wherton, J., Hughes, G., & Greenhalgh, T. (2017). Studying scale-up and spread as social practice: Theoretical introduction and empirical case study. *Journal of Medical Internet Research, 19*(7), e244.

Smets, M., & Jarzabkowski, P. (2013). Reconstructing institutional complexity in practice: A relational model of institutional work and complexity. *Human Relations, 66*(10), 1279–1309.

Straus, S. E., Tetroe, J. M., & Graham, I. D. (2011). Knowledge translation is the use of knowledge in health care decision making. *Journal of Clinical Epidemiology, 64*(1), 6–10.

Teulier, R., & Rouleau, L. (2013). Middle managers' sensemaking and interorganizational change initiation: Translation spaces and editing practices. *Journal of Change Management, 13*(3), 308–337.

Van de Ven, A. H., & Johnson, P. E. (2006). Knowledge for theory and practice. *Academy of Management Review, 31*(4), 802–821.

Waring, J., Marshall, F., & Bishop, S. (2015). Understanding the occupational and organizational boundaries to safe hospital discharge. *Journal of Health Services Research & Policy, 20*(1_suppl.), 35–44.

Wartman, S. (2015). *The transformation of academic health centers—Meeting the challenges of healthcare's changing landscape.* San Diego, CA: Elsevier.

Washington, A. E., Coye, M. J., & Boulware, L. E. (2016). Academic health systems' third curve: Population health improvement. *JAMA, 315*(5), 459–460.

Wilkinson, H., Gallagher, M., & Smith, M. (2012). A collaborative approach to defining the usefulness of impact: Lessons from a knowledge exchange project involving academics and social work practitioners. *Evidence & Policy: A Journal of Research, Debate and Practice, 8*(3), 311–327.

Yin, R. K. (2013). *Case study research: Design and methods.* Thousand Oaks, CA: Sage.

Zietsma, C., & Lawrence, T. B. (2010). Institutional work in the transformation of an organizational field: The interplay of boundary work and practice work. *Administrative Science Quarterly, 55*(2), 189–221.

15

Developing Pragmatic Boundary Capabilities: A Micro-Level Study of Boundary Objects in Quality Improvement

Catherine E. French, Laura Lennox and Julie E. Reed

A major challenge facing healthcare organisations is how to improve quality of care for patients in complex, multidisciplinary environments. In recent years, there has been a substantial increase in developing and

C. E. French (✉) · L. Lennox · J. E. Reed
National Institute for Health Research Collaboration for Leadership in
Applied Health Research and Care (NIHR CLAHRC) Northwest London,
Imperial College London, Chelsea and Westminster Hospital,
London, UK
e-mail: catherine.french@gstt.nhs.uk

C. E. French
Guy's and St Thomas' NHS Foundation Trust, London, UK

L. Lennox
Department of Primary Care and Public Health,
Imperial College London, London, UK
e-mail: l.lennox@imperial.ac.uk

J. E. Reed
e-mail: julie.reed02@imperial.ac.uk

© The Author(s) 2020   **347**
P. Nugus et al. (eds.), *Transitions and Boundaries in the Coordination
and Reform of Health Services*, Organizational Behaviour in Healthcare,
https://doi.org/10.1007/978-3-030-26684-4_15

implementing managerial approaches to quality improvement (Radnor and Boaden 2008). Packages of tools, such as Lean and six-sigma, are sold to healthcare provider organisations with promises of providing blanket solutions to solving problems in care (Waring and Bishop 2010; Radnor et al. 2012). These managerial logics are often sedimented (Cooper et al. 1996; Kitchener 2002) onto complex organisations with established professional and organisational power structures and potentially vested interests in maintaining the status quo, and can fail to result in promised outcomes for staff and patients (Radnor et al. 2012). Top-down approaches may not pay sufficient attention to the micro-level processes required for quality improvement at the clinical level.

Even if small-scale improvement projects may not lead to system-wide outcomes (Dixon-Woods and Martin 2016), improving care requires micro-level work across knowledge boundaries between different organisations, professions and lay perspectives (Waring et al. 2013), where knowledge is embedded in practice and the communities in which it is developed. Although the quality improvement literature demonstrates many structured micro-level descriptors of improvement projects, micro-level knowledge boundary processes remain under-examined and under-theorised.

The professional boundaries literature has tended to focus on how and why boundaries are constructed, negotiated and defended between areas of professional jurisdiction (Abbott 1988). Empirical studies have focused on day-to-day boundary work between multidisciplinary teams (e.g. Liberati et al. 2016). Less is known about the conditions which are required to support boundary practices that can transform ways of working rather than maintain the status quo.

We contribute to addressing these two gaps by using Carlile's (2004) knowledge boundary framework based on analysis from new product innovation to understand how bottom-up, facilitated quality improvement approaches can surface knowledge from different domains and support improved practice. Using QI tools as tracer cases, our empirical study draws on 17 QI initiatives in Northwest London, UK, to explore boundary interactions at the micro-level. We analyse specifically how objects (Star and Griesemer 1989) support the creation of common lexicons, meanings and interests at professional, organisational and lay intersections.

The chapter is structured as follows. First, we outline our theoretical approach to the study by discussing how we conceptualise knowledge and boundaries in quality improvement. We then outline our methods for this study and introduce our case context. We present the findings from our analysis and discuss how objects can drive change by surfacing and transforming knowledge between different professional groups.

Conceptualising Knowledge and Boundaries for Quality Improvement

The natural state for professions is to protect their interests and maintain jurisdiction of a body of knowledge by defending boundaries (Abbott 1988). Consequently, professional and organisational boundaries can slow the spread of innovation and improvements in care (Ferlie et al. 2005; Powell and Davies 2012; Liberati 2017). After all, the knowledge required to influence change resides in these different communities that operate in separate professional and organisational domains.

Part of the challenge of delivering improvements in care is surfacing and sharing separate bodies of knowledge and developing new practices from them. Constructing the development of new practices as quality improvement can motivate workers and act as a boundary concept (Löwy 1992) for professional boundary work, particularly at the micro-level of clinical practice.

Through his seminal study of innovations in new product development, Carlile (2004) developed a framework exploring the properties of knowledge boundaries (and managing knowledge across them). He conceptualises three progressively complex forms of boundary (syntactic, semantic and pragmatic) and ascribes capabilities to each of them. The least complex, *syntactic* boundaries are associated with information processing and are based on a technical conception of knowledge that is unproblematic and requires 'transferring' from one community to another.

The transition from a syntactic to a *semantic* boundary 'occurs when novelty makes some differences and dependencies unclear or some meanings ambiguous' (p. 558). Here, the shared meanings developed in communities of practice (Brown and Duguid 1991; Lave and Wenger 1991; Orr 1996) require translation across the boundaries between them and therefore more skilled levels of boundary work.

Pragmatic boundaries occur when a political element is introduced to the knowledge mobilisation process (i.e. when the actors have different interests that need to be resolved). The resolution of these different interests across boundaries is only facilitated through knowledge transformation which results in trade-offs between the different communities. Swan et al. (2007) draw on this tripartite framework to examine boundary processes in genetics knowledge parks.

The move through the different types of boundary, Carlile suggests, depends on distinguishing three aspects of knowledge which, as they diverge, indicate the complexities of the boundary work required to mobilise knowledge: difference, dependence and novelty. By *difference*, Carlile posits that the more diverse the amount and type of domain-specific knowledge accumulated, the more complex the boundary work. The knowledge required to make improvements in health care comes in a variety of forms, some codified in the form of research outputs to 'implement', and most embedded in micro-level practices in health-care settings (Gabbay and Le May 2010). Combining knowledge about processes of care in local settings, seeing how different individuals and teams work and taking into account patient perspectives can lead to the co-production of new knowledge to support ongoing improvement (Renedo et al. 2017).

Carlile (2004) framed the *dependence* of knowledge as the situation of those in different domains who are more reliant on the knowledge accumulated by other communities requiring more complex boundary work. In health care, those working in multidisciplinary teams are dependent on knowledge from other domains to make care decisions. For example, in cancer care, decisions are made together by teams who bring knowledge across either inter- or intra-professional boundaries (Oborn and Dawson 2010).

Carlile (2004) views the *novelty* of knowledge as the extent to which the knowledge shared at boundaries is new to the other domain. The aim of quality improvement is to change current practices for the benefit of patients. Thus, the activity taking place at boundaries is the creation of new knowledge that will drive new practices and may challenge vested interests.

For these reasons, we suggest that boundary work to drive improvement needs to operate across pragmatic knowledge boundaries. Common interests need to be aligned to drive change, and knowledge is required to transform common interests into new practices. To develop the skills of healthcare teams and, therefore, the conditions required for developing boundary practices, capacity needs to be developed at each level of transferring, translating and transforming knowledge.

Boundary Objects for Pragmatic Work

To build pragmatic boundary capability, Carlile (2002) paid particular attention to the role of boundary objects in this process and how different types of objects support different types of boundary work. Boundary objects are flexible artefacts that act as translation devices at the boundaries between different domains of practice. The term originated in Star and Griesemer's (1989) study of Berkeley's Museum of Vertebrate Zoology in which they characterise a boundary object as an 'object that lives in multiple social worlds and has different identities in each'. The key feature of a boundary object is that it is flexible and can be interpreted differently by different groups on either side of the boundary (Bijker et al. 1987; Bechky 2003). Despite the risk of boundary objects becoming a portmanteau concept that attempts to explain all boundary interactions (Nicolini et al. 2012), the idea has been widely applied in both healthcare and biomedical research settings, for example, to reference standard forms in multidisciplinary meetings (Oborn and Dawson 2010), care pathways (Allen 2009) and telemedicine (Constantinides and Barrett 2006).

Carlile's (2004) framework suggests that different types of boundary object are used, depending on the form of collaborative work. When the situation is routine and familiar, and information simply needs to be transferred, a simple object such as a single word will suffice (syntactic co-ordination). If the situation is more complex, actors may need to establish common meanings and the boundary object would need to contain more information (semantic co-ordination). Finally, if negotiation and compromise are required, the object requires flexibility to enable a change or transformation (pragmatic co-ordination).

Boundary objects have both instrumental and symbolic value. They can be used to signify status as well as shared understanding, thus reinforcing boundaries through symbolic power (Bechky 2003; Levina and Vaast 2005). For example, in the biomedical field, Swan et al. (2007) demonstrate that when objects are symbolically associated with positive ideology and values, it is this phenomenon that is crucial in facilitating interaction across boundaries, rather than the instruments (such as databases) themselves. Their study identified that objects with high levels of flexibility in how they could be interpreted had considerable symbolic value, which could be leveraged across a range of communities to raise interest in the initiative. The symbolic association also corresponded with pre-existing positive policy discourses.

Although the boundaries literature highlights the role of different objects in different types of boundary work, less is known about how objects can transition in terms of their role when they are foregrounded and the impact this can have on collaboration (Nicolini et al. 2012). For instance, can the same objects support syntactic, semantic and pragmatic boundary work at different stages in a transformative process? If so, does the trajectory of objects through these stages support the development of boundary practices and increase pragmatic capabilities?

This study contributes to addressing this gap by considering the role objects play in knowledge boundary negotiation, in this case activities (with positive policy discourses), to improve micro-level processes in health care. The study focuses on the role of QI tools in how boundary practices were developed at the micro-level, highlighting some of the conditions required for attentive and overt boundary negotiation. Specifically, it considers how shared understandings of problems are important in influencing knowledge integration across professional boundaries.

Understanding Boundary Capabilities for Quality Improvement

Cases and Context

We used a case study design (Yin 2009) to examine 17 improvement initiatives in Northwest London, UK (2014–2017). This method enables a holistic examination of complex social processes in their real-life contexts which enhances the prospect of theory building (Eisenhardt 1989). All initiatives were supported by NIHR CLAHRC Northwest London, which was funded to conduct and implement applied health research in the NHS to improve care for patients (Howe et al. 2013).

The improvement initiatives were designed to mobilise research knowledge into clinical settings in the NHS and community within the geographical area of Northwest London. Initiatives were selected through a competitive process which required evidence of a clearly defined quality gap and a multi-professional and patient-centred approach.

In contrast to other improvement approaches, initiatives were 'bottom up' in nature, that is, driven by clinicians who, with some organisational support, applied independently for the 'researcher led' call. The proponents of each initiative were asked to identify a multidisciplinary team who were responsible for the delivery of the programme, and each initiative also had a wide variety of stakeholders involved. Initiatives were predominantly based on acute care and mental health settings, and multidisciplinary teams included doctors, nurses, allied health professionals and patients as well as a project manager. The aims of each initiative are summarised in Table 15.1.

The initiatives were supported through a central team that provided support, through facilitation, coaching, site visits, team and one-to-one training and eLearning. Support was provided for the use of different QI methods including process mapping, engaging patients and the public, stakeholder management and Plan Do Study Act cycles (Taylor et al. 2014). The central team also provided bespoke technical support through face-to-face contact and an online support tool for measuring

Table 15.1 Shared aims of improvement initiative cases

Initiative number	Initiative aim (determined by action effect method)
Initiative 1	To improve delivery of specialist allergy services in a secondary care setting
Initiative 2	To improve the physical well-being of people with serious mental illness
Initiative 3	To improve the quality of life and experience of care for patients who are primarily diagnosed with acute heart failure
Initiative 4	To sustainably improve our delivery of consistent, high-quality medicines optimisation to achieve better patient experience and outcomes
Initiative 5	To improve the quality of care for patients with an acute exacerbation of Chronic Obstructive Pulmonary Disease (COPD)
Initiative 6	To improve quality of care and healthcare outcomes (including stroke prevention) for people with or at risk of Atrial Fibrillation
Initiative 7	To improve the experience of care for in-patients who are alcohol dependent
Initiative 8	To improve health, well-being and quality of life of people living with asthma
Initiative 9	To improve patient experience and outcomes following surgery for oesophago-gastric cancer patients
Initiative 10	To improve the health and wellness of care-home residents by focusing on hydration and to ensure residents have enough to drink throughout the day as part of their personalised care
Initiative 11	To improve the quality of care, reducing anxiety/stress and increasing confidence in care pathway for patients with a pregnancy of unknown location
Initiative 12	To improve the quality of care for patients who receive acute non-invasive ventilation
Initiative 13	To increase patient and staff confidence in the quality of care for patients with hand/wrist fractures
Initiative 14	To improve the experience of parents with a baby being cared for in the neonatal unit
Initiative 15	To improve the quality of care for out-patients with Inflammatory Bowel Disease
Initiative 16	To improve the quality of life, physical health and life expectancy of people with long-term mental health needs through delivering a holistic approach to service users' care
Initiative 17	To improve people's experience and maintain and build on existing service standards in a hospice setting

for improvement, to enable teams to design and analyse process and outcome measures specific to their initiative aims.

It is beyond the scope of this paper to outline the trajectories of boundary work and the relationship to improvement in each initiative case (a sample of these will be published elsewhere). Rather, we focus on exploring how QI tools and facilitators supported the sharing and co-creation of knowledge across professional and occupational boundaries at the micro-level.

Data were collected using three methods to enable methodological triangulation (Denzin 1970). Firstly, semi-structured interviews ($n = 38$) were conducted with initiative and central team members to ascertain their experiences of using QI tools and the role of facilitation to support their use (Fitzgerald and Dopson 2009). Interviews explored participants' experiences of the QI project generally and then focused on experiences of how specific tools were used. Secondly, researchers conducted non-participant observations (approximately 90 hours) of how tools were used in practice, using a loosely structured observation sheet to prompt the capturing of key information relating to setting, seating arrangements and participants (Brannan and Oultram 2012). In some cases, the researchers were peripherally known to the participants (through interviews and observations). Thirdly, we conducted documentary analysis (Shaw et al. 2004) of tool artefacts, such as diagrams and completed questionnaires, over the course of the improvement initiatives, as well as reviewing minutes of review meetings (approximately 270 documents).

Data were analysed using both inductive and deductive approaches (Blaikie 2007; Fulop et al. 2001). Deductively, researchers approached the data with the loose theoretical framing of boundary work, looking to identify different professional and occupational domains and how quality improvement initiatives shaped any boundary activity and knowledge mobilisation. Inductively, data documents were analysed to determine other themes not captured through a boundary framework. Both approaches involved close reading of observation templates, interview transcripts and documents, including diagrams and texts produced by facilitators and teams as part of the improvement initiative (Mays and Pope 2000). This was followed by a process of interpretation (by two of the researchers, CF and LL) in which sections of data were coded and compared for their consistency and then recoded as higher-order codes and themes. The study received approval from the National Health Service Health Research Authority (IRAS188851).

The Role of Boundary Objects in Quality Improvement Interventions

The findings presented here draw on analysis across the range of tools, approaches and interactions in the 17 improvement initiative cases. A consistent QI approach was taken to each of the initiatives, supported by the central team. This 'systematic approach' includes eight different QI tools/methods designed for both engagement and to support 'technical' aspects of QI. For clarity and to present our key themes, we use two tools/methods as tracer cases to explore the impact of micro-level boundary processes for quality improvement on knowledge mobilisation across different professional and occupational groups. We selected these two tools because, although they have different purposes and methods, both were designed to encourage collaboration, they provided an artefact of this collaboration, and their use might illuminate boundary processes.

Both tools were designed to be used throughout the improvement initiatives and had different purposes. The first tool, the Action Effect Method (AEM), was designed to support improvement initiatives to develop a shared aim and 'programme theory' for the initiative. The second tool, the Long Term Success Tool (LTST), was to enable initiative teams to plan for sustainability of improvements in the complex social systems in which they were working. After outlining the use of both tools, we identify two broad themes: (1) the way in which objects were co-created influenced how their use changed over time in supporting syntactic, semantic and pragmatic work; and (2) the resistance to and adaptation of tools by healthcare professionals to local contexts.

Tool 1—Action Effect Method: Developing a Shared Aim and Outlining a Programme Theory

QI scholars have suggested that more explicit and informed use of theory can strengthen improvement programmes (Davidoff et al. 2015). From a practitioner perspective, theory is useful when it can help achieve real world improvements. The AEM was designed to support improvement teams to develop a shared aim, potential interventions to achieve this aim, anticipated cause-effect relationships between the interventions and the aim and measures to monitor improvement (Reed et al. 2014).

The AEM consists of a boundary interaction (Wenger 1998) in the form of a facilitated workshop, knowledge brokering (Gould and Fernandez 1989) by quality improvement facilitators and the co-creation of a boundary object—a diagrammatic representation of a programme theory of an improvement initiative (the Action Effect Diagram (AED). The relationship between these three aspects of boundary work appeared to facilitate work across syntactic, semantic and pragmatic boundaries.

Tool 2—The Long Term Success Tool: Developing a Shared Understanding to Plan for Sustainability of Improvement Initiatives

QI scholars have suggested that for improvement initiatives to be sustained they need to adapt to changing conditions and planning throughout the initiative (Chambers et al. 2013). The second tracer case 'tool', the LTST, was designed to support the planning for sustaining improvement initiatives in complex social systems. The tool, a boundary object in the form of a 'standardised form' (Star and Griesemer 1989), aims to 'support those implementing improvements to reflect on 12 key factors to identify risks and prompt actions to increase the chances of sustainability over time' (Lennox et al. 2017).

The tool was developed with stakeholders and end-users to provide an evidence-based, user-friendly approach for improvement teams to consider the sustainability of their initiatives. The factors are:

'*Commitment to the improvement, Involvement, Skills and capabilities, Leadership, Team functioning, Resources in place, Evidence of benefits, Progress monitored for feedback and learning, Robust and adaptable processes, Alignment with organisational culture and priorities, Support for improvement, and Alignment with external political and financial environment*' (Lennox et al. 2017).

The tool was used by the improvement teams at varying intervals throughout their initiatives following training in how to use it by a QI facilitator (as knowledge broker). Tool responses were collected on a paper questionnaire form, online Qualtrics survey or a custom-made web-based portal. The questionnaire consisted of 12 questions rated on a 5-point Likert scale (Very good to Very poor) as well as 'no opinion' and 'don't know' options. Each question included an area for free text comments for each factor. Team members were asked to answer 12 questions within the tool individually and anonymously. Team scores were collated to produce reports which included simple statistics such as range and mean, visual charts as well as comment lists for each factor. These reports were designed to be discussed as a team (in a boundary interaction) to determine which aspects of sustainability needed to be addressed. The method appeared to enable syntactic and semantic co-ordination, as the reports were used to collate information from different professional groups in one codified object.

Supporting Pragmatic Boundary Practices: The Nature of Object Co-creation

The tools, and the way in which they were used, supported knowledge mobilisation across communities. For example, with the AEM, many participants reflected that it was the process by which the diagram was developed that was beneficial to the improvement initiative.

The workshops held to develop the AED included a process of 'real time' co-creation of two artefacts of the collaboration that supported syntactic, semantic and the beginnings of pragmatic boundary work. Participants were able to see how their input to the workshop developed before their eyes. Firstly, through 'emotional' mapping, participants individually indicated the emotional experiences of patients at each part of a care pathway. These data were then analysed by members of the facilitation team and fed back to the participants later in the same workshop in the form of a word cloud. This feedback supported syntactic boundary work, enabling a shared lexicon to be developed around the scope of the initiative and shared aim.

Secondly, when the AED was created, participants were able to contribute thoughts and ideas to a shared aim for the initiative. This was also analysed by the facilitation team and fed back in real time. The AED and facilitator feedback supported semantic boundary work, as common meanings were developed by the group through the interactive process. Knowledge brokers used facilitation techniques to ensure the views of all participants were heard. They included purposively selecting the order in which participants fed back from discussions, use of 'silent' input (writing ideas on post it notes) and ensuring that everyone spoke during the session. The way in which object co-creation was visualised by participants was important:

> So, ... it was a very interesting session where I think it was about 20 people who gathered in a room and we had a lot of support with voting and readymade results using the screen. So, that part of the process was very interesting and that you get the results at the moment, and then you get direct help in actually implementing them. [P60, Improvement team member, Doctor]

Participants reflected that the workshops enabled pragmatic boundary work, as different professional groups were able to discuss their perspectives on scoping the improvement initiative:

> I thought it was interesting [that] you could see in the initial phases some of the professional groups going to their default positions. So, ... the allied health professionals started to get very hung up about which [clinical equipment] to use – but everyone needs a starting point from somewhere, don't they? ... Everyone comes from their own perspective, but by the end we had a more homogenous view. [P40, Improvement team member, Physiotherapist]

The LTST appeared to support syntactic and semantic boundary work between professional and occupational groups. Completing the tools enabled a common lexicon to be developed around sustaining processes:

> We had stakeholders in the room [who] were really pleased that we were redesigning secondary care settings. But, for some other people, it was an absolute disaster that we couldn't go in the community. So it's about really balancing that, and that's what the tool really allows is to understand – that ... you will have the same approach ... That really comes through the tool because people will be really, really green and really happy with what they're doing, and other people would be really red and really unhappy with what they were doing. [I15, Improvement team member, Nurse]

Unlike what occurred using the AEM, discussions took a free-flowing form outside of the facilitated workshop setting. In addition, the individual nature of completing the questionnaire enabled those who were less confident or powerful to express themselves:

> The comments section has been completed by people who feel they can't say things in a meeting; ... they say it in the comments section instead. [I6, QI Facilitator]

When the outcomes of the questionnaires were collected and discussed in a team setting, it enabled semantic work by ascribing common meanings to feelings and concepts:

> One thing that I feel like the long term success tool really did for us was ... to really understand that we were all struggling with the concept of not feeling that there was enough support, and [that] really empowered us to understand that it wasn't just one person rowing against the tide ... It was a tool that really enabled us as a team to be more cohesive ... because it really made us realise that they also feel the same – like, 'oh, I'm not here on my own.' [I15, Improvement team member, Nurse]

In summary, the tools as boundary objects appeared to support both pragmatic boundary work and boundary work at syntactic and semantic levels, but the pragmatic work was enacted particularly when the object was co-created in a shared and facilitated space.

Resistance to and Adaptation of Boundary Objects for Pragmatic Work

In common with the findings of Waring and Bishop's (2010) analysis of Lean, professional groups were initially resistant to QI methods (despite the bottom-up nature of the selection process for initiatives):

> *I suspect other people thought, 'here we go, here's another (QI facilitation) thing, oh bloomin' heck, what will they think of next, what are they chucking at us now? – and you fill out the form.* [I1, Improvement team member, Doctor]

In addition, professional groups rarely adopted the QI methods uncritically and often adapted them to their own needs within professional domains. Specifically, doctors appeared to adapt and shape knowledge created through the QI methods (in particular, the AEM) to fit in the jurisdictions of their body of knowledge:

> *Before the AED meeting ... I had created my own AED diagram, just from the theory of what is the AED method. I went home and I made one, and then, from having the interactive session we ... created one with [the facilitator], and it was just so interesting how they were very similar but very different at the same time.* [P45, Improvement team member, Doctor]

Other professional groups felt that the method had a closer fit to their professional epistemic cultures (Knorr Cetina 1999):

> *So, the actual tool itself to me just very much makes sense. It's about identifying what your objective is, what success looked like in order to hit that objective, what are the steps that you need to go through in order to have success, and then breaking that down into further actions. And I think that is very similar to things that, as a physio, I do in my everyday clinical practice.* [P4 Improvement team member, physiotherapist]

Professional groups continued to adapt the tools throughout the improvement initiative, and as such the artefacts of the collaboration took on different roles over time. For example, the AED drove pragmatic collaboration in its creation but then was used with less contention as a representation of programme theory or a project plan over the life cycle of the initiative. Teams used the AED both to describe the scope of the initiative to external stakeholders and to measure and monitor progress towards their shared aim:

I think also what was really good was the fact that we [drafted] AED on the day as well. So, I think that really helped to then put it in perspective, 'oh, so all of this stuff is now on there' – and actually that really makes sense, and although since then we've gone through, I think, we're on our 12th AED now, not a massive amount has changed, which is maybe reassuring that actually we're all pretty much on the same wavelength to start with, that everyone felt that this is what they wanted to achieve out of the project, and the fact that we've carried that through and other project teams haven't had too much influence over other people's ideas of what the project should look like. [P53 Improvement team member, Project Manager]

Other teams demonstrated how they had used the tools in a way that suited their project, which may have differed from conventional use of the tool (Taylor et al. 2014):

I get the feeling that our [QI facilitators] feel that we should be using [the AED] more practically too. … We've been told that it's an interactive thing; it's a live thing. It's not just something that you do when you leave – which I understand, but I think to this date, in the practical sense, I don't think that we've done that yet – not because we refuse to do it. It's just that it hasn't been needed … We've proved that it goes from A to B and everyone's on board and everyone's engaged. [P45, Improvement team member, Doctor]

The ability to adapt the objects over time was an important condition of the development of boundary practices to enable pragmatic boundary negotiation. Following initial co-creation, professional groups then adapted tools to suit their settings and clinical jurisdictions.

The Systemic Contribution of Micro-Level Interactions to Boundary Capabilities

Our findings outline how quality improvement tools can act as boundary objects and can support the development of pragmatic boundary practices and capabilities. The tools were often met with resistance and they were not adopted uncritically (Waring and Bishop 2010). When tailored to align with clinical practices, however, they developed some key boundary object features that also had a trajectory supporting syntactic, semantic and pragmatic work as the collaboration matured.

This paper makes two main (empirical) contributions. Firstly, we contribute to the boundaries literature (Lamont and Molnár 2002) by demonstrating how co-creation and adaptation of boundary objects can develop pragmatic boundary capabilities in healthcare teams.

Our cases demonstrate that the way in which objects are co-created may have an impact on the extent to which they can support boundary practices, and how objects can transition in terms of their primary role in collaboration. Objects that are not co-created through boundary negotiation (Renedo et al. 2017), or facilitated, reach a limit of syntactic and semantic boundary work. They can create a common lexicon or common meanings to be ascribed. In contrast, even objects which are brought by 'outsiders' (liaisons) (Gould and Fernandez 1989) to the group can be used to transform knowledge at pragmatic boundaries if participants view the content as co-created. These 'imported' objects can be negotiated with effective knowledge brokers in environments that support all participants, regardless of professional or occupational group, to surface and share practice-based knowledge. Knowledge brokers played an important part in facilitating the processes of co-creation and were required to drive pragmatic work.

The artefacts of the collaborations identified in our cases also display both instrumental and symbolic characteristics (Swan et al. 2007). Some teams used the artefacts (the AED and the 'pooled' knowledge from the LTST) as instrumental tools to drive the improvement initiatives. Moreover, the symbolism of the 'shared' and 'co-created' nature of the knowledge was important to bring groups together.

Secondly, we contribute to the sociocultural literature on quality improvement by providing an analysis of the micro-level boundary processes involved in using tools and facilitation of bottom-up quality improvement initiatives. Complementing other studies of top-down implementation of management approaches, for example Lean, our cases are primarily examples of bottom-up improvement initiatives driven locally by clinicians and supported by external facilitators.

Limitations

There are two limitations to this study. Firstly, there is the possibility of biases in the data collection and analysis, as some members of the research team were also involved in developing the tools and facilitating QI teams. In particular, in interviews we were aware that QI team members might try to state what they thought we wanted to hear. We mitigated against this risk by having independent researchers conduct the interviews and observations, and the researchers (CF and LL) not involved in QI facilitation conduct the analysis. Secondly, by focusing on the role of tools, we might have missed other mechanisms for boundary work that exist in QI approaches. The benefit of adopting this approach, however, was to contribute empirically and specifically to the boundary object literature.

Conclusion

Analysis of micro-level processes for quality improvement can help us understand how objects enable knowledge mobilisation for pragmatic boundary work and support the development of boundary practices. Understanding and working with professional and occupational interests, and being attentive to boundary negotiation, may support improvements in care. When QI methods are not imposed but allowed to be adapted to local clinician demands, they may be more effective. Further empirical research is needed to examine how other approaches to quality improvement may support complex work at the boundaries of health care.

References

Abbott, A. (1988). *The system of professions: An essay on the division of expert labor*. Chicago: University of Chicago Press.

Allen, D. (2009). From boundary concept to boundary object: The practice and politics of care pathway development. *Social Science and Medicine, 69*, 354–361.

Bechky, B. A. (2003). Sharing meaning across occupational communities: The transformation of understanding on a production floor. *Organization Science, 14*, 312–330.

Bijker, W. E., Hughes, T. P., & Pinch, T. J. (Eds.). (1987). *The social construction of technological systems: New directions in the sociology and history of technology*. Cambridge, MA: Massachusetts Institute of Technology.

Blaikie, N. (2007). *Approaches to social enquiry*. Cambridge: Polity Press.

Brannan, M. J., & Oultram, T. (2012). Participant observation. In G. Symon & C. Cassell (Eds.), *Qualitative organizational research*. London: Sage.

Brown, J. S., & Duguid, P. (1991). Organizational learning and communities of practice: Towards a unified view of working, learning and innovation. *Organization Science, 2*, 40–57.

Carlile, P. R. (2002). A pragmatic view of knowledge and boundaries: Boundary objects in new product development. *Organization Science, 13*, 442–455.

Carlile, P. R. (2004). Transferring, translating, and transforming: An integrative framework for managing knowledge across boundaries. *Organization Science, 15*, 555–568.

Chambers, D. A., Glasgow, R. E., & Stange, K. C. (2013). The dynamic sustainability framework: Addressing the paradox of sustainment amid ongoing change. *Implementation Science, 8*, 117.

Constantinides, P., & Barrett, M. (2006). Negotiating ICT development and use: The case of a telemedicine system in the healthcare region of Crete. *Information and Organization, 16*, 27–55.

Cooper, D. J., Hinings, B., Greenwood, R., & Brown, J. L. (1996). Sedimentation and transformation in organizational change: The case of Canadian law firms. *Organization Studies, 17*, 623–647.

Davidoff, F., Dixon-Woods, M., Leviton, L., & Michie, S. (2015). Demystifying theory and its use in improvement. *BMJ Quality & Safety, 24*(3), 228–238.

Denzin, N. K. (1970). *The research act: A theoretical introduction to sociological methods*. Chicago: Aldine.

Dixon-Woods, M., & Martin, G. P. (2016). Does quality improvement improve quality? *Future Hospital Journal, 3,* 191–194.

Eisenhardt, K. M. (1989). Building theories from case study research. *The Academy of Management Review, 14,* 532–550.

Ferlie, E., Fitzgerald, L., Wood, M., & Hawkins, C. (2005). The nonspread of innovations: The mediating role of professionals. *Academy of Management Journal, 48,* 117–134.

Fitzgerald, L., & Dopson, S. (2009). Comparative case study designs: Their utility and development in organizational research. In D. Buchanan & A. Bryman (Eds.), *The Sage handbook of organizational research methods.* London: Sage.

Fulop, N. J., Allen, P., Clarke, A., & Black, N. (Eds.). (2001). *Studying the organisation and delivery of health services: Research methods.* London: Routledge.

Gabbay, J., & Le May, A. (2010). *Practice-based evidence for healthcare: Clinical mindlines.* London: Routledge.

Gould, R. V., & Fernandez, R. M. (1989). Structures of mediation: A formal approach to brokerage in transaction networks. *Sociological Methodology, 19,* 89–126.

Howe, C., Randall, K., Chalkley, S., & Bell, D. (2013). Supporting improvement in a quality collaborative. *British Journal of Healthcare Management, 19,* 434–442.

Kitchener, M. (2002). Mobilizing the logic of managerialism in professional fields: The case of academic health centre mergers. *Organization Studies, 23,* 391–420.

Knorr Cetina, K. (1999). *Epistemic cultures: How the sciences make knowledge.* Cambridge, MA: Harvard University Press.

Lamont, M., & Molnár, V. (2002). The study of boundaries in the social sciences. *Annual Review of Sociology, 28,* 167–195.

Lave, J., & Wenger, E. (1991). *Situated learning: Legitimate peripheral participation.* Cambridge: Cambridge University Press.

Lennox, L., Doyle, C., Reed, J. E., & Bell, D. (2017). What makes a sustainability tool valuable, practical and useful in real-world healthcare practice? A mixed-methods study on the development of the long term success tool in Northwest London. *British Medical Journal Open, 7,* e014417.

Levina, N., & Vaast, E. (2005). The emergence of boundary spanning competence in practice: Implications for implementation and use of information systems. *MIS Quarterly, 29,* 335–363.

Liberati, E. G. (2017). Separating, replacing, intersecting: The influence of context on the construction of the medical-nursing boundary. *Social Science and Medicine, 172*, 135–143.

Liberati, E. G., Gorli, M., & Scaratti, G. (2016). Invisible walls within multidisciplinary teams: Disciplinary boundaries and their effects on integrated care. *Social Science & Medicine, 150*, 31–39.

Löwy, I. (1992). The strength of loose concepts: Boundary concepts, federal experimental strategies and disciplinary growth: The case of immunology. *History of Science, 30*, 373–396.

Mays, N., & Pope, C. (2000). Assessing quality in qualitative research. *British Medical Journal, 320*, 50–52.

Nicolini, D., Mengis, J., & Swan, J. (2012). Understanding the role of objects in cross-disciplinary collaboration. *Organization Science, 23*, 612–629.

Oborn, E., & Dawson, S. (2010). Learning across communities of practice: An examination of multidisciplinary work. *British Journal of Management, 21*, 843–858.

Orr, J. E. (1996). *Talking about machines: An ethnography of a modern job*. Ithaca: Cornell University Press.

Powell, A. E., & Davies, Huw T. O. (2012). The struggle to improve patient care in the face of professional boundaries. *Social Science and Medicine, 75*, 807–814.

Radnor, Z., & Boaden, R. (2008). Editorial: Lean in public services—Panacea or paradox? *Public Money & Management, 28*, 3–7.

Radnor, Z. J., Holweg, M., & Waring, J. (2012). Lean in healthcare: The unfilled promise? *Social Science and Medicine, 74*, 364–371.

Reed, J. E., Mcnicholas, C., Woodcock, T., Issen, L., & Bell, D. (2014). Designing quality improvement initiatives: The action effect method, a structured approach to identifying and articulating programme theory. *BMJ Qual Saf, 23*, 1040–1048.

Renedo, A., Komporozos-Athanasiou, A., & Marston, C. (2017). Experience as evidence: The dialogic construction of health professional knowledge through patient involvement. *Sociology, 52*, 1–18.

Shaw, S., Elston, J., & Abbott, S. (2004). Comparative analysis of health policy implementation: The use of documentary analysis. *Policy Studies, 25*, 259–266.

Star, S. L., & Griesemer, J. R. (1989). Institutional ecology, 'translations', and boundary objects: Amateurs and professionals in Berkeley's museum of vertebrate zoology, 1907–1939. *Social Studies of Science, 19*, 387–420.

Swan, J., Bresnen, M., Newell, S., & Robertson, M. (2007). The object of knowledge: The role of objects in biomedical innovation. *Human Relations, 60*, 1809–1837.

Szulanski, G., & Cappetta, R. 2003. Stickiness: Conceptualizing, measuring, and predicting difficulties in the transfer of knowledge within organizations. In *The Blackwell handbook of organizational learning and knowledge management* (pp. 513–534). Malden, MA: Blackwell.

Taylor, M. J., Mcnicholas, C., Nicolay, C., Darzi, A., Bell, D., & Reed, J. E. (2014). Systematic review of the application of the plan–do–study–act method to improve quality in healthcare. *BMJ Quality & Safety, 23*, 290–298.

Waring, J., Currie, G., Crompton, A., & Bishop, S. (2013). An exploratory study of knowledge brokering in hospital settings: Facilitating knowledge sharing and learning for patient safety? *Social Science and Medicine, 98*, 79–86.

Waring, J. J., & Bishop, S. (2010). Lean healthcare: Rhetoric, ritual and resistance. *Social Science and Medicine, 71*, 1332–1340.

Wenger, E. (1998). *Communities of practice: Learning, meaning and identity.* Cambridge: Cambridge University Press.

Yin, R. K. (2009). *Case study research: Design and methods.* London: Sage.

Conclusion: Learning Health Systems: Complexity, Coordination & Integration

These chapters, mostly based on selected empirical research, have shown the dynamics, opportunities and challenges of working across professional, institutional and conceptual boundaries in health systems. Central to boundary-work in organized healthcare delivery is the relationship between overt, system-wide reform and the sustainability of local capacity to innovate to meet the needs of local communities and individuals. This tension requires increasing research attention to work *within* the boundaries of health services and systems, and not merely *across* them. Complex adaptive systems (CAS), characterising health services and systems, have porous boundaries around their systems and with sub-systems, allowing mutual influence between system-wide and local innovations. The boundaries of CAS themselves have agency. Scientifically, healthcare reform need not be constrained by the potentially stultifying distinction between (systemic) structure and the (individual) agency of freely-acting persons. It is the everyday interactive relational work *within* boundaries that generates structures that might support care coordination, and ought to be a defining feature of what has been called "learning health systems".

For all of us who value understanding healthcare systems, as a foundation for their continuous self-improvement, challenges remain. Fear of death in western society perverts the allocation of scarce resources. Healthcare continues to be narrowly identified with curative biomedicine, relatively de-coupled from broader political, institutional, economic and social influences, such as systemic poverty in developed as well as resource-poor environments. Systemic inequality is reflected and reinforced by health system and service structures. Inequality and limited healthcare access are exacerbated by unaffordable housing, inadequate public transportation, lack of public spaces, social isolation, and neo-liberal valuing of financial production over other forms of social contribution. The latter affects the way we treat older people, in particular.

Healthcare systems are traditionally organized around and delivered according to habitual and relatively narrow ways by which we understand healthcare. Despite ageing populations and increasing rates of chronic diseases, such as mental health conditions and Alzheimer's disease, our health systems and services lack sufficient electronically-enabled information-sharing, and timely and individual-focused integration of health and social services. There is still a long way to go for patients' and citizens' voices to be sufficiently well heard and understood in organised healthcare delivery systems. This is especially the case for indigenous voices and those from the global south, whose voices are also muted in broader health systems research.

In a context that enormously privileges technological intervention and specialisation, medical and other health professions education systems have experienced profound reforms over the last decades. Inter-professional and inter-organisational collaboration have been put forward as means for making healthcare delivery not only of higher quality but also, due to the escalation healthcare delivery costs, more sustainable and equitable. However, effective teamwork among self-defined autonomous healthcare professionals is exceptionally difficult to enact. Professional and organisational silos—in particular, the disproportionate influence of narrow bio-medical priorities—impede the scope of practice of many health professionals and realistic plans for inter-professionalism. Global migration and environmental degradation also pose challenges to the way healthcare is conceived, governed, organised and delivered. We have yet to find sustainable ways, through our communication and information-sharing systems, to foster local adaptation and innovation, while sharing lessons across health services and systems. There is more than enough to keep us busy.

Index